HISTORIC PHOTOS OF
ROCHESTER

TEXT AND CAPTIONS BY
RUTH ROSENBERG NAPARSTECK

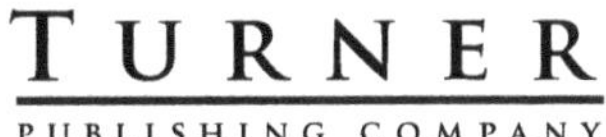

Sometime near the turn of the century, people look over the rail of the Court Street Bridge at the Genesee River, perhaps wondering if its waters will overrun the banks, which frequently happened in the spring. Flooding was considered an uncontrollable annual occurrence until the opening of the Mt. Morris Dam in the mid–twentieth century.

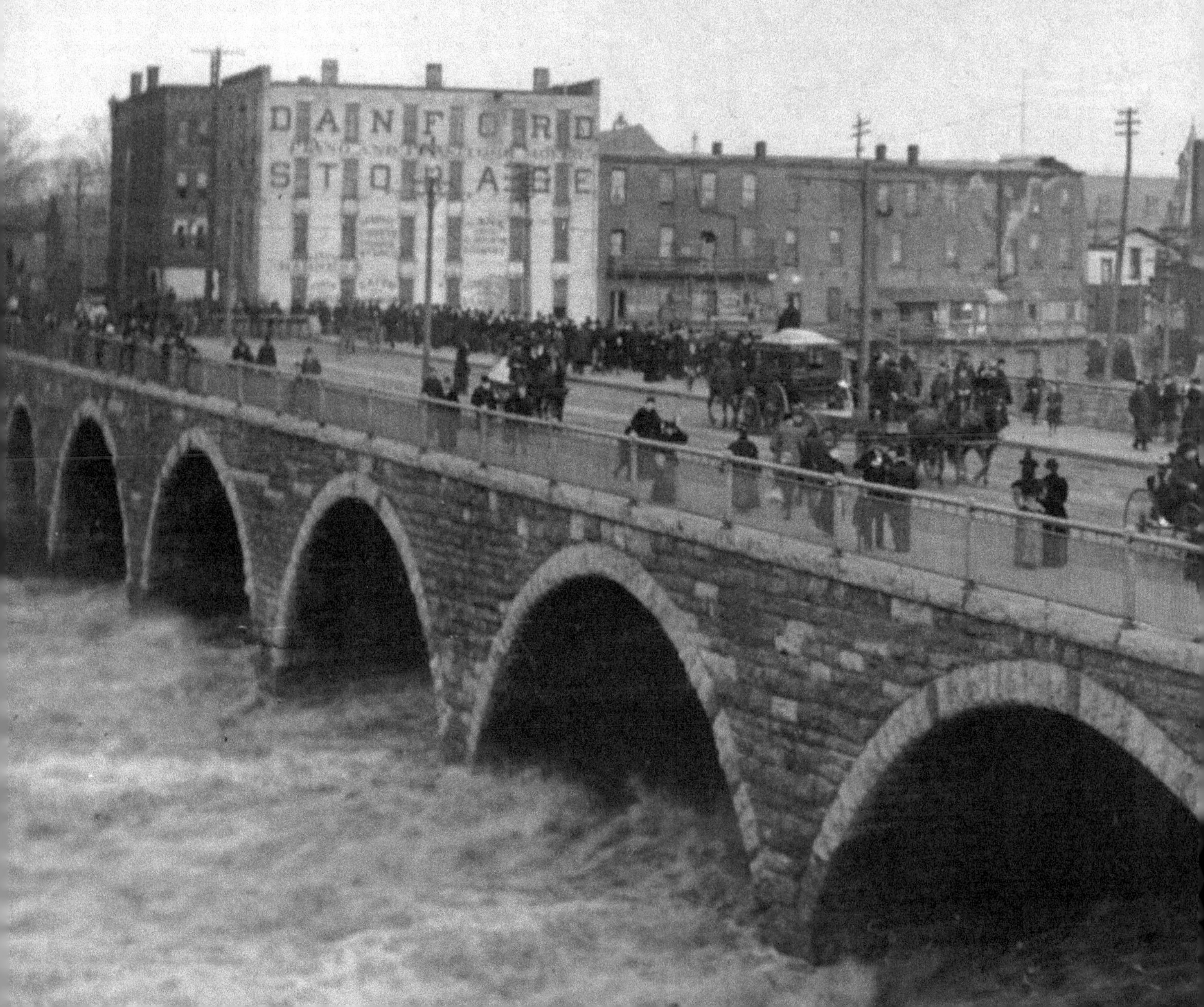

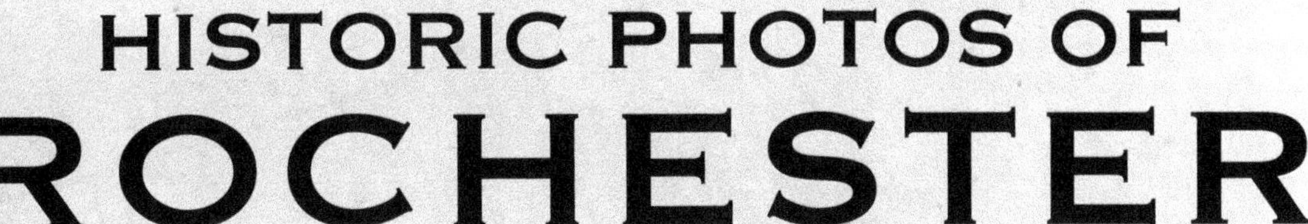

HISTORIC PHOTOS OF ROCHESTER

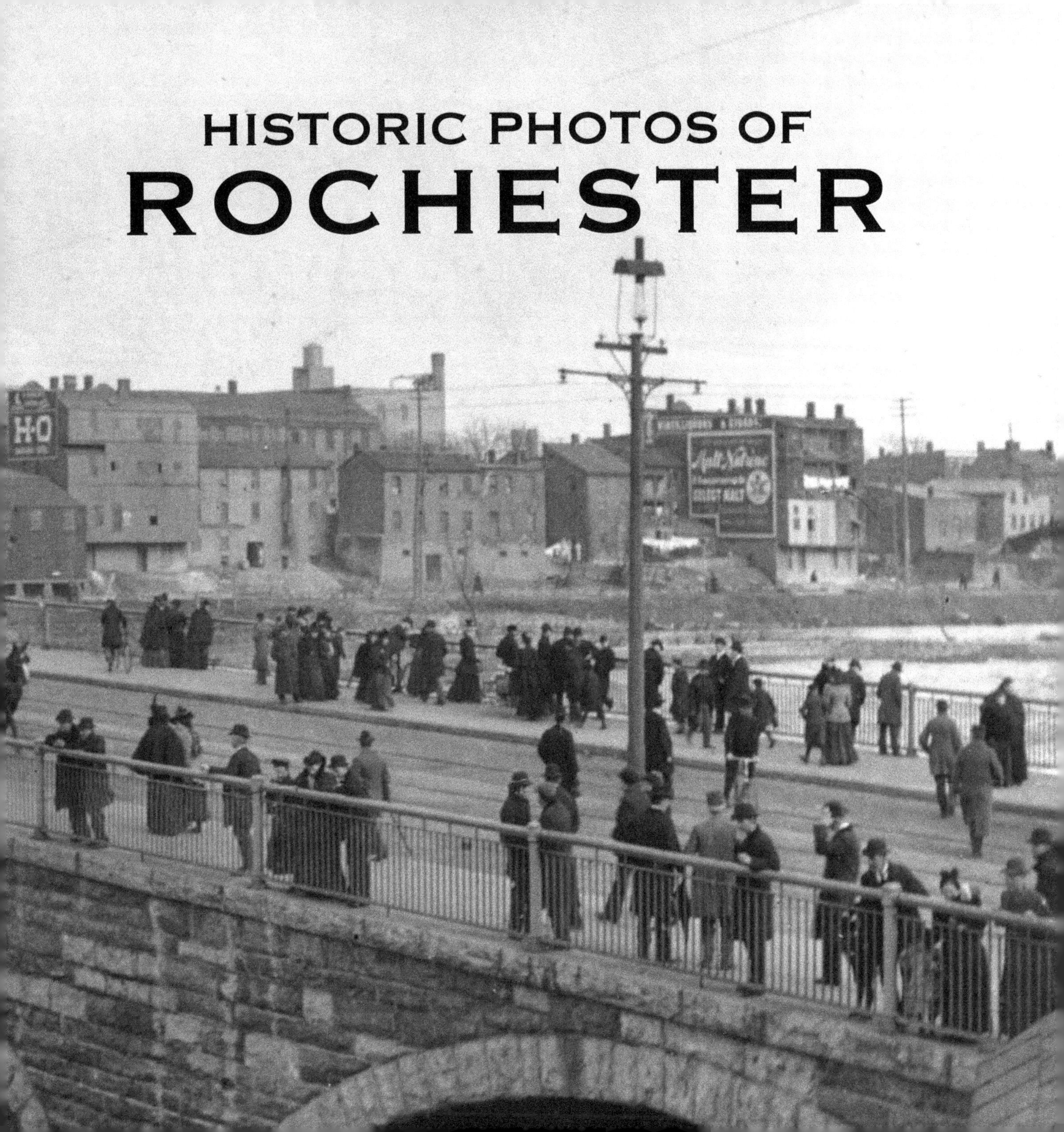

Turner Publishing Company
www.turnerpublishing.com

Historic Photos of Rochester

Library of Congress Control Number: 2006937033

ISBN: 978-1-59652-321-0

ISBN 978-1-68336-936-3 (hc)

Contents

Acknowledgments vii

Introduction viii

From Civil War to Growing City
(1865–1879) 1

A City of Immigrants
(1880–1899) 15

Great Expectations
(1900–1919) 75

Rochester Rises to the Challenge
(1920–1939) 137

United to Win the War
(1940–1949) 167

Growth and Change
(1950–1970s) 185

Notes on the Photographs 200

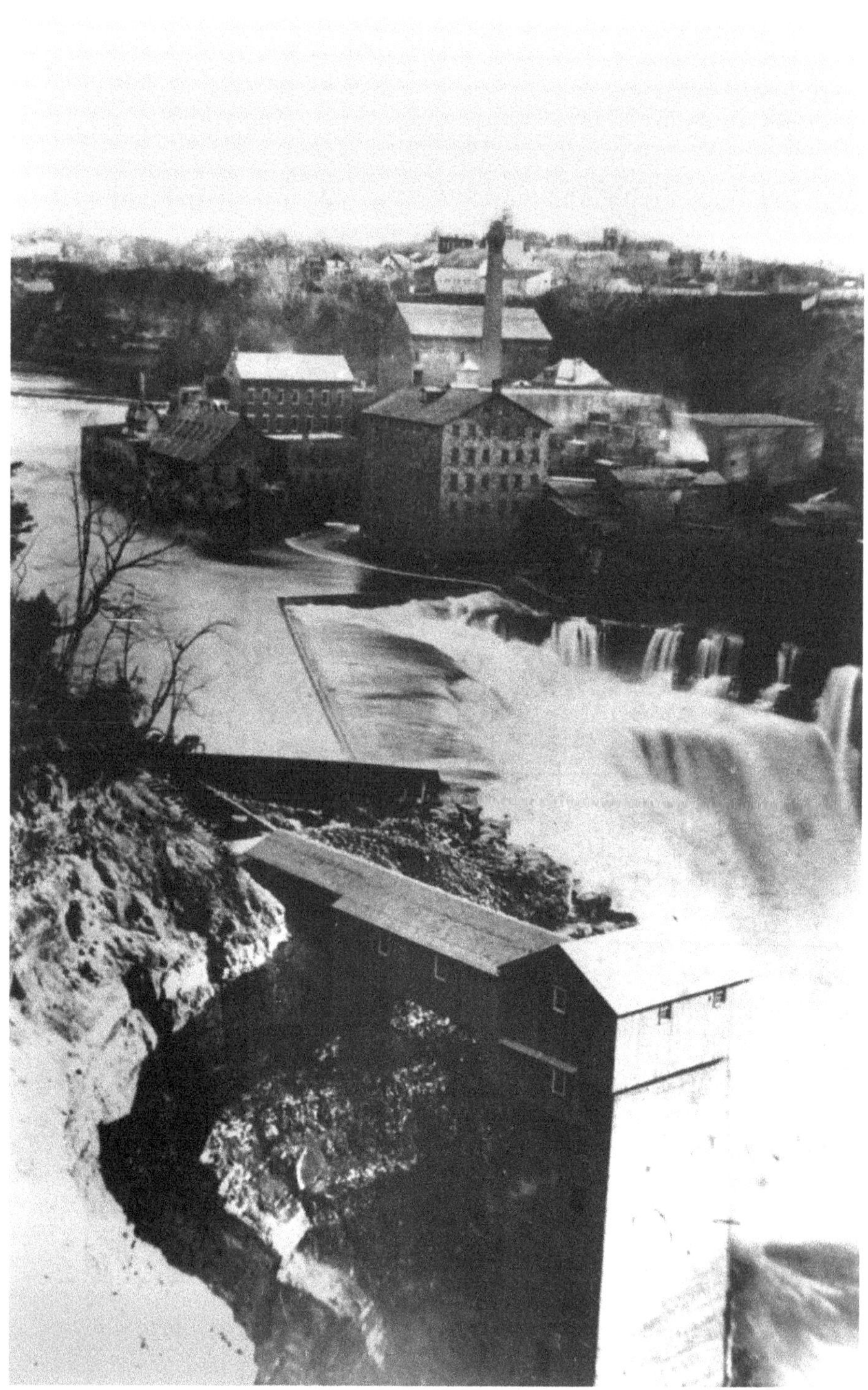

Using the inexhaustible water of the Lower Falls, an electric power generation plant is visible in the center foreground of this photograph. In the background is a paper mill and the Middle Falls, which are barely visible. Just north of the Lower Falls, the energy of the river and its urban, fast-paced life give way to a peaceful flow into Lake Ontario.

Acknowledgments

This volume, *Historic Photos of Rochester,* is the result of the cooperation and efforts of many individuals and organizations. It is with great thanks that we acknowledge in particular the valuable contribution of Rochester Public Library's City Hall Collection, Local History Collection, and Municipal Archives Collection.

This project represents countless hours of review and research. The researchers and writer have reviewed thousands of photographs. We greatly appreciate the generous assistance of the archives listed here, without whom this project could not have been completed.

The goal in publishing this work is to provide broader access to a set of extraordinary photographs. The aim is to inspire, provide perspective, and evoke insight that might assist officials and citizens, who together are responsible for determining Rochester's future. In addition, the book seeks to preserve the past with respect and reverence.

With the exception of touching up imperfections that have accrued with the passage of time and cropping where necessary, no other changes have been made. The focus and clarity of many images is limited to the technology and the ability of the photographer at the time they were taken.

We encourage readers to reflect as they explore Rochester, stroll along its streets, or wander its neighborhoods. It is the publisher's hope that in making use of this work, longtime residents will learn something new and that new residents will gain a perspective on where Rochester has been, so that each can contribute to its future.

—*Todd Bottorff, Publisher*

INTRODUCTION

In *Sketches of Rochester,* the first real history of Rochester, Henry O'Reilly wrote in 1838 of the geological wealth and geographical advantages of the Genesee River Valley, upon which the city of Rochester is built at its outlet. The people, he wrote, need only take advantage of what was offered.

Coming from the New England states, the first white settlers brought with them the Puritan work ethic and the vision of a New England community that they set about reproducing both architecturally and culturally. There was work to be had by the wealthy entrepreneur as well as the barber who owned nothing more than a pair of scissors and a comb. The back-breaking labor of cutting wood, clearing trees for fields and roads, hauling stone, making bricks, and carting sawed lumber to building sites kept the unskilled settler busy.

Six settlements that eventually became Rochester, dotted the Genesee River's edge in the first decade of the nineteenth century. Each settlement believed it had the advantage that would make it the center of commerce. To name a few: Charlotte had the shipping port at its mouth, but ports nearer to the Lower Falls took away much of Charlotte's business; Carthage had a bridge that connected the east and west ends of Ridge Road, but the bridge collapsed after only fifteen months; Castletown lost its purpose as a transfer point when riverboats began to take the bypass to the Erie Canal; other settlements were not able to develop their assets before the rapid transformation of the One Hundred Acre Tract sealed their fate in the absorption of Frankfort into the formation of Rochesterville.

Colonel Nathaniel Rochester, the primary partner with William Fitzhugh and Charles Carrol, guided the One Hundred Acre Tract to become the path for the state road over the Main Street bridge and the Erie Canal aqueduct as well as the site of the Court House for newly formed Monroe County. The intersection of Main Street (toward Buffalo) and Lake Avenue (for shipping) ensured that both surface and lake travel would be centered in Rochesterville. Colonel Rochester helped to charter the village's own bank, which further stimulated growth. The opening of the Erie Canal in 1825 brought growth more rapid than anyone could have imagined. The fields to the south were so fertile that the grain sent to Rochester's mills made the Genesee River Valley the breadbasket of America. Lumber in the hills to the south helped to build boats and buildings.

Rochester was attractive to waves of immigrants who not only found Rochester a welcome home, but found a ready use for their skills. The assets the city held in the skills of its people alone made Rochester wealthy. This wide array of skills—in carpentry, masonry, brewing, shoe and clothing manufacture, agriculture and horticulture, optics and precision instruments—as well as the diversity of manufacturing they made possible, protected the city from the effects of economic downturns better than cities that depended on one industry.

The following collection of photographs reveals the city over a century as it grew from adolescence in the mid–nineteenth century to maturity shortly after the mid–twentieth century. In 2006, still on the leading edge of technology, innovation, medical science, and education, Rochester is seeking a redefinition of its image. This collection is published with a view toward that goal.

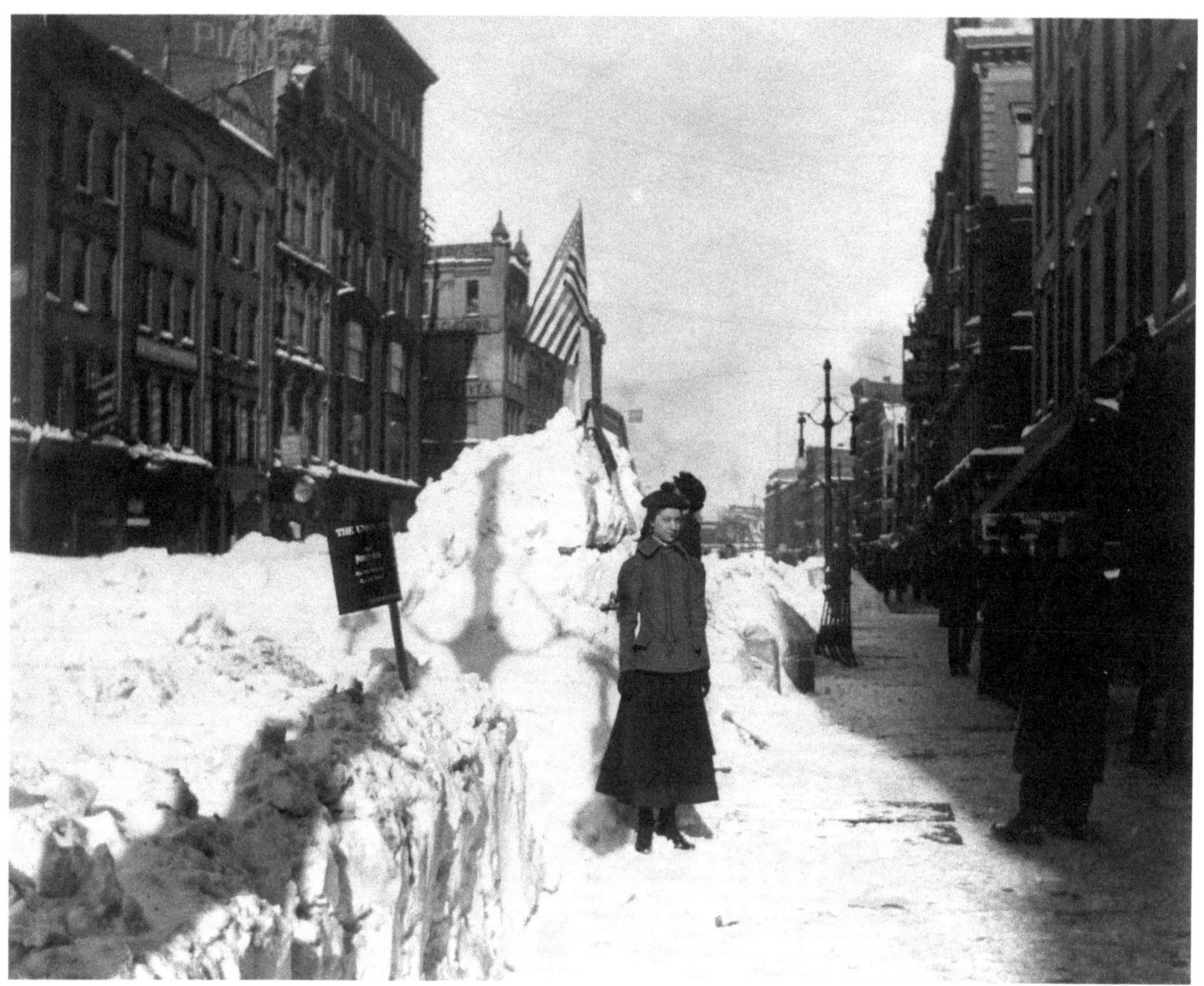

Snow removal in Rochester and other lakeside communities in the north was a great challenge at the turn of the century. Heavy equipment was designed to plow and remove the snow to let emergency equipment pass through the streets. Fire fighters were especially challenged by the deep snows. Fortunately many of the heavy snowstorms occurred in the spring when snow melt was not far off.

From Civil War to Growing City

(1865–1879)

When news of the surrender of Robert E. Lee reached Rochester, church bells all over the city began to ring, calling the people to the Four Corners of downtown Rochester for an announcement. Mayor Daniel D. T. Moore stood on the steps of the Powers Bank, but his words were lost in the cheers of the people. Soon the soldiers would be home. Scarcely had that news been received when the joy became sadness upon learning of the assassination of President Abraham Lincoln.

People were further saddened when the businesses and jobs that the returning soldiers expected to assume were severely damaged by the worst flood in the city's history on March 17, 1865. When the water receded three days later, thousands of dollars were lost in inventory and buildings were heavily damaged.

A financial slump in 1873 temporarily slowed the growth of postwar business. War contracts ended in 1865 and industries were changing. A brilliant businessman, banker Daniel Powers placed thousands of dollars in cash in the window of his bank at the corner of State and Main streets so that people could see that his bank was secure in the recession.

Powers held great influence on the businessmen in the city, his bank holding a key location at the Four Corners. In 1874 the Holly Water Works was constructed at Browns Race to increase the water pressure in the fire hydrants downtown. Powers opposed the construction of the system, believing his building to be fireproof, but when the great Chicago fire destroyed a cast-iron building there, he decided to support the system, despite his opposition to the tax increase it could bring.

Perhaps one of the most visible changes was in transportation. Horse-drawn streetcars were being replaced with electric cars. George Selden tested his gasoline-powered automobile in New York City successfully and began to manufacture them, but Selden's loss of a patent suit after an eleven-year battle with Henry Ford would make Detroit, rather than Rochester, the automobile manufacturing center of America.

Shoes, optical products, precision instruments, and other products strengthened Rochester's diversified manufacturing base. Railroads were helping to extend the market reach of Rochester's businesses to the growing Midwest. The Erie Canal continued to carry goods and passengers, but the railroad was challenging the waterway, expanding market reach from regional to nationwide.

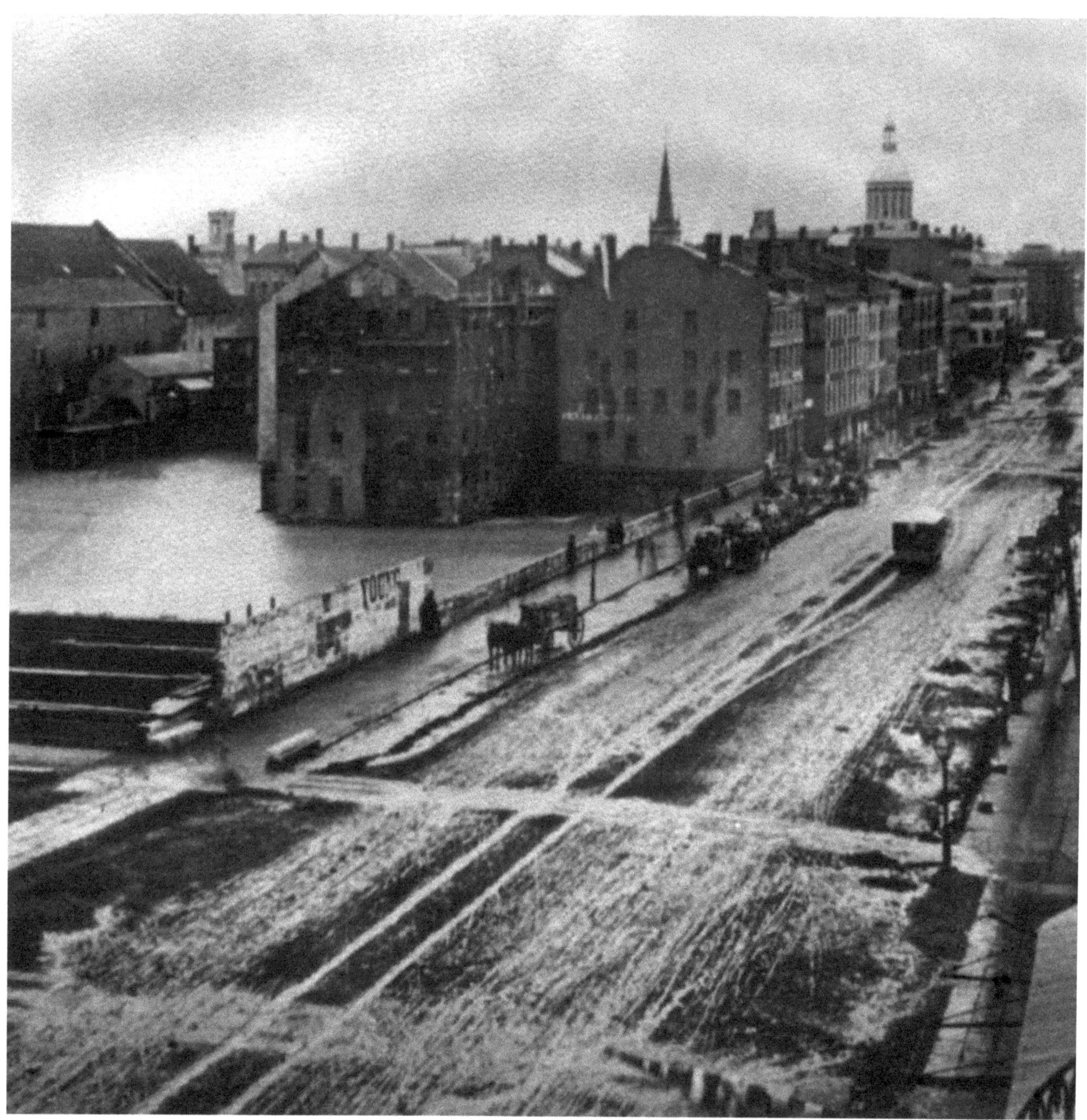

A view west across Main Street toward what was once Buffalo Street, now west Main Street, about 1860. The Monroe County Court House, now the County Office Building, can be seen in the distance. By the end of the decade the First Presbyterian Church in the background had burned.

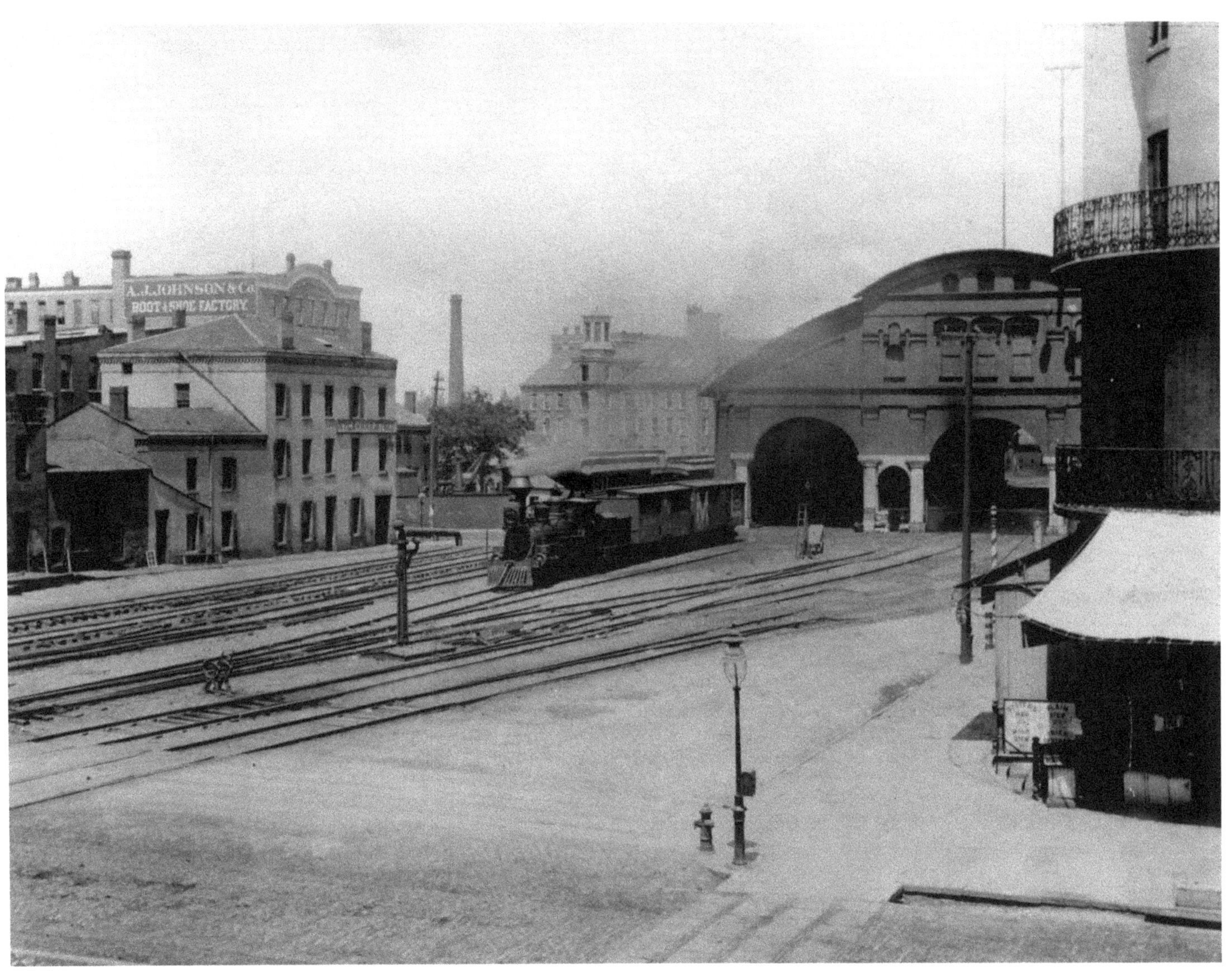

Built in 1852 to replace the wooden Auburn Railroad Station, this New York Central Railroad Station stood until 1883 when it was replaced with a more modern edifice. Abraham Lincoln stopped near this station in 1860 on his way to Washington to take the oath of office as president of the United States. Five years later his funeral train came through. First Lady Mary Lincoln also passed through Rochester, dining at the Waverly House seen on the right.

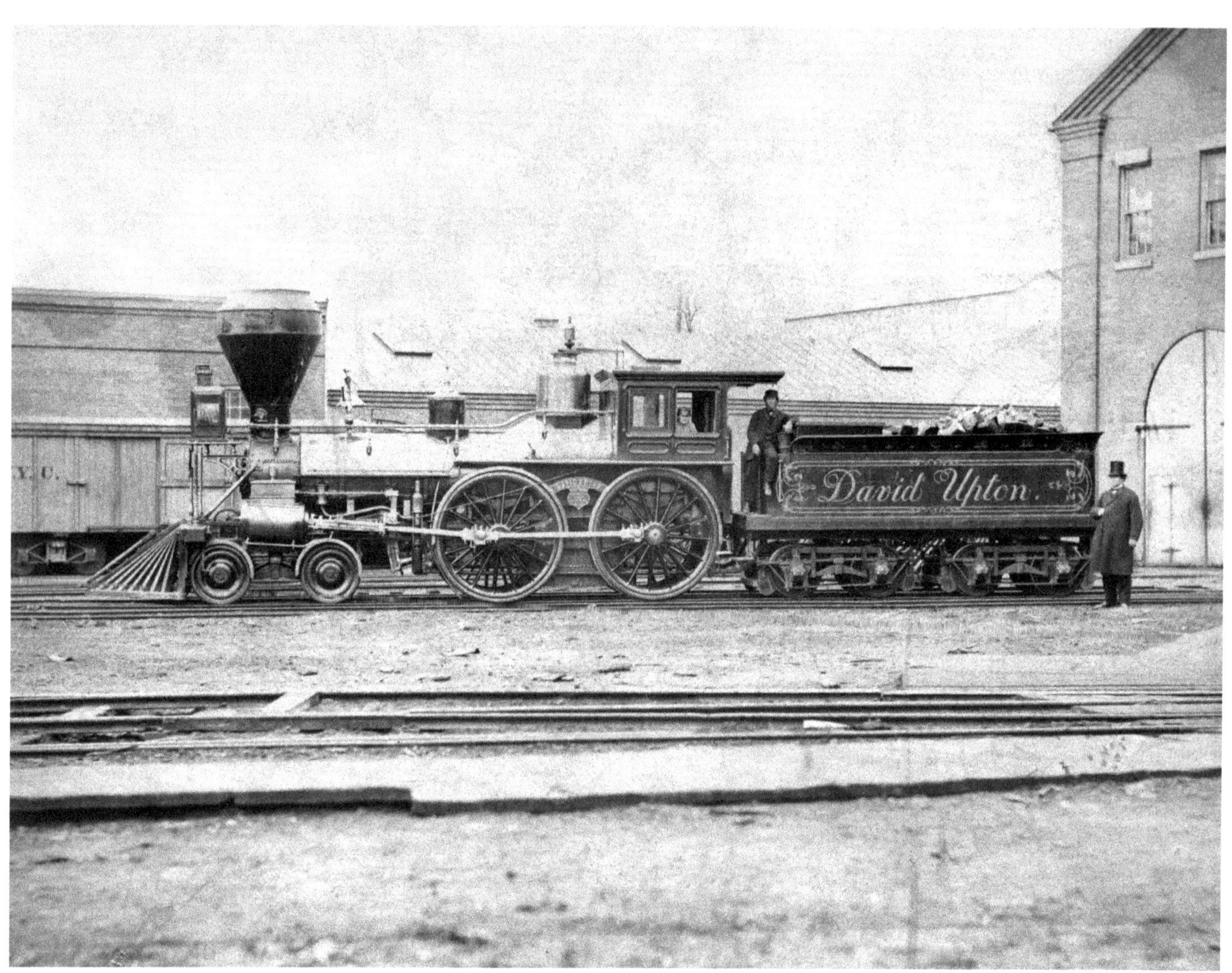

This early 1860s locomotive was named for David Upton (1816–1885), once master mechanic and superintendent in the western division for New York Central Railroad. In 1865 Upton arranged for several railroad cars to carry dignitaries joining the funeral cortege of the assassinated president Abraham Lincoln.

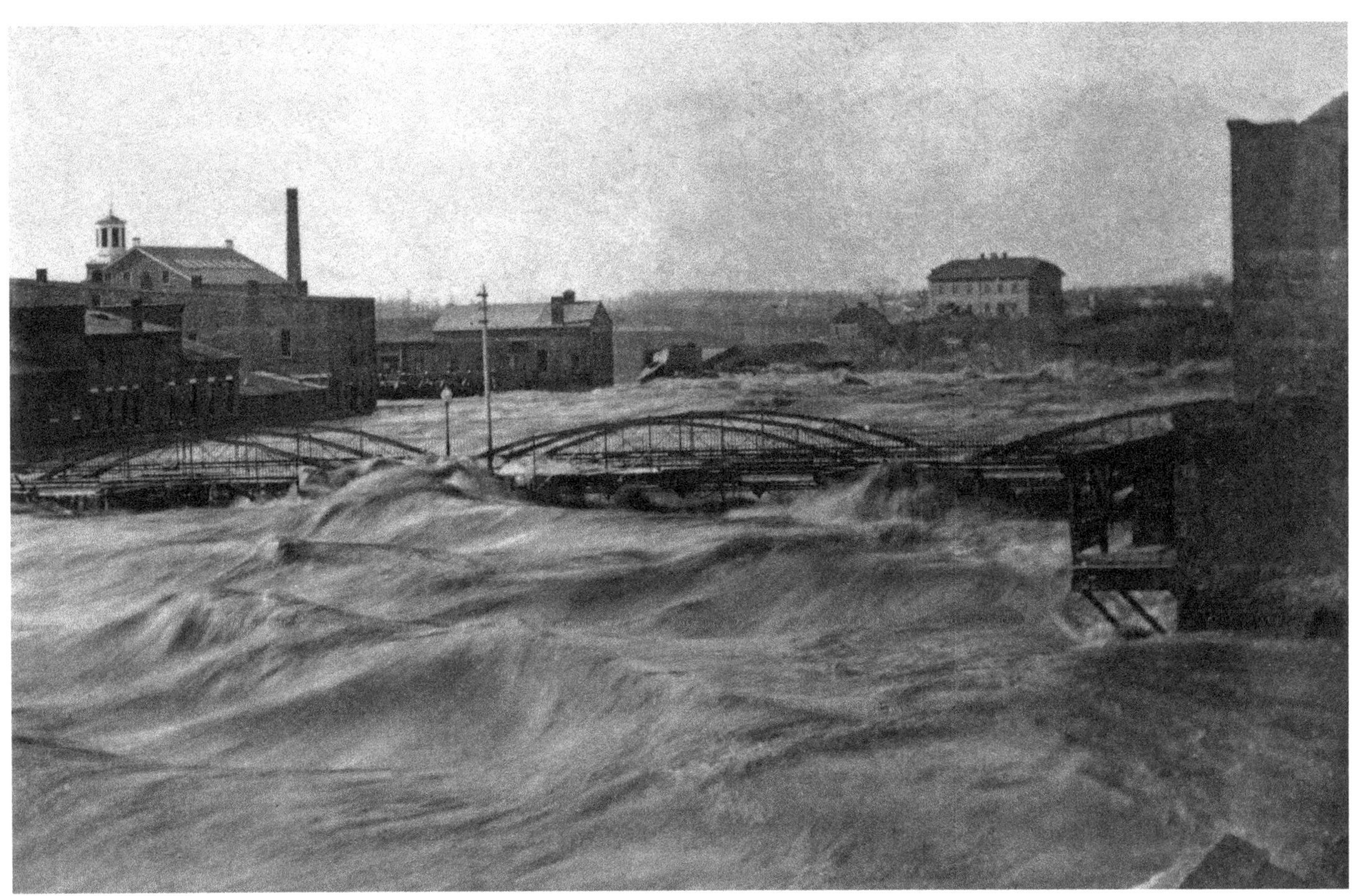

Rain and snowmelt from the Pennsylvania hills where the Genesee River originated sent 54,000 cubic feet of water per second rushing northward during the St. Patrick's Day flood in 1865. The Andrews Street Bridge was nearly destroyed. The city's streets were flooded for three days. There has never been a more damaging flood in the city, partly owing to the 1952 opening of the Mt. Morris Dam sixty miles south of the city.

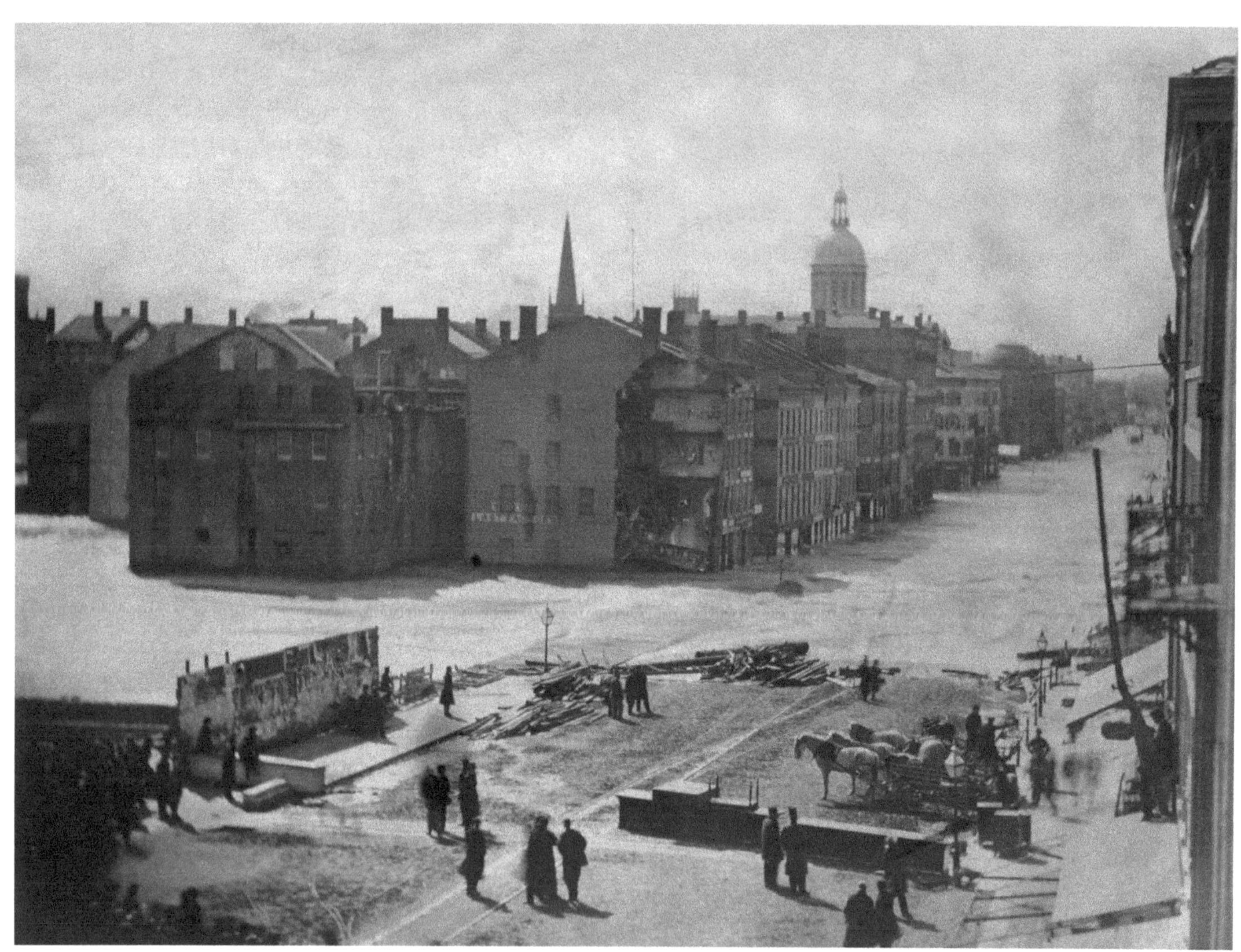

The floodwaters of the Genesee River in 1865 were carried north through the Genesee Valley Canal and east and west through the Erie Canal. The gas company feared gas explosions in the public street lamps, but fortunately no fires or explosions erupted. This photograph emphasizes the depth of the waters.

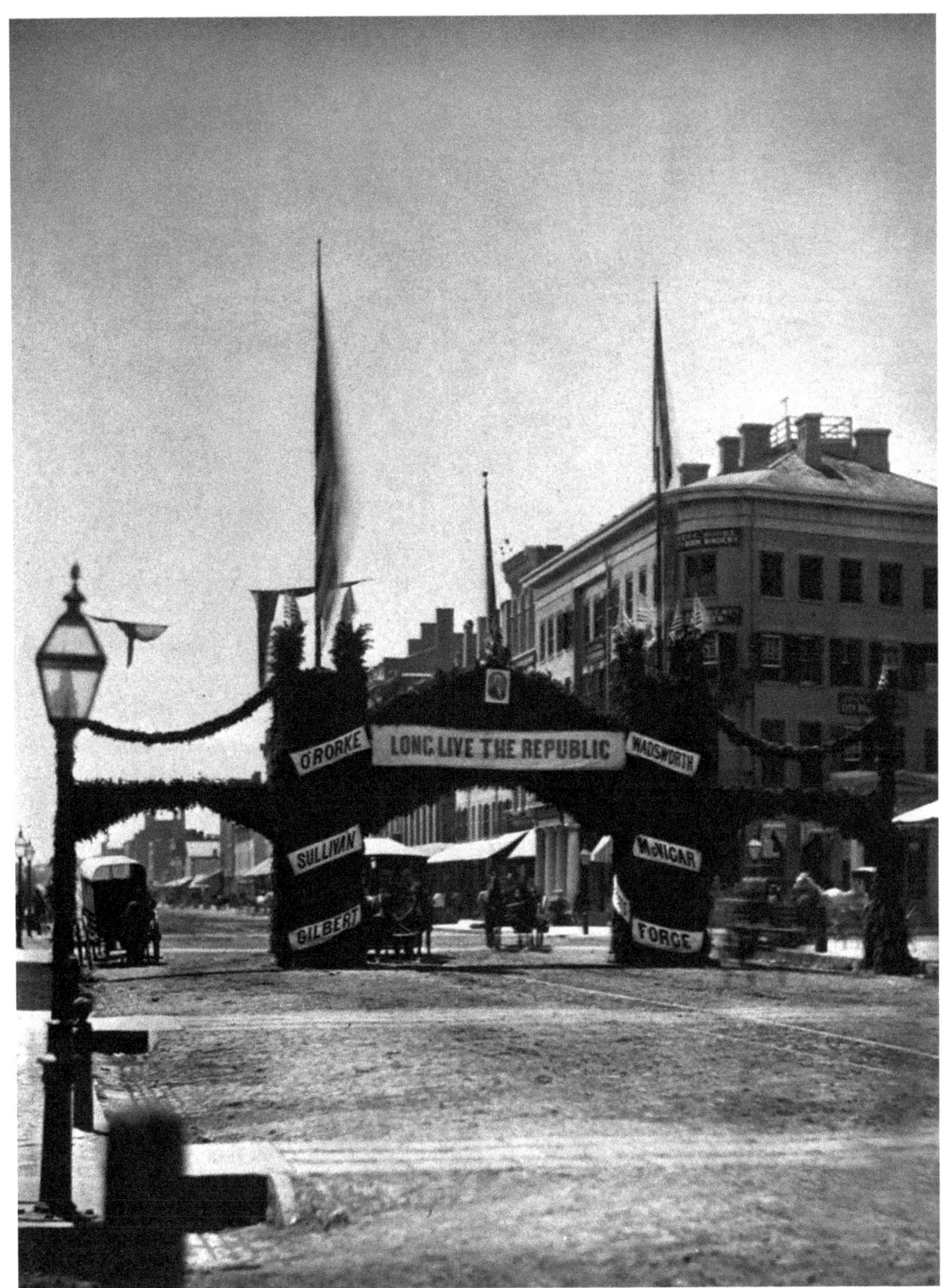

Following the Civil War, a Victory Arch was erected over Main Street near the Four Corners at State Street. Local nurseryman Edward Allen Frost financed the arch, which cheered "Long Live the Republic" while individually recognizing the contributions of six men who served.

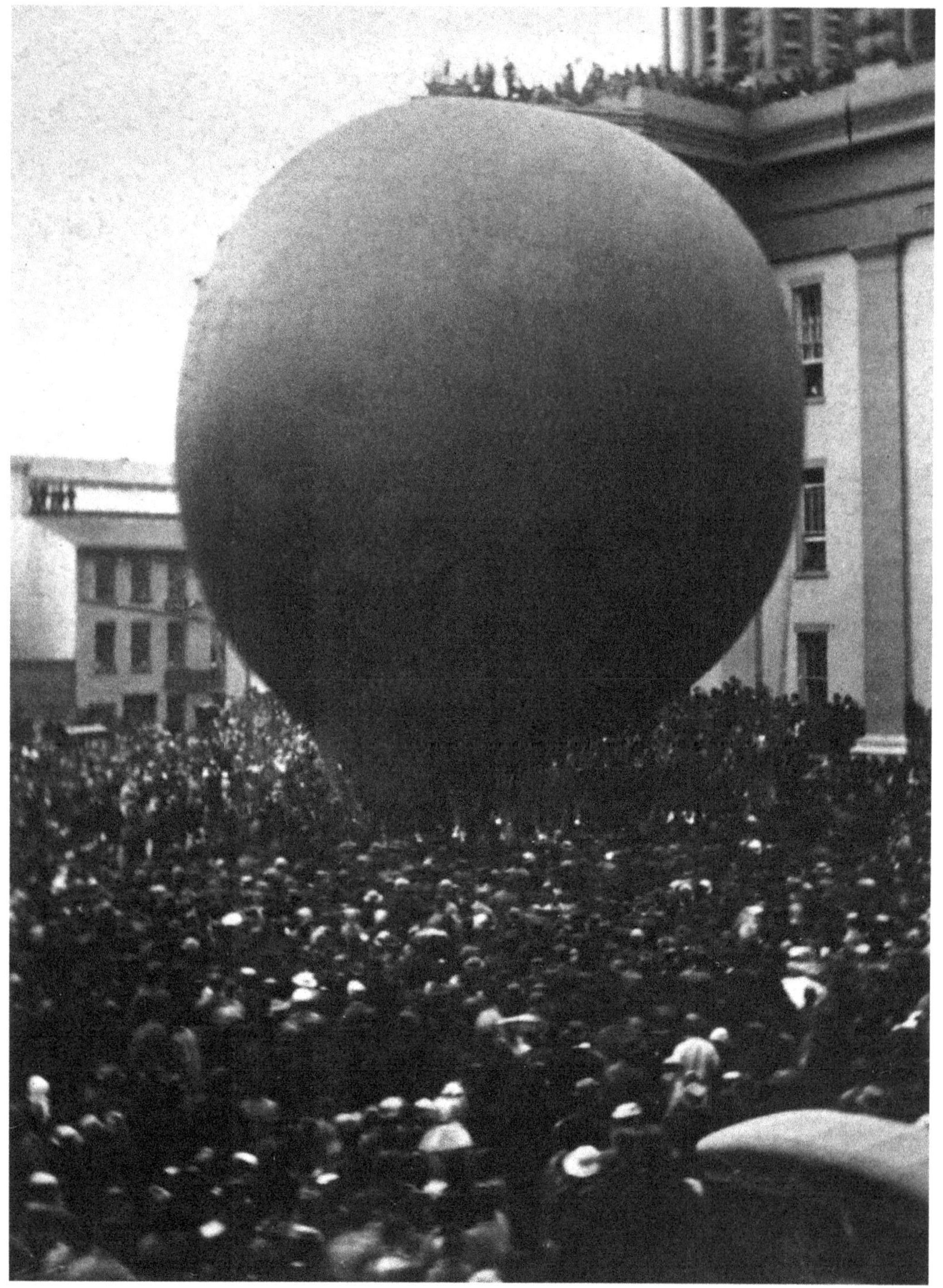

On October 19, 1869, the hot-air balloon *Hyperion* launched from downtown Rochester to Cazenovia near Syracuse. A large crowd watched as Professor S. A. King piloted the balloon carrying several other people. Though King had a very rough landing, which was reported in Rochester newspapers, flying remained an interest to which many in Rochester contributed.

The *American Rural Home* and the German language *Rochester Beobachter* newspapers were published in the Rochester Evening Express Building at the southwest corner of Aqueduct and west Main (then Buffalo) streets in the early 1870s. Evening Express building owners C. D. Tracy and F. S. Rew leased to other businesses, like the Cigar and Tobacco Manufactory of Solomon F. Hess and the busy hardware store of Arthur S. Hamilton and James W. McKindley.

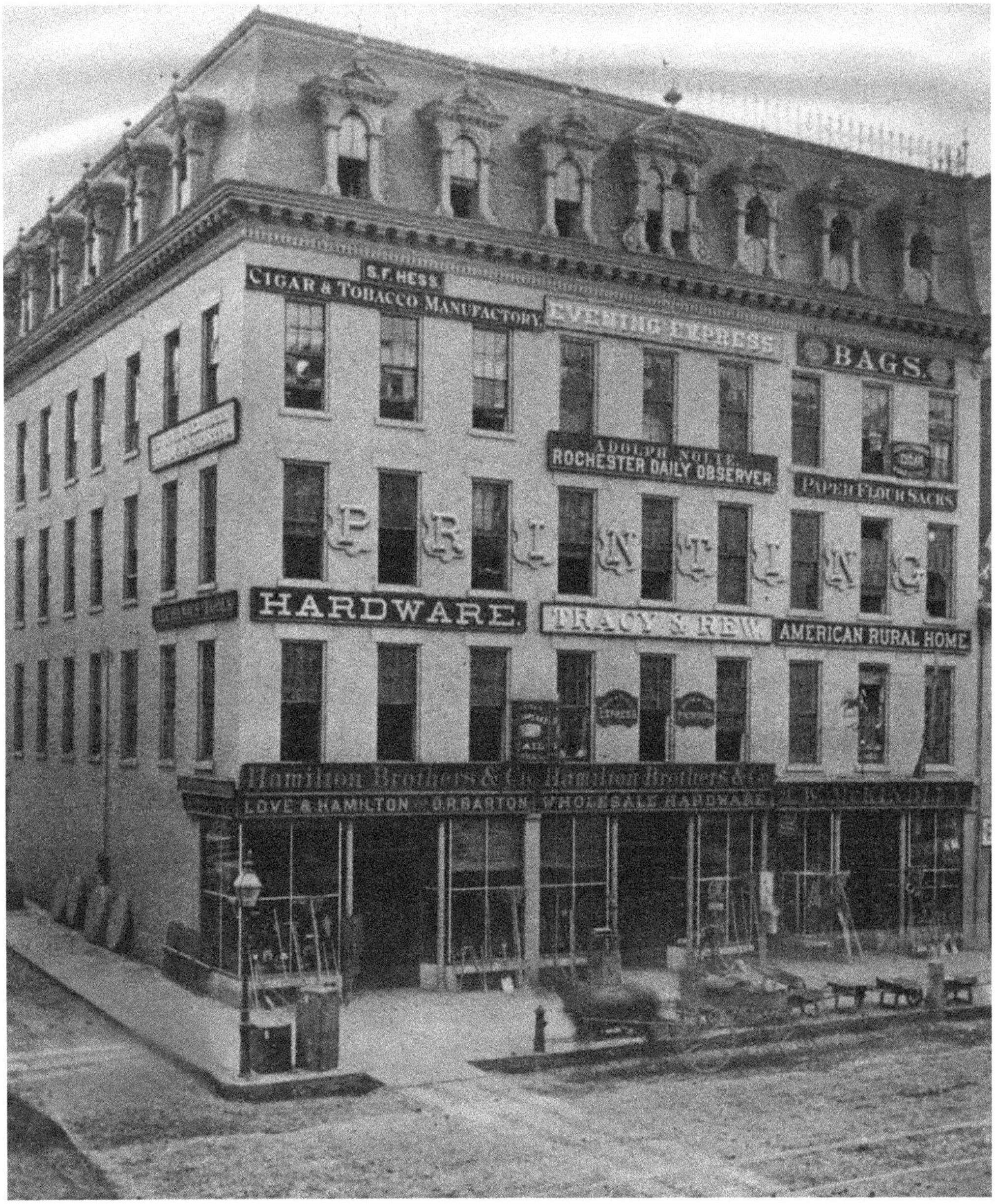

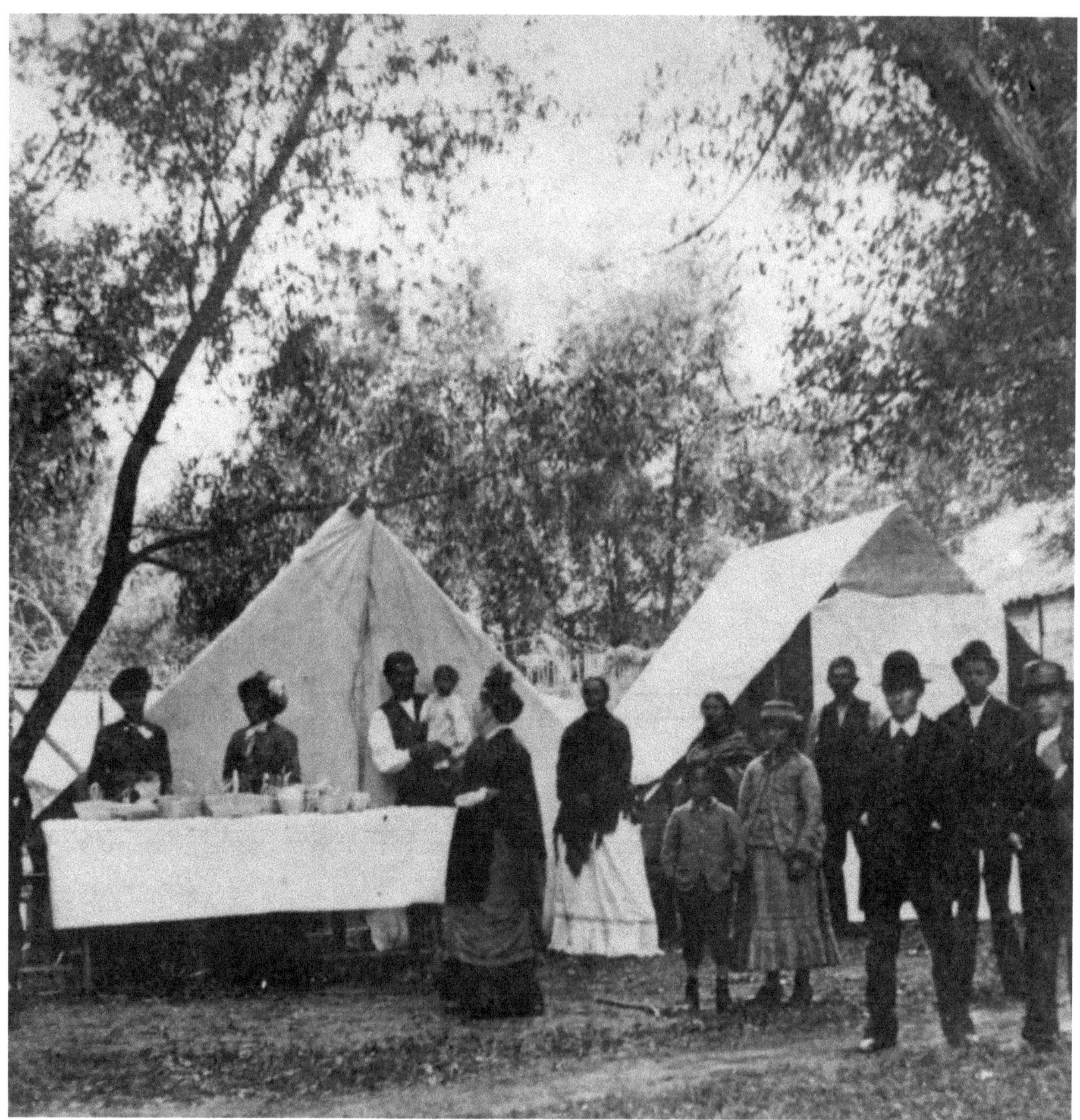

Native American families gathered at Maplewood Park in the early 1870s for Indian Day. Then known as Maple Grove, the Genesee country remained home to many of the Seneca Indians after the claim to their lands was sold to Oliver Phelps and Nathaniel Gorham in 1788. Today they hold festivals in the Rochester area and keep their traditions.

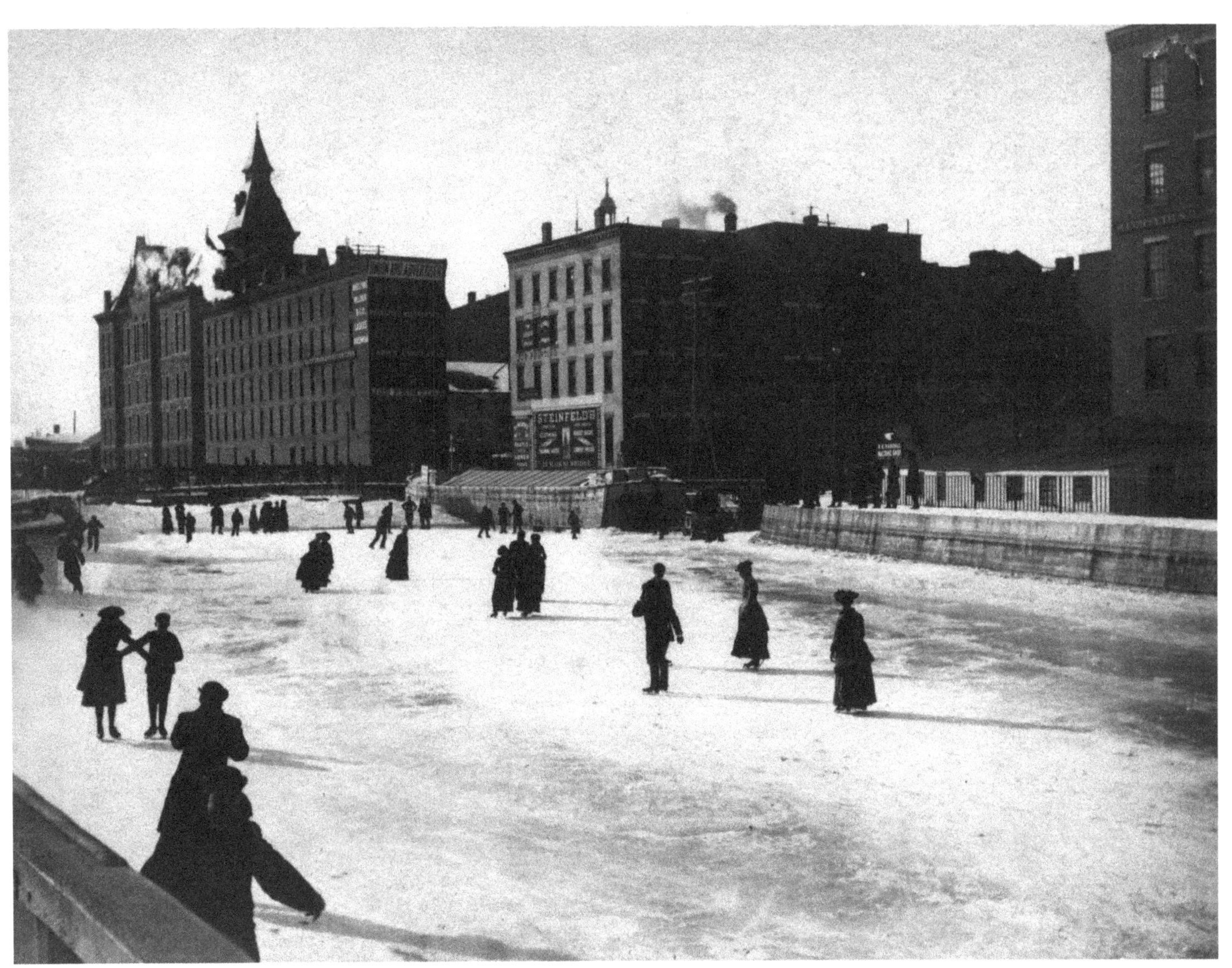

Ice skaters enjoy late-afternoon recreation among canal boats tied up for the winter on the Erie Canal aqueduct in the early 1800s. In season between May and late November, this aqueduct bed was busy with boat traffic.

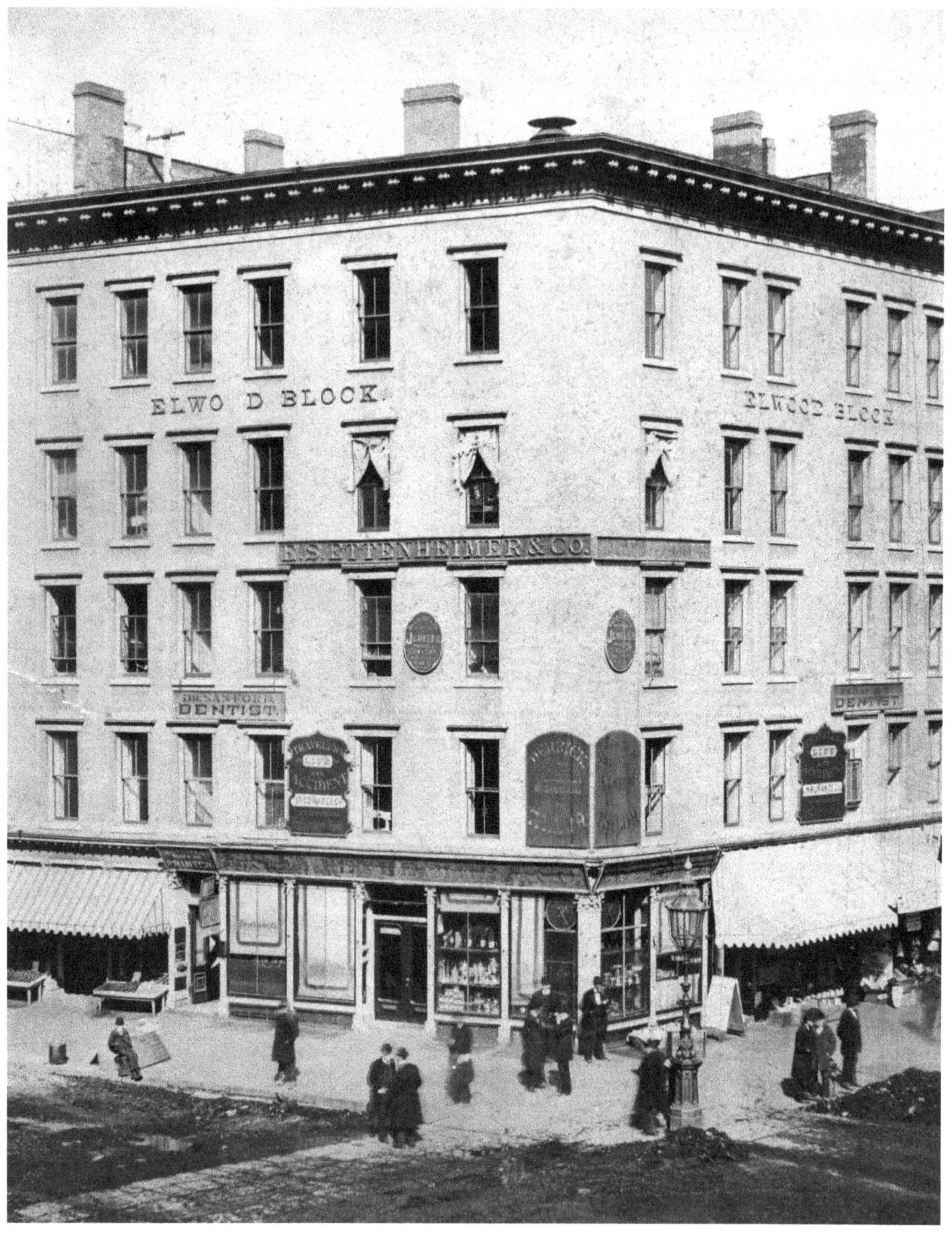

The busy intersection of Main and State streets, known as the Four Corners, was the site of a stone building in 1818. Expanded several times, the five-story building was known as the Burns Block about 1846. In 1864 the name changed to the Elwood Block. It was demolished and replaced with the Elwood Building in 1879. Pictured here before 1879, the Elwood Block is leased to tailor Timothy Derrick, dentist John F. Sanford, and jeweler Elias S. Ettenheimer.

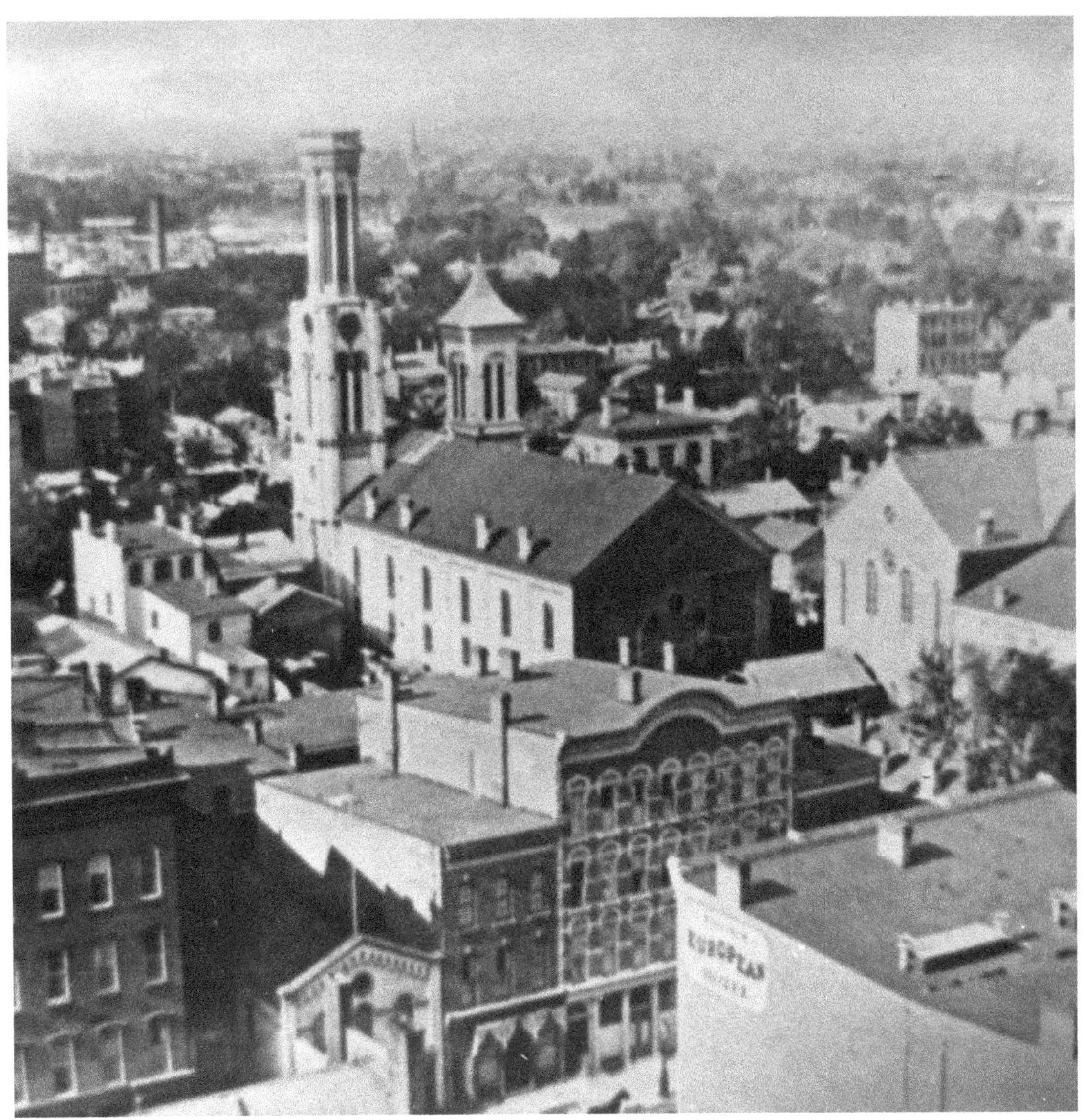

The Central Presbyterian Church on Plymouth Avenue (then Sophia Street) and the First Baptist Church to the right are seen in this (ca. 1870s) northwest view of downtown Rochester from atop the Powers Building at the Four Corners. A portion of Fitzhugh Street shows in the foreground.

People said Abelard Reynolds took a great financial risk building the Reynolds Arcade in 1828. The four-story building cost $30,000, making it the largest, most expensive building west of the Hudson River. Just a decade after Rochester became a village, the arcade became the center of activity, housing a post office, Western Union, and Dewey's Books. Pictured here about 1877, this building stood until 1932, when it was demolished and replaced with the second Reynolds Arcade.

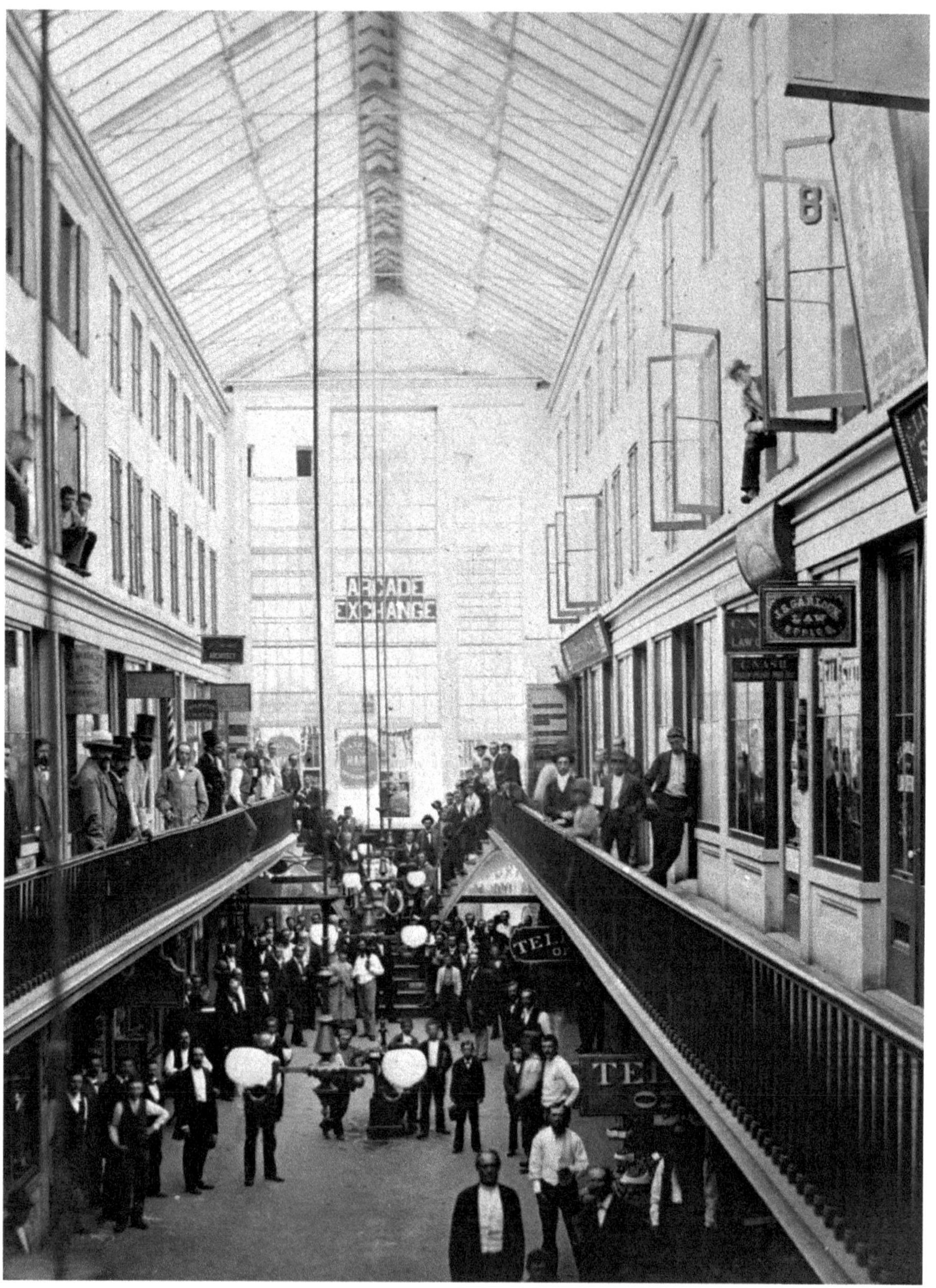

A City of Immigrants

(1880–1899)

The Irish who had arrived in large numbers in the 1840s and 1850s were being succeeded by German immigrants who brought skills in shoe manufacturing, brewing, optics, precision instruments, and agriculture. By the 1880s Italians were arriving, giving rise to the clothing industry, which soon outstripped the other industries in dollar value. Street names and names of businesses reflected the changes as one group of immigrants gave way to another. Second-generation Italians moved primarily to Irondequoit where they could grow produce. Rising at 3:00 A.M. to load up their products to open at the market by 5:00 A.M., they supplied the restaurants and city residents with some of the best produce in the nation. Italian and German language newspapers helped to keep the new immigrants informed about events in their native countries as well as their adoptive home.

Modern architectural designs allowed buildings to be built taller. When the seven-story Elwood Building was constructed in 1879, Daniel Powers felt challenged and added a seventh story with a second mansard roof in order to maintain his dominance on the skyline. In 1881 Powers added a hotel along Main Street that rivaled the elegance of the Palmer House in Chicago. Near the end of the decade, Frederick Cook built an eleven-story building on Main Street to house the German Insurance Company. Banker Samuel Wilder matched Cook with the construction of his eleven-story bank diagonally across the Four Corners from the Powers Bank. Not to be outdone, Powers again added two stories and a third mansard roof.

The protection offered by the Holly fire hydrants at Browns Race encouraged construction of new factories along St. Paul Street. As many as fifty-seven new buildings were built in the business section in the 1880s. By the end of the decade, the clothing industry was centered on St. Paul Street. Banks, hotels, legal offices, and government offices were centered on the Four Corners, which before had been the center of everything. Retail businesses moved down East Main Street, extending the footprint of downtown.

The celebration of the city's first half century brought a recitation of accomplishments from business and government leaders. A look down the busy Main Street was beyond the pioneers' visions a short lifetime before.

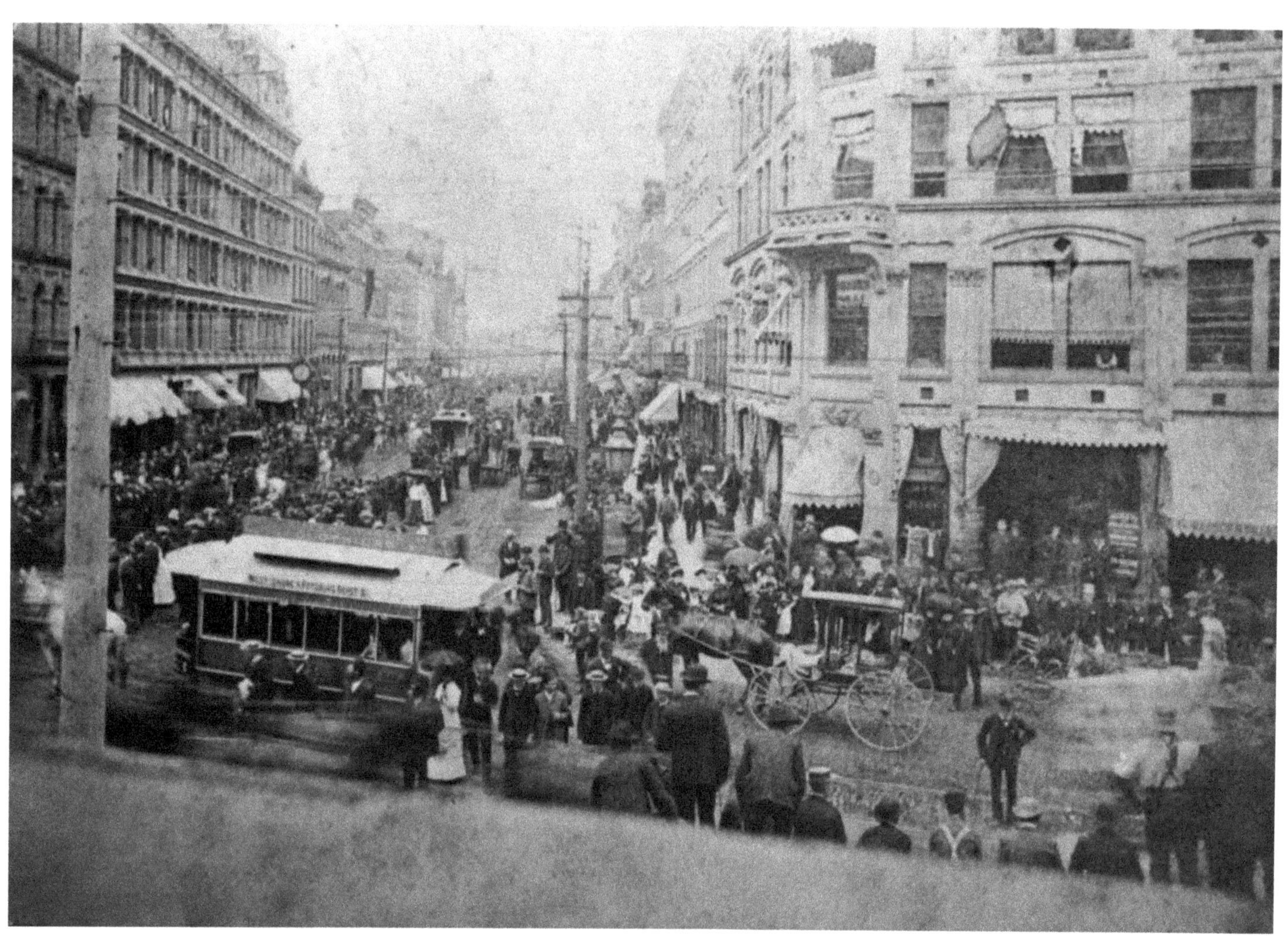

This view north from the Four Corners at State Street and Main about 1880 shows the nearly locking traffic of the busy downtown as wagons, horse-drawn streetcars, and pedestrians make their way through. A policeman stands in the street to help maintain order. The Powers Building can be seen on the left and the new Elwood Building on the right. State Street, which becomes Lake Avenue, was one of the first plank roads constructed.

Facing west from the Elwood Building at the Four Corners, the Powers Building can be seen on the right and Smith's Arcade on the left. In the distance is the Monroe County Court House, recognizable by its domed roof. The historic Rochester Savings Bank dominates at center.

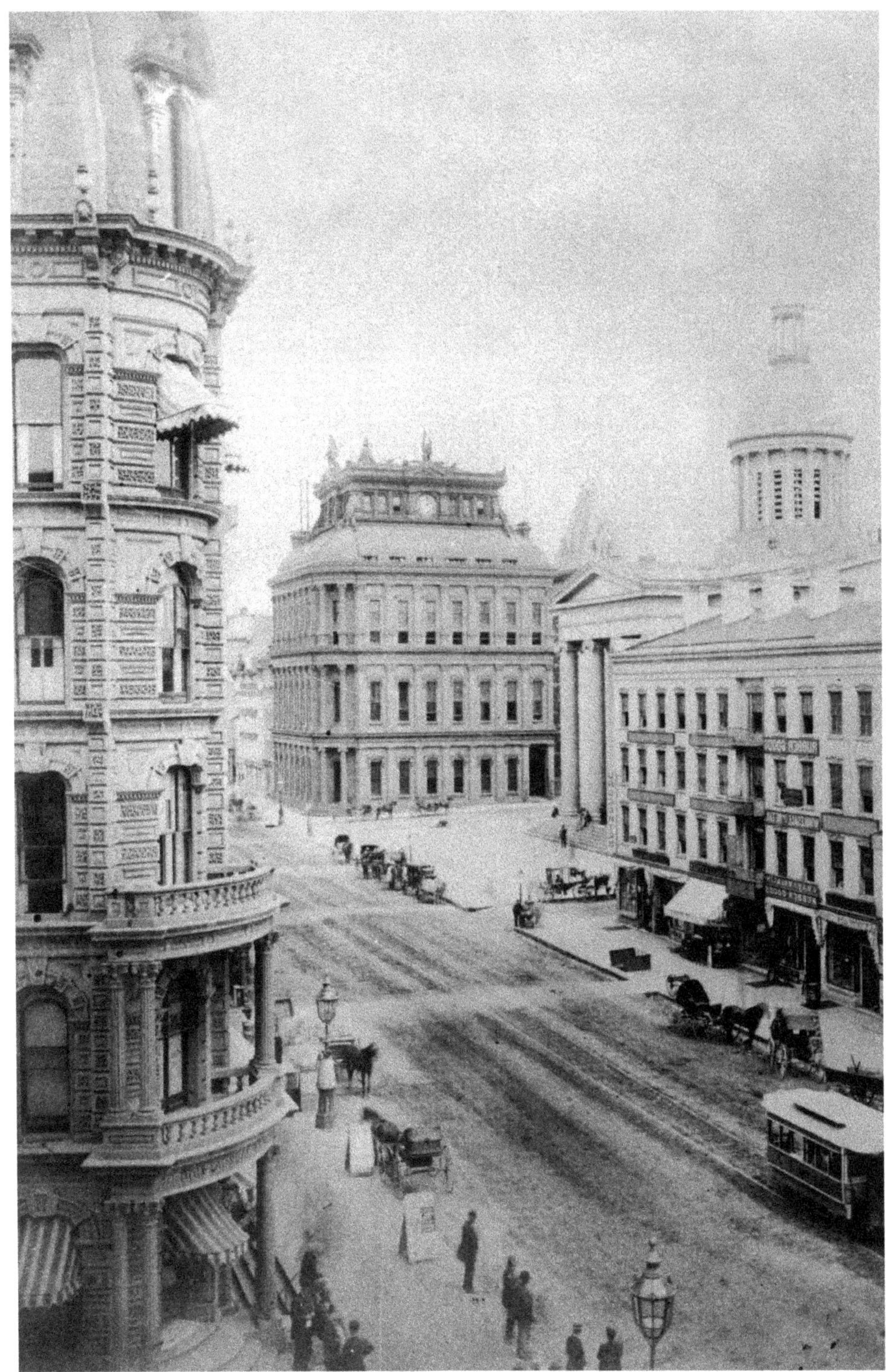

This image (ca. 1880) shows the Steam Fire Engine Co. No. 2 (organized in 1863) and Hook and Ladder Co. No. 2 (organized in 1878) at the Stillson Street firehouse between East Main and Achilles streets.

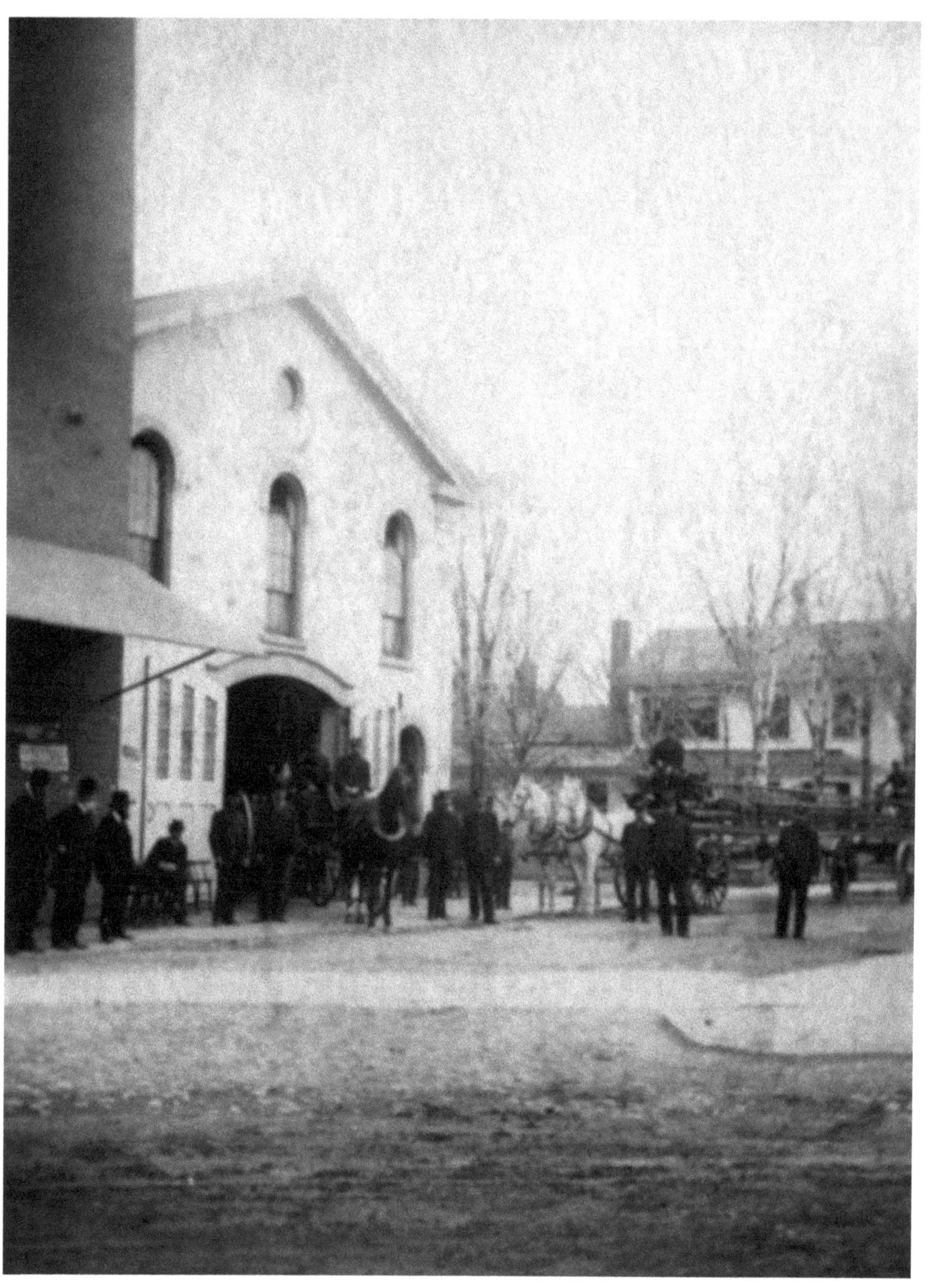

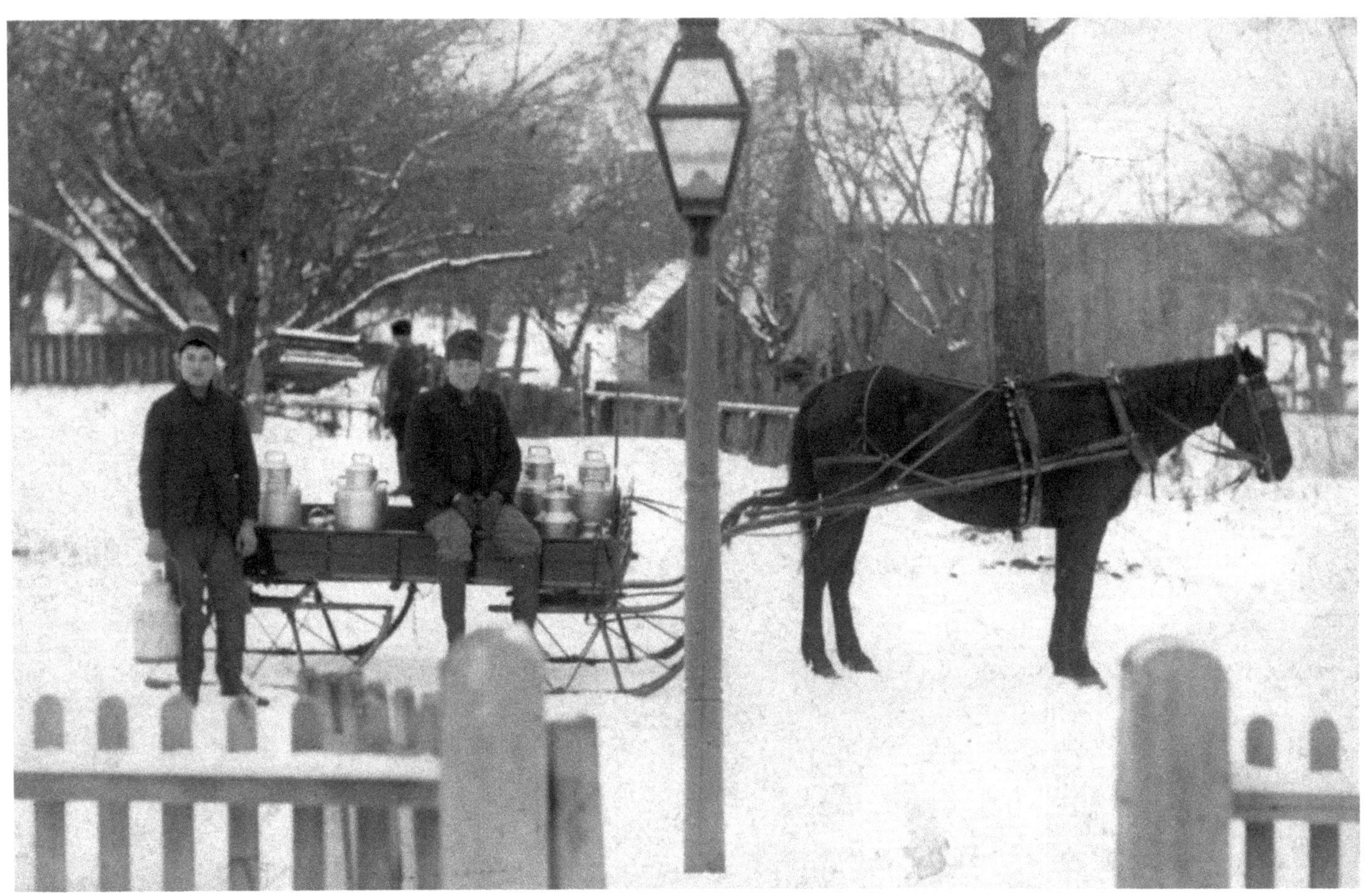

Residents in the city commonly had their milk delivered daily by local farmers, who rose in the wee hours of the morning to provide that service. Many houses in the city still have milk delivery doors near the side or rear doors. This photograph (from 1880 or before) shows Josh Kintz on the left and Milton Kintz seated on the sleigh.

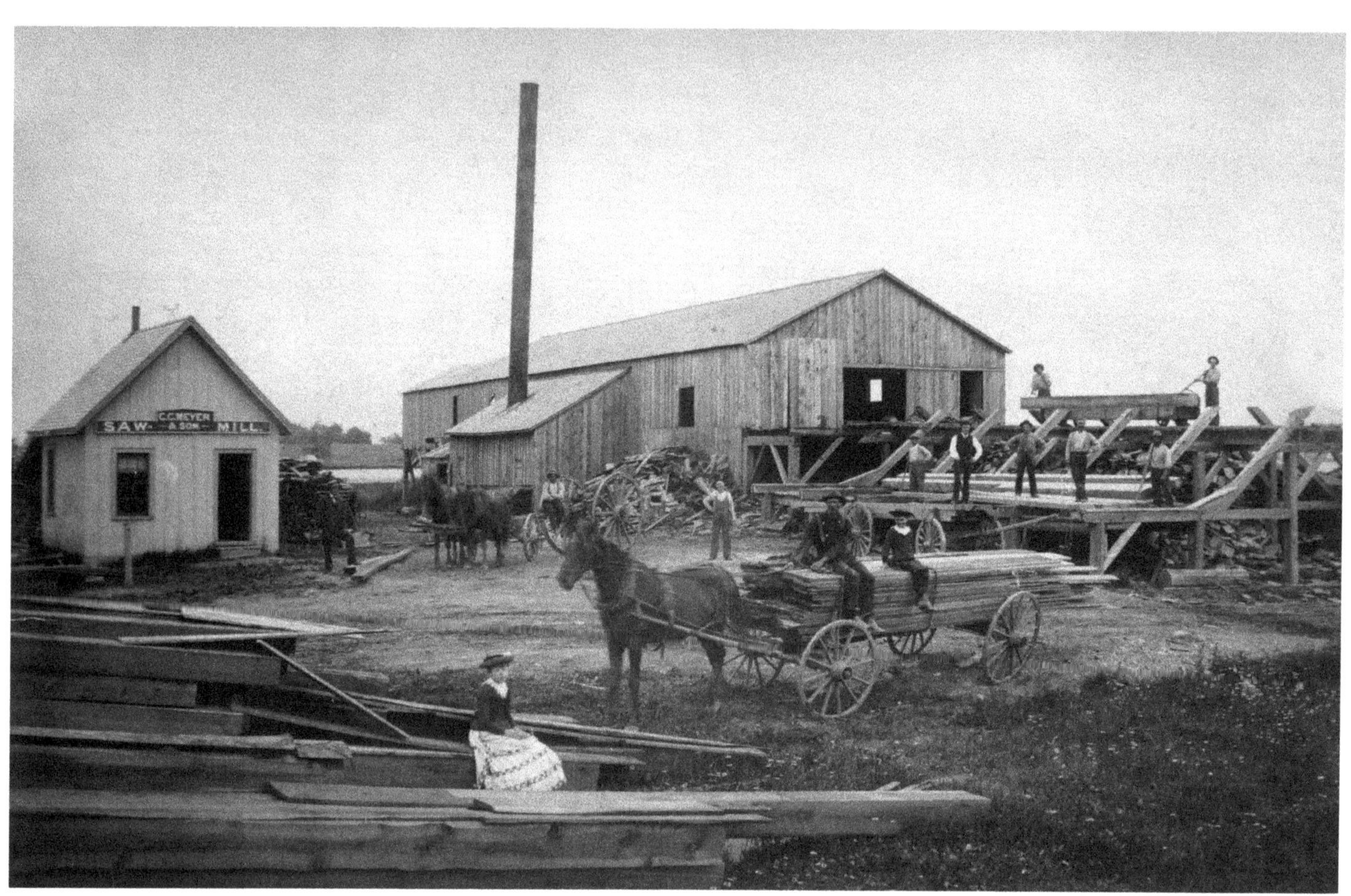

Near the intersection of Monroe Avenue and the Erie Canal, the C. C. Meyer and Son Steam Sawmill filled orders for lumber and building supplies for buildings and boats in the growing city of Rochester. One buckboard wagon is loaded with lumber as its passengers wait. A young girl in a dress in the foreground is possibly waiting for an order to be filled.

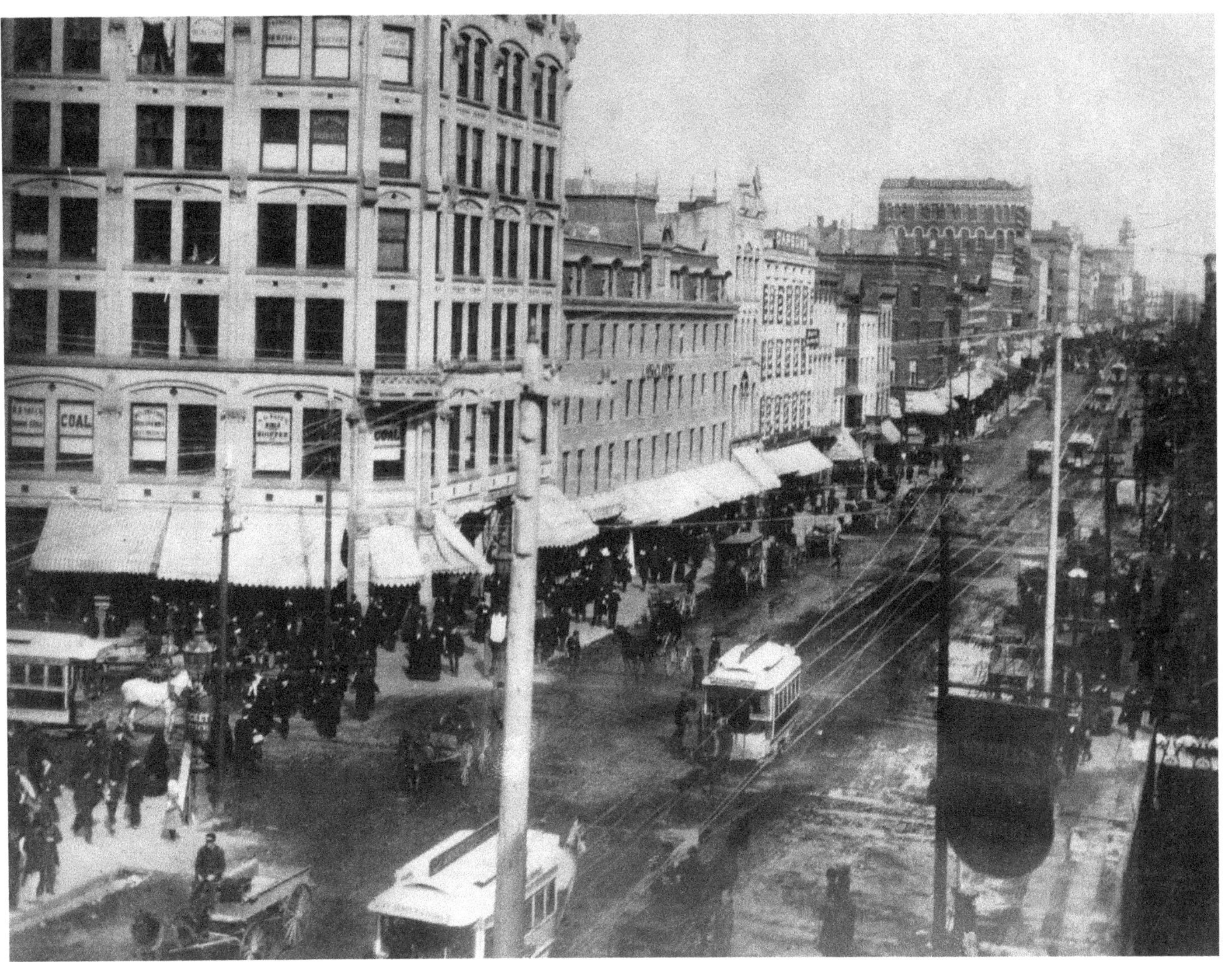

The Elwood Building can be seen at left in this view of Main Street looking east from the Four Corners. The Reynolds Arcade is still a center to the city's busy commerce and communications here in the 1880s. The horse-drawn streetcars have given way to electric cars and telephone lines now crisscross the city's streets.

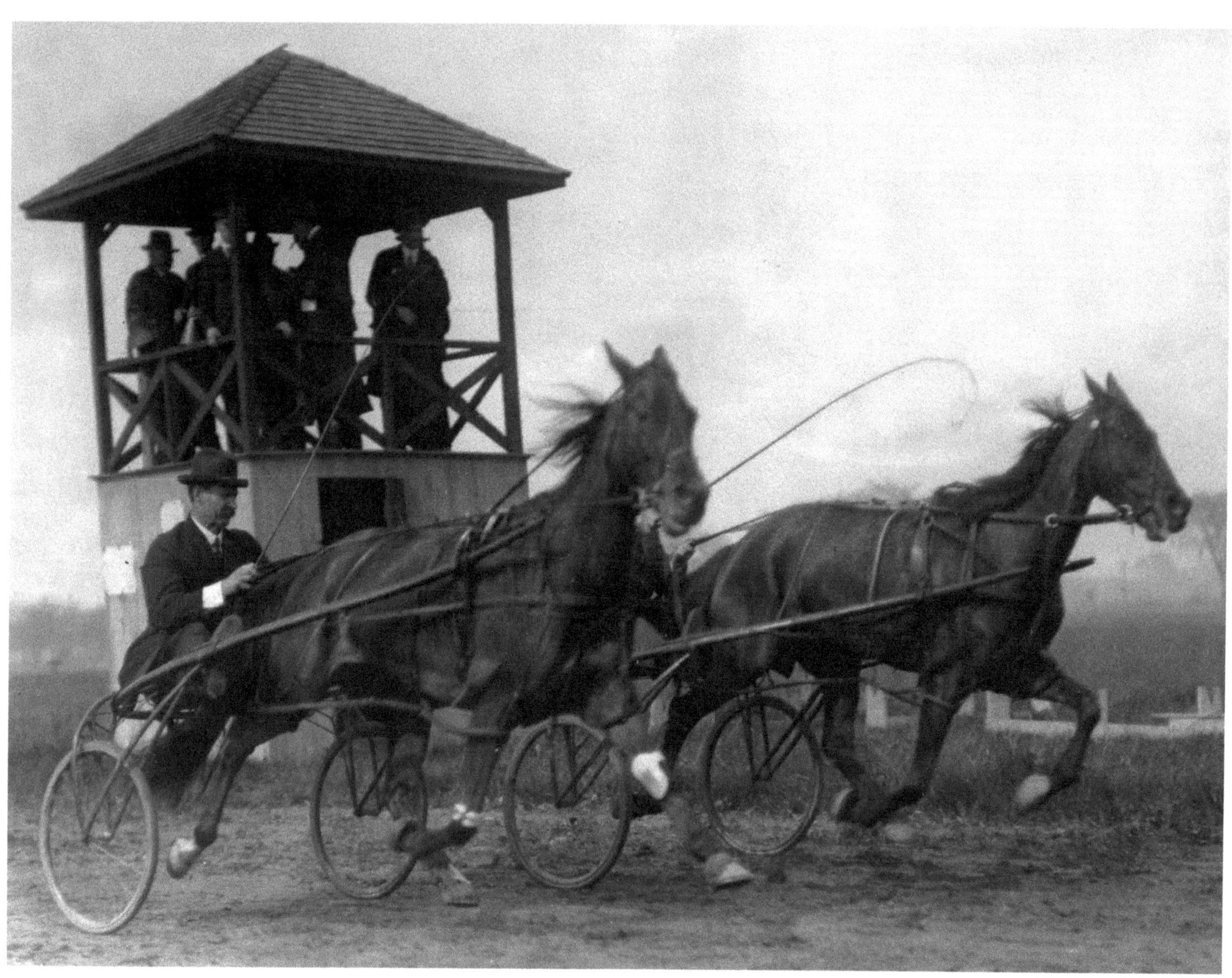

In the early 1900s Driving Park Race Track attracted hundreds to watch the sulky races. A sulky driver races past the judges' stand in this photograph from around the turn of the century. When the horse races ended, dog races were held for a few seasons before they were banned. Once a part of Greece, the land occupied by Driving Park became a part of the city.

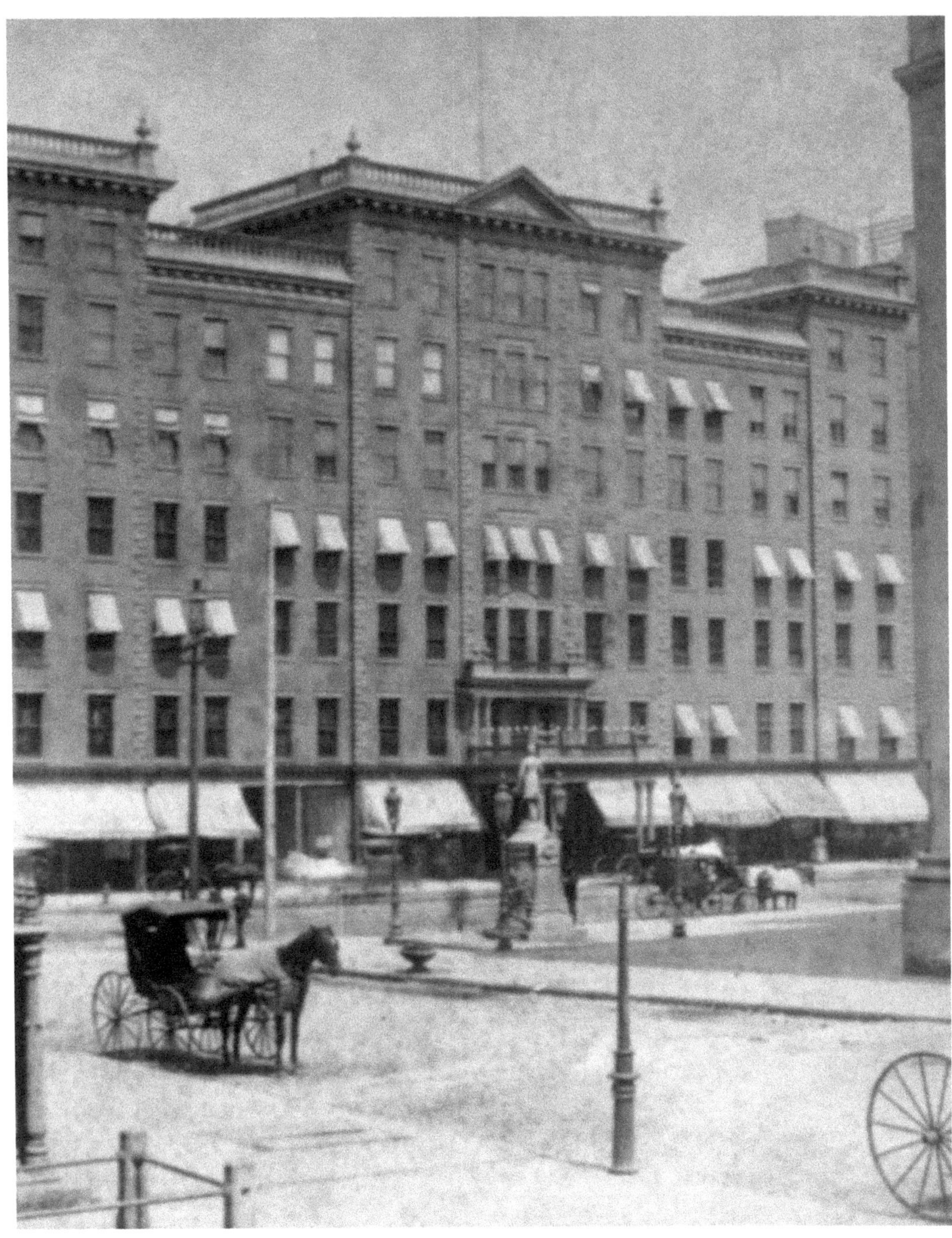

The Coggswell Fountain, donated by Henry D. Coggswell, stood in front of the Monroe County Court House to encourage those inclined "to wet their whistle" in a downtown tavern to drink water instead. The temperance movement was very strong throughout the last decades of the nineteenth century, culminating in the Prohibition laws of the twentieth century. In 1885 the fountain disappeared in what were considered "suspicious" circumstances.

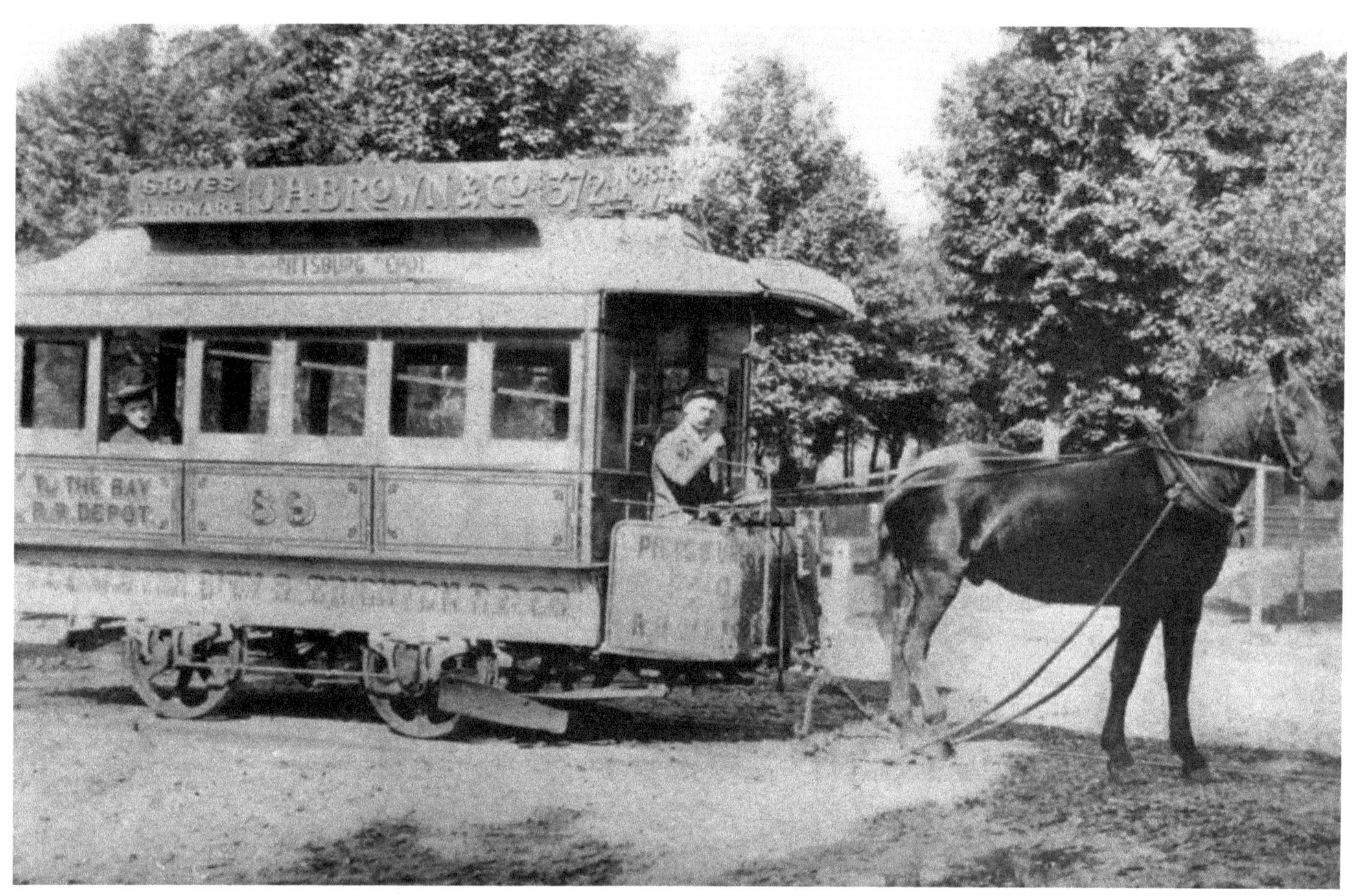

As residents of the city moved farther from downtown, horse-drawn streetcars filled the need for mass transportation. This Rochester City and Brighton Railroad Company began in 1863. In 1890 it sold to the Rochester Railway Co., which electrified the line. Fewer people kept their own horses and buggies as the city grew, relying instead on the streetcars and liveries.

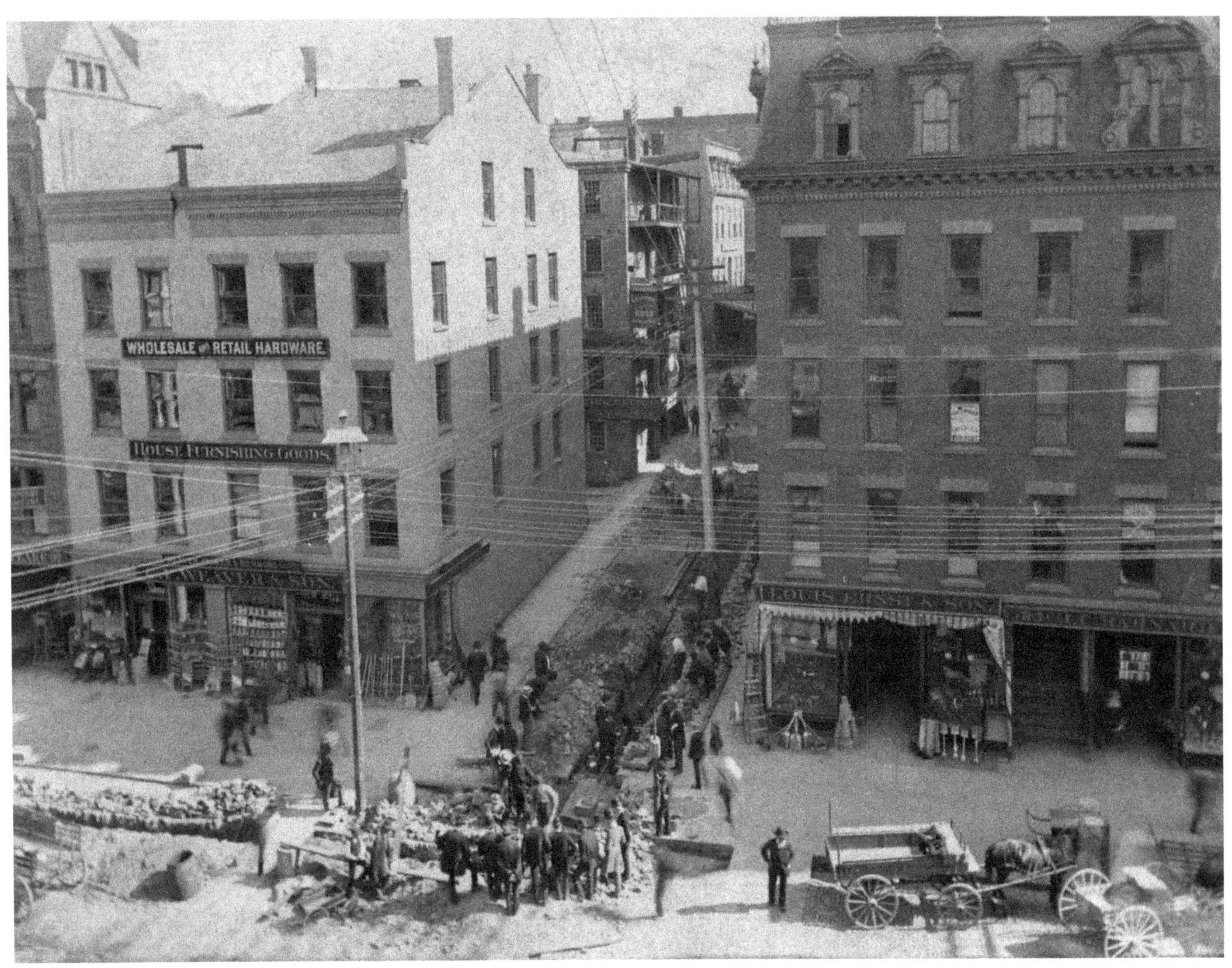

A rare view of Aqueduct Street from the south side of East Main Street shows loaded wagons and busy pedestrians in front of businesses like C. F. Weaver and Sons, Louis Ernst and Son, and J. C. Barnard.

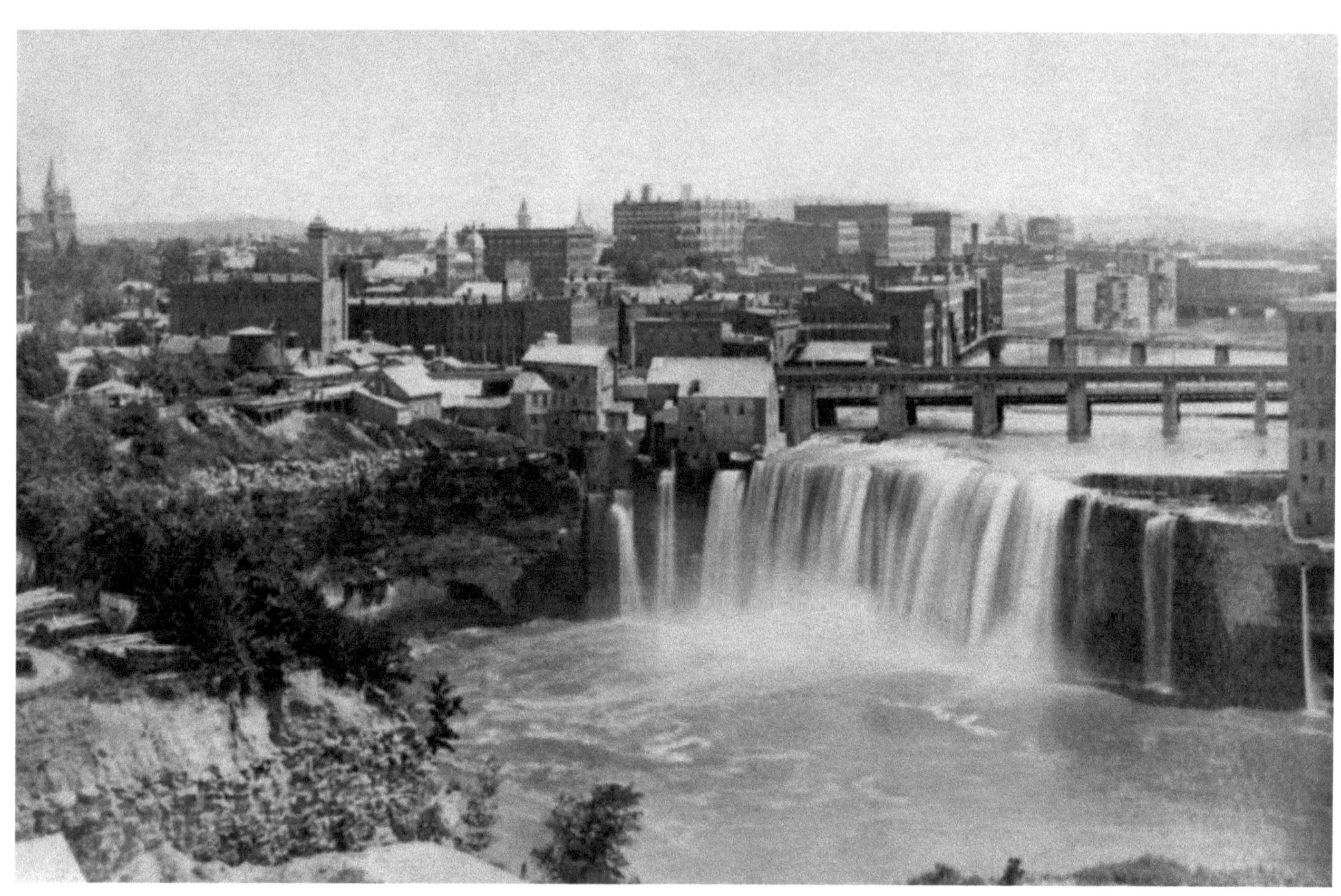

The Main, Genesee, or Upper Falls, today called the High Falls, about 1885 as seen from the roof of the Standard Brewery on the northeast side of the Genesee River. The New York Central Railroad, Andrews Street, and Main Street bridges can be seen, looking south on the north-flowing river. The ledge on the right is the site from which the famous daredevil Sam Patch leaped to his death on November 13, 1829.

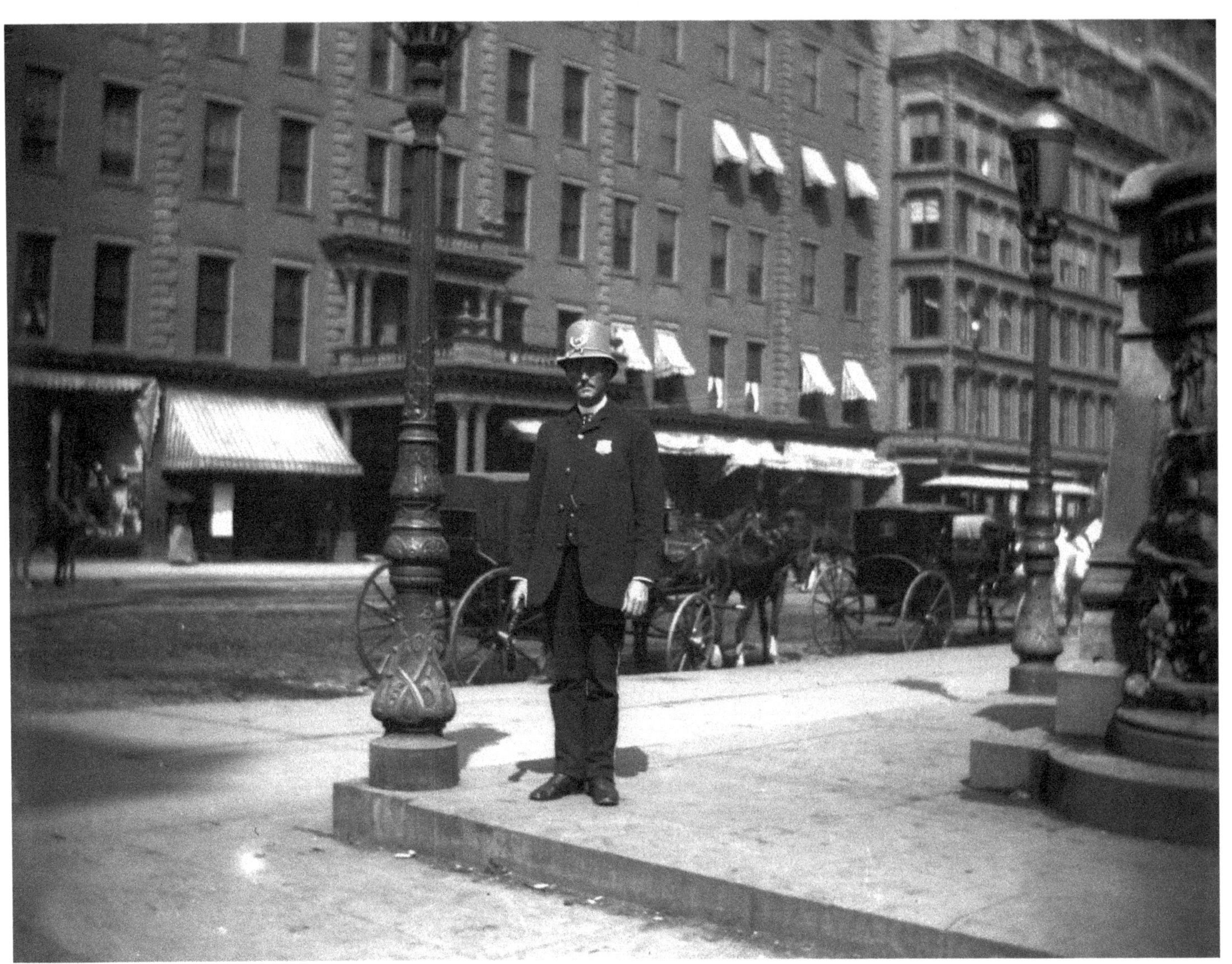

A policeman stands watch at the intersection of Main and Fitzhugh streets across from the Powers Building between 1883 and 1885. The famous Coggswell Fountain, placed at the front of the Monroe County Court House by temperance-minded Henry Coggswell, is visible at right. By this time, Rochester had been a city for half a century and was home to newly arriving German and Italian immigrants.

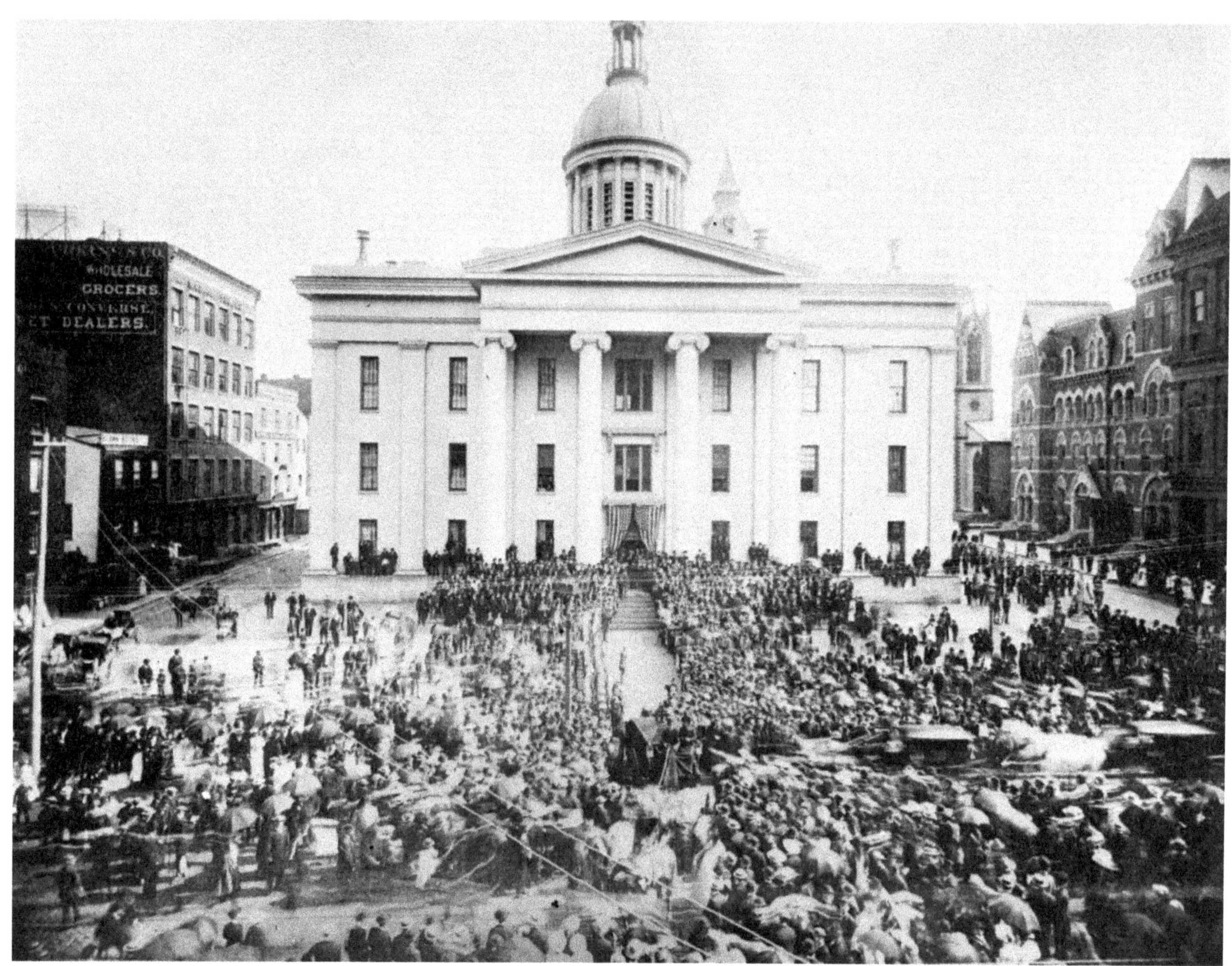

Hundreds of people gathered outside the second Monroe County Court House for the funeral of Lieutenant Frederick F. Kislingbury, who died on the arctic expedition of Adolphus Greely in 1884. Second in command, Kislingbury died of starvation along with several others in his unit, after a supply boat was unable to reach their ice-locked location. A few of his men survived to be rescued and rumors of cannibalism circulated. Kislingbury's remains were exhumed from his grave at Mt. Hope Cemetery. An autopsy confirmed cannibalism in one of America's most tragic expeditions.

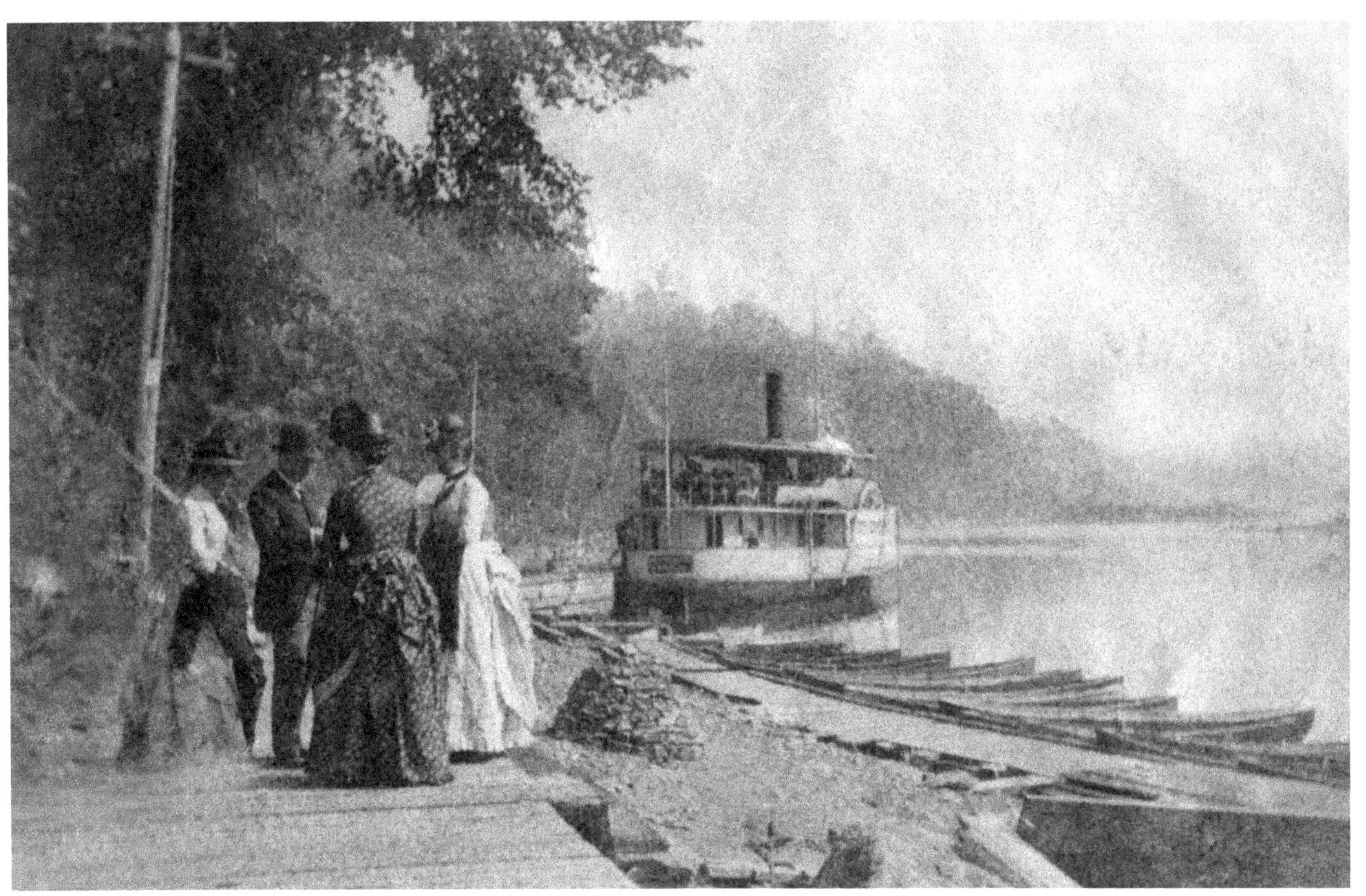

Passengers await boarding of the *City of Rochester* steamboat at the popular Glen House on the north side of the Lower Falls just below today's Maplewood Rose Garden. Boats came in and out of the Genesee River to Lake Ontario. Many boats traveled along the south shore of the lake, stopping at other lakeside communities and moving on to Canada or out for day trips for tourists and day trippers. Construction of a sewer main nearby ended the attractiveness of the popular restaurant and hotel.

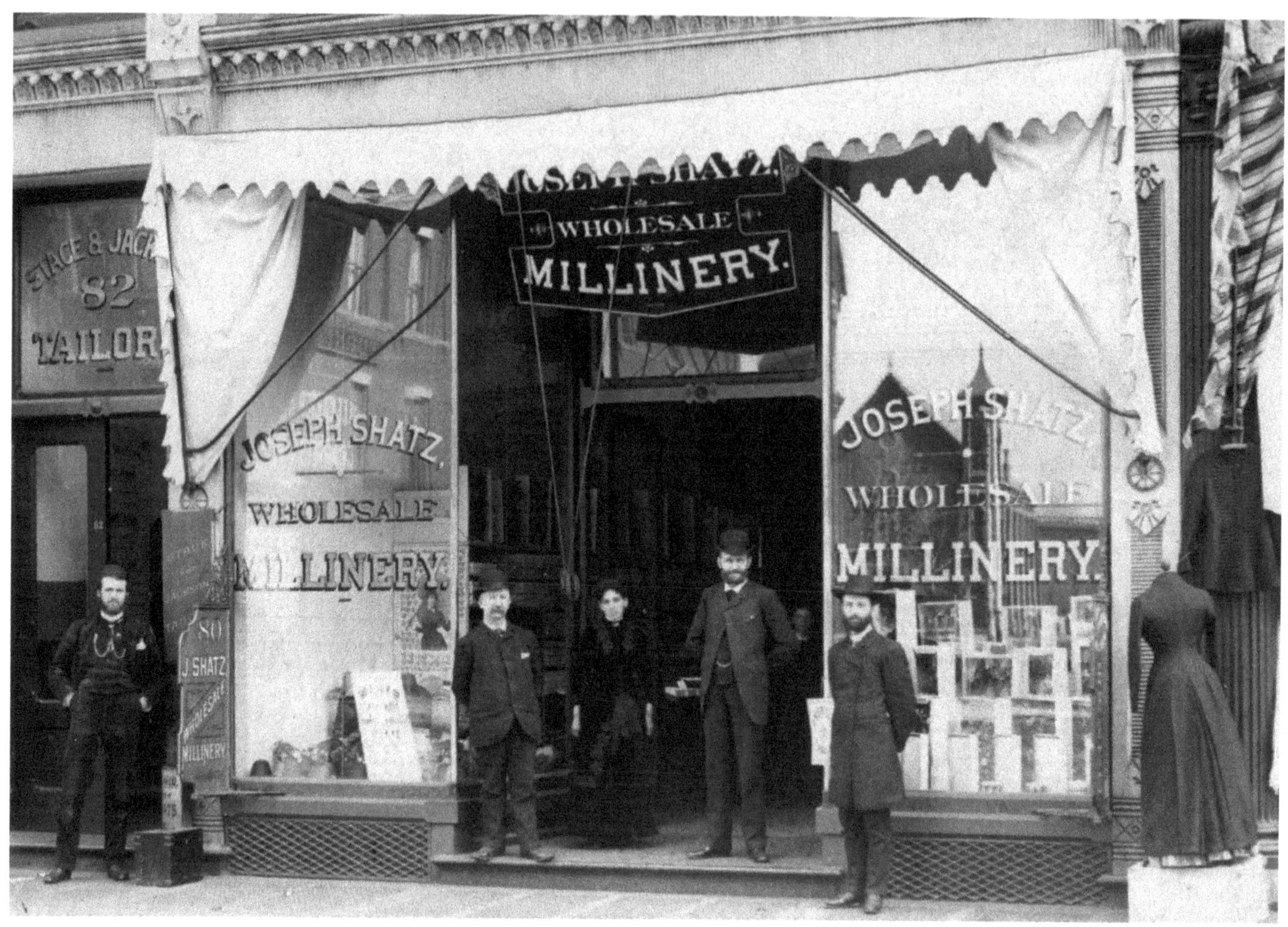

Several people stand in the doorway of wholesale milliner Joseph Shatz on State Street. A little off balance and without a hat, a woman's dress is displayed in front of the business next door. Women's hats were fashionable in the late nineteenth century. Many immigrant and single or widowed women in Rochester learned to make hats in night school.

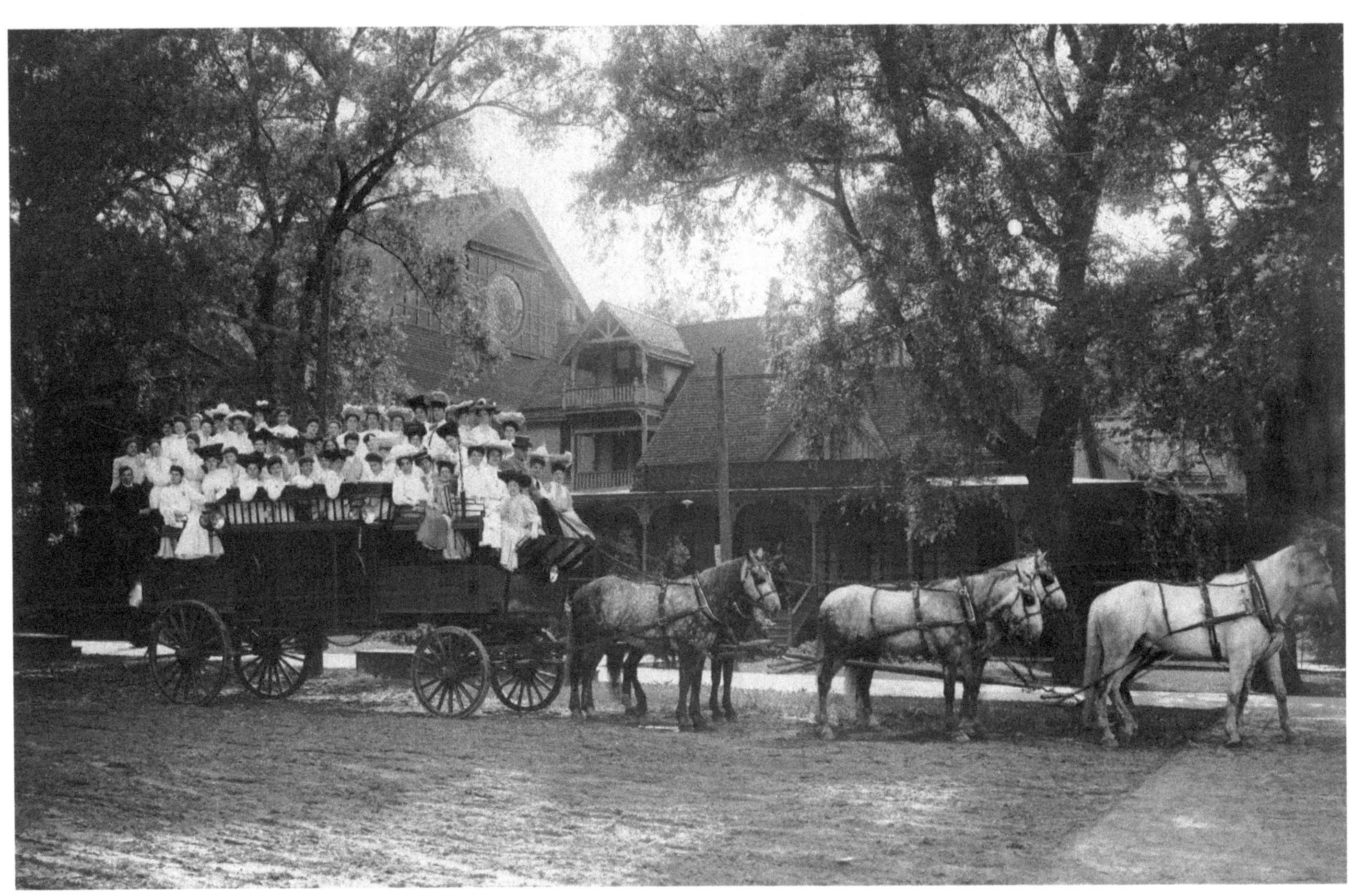

Bartholomay Cottage Hotel, run by Bartholomay Brewery, was a popular nineteenth-century site for picnics and other celebrations on Lake Ontario. The occasion is unknown in this photograph of a six-horse-drawn "carryall" wagon in front of the hotel.

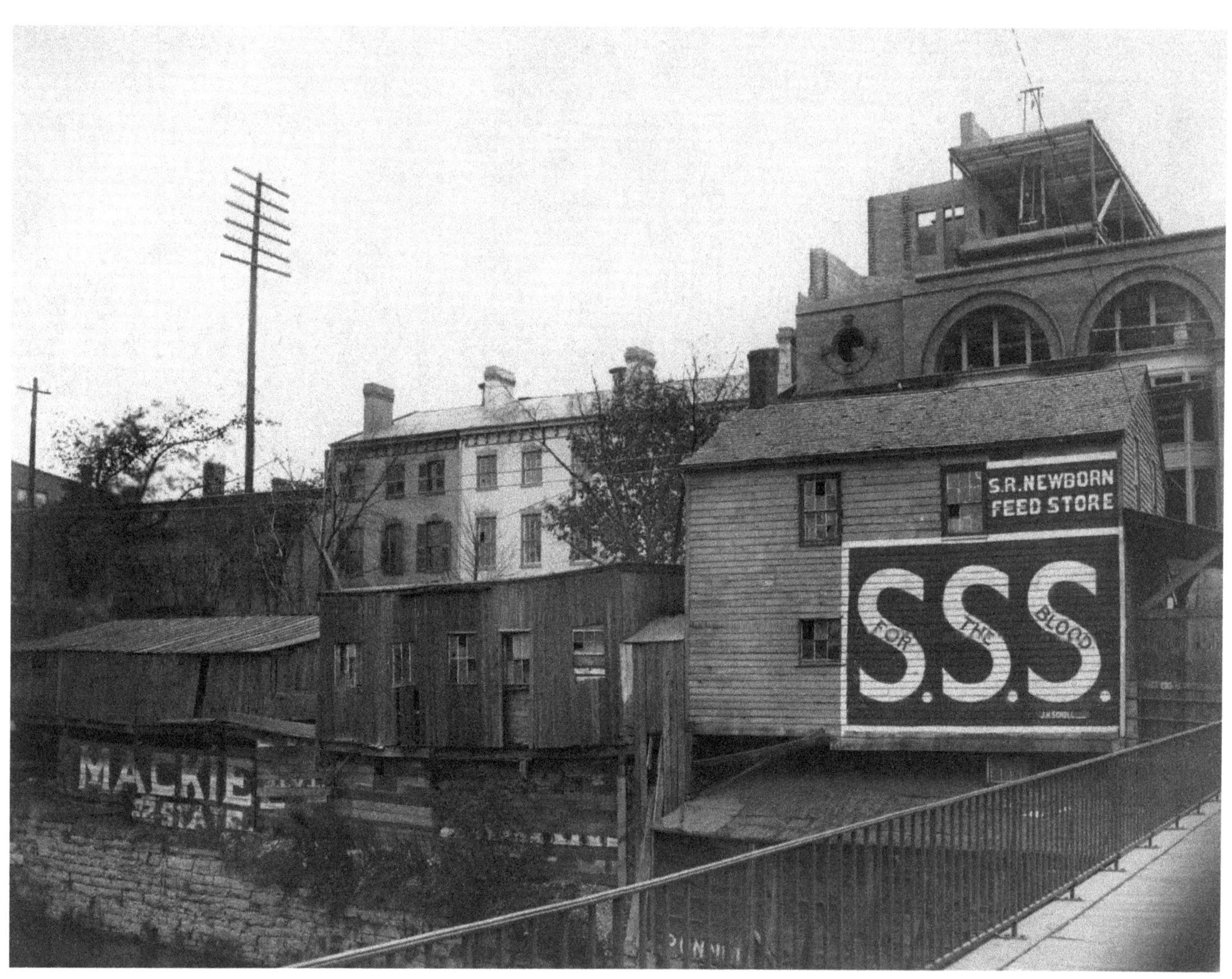

S. R. Newborn Feed Store displays a stenciled advertisement facing the Genesee River. Shown here are the backsides of deteriorating buildings along South St. Paul Street between Court Street and the Erie Canal aqueduct. (ca. 1875–1893)

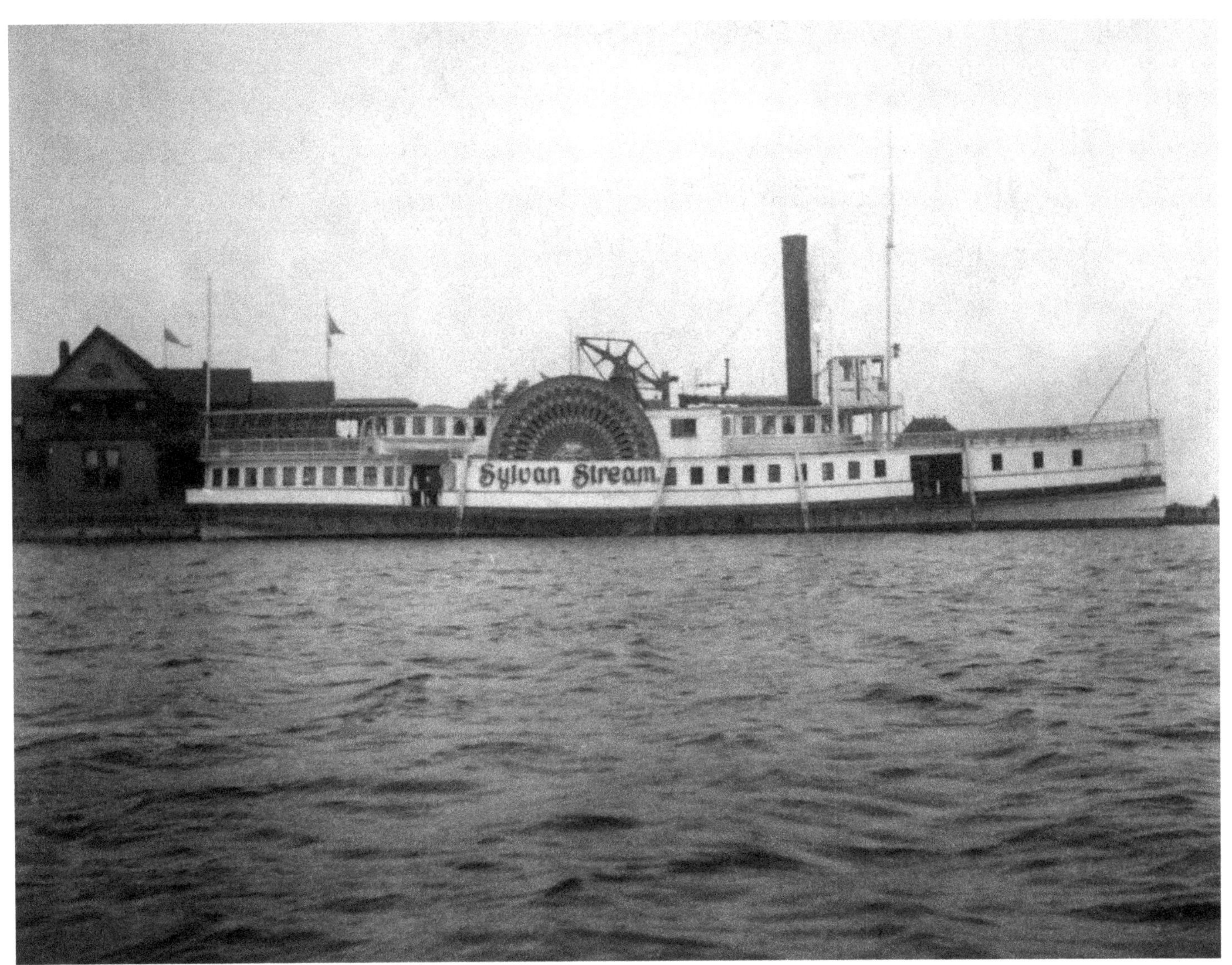

The sidewheeler steamer *Sylvan Stream,* owned by the Lake Ontario Steamboat Company, made daily summer trips between the Glen House and Charlotte. The sidewheeler could carry up to 800 passengers. In the late nineteenth and early twentieth centuries, steamboat travel on the lake was common.

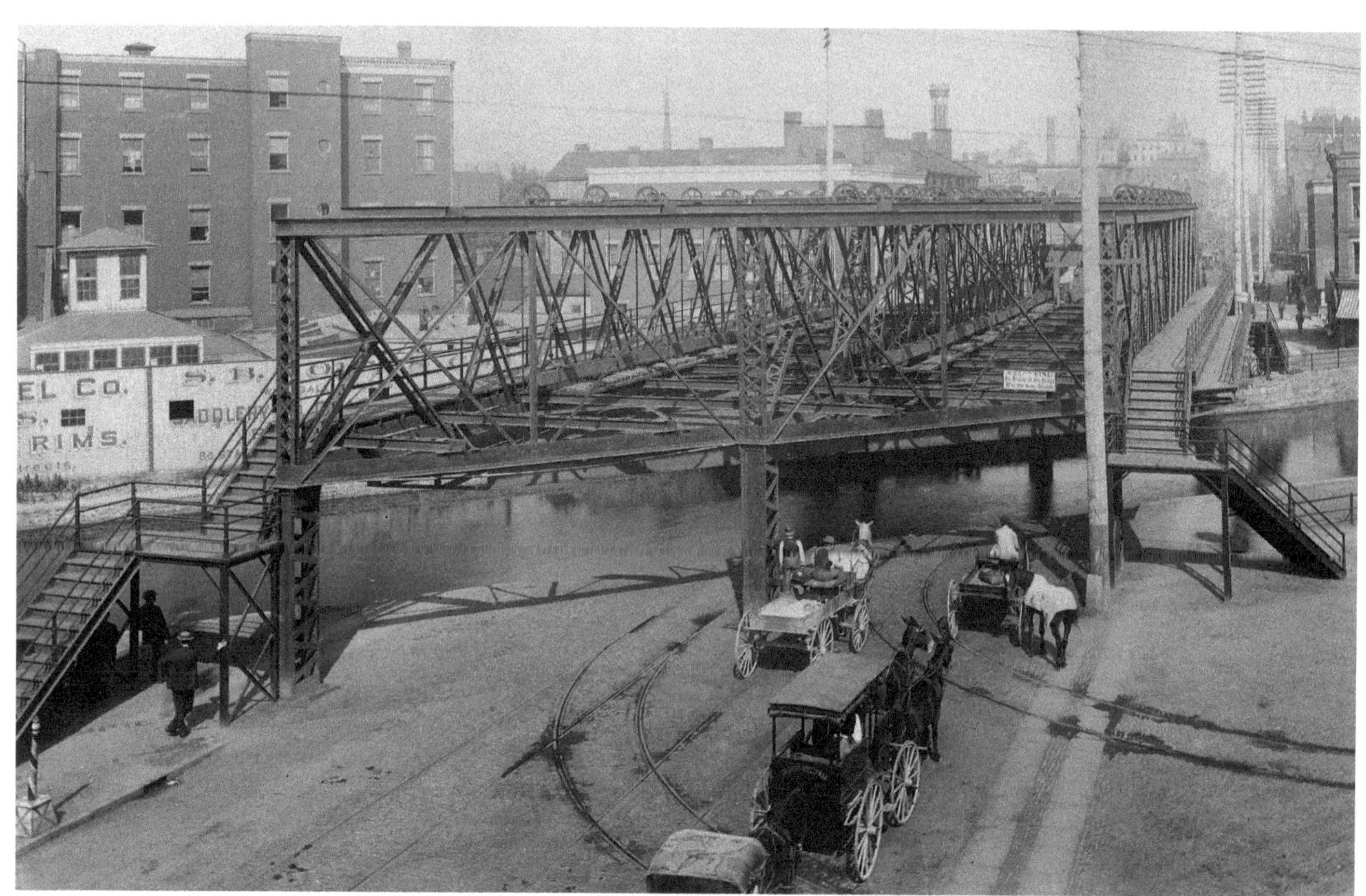

Several horse-drawn wagons wait for the signal to cross the West Avenue lift bridge at the Erie Canal. This bridge replaced the old swing bridge. The sign warns carriage drivers of a $25 fine for driving on the bridge after the gong sounds, alerting them that the bridge will be lifted.

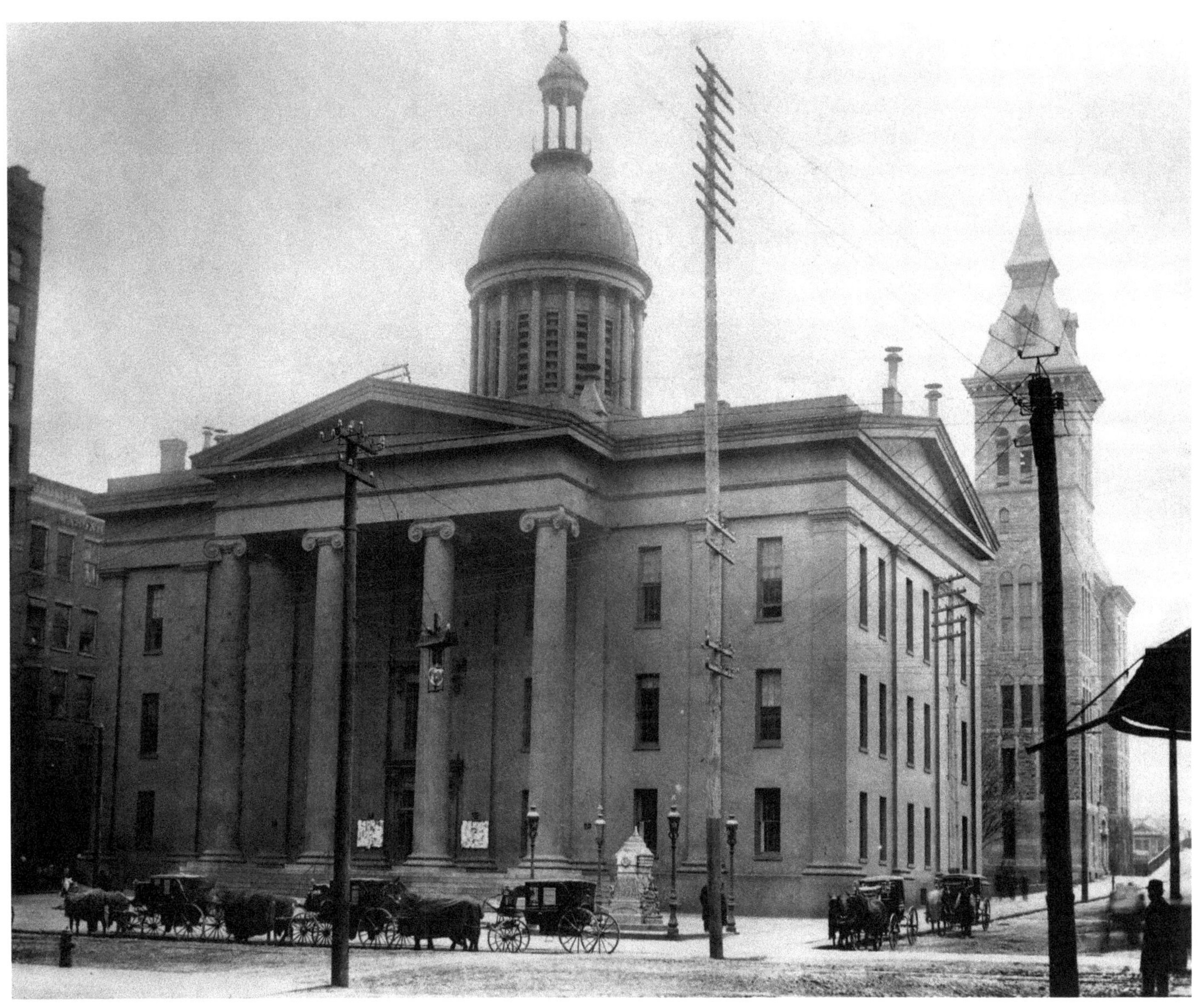

This second Monroe County Court House was built in 1850 and demolished in 1894 to make way for the third Court House, now referred to as the Monroe County Office Building. Old City Hall is in the background at right.

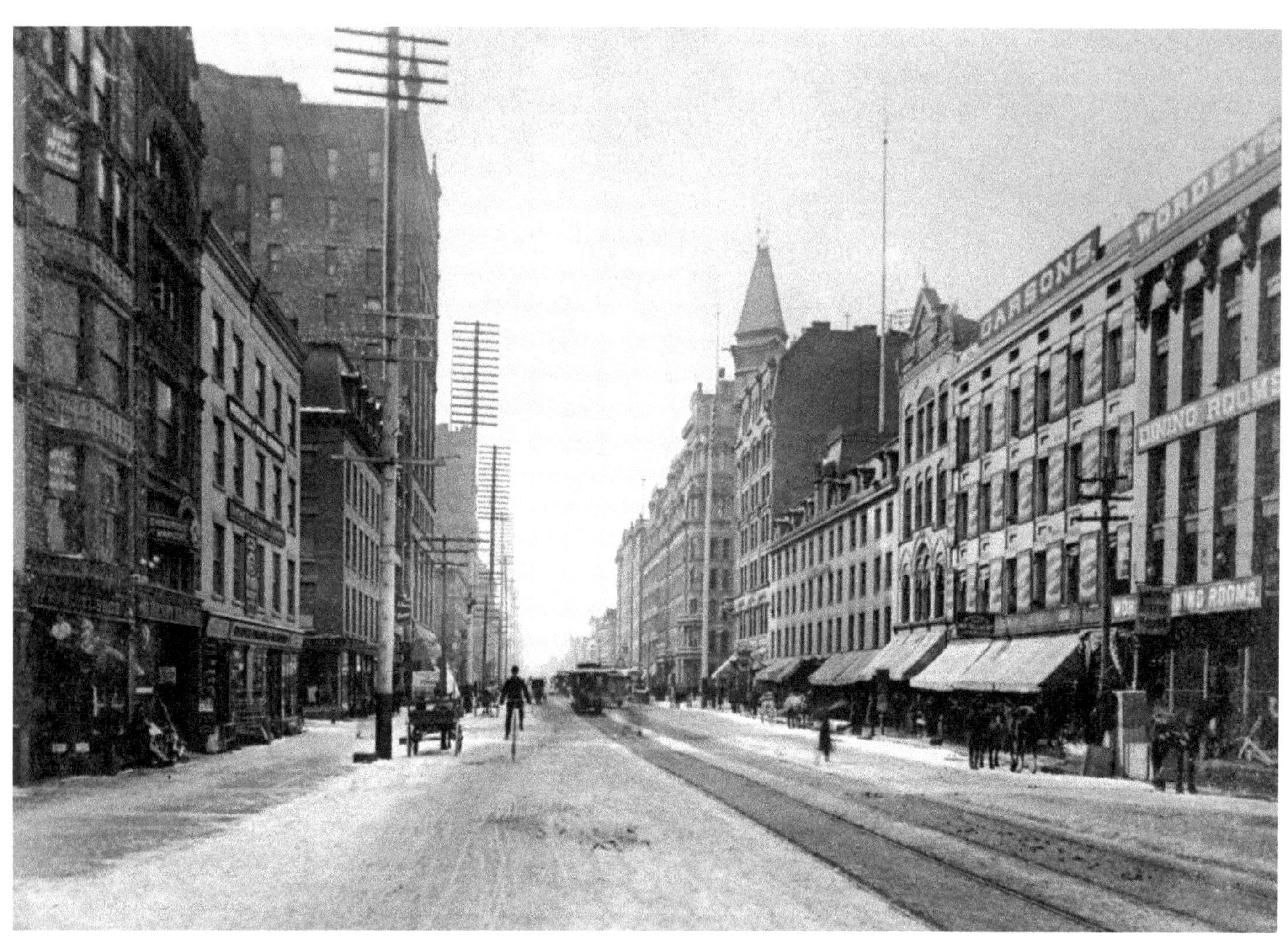

Main Street facing west about 1888. Worden's Eating House, Garson's Department Store, the Elwood Building, and the Powers Building are visible on the north side of the street. The Wilder Building is on the south side at left.

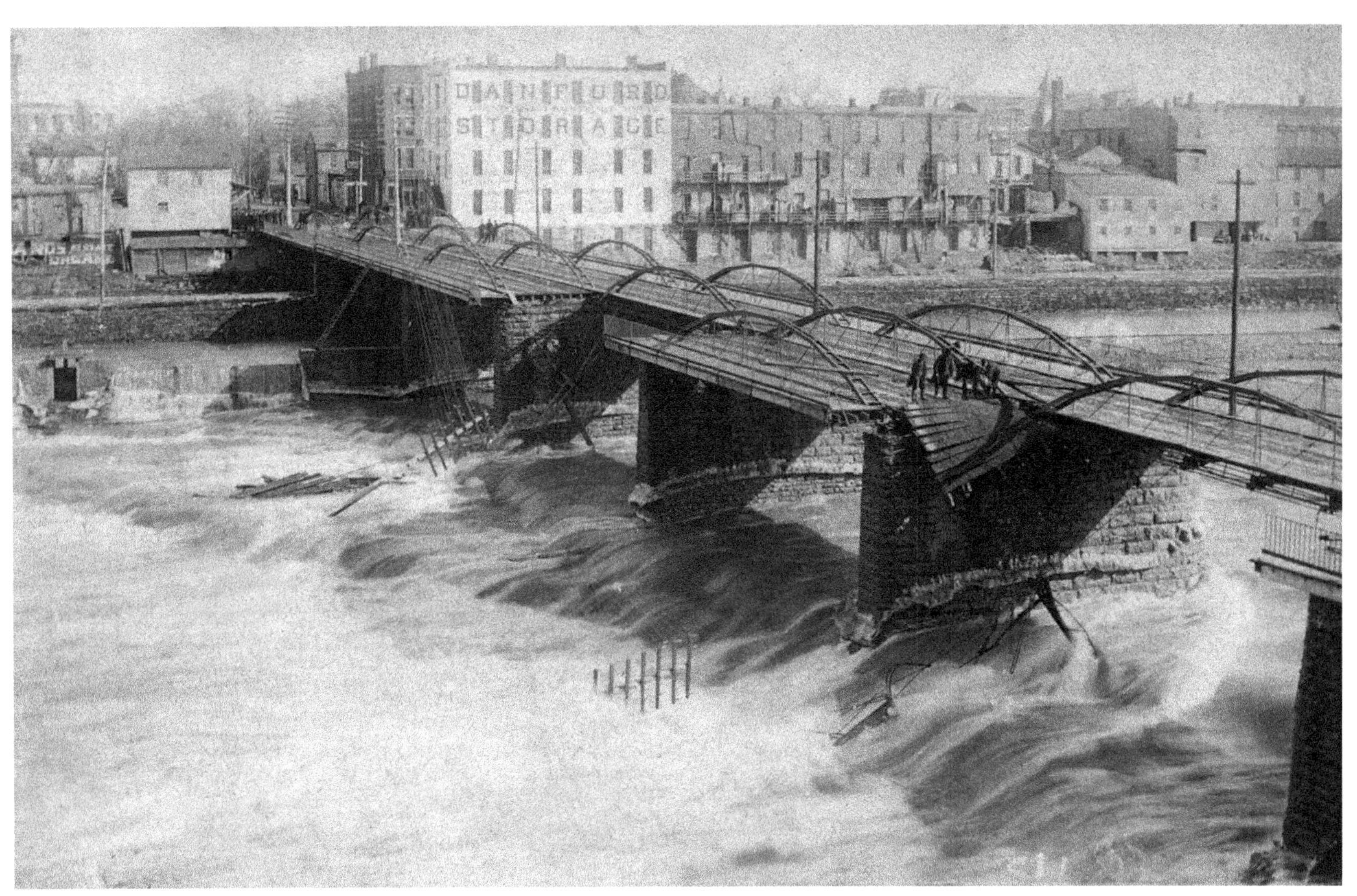

On February 18, 1887, a severe storm with heavy winds tore out a section of the Court Street bridge, pulling out the paving planks and wire poles. Curious spectators stand precariously at the edge of a fallen section, heedless of the story of a woman swept over the bridge and drowned when the bridge was damaged.

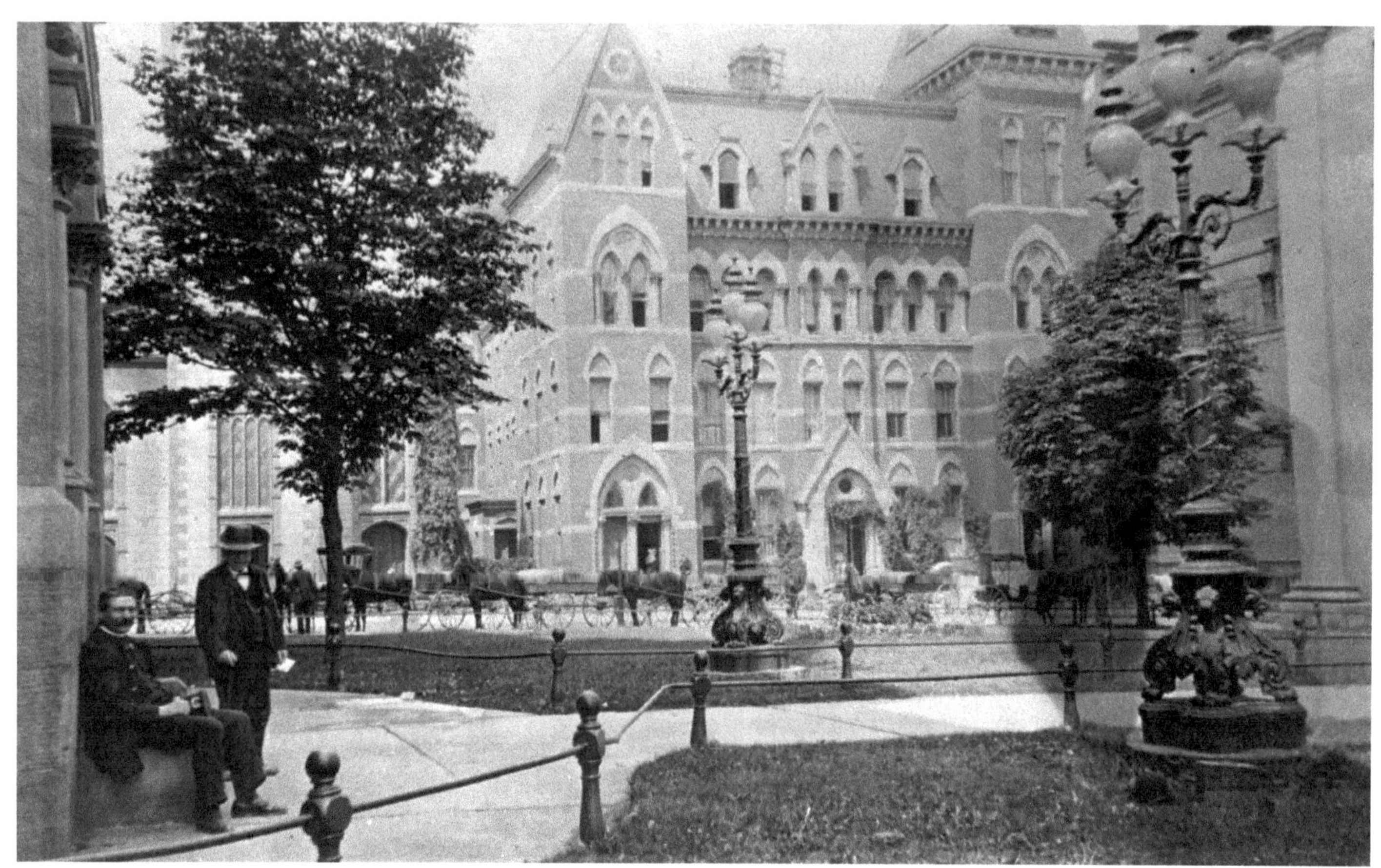

The beautiful Rochester Free Academy stands across from the peaceful plaza between old City Hall and the second Monroe County Court House. St. Luke's Church is visible on the left next to the academy. The plaza is gone, but all of these buildings still stand today.

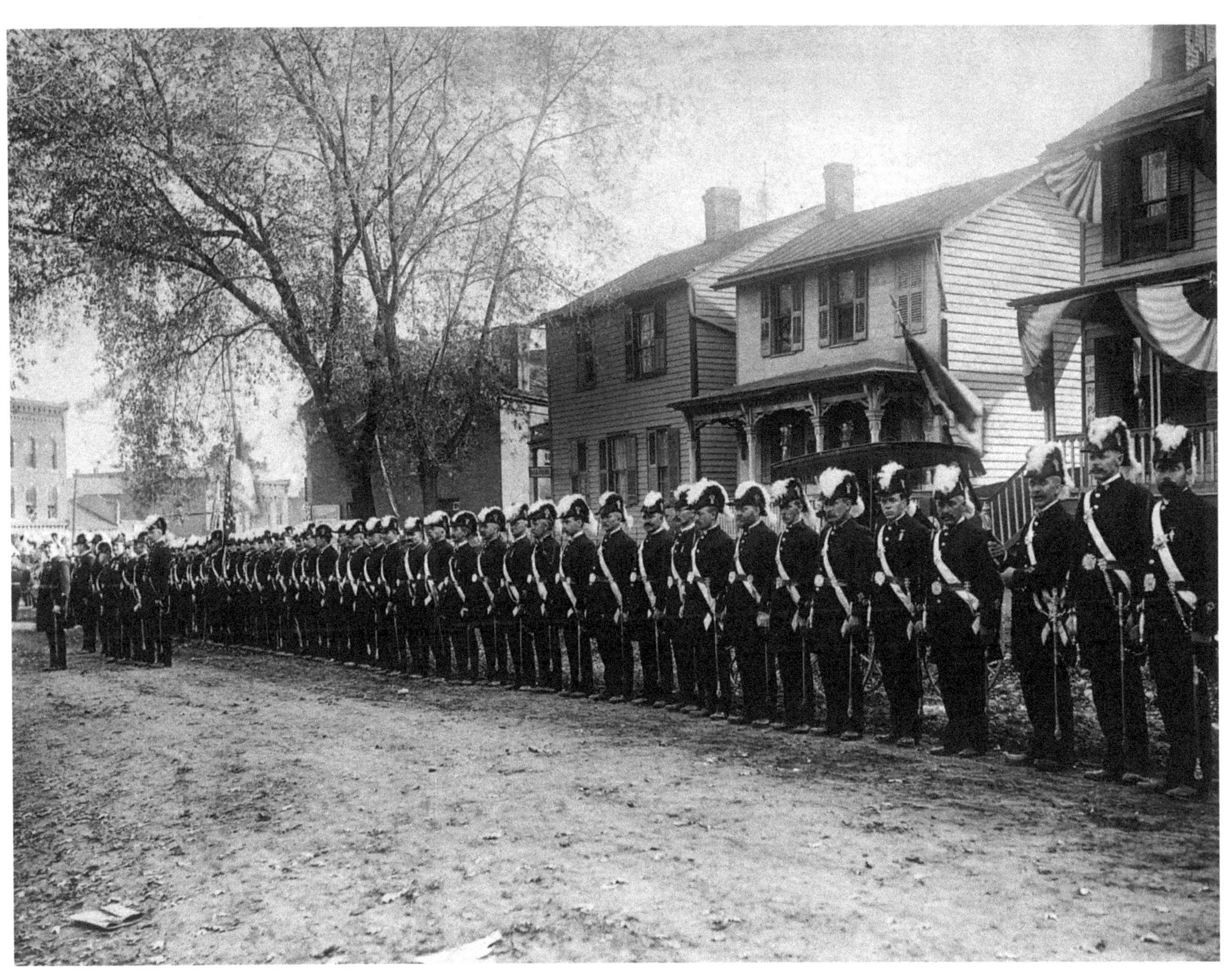

The Monroe Commandery No. 12 of the Knights of Templar, dressed in full uniform, practice precision drills at an unnamed location around the turn of the century.

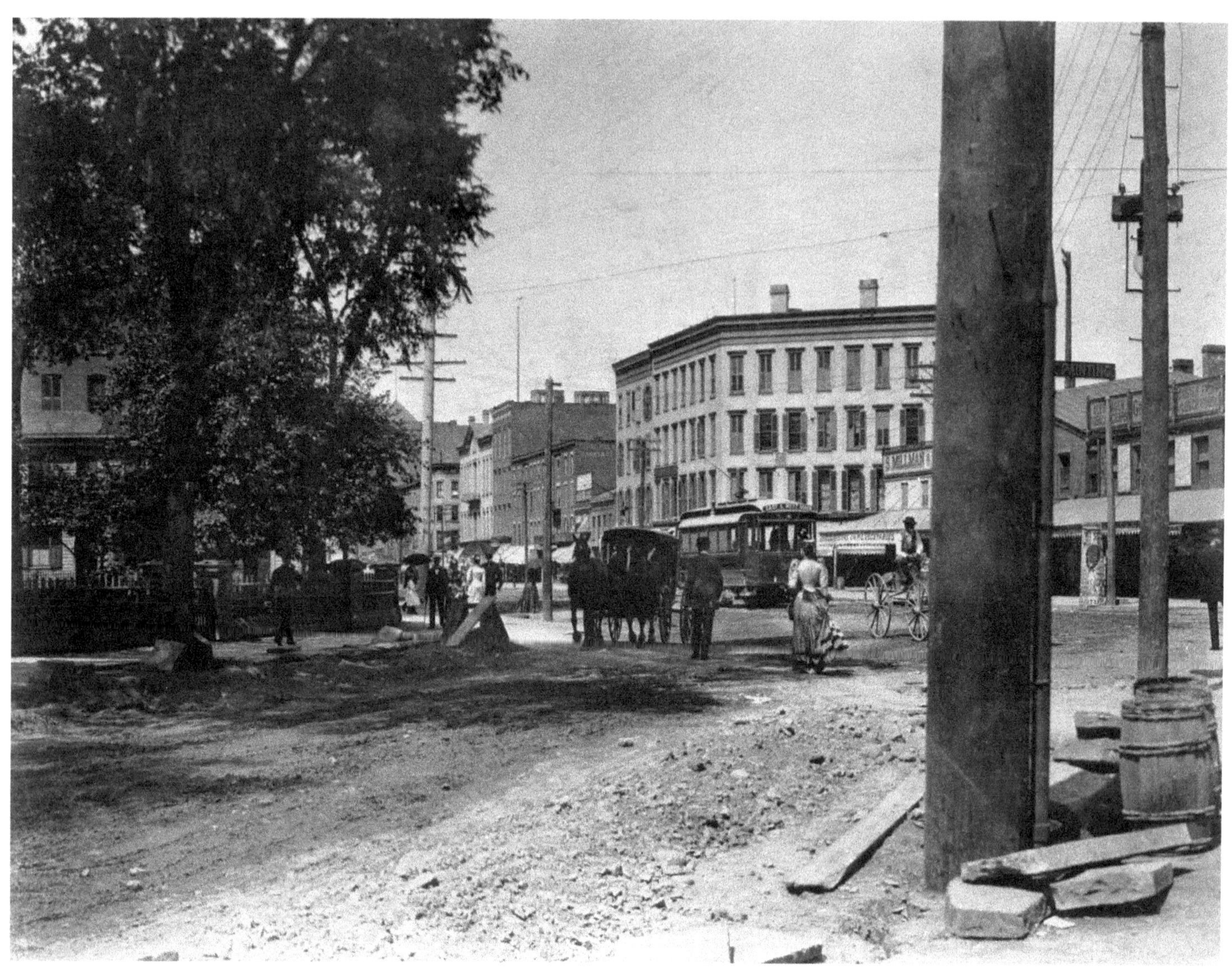

In this view west down Main Street, wagons and a streetcar are seen in the background at the intersection of East Avenue. In the foreground, street construction appears to be under way. (ca. 1890)

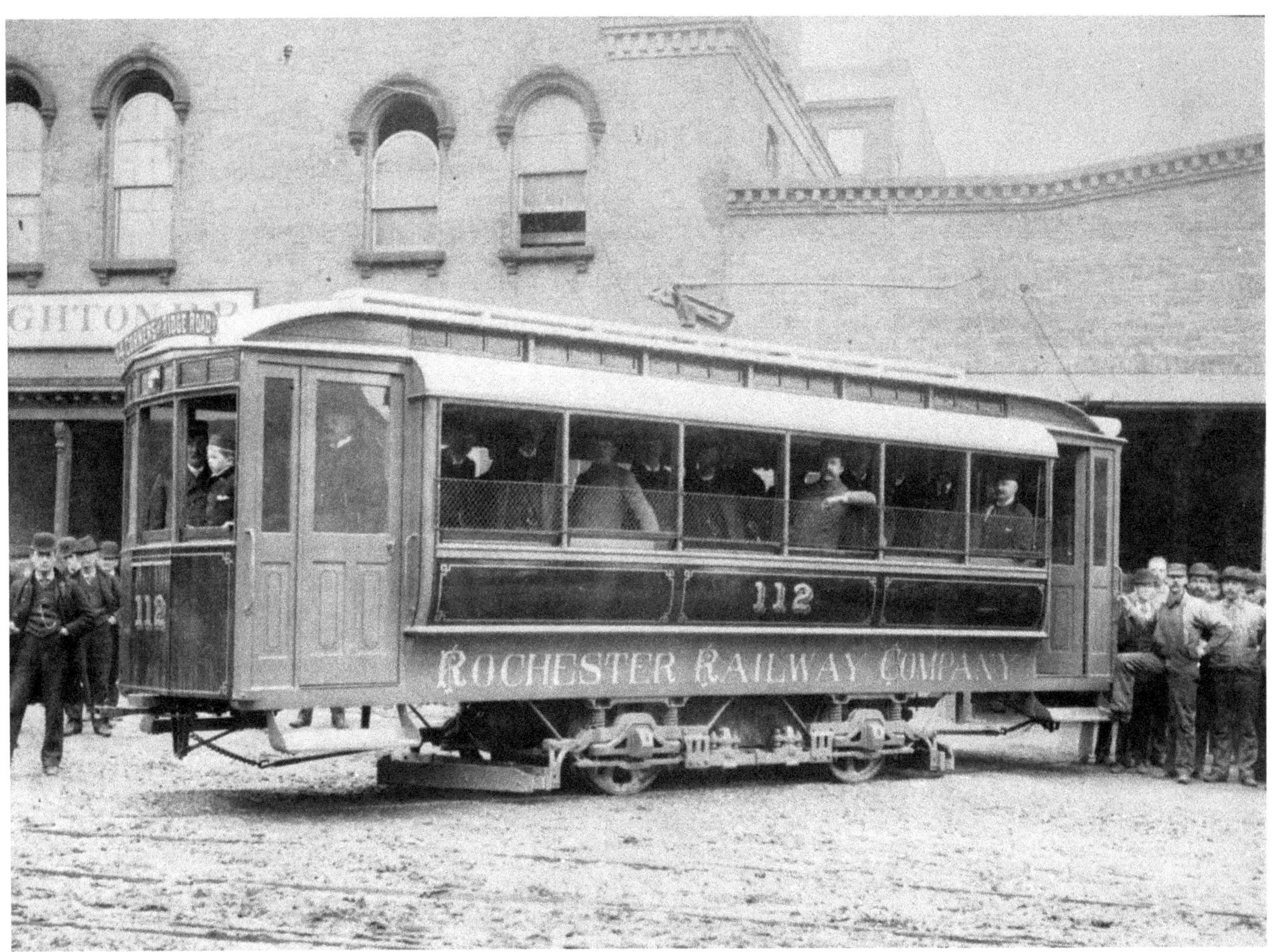

Rochester Railway Company's Car No. 112 was the first electric streetcar to run in the city of Rochester. The red and yellow car ran along Lake Avenue on its first run in November 1890. In 1909 the company merged with New York State Railways.

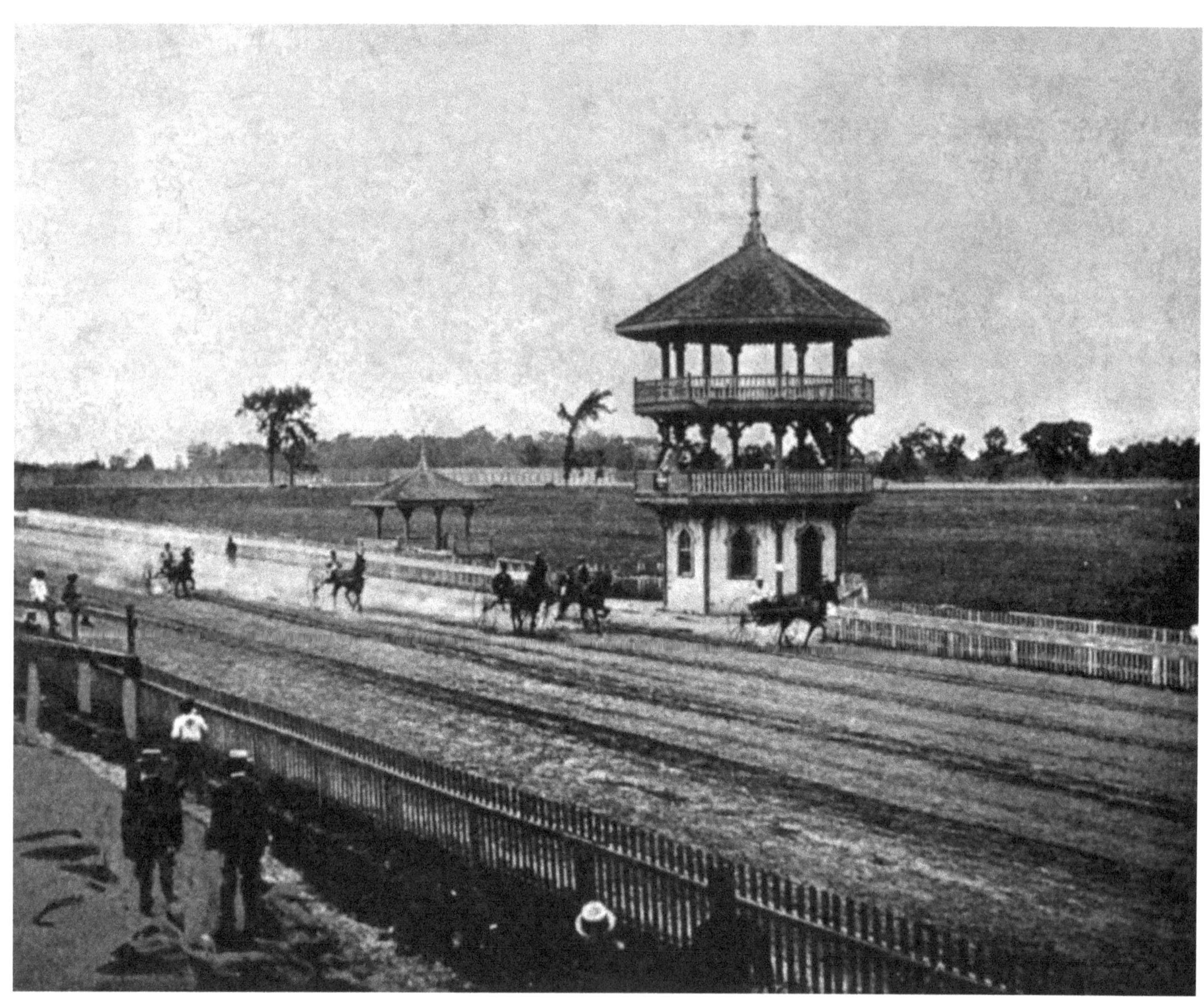

The Rochester Driving Park Race Track, bounded by Dewey and Driving Park avenues, the New York Central Railroad tracks, and Bryan Street, was a popular horse-race track and later, dog track. The park was a part of the Grand Circuit in horse racing from its opening in 1874 to its closing in 1895. By 1906 the property that was once a mile-long track, stables, offices, and a hotel, became building lots.

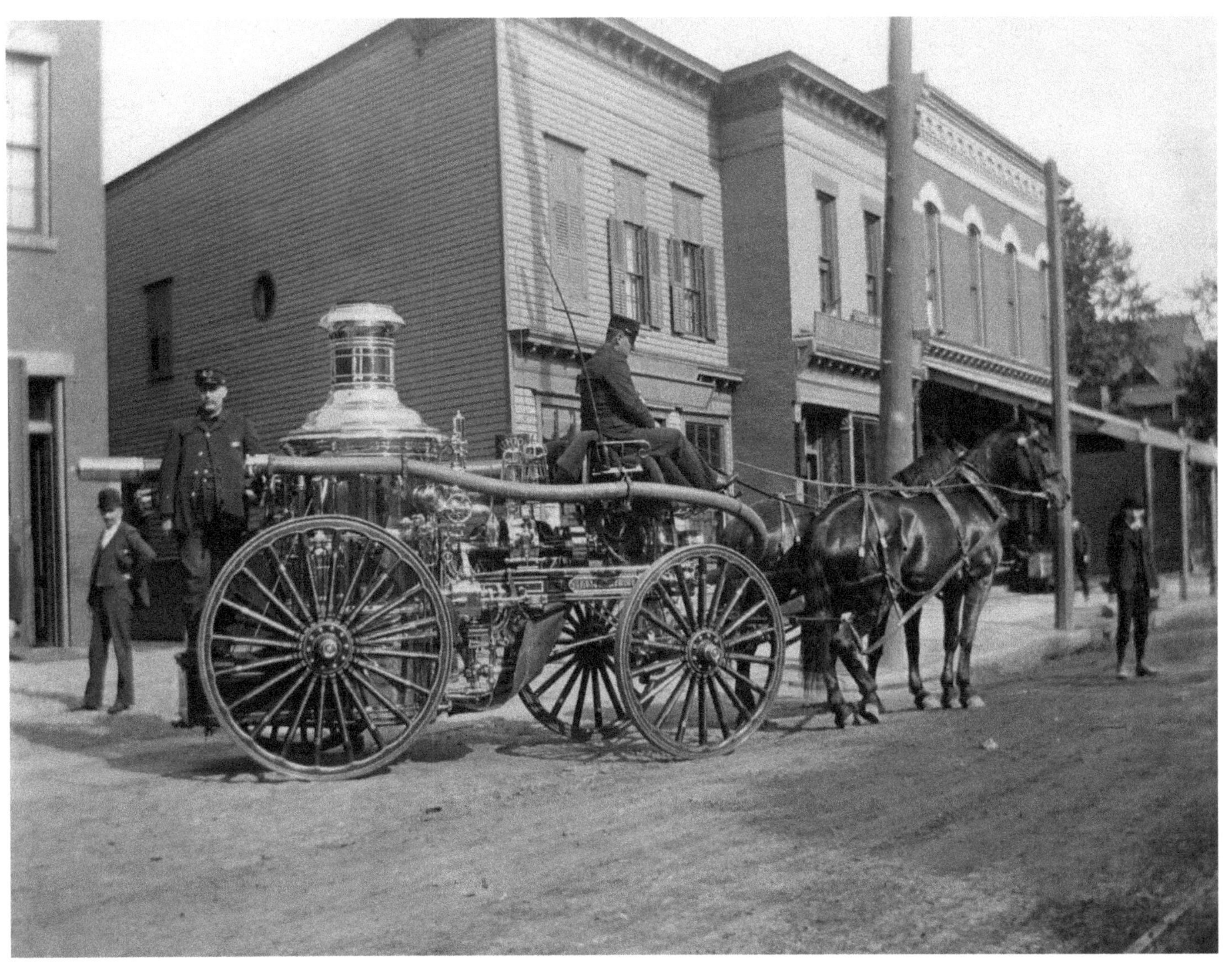

Driver Edward Klippert and engineer Frank J. Brennan, at rear, display Rochester Fire Department's Steamer No. 2 on North Clinton Avenue near Lowell Street. At left is the corner of Hose Co. No. 2 and Steamer No. 2.

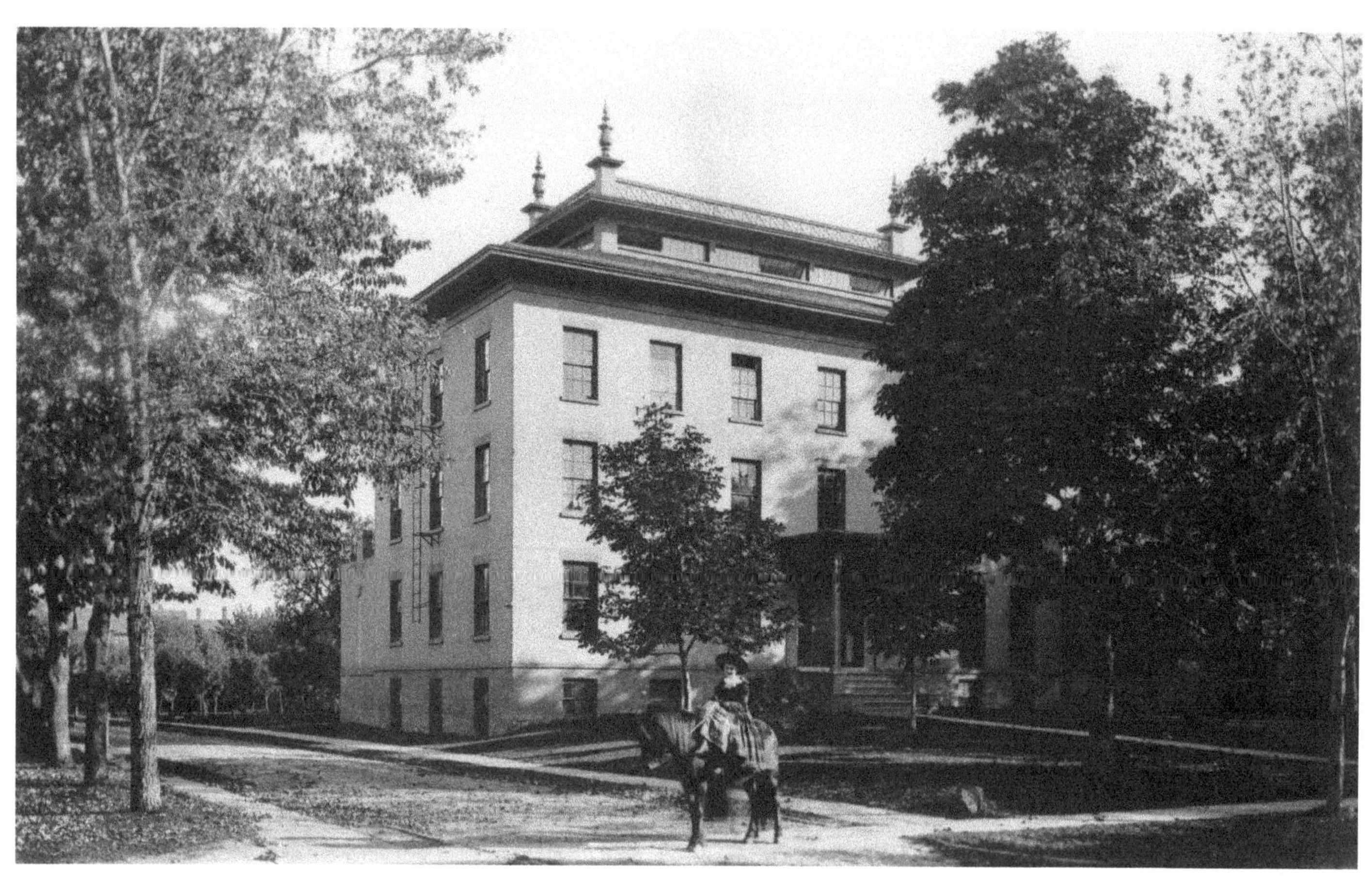

A young girl sits astride a pony in this view of the German Theological Seminary at Alexander and Tracy streets (ca. 1890). This is probably the newer of two buildings on this site.

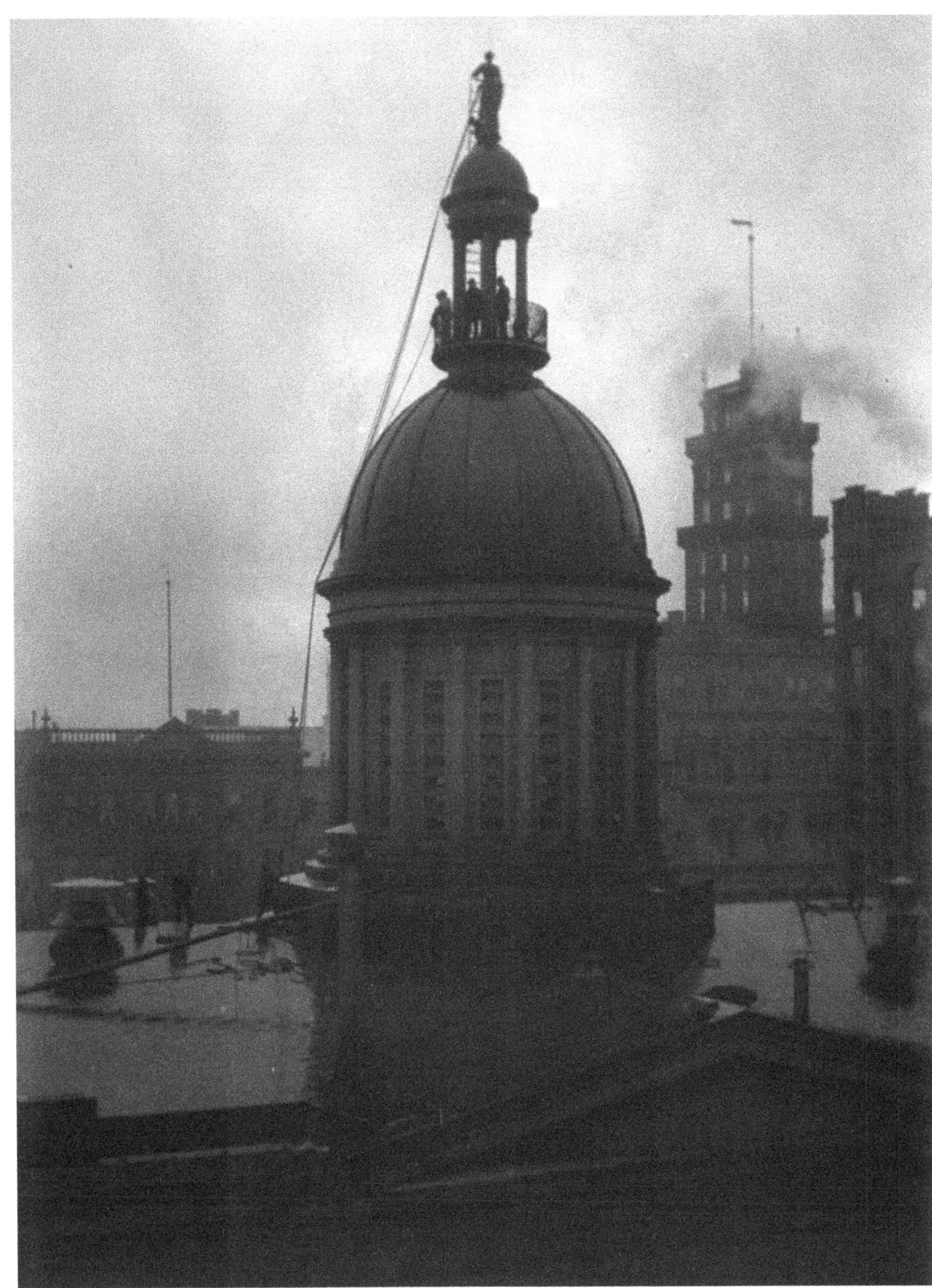

Repairmen work atop the dome of the second Monroe County Court House in the late 1880s. At right is the Powers Building at the Four Corners at State and Main streets.

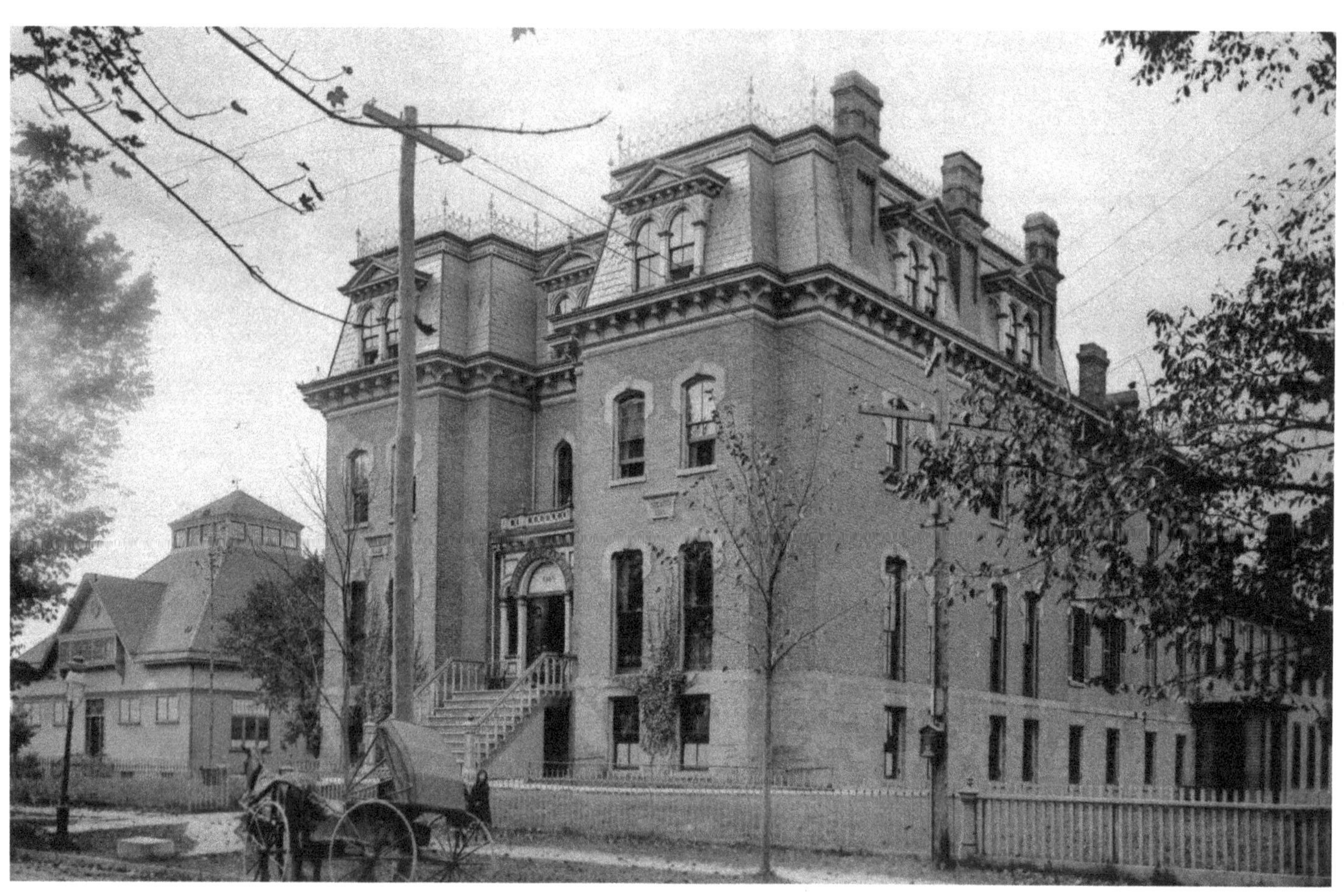

The Rochester School for the Deaf about 1890 at 263 North St. Paul Street. Established in 1874 by Mrs. Gilman Perkins, the school offered innovative education to the hearing impaired. Instruction in speech and sign language was innovative and became known as the Rochester method. Alexander Graham Bell visited Rochester and worked with the school on several occasions. The school is still located on St. Paul Street.

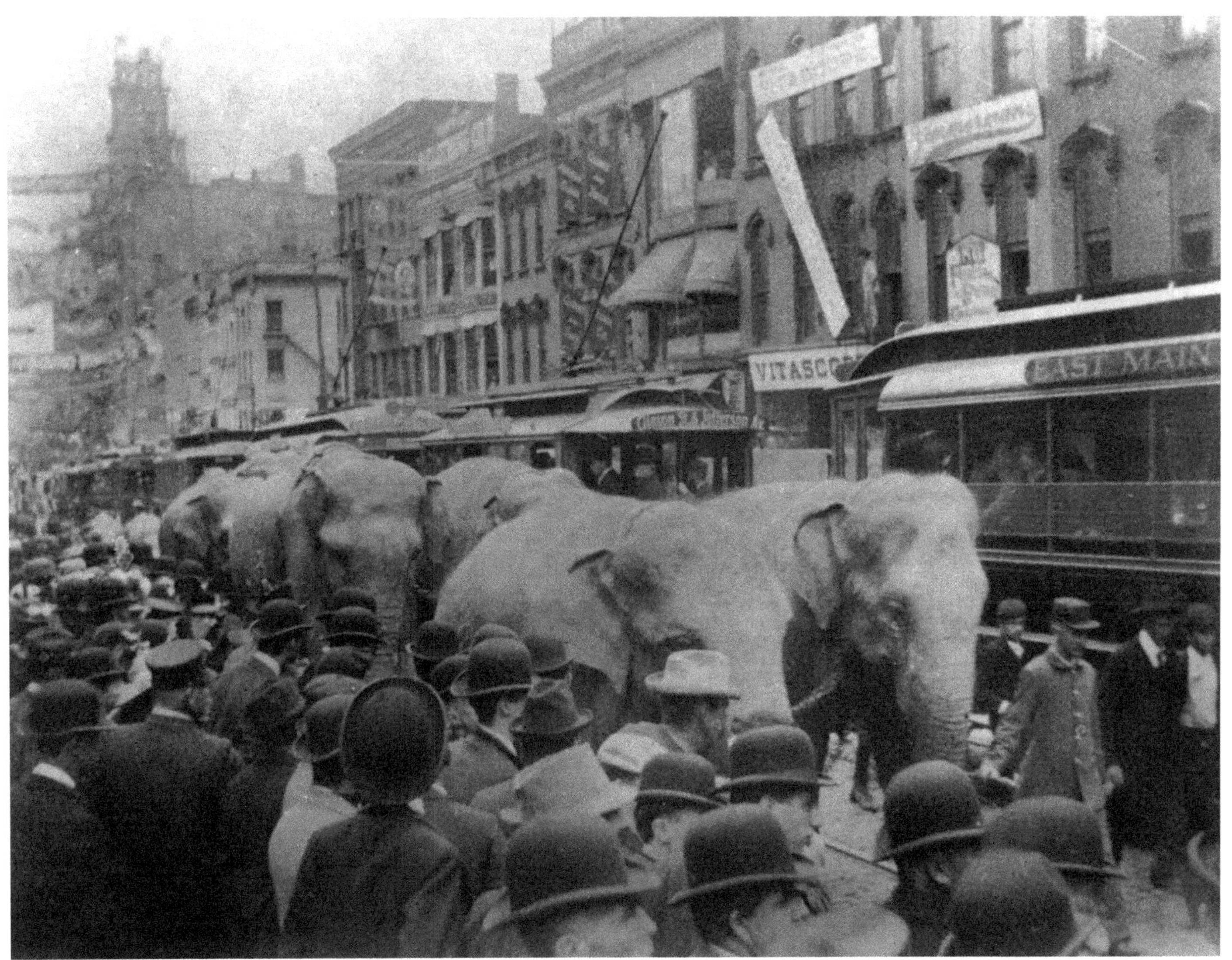

In a view looking northwest, elephants pass down Main Street in the late 1890s. Streetcars wait in the crowded street. The circus worker at far-right can be seen leading an elephant at the front of the line.

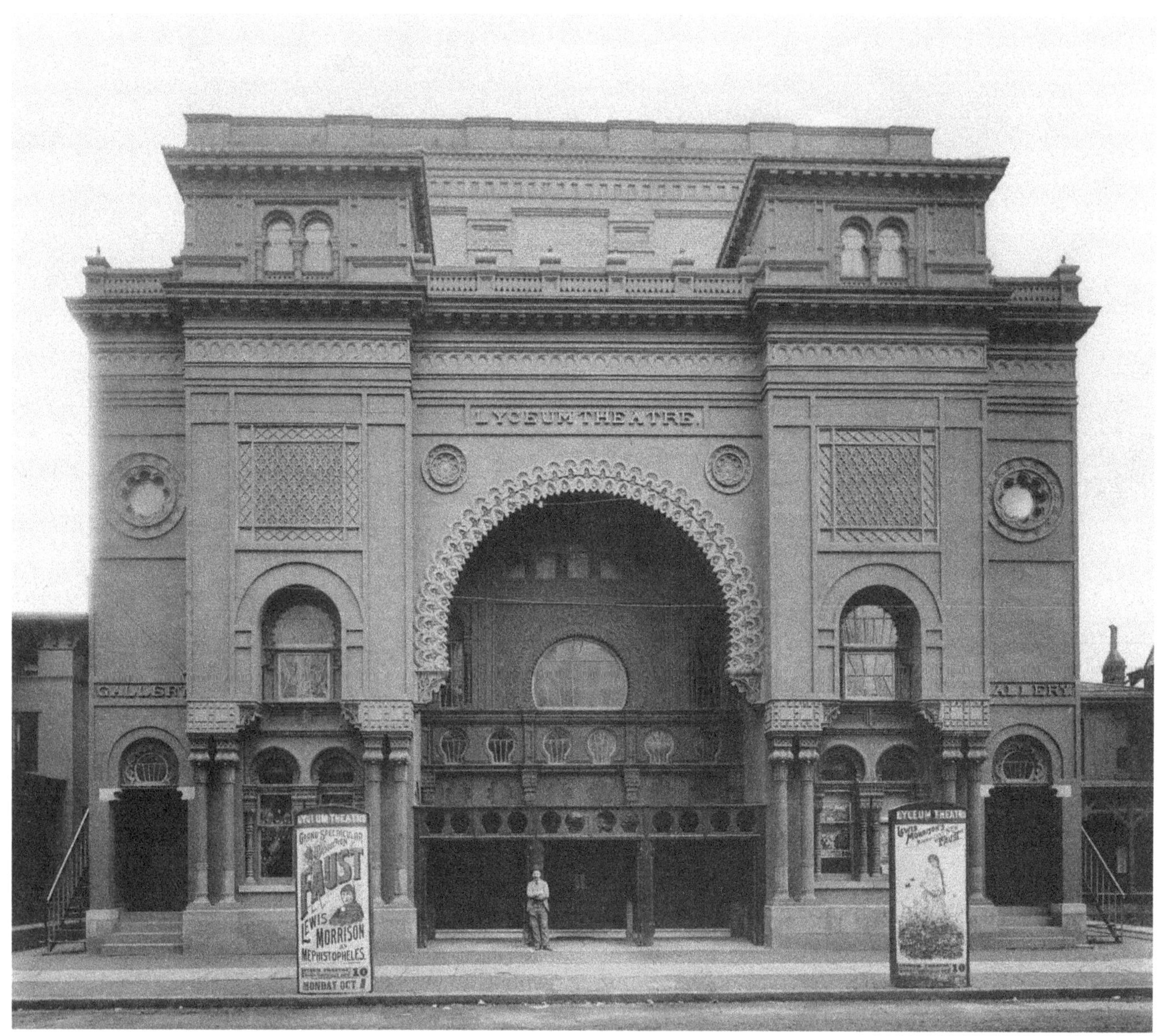

Clinton Avenue was once lined with movie theaters. About 1890 a man stands in the entrance of the Lyceum Theatre, built in 1888 by Rochester architects Warner and Brockett on a design by Leon Lempert. It was one of the largest in the nation. The posters on the sidewalk beckon passers-by into the theater. The building was razed in 1934.

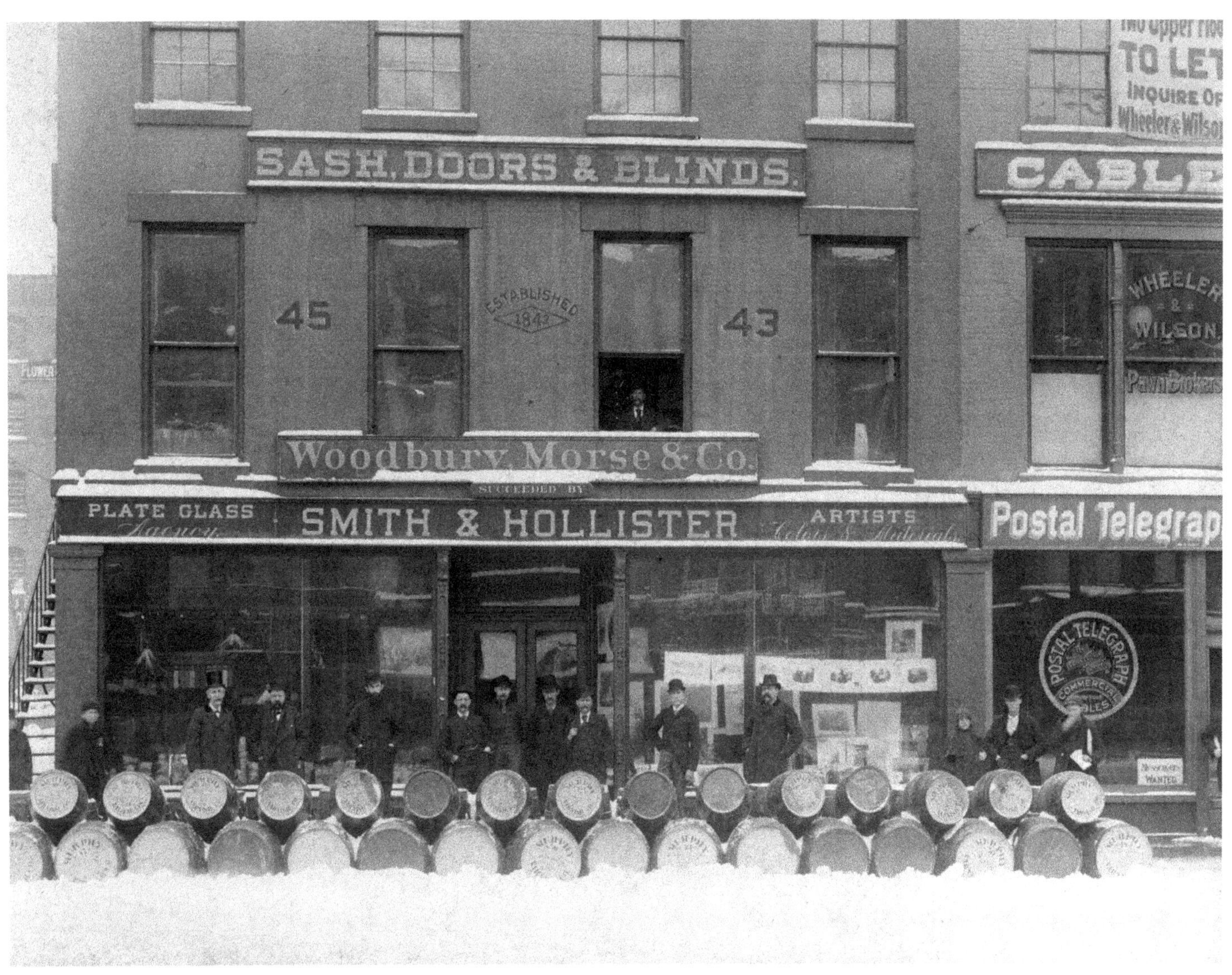

Established in 1842 as Woodbury, Morse and Co., this art-supply store at the corner of East Main and Graves streets became Smith and Hollister in 1889. In this photograph taken about 1893, varnish barrels are stacked in front of the store. Window sashes, doors, and blinds are available in the business upstairs.

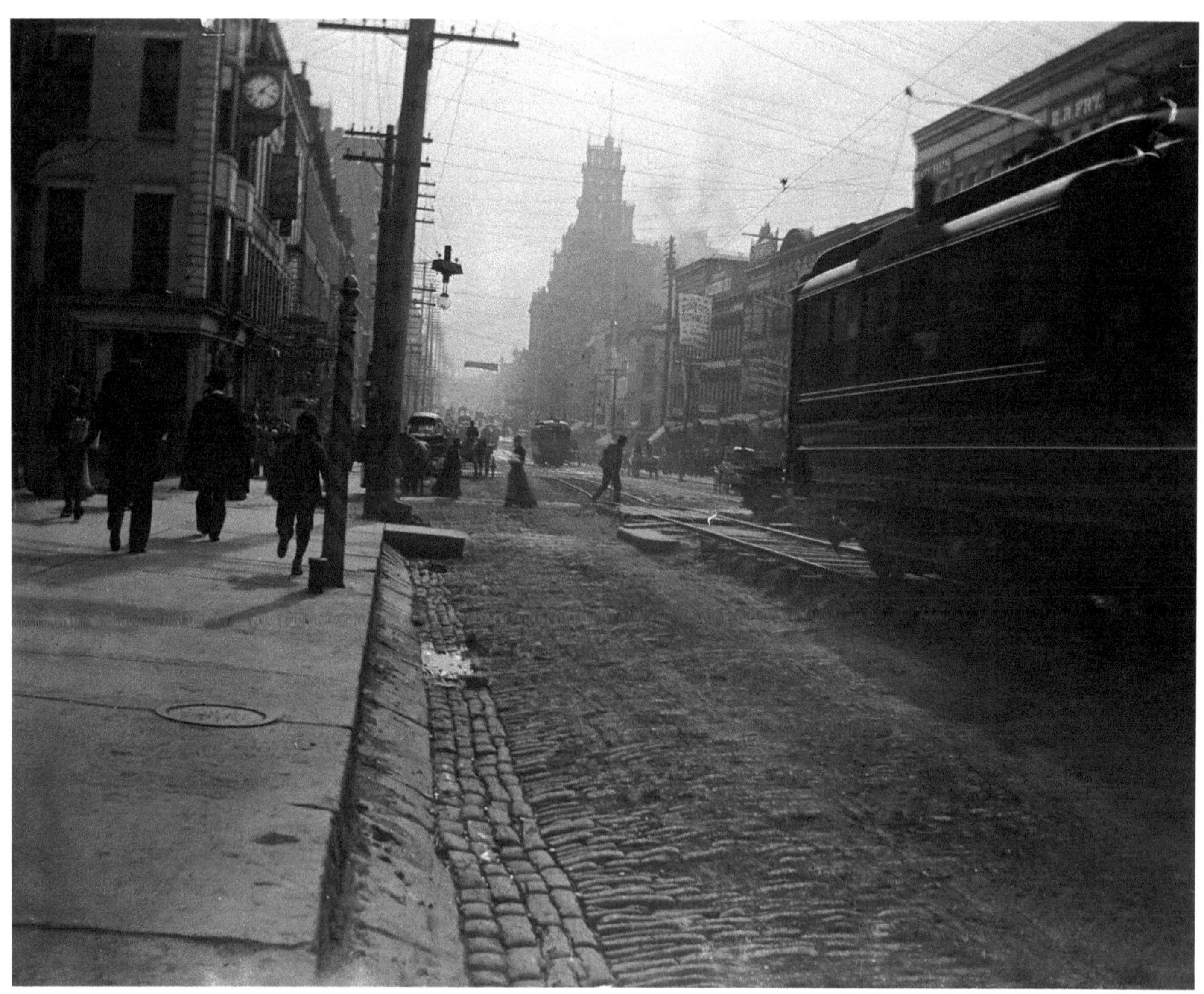

A young boy runs westward along Main Street at North Water Street in April of 1893. An electric streetcar passes by on tracks raised above the brick street surface. The gutter at the side of the street helps to drain the rainwater, which formerly sat stagnant with horse droppings, plaguing the city with pathogens. A stone step from the sidewalk to the street helps to keep pedestrians clean during muddy days.

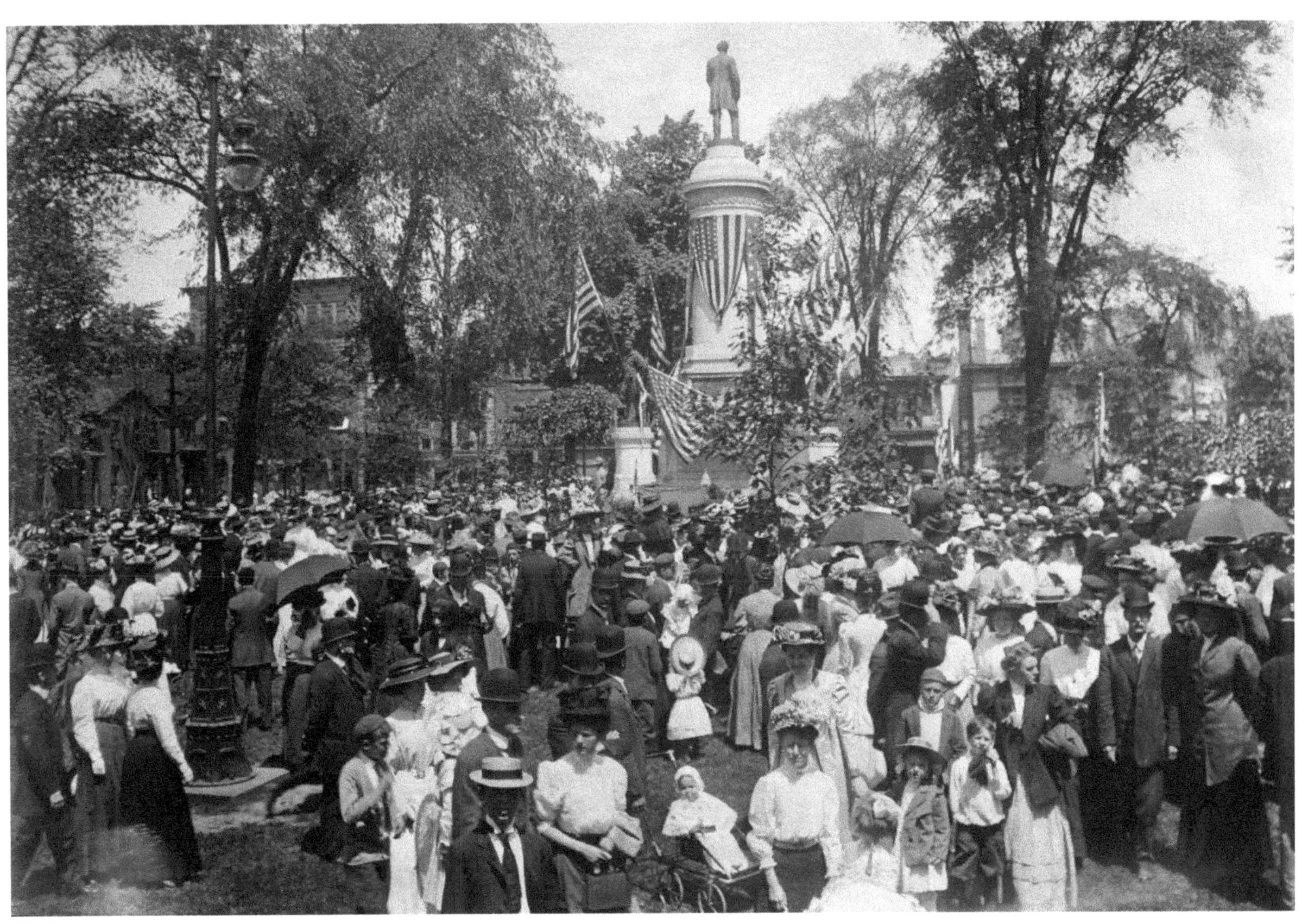

A larger-than-life statue of Abraham Lincoln stands atop the Soldiers and Sailors Monument at the dedication May 30, 1892, at Washington Square near the intersection of Court Street and Clinton and South avenues. The monument was designed by Leonard Volk. Hundreds of people dressed patriotically for the occasion.

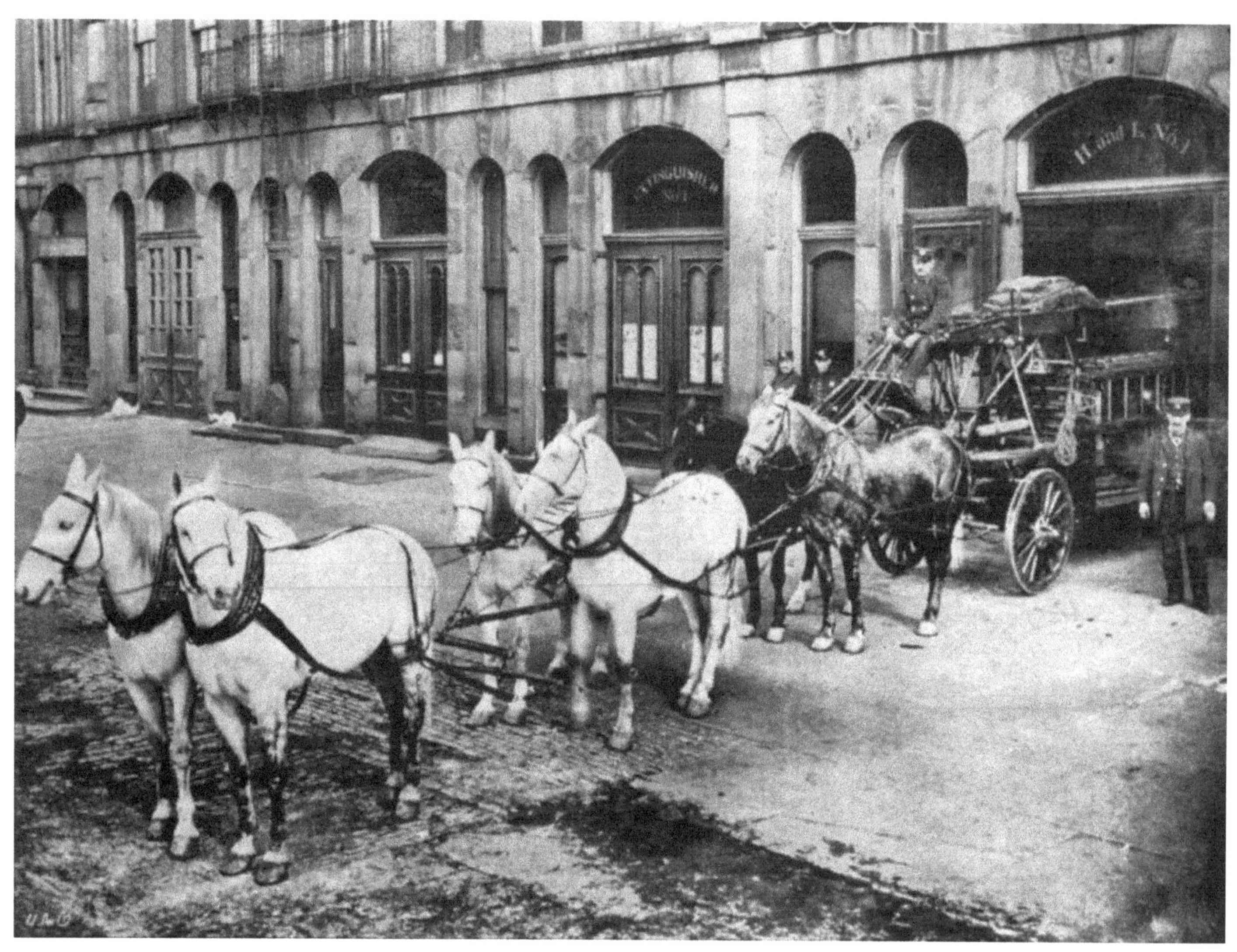

Driver John Hammond required a lot of skill to manage this six-horse team and their new fire truck seen here in 1895 in the doorway of the Hook and Ladder Co. No. 1 on Front Street. Standing at right is probably Captain Patrick O'Meara.

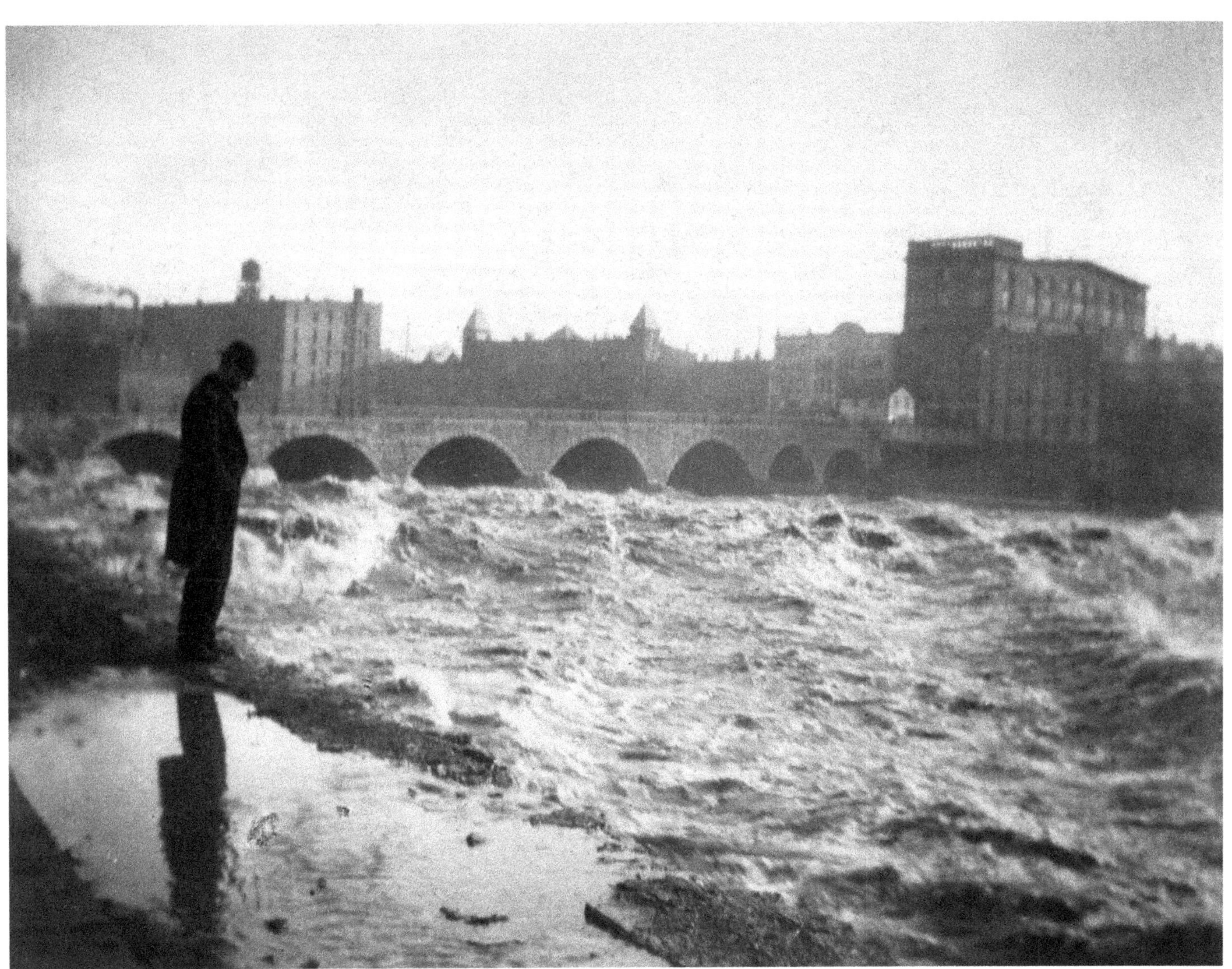

Until the Mt. Morris Dam opened in 1952, the Genesee River was free to flood. An unidentified man stands at the edge of a flooding Genesee River on the south side of the Court Street Bridge in April of 1896.

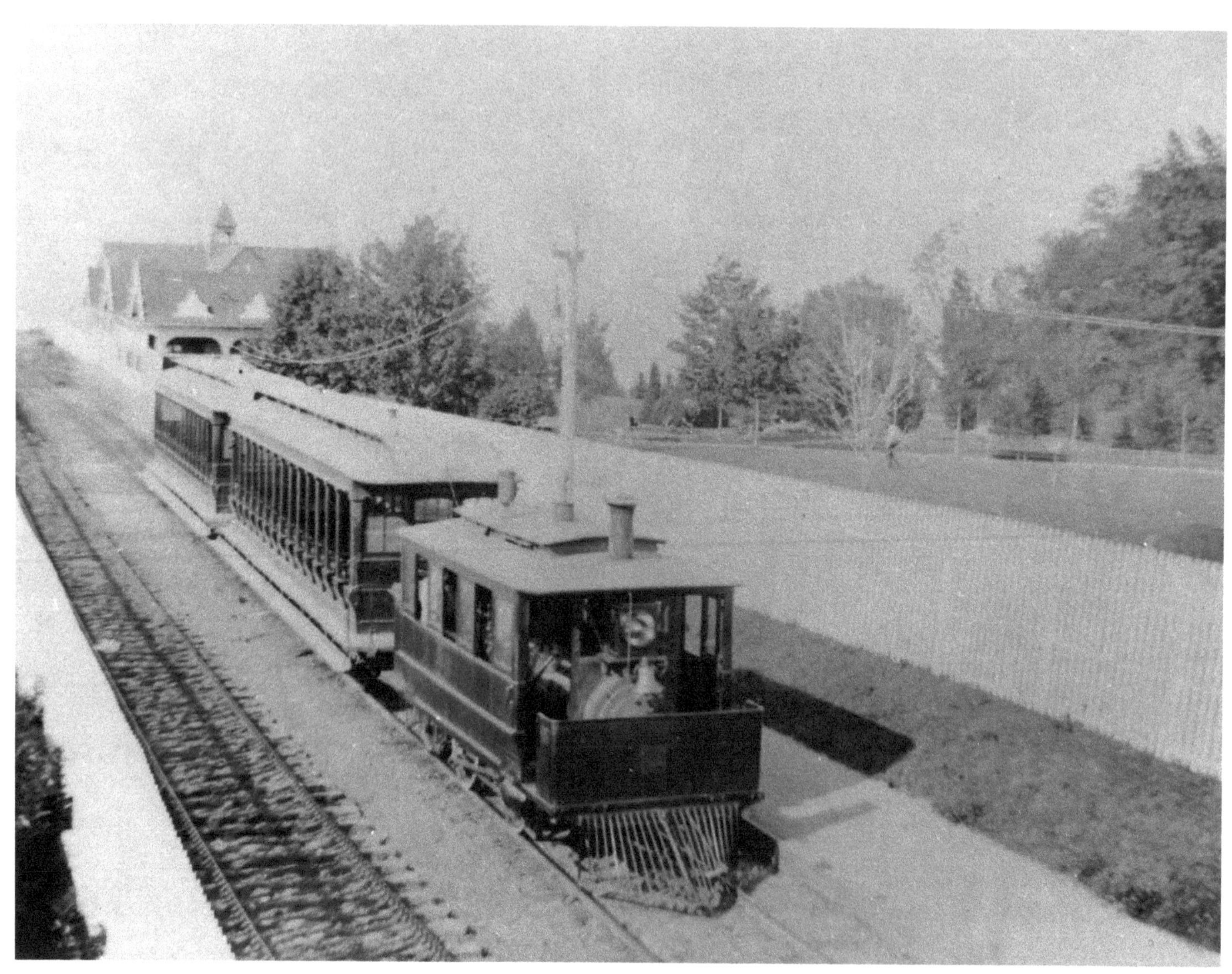

This photograph taken about 1894 shows a Baldwin 0-4-2 engine and its train, owned by the Rochester and Lake Ontario Railroad. The railroad operated the Bay Road Line, which ran from Bay Street to Portland Avenue to Ridge Road to Sea Breeze.

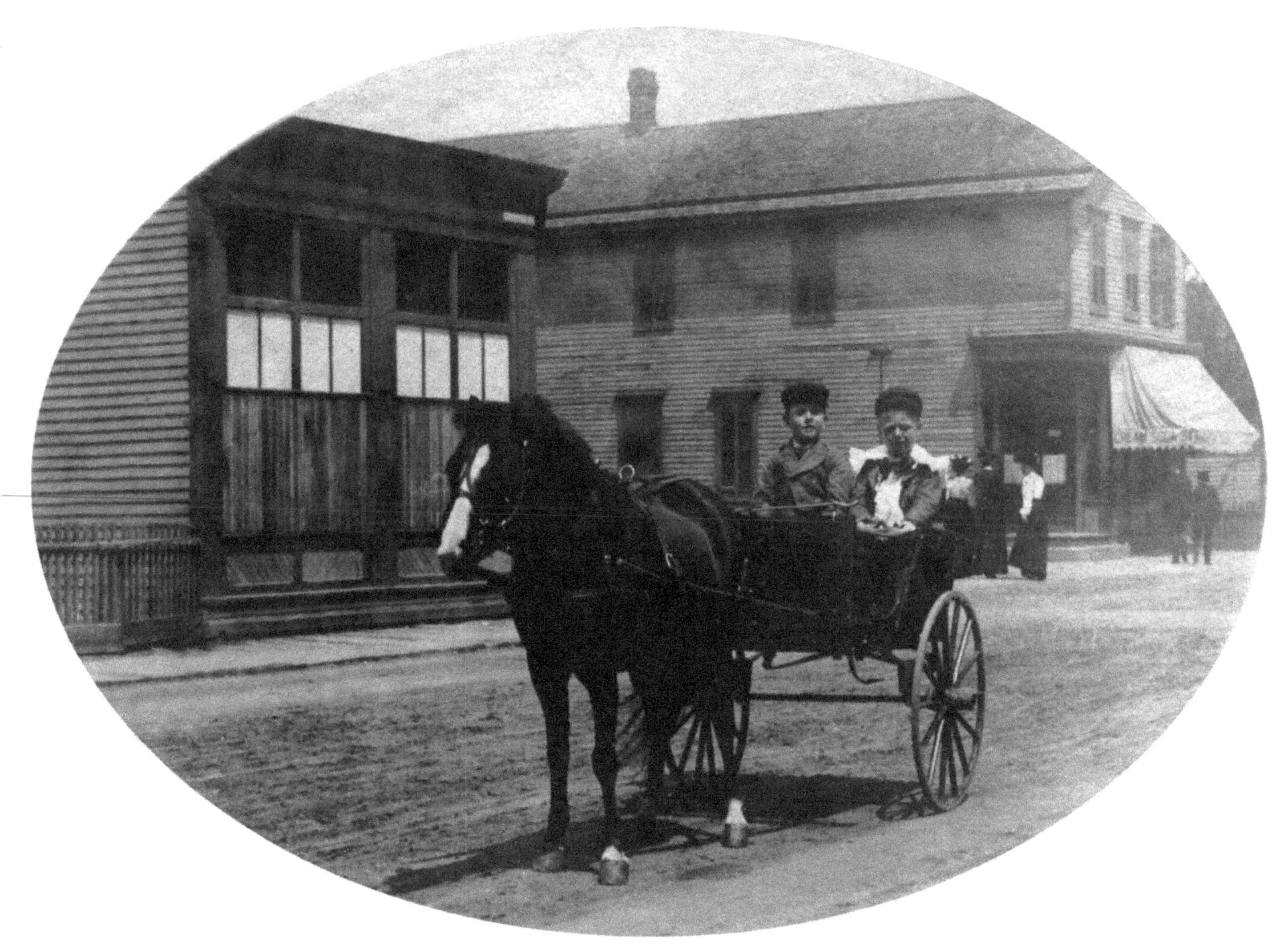

At the turn of the century two young boys drive a pony cart to School #26.

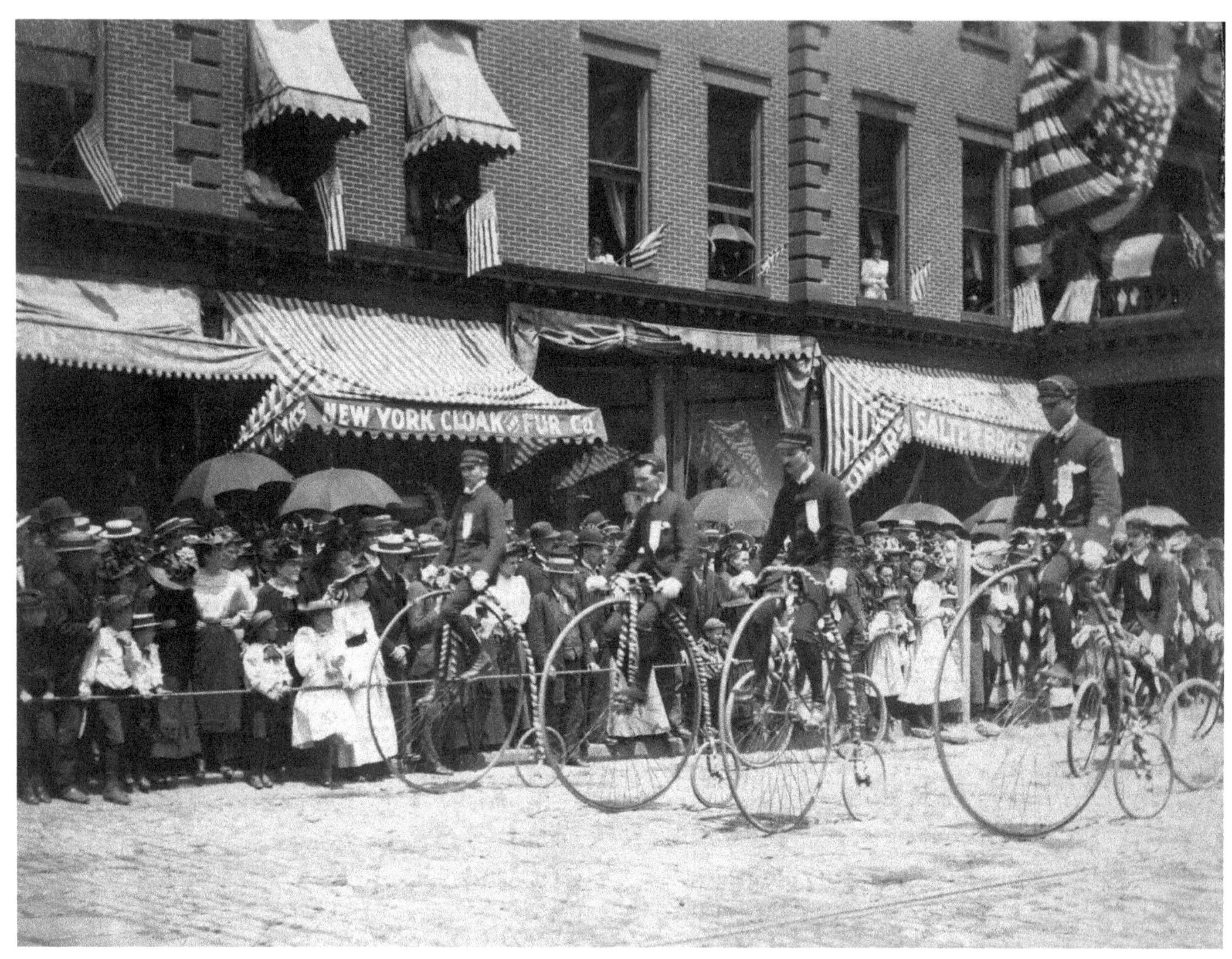

Penny farthing bicyclists pass spectators in a 4th of July parade on East Main Street in downtown Rochester. New York Cloak and Fur Co. and Salter Bros. Florist are visible in the background.

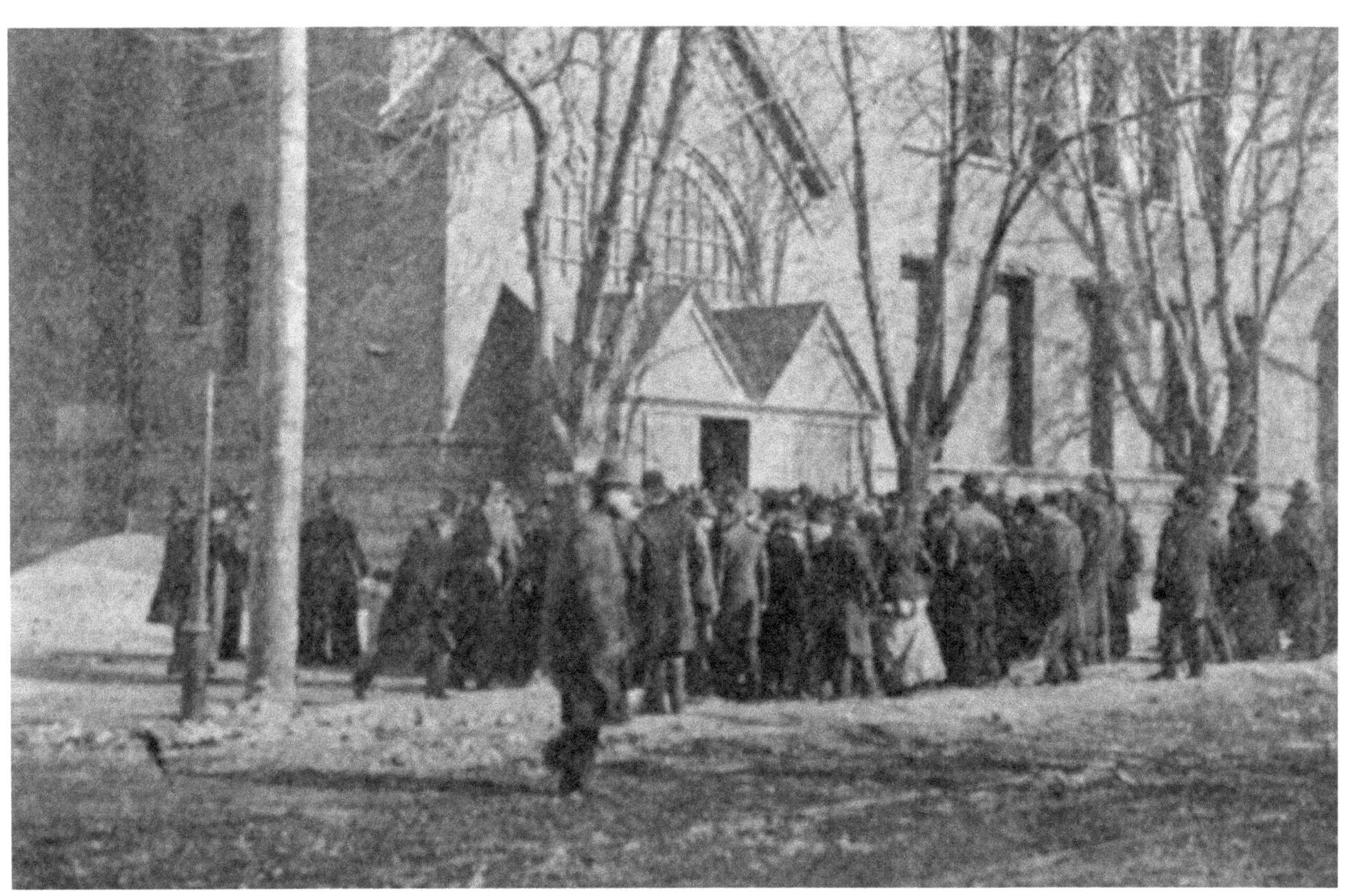

Hundreds gather outside the Central Presbyterian Church on the corner of South Plymouth Avenue and Church streets for the funeral of noted abolitionist Frederick Douglass on March 2, 1895.

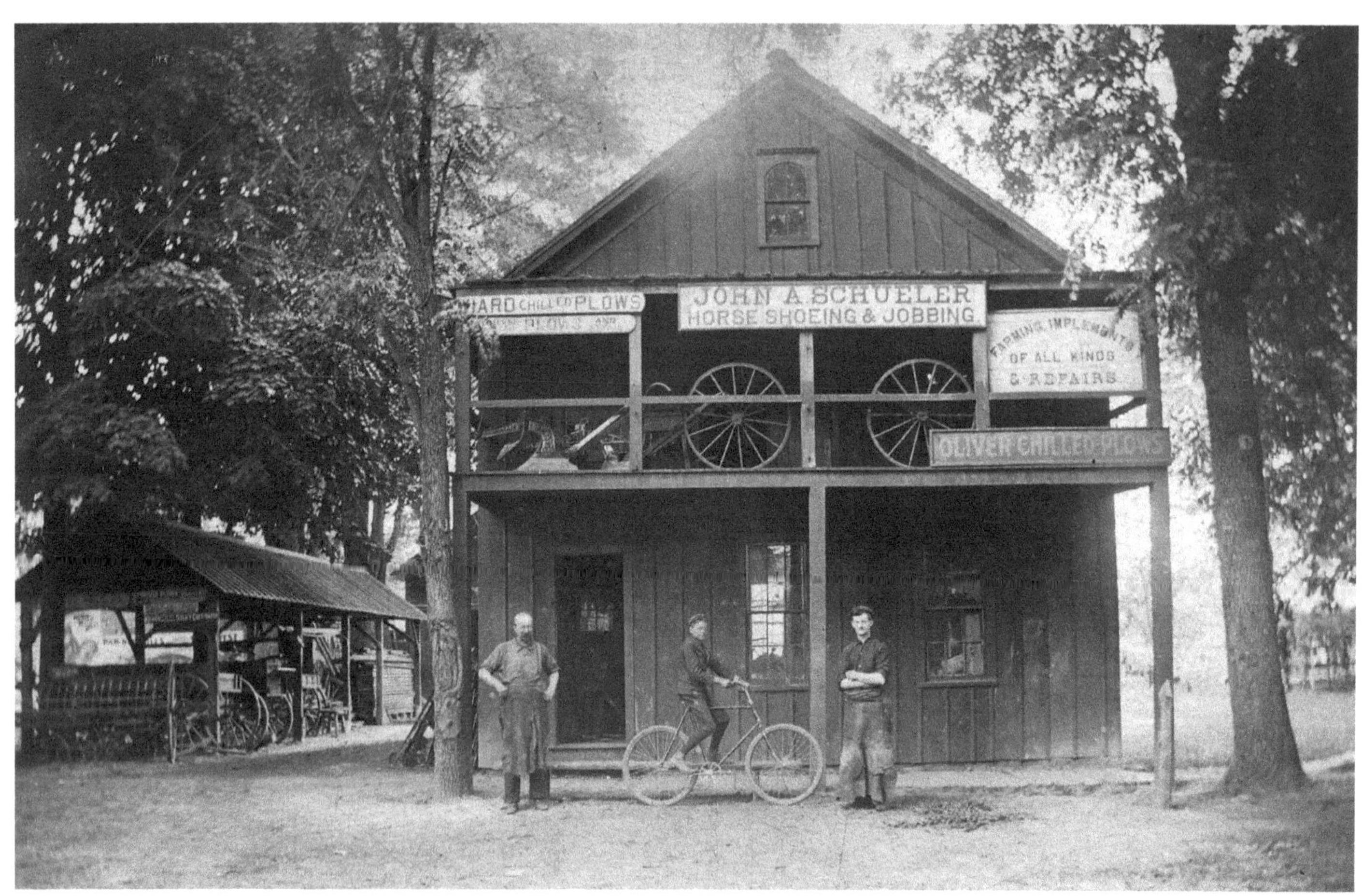

Signs for Oliver's and Ward's chilled plows and farming implements advertise the agricultural tools that could be purchased or repaired in this Penfield building that was John A. Schueler's blacksmith shop in the 1890s.

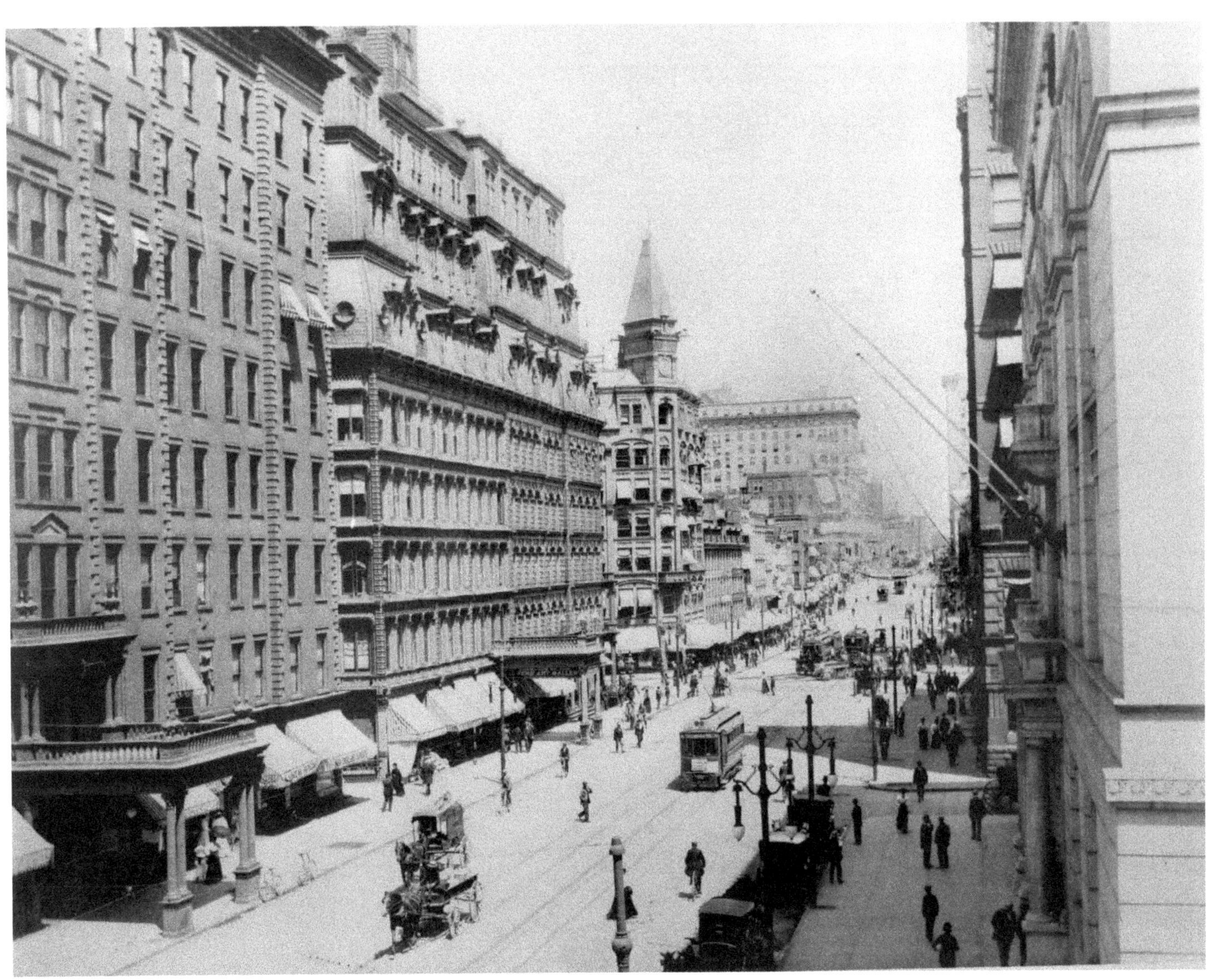

The Powers Hotel and Powers Building on the left dominate Main Street in this view facing east from Fitzhugh Street near the Monroe County Court House.

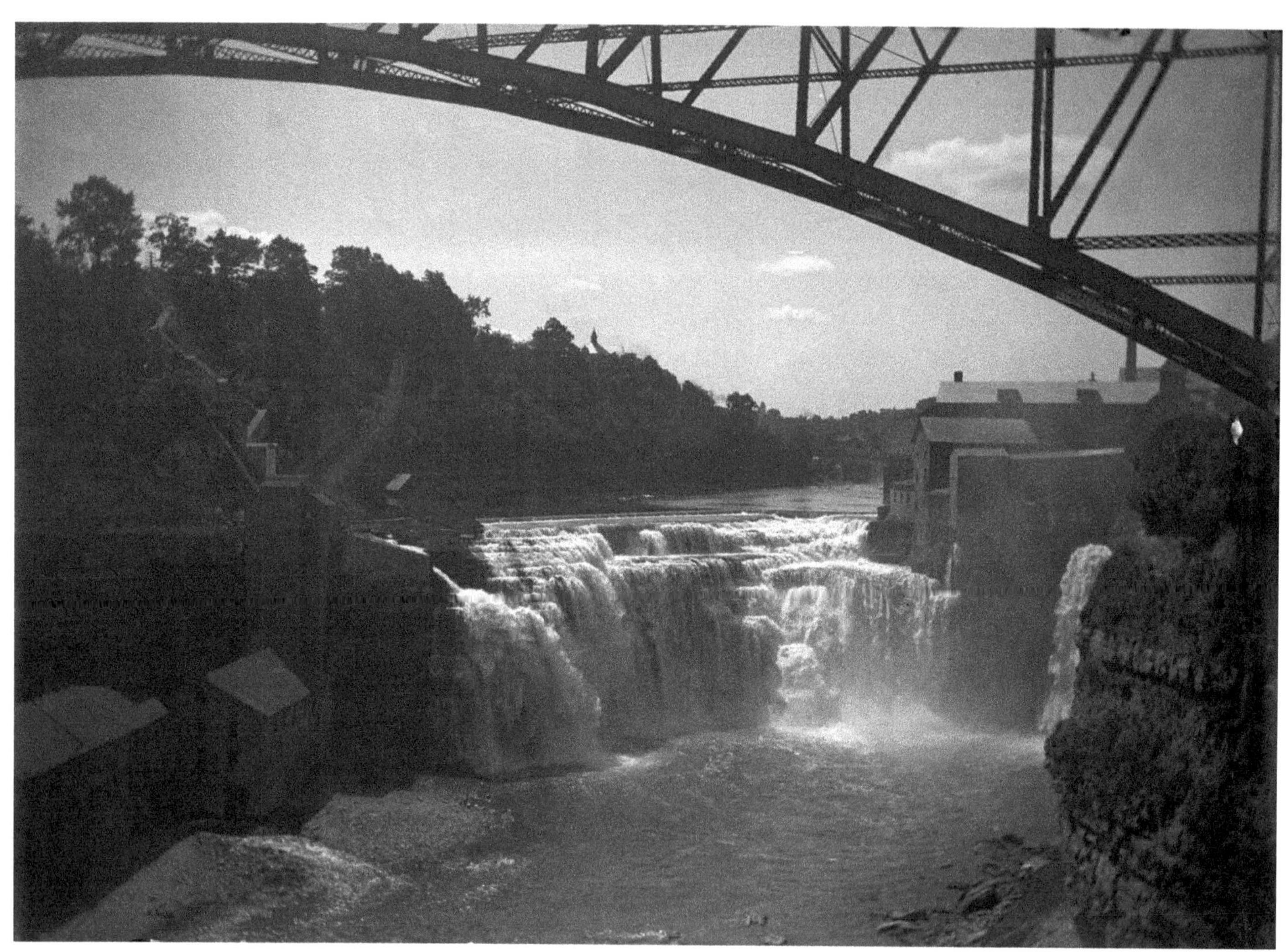

Looking south from the Driving Park Bridge, the graceful bend of the Lower Falls is seen dropping the Genesee River about 80 feet to a more leisurely flow. The first Carthage Bridge was built on this site in 1818 to connect the east and west portions of the Ridge Road. It fell after fifteen months, crashing the financial hopes of its investors.

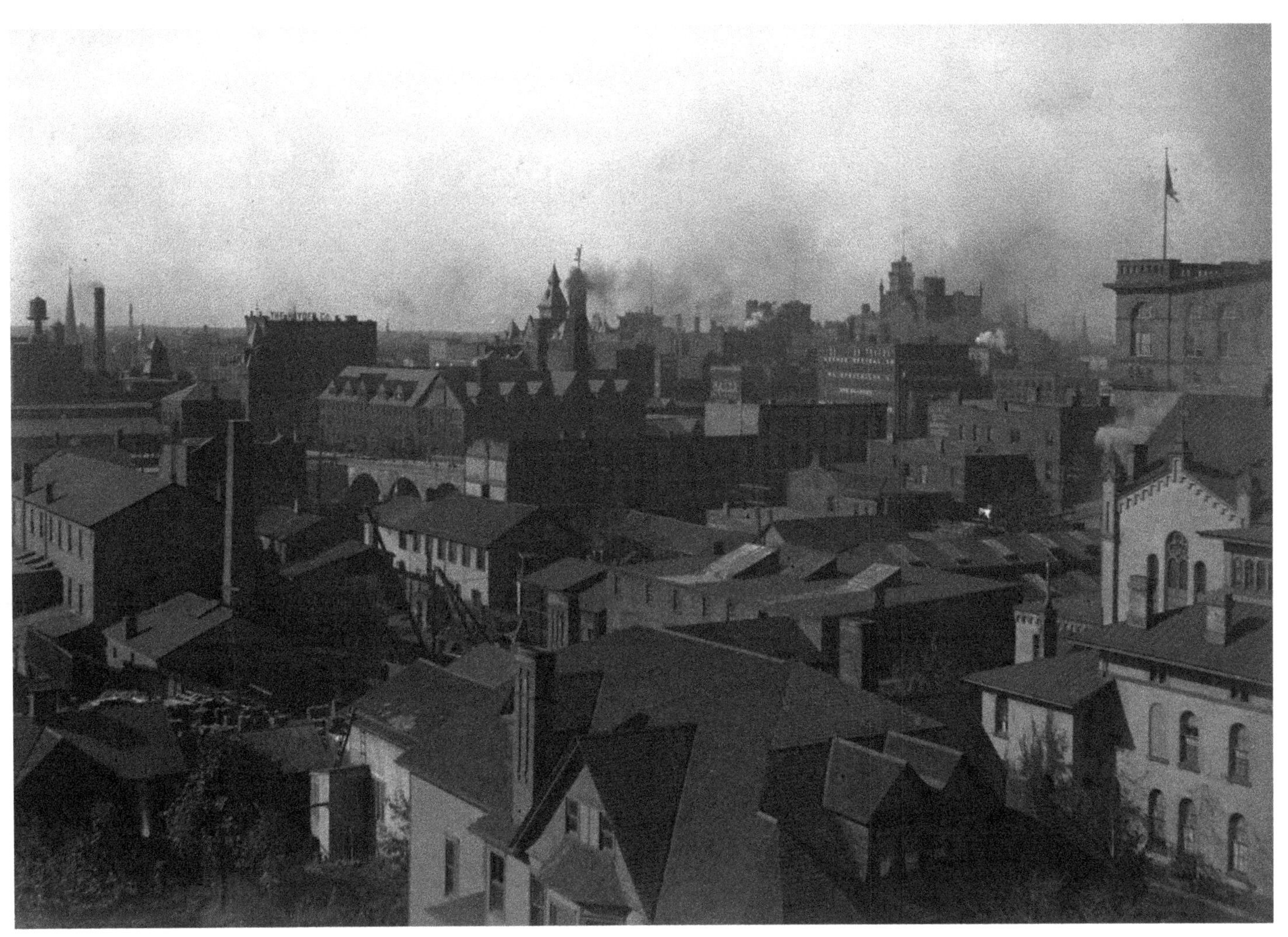

In this view facing northwest from the old armory (now GEVA Theatre), the rooftops of St. Mary's Church and the YMCA Building are visible on the right. In the distance at center, the Kimball Tobacco Factory, now the site of the Rochester War Memorial, can be seen with its statue of Mercury atop the smokestack. The old City Hall and the tower of the Powers Building are visible near the smokestack.

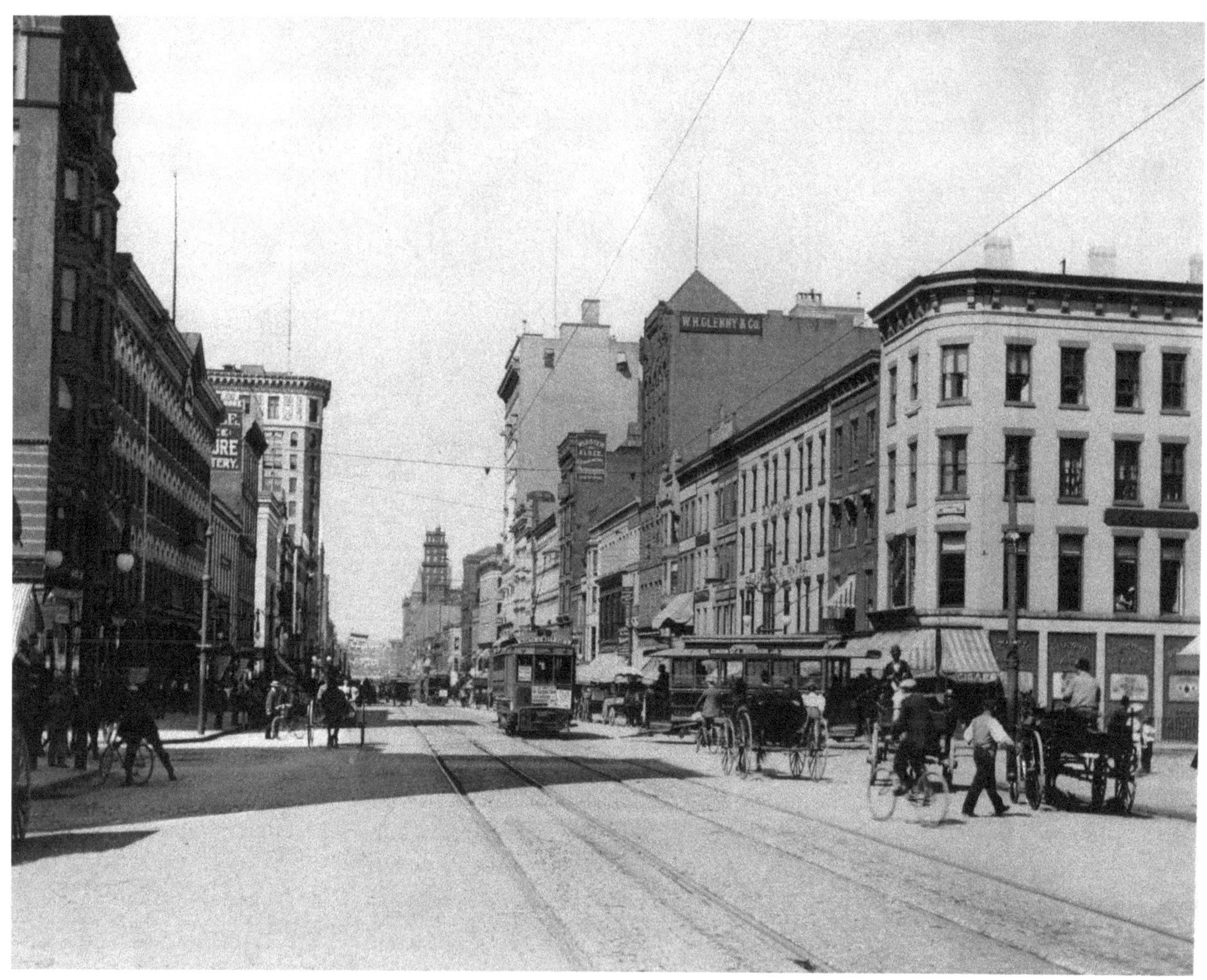

The Whitcomb House, the Temperance Hotel, the Granite Building, and the Powers buildings are visible in this view of Main Street looking west from Clinton Avenue. The street is busy with wagons, a bicycle, pedestrians, and a streetcar.

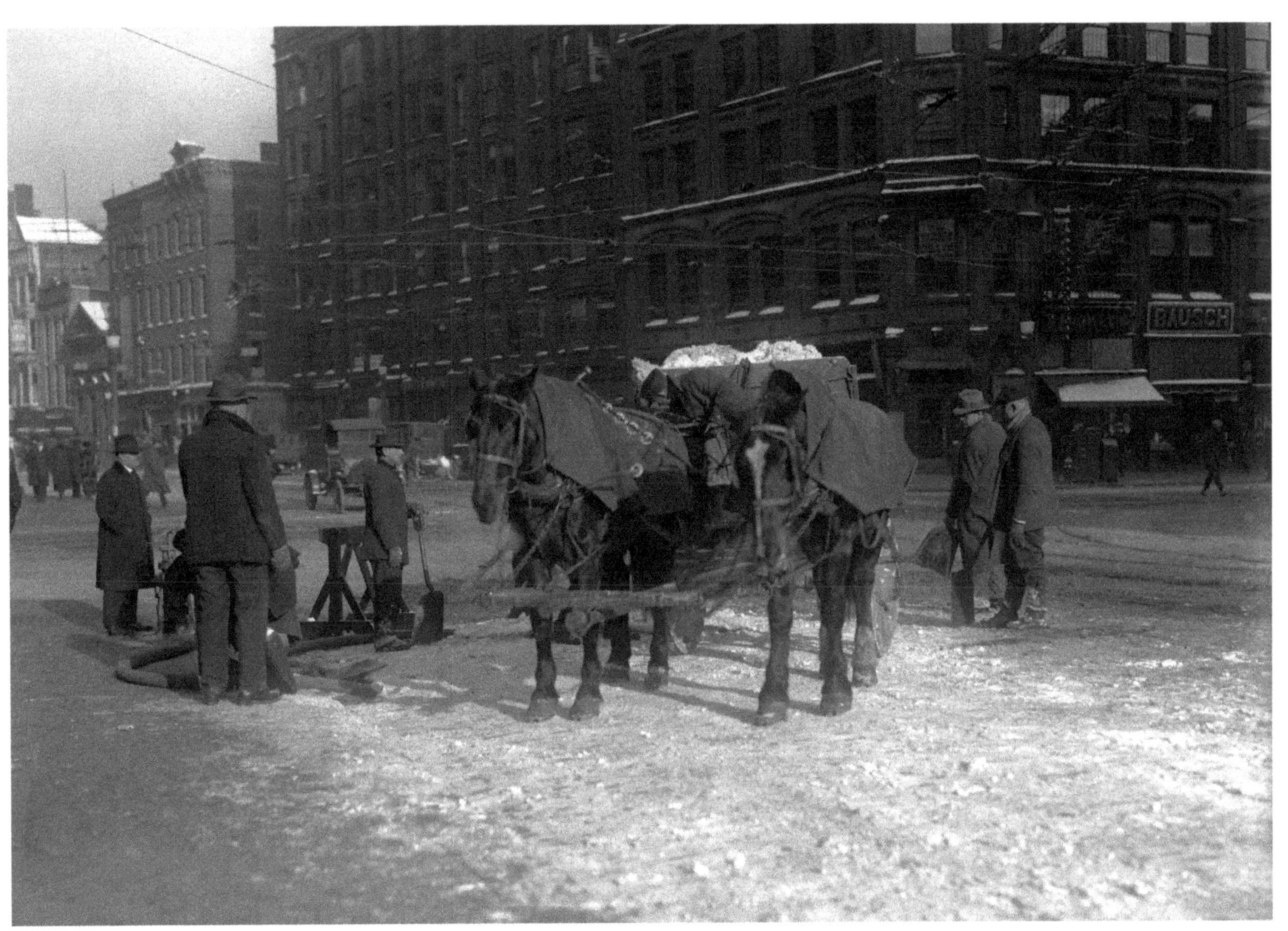

At the intersection of Main and State streets looking northeast, horses stand blanketed as men work to remove snow from the Four Corners near the Elwood Building. (1890s)

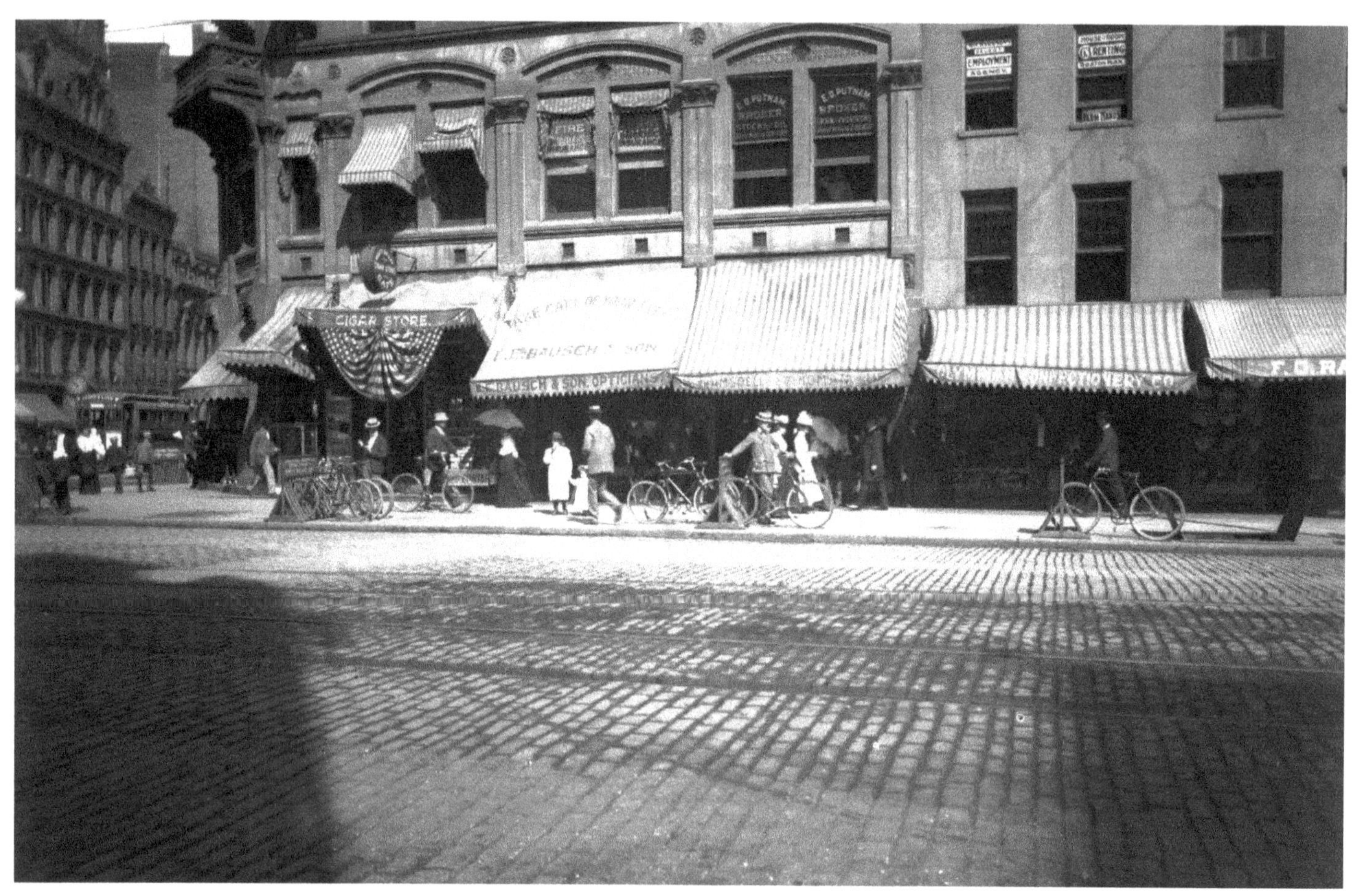

This seven-story Elwood Building, built by Frank Elwood in memory of Isaac R. Elwood in 1879, cost $100,000, at the time a vast sum. The shop of opticians E. E. Bausch and Sons occupied the ground floor. The Powers Building is across State Street at left. Numerous bicycles, here and in other images, suggest that this mode of travel was relied on by many.

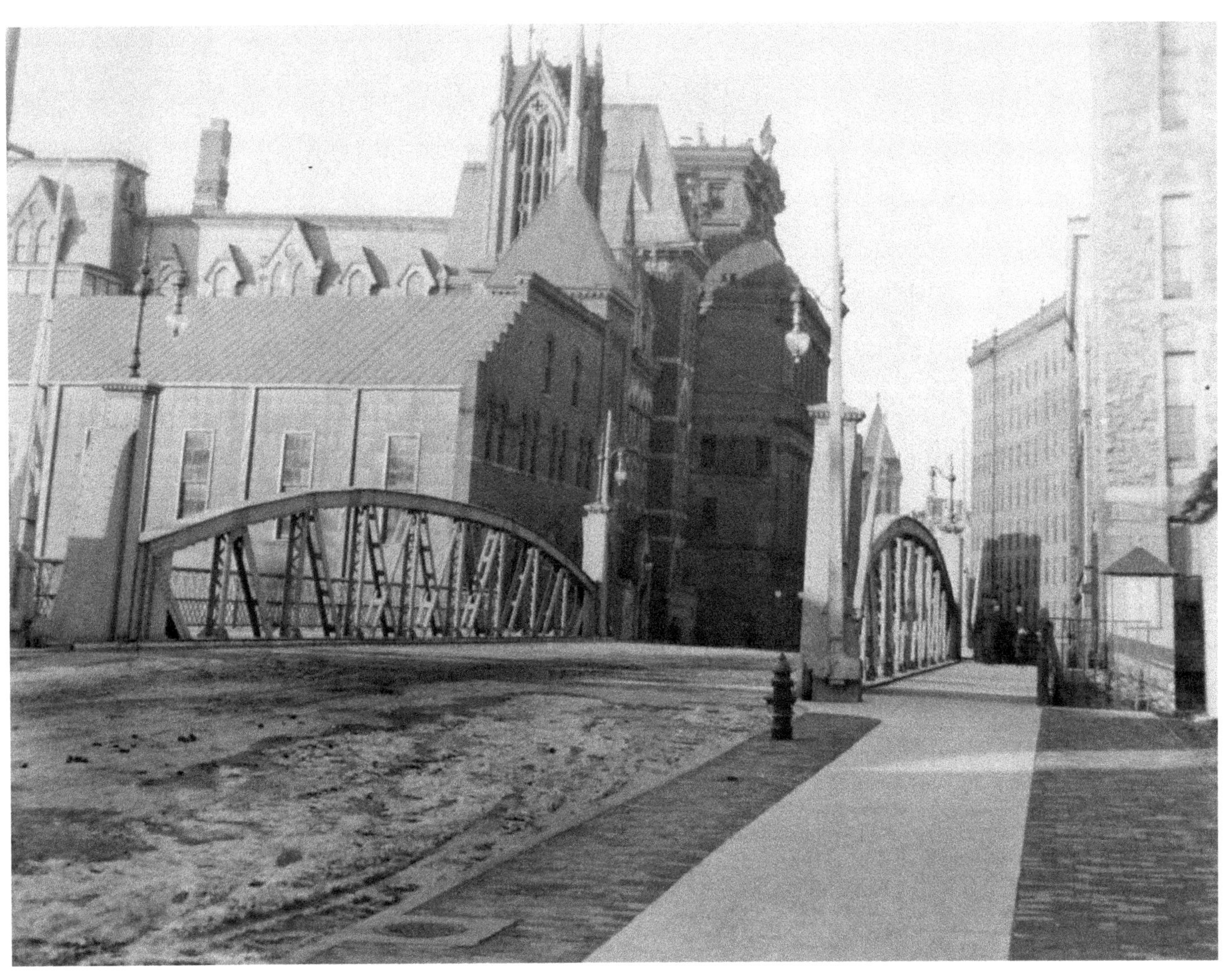

A view of the Fitzhugh Street Bridge built over the Erie Canal in 1899. The square steeple of St. Luke's Church can be seen at top-center. The Erie Canal flowed through downtown from 1825 to 1919, when it was rerouted south of the city through the Genesee Valley Park, for lack of room to widen the busy canal among the buildings and roads downtown.

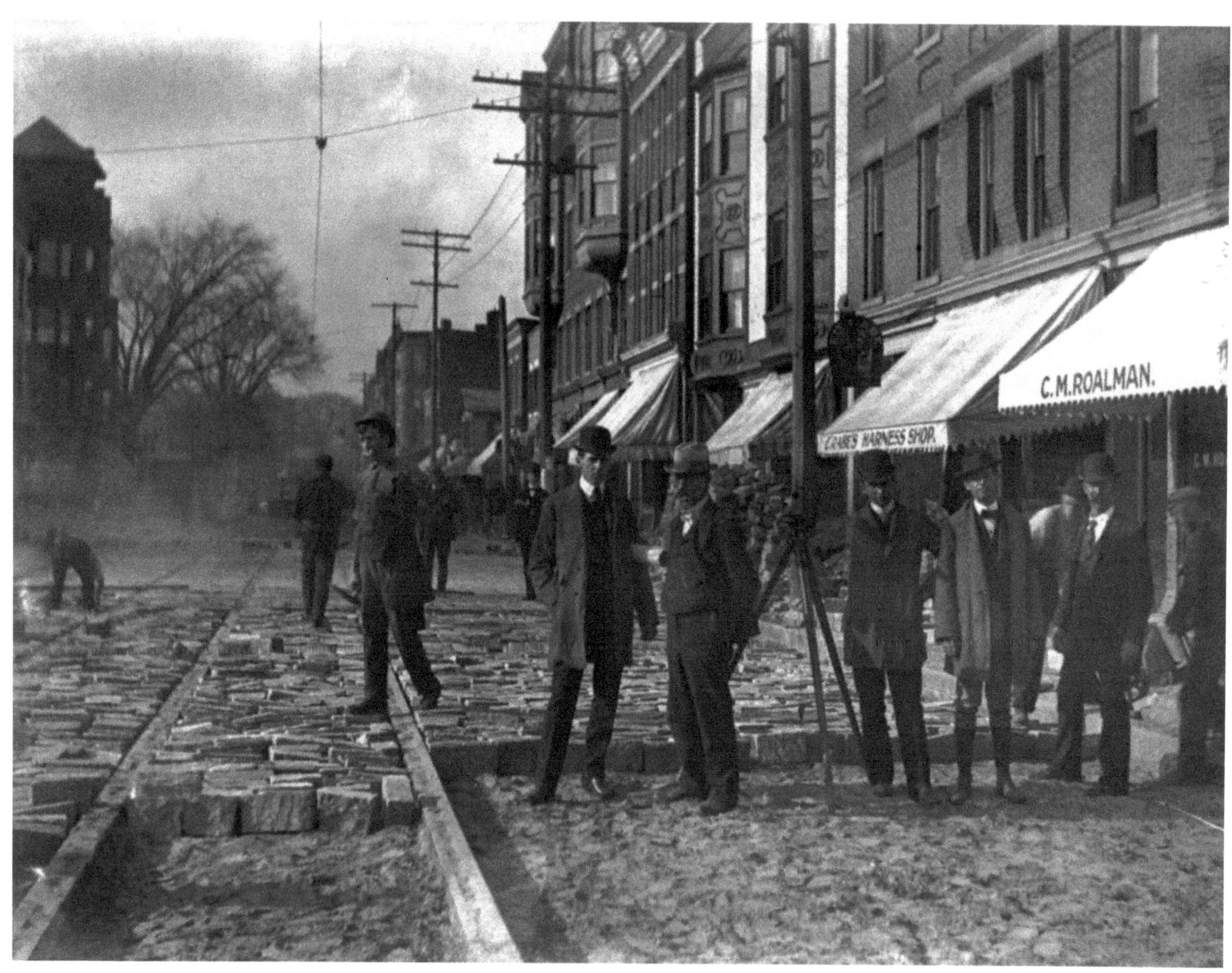

Looking west on Monroe Avenue from Manhattan Street, in front of Charles M. Roalman's Market and Edward Rabe's Harness Shop, a surveyor stands among workmen who lay paving bricks on the roadbed and fit them snugly along the streetcar tracks.

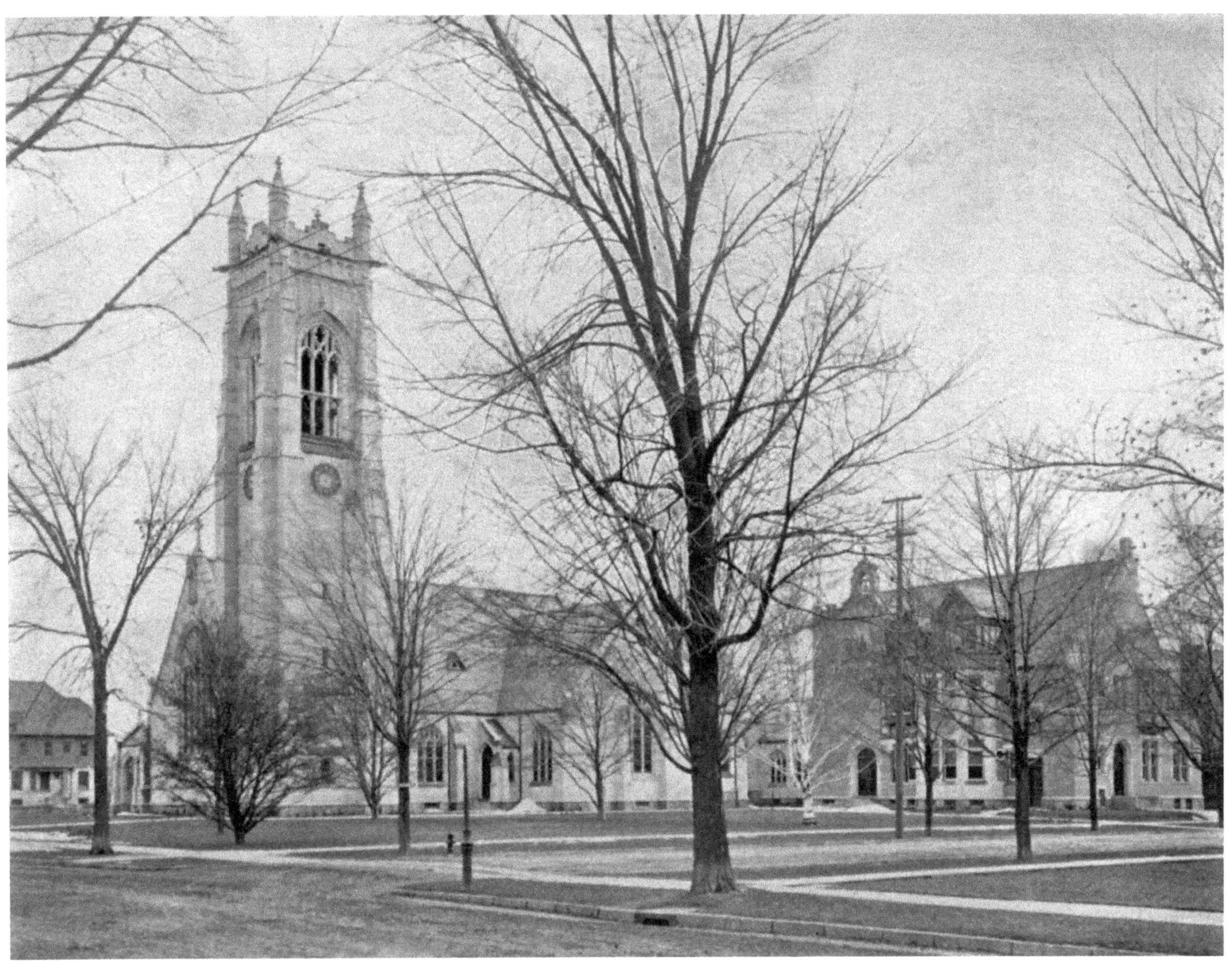

Organized in 1827, St. Paul's Episcopal Church congregation built its church on St. Paul Street in 1830, moving to East Avenue at Vick Park B in 1897. Shown here are the church and parish house around 1899. The young trees are today mature, with more than a century of growth.

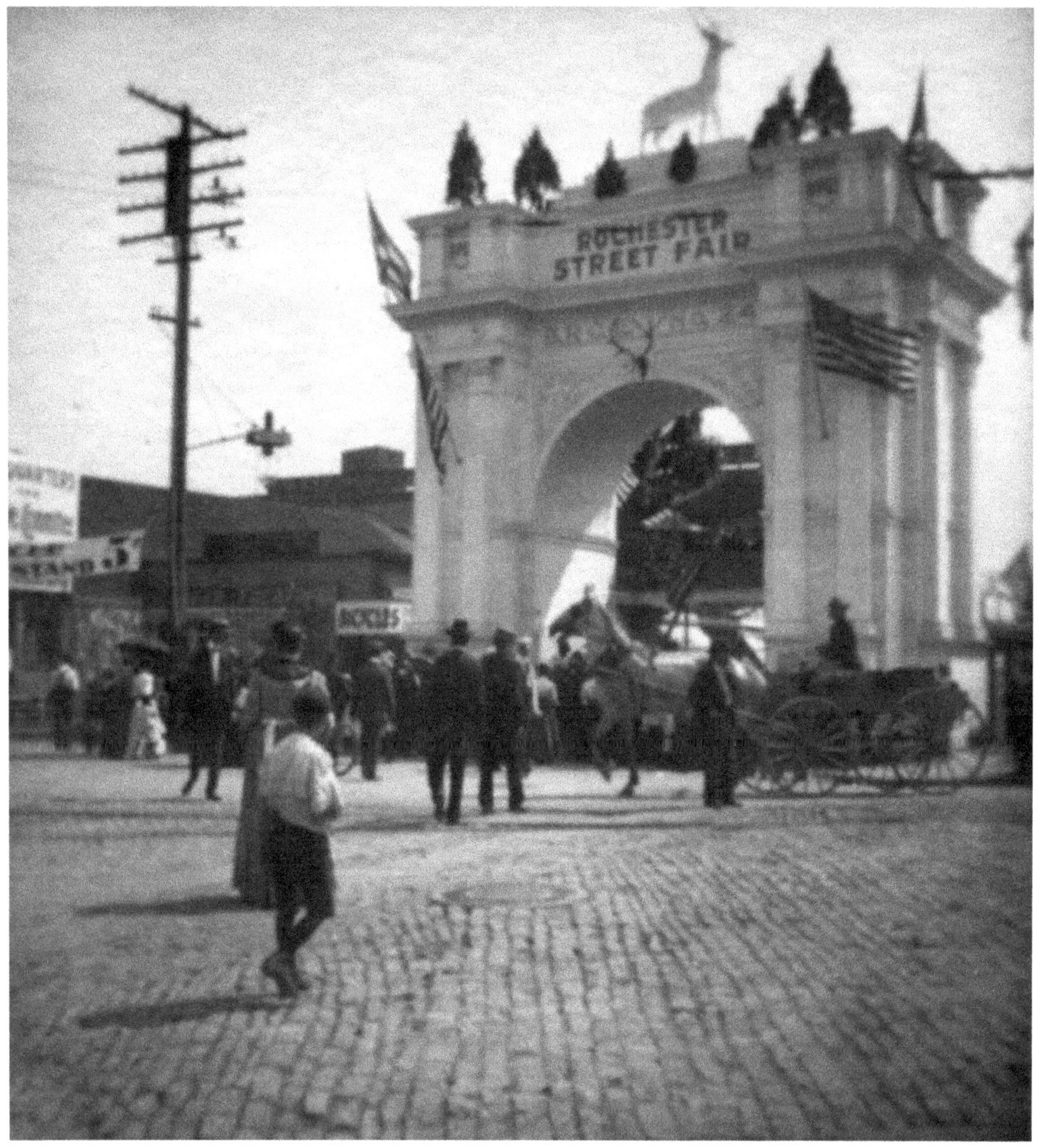

In August 1899, fair goers are attracted to the entrance arch of the Rochester Street Fair, a weeklong carnival offered by the B.P.O.E. No. 24. The arch is decorated with elk antlers, trees, and flags perhaps in celebration of Elk's Day.

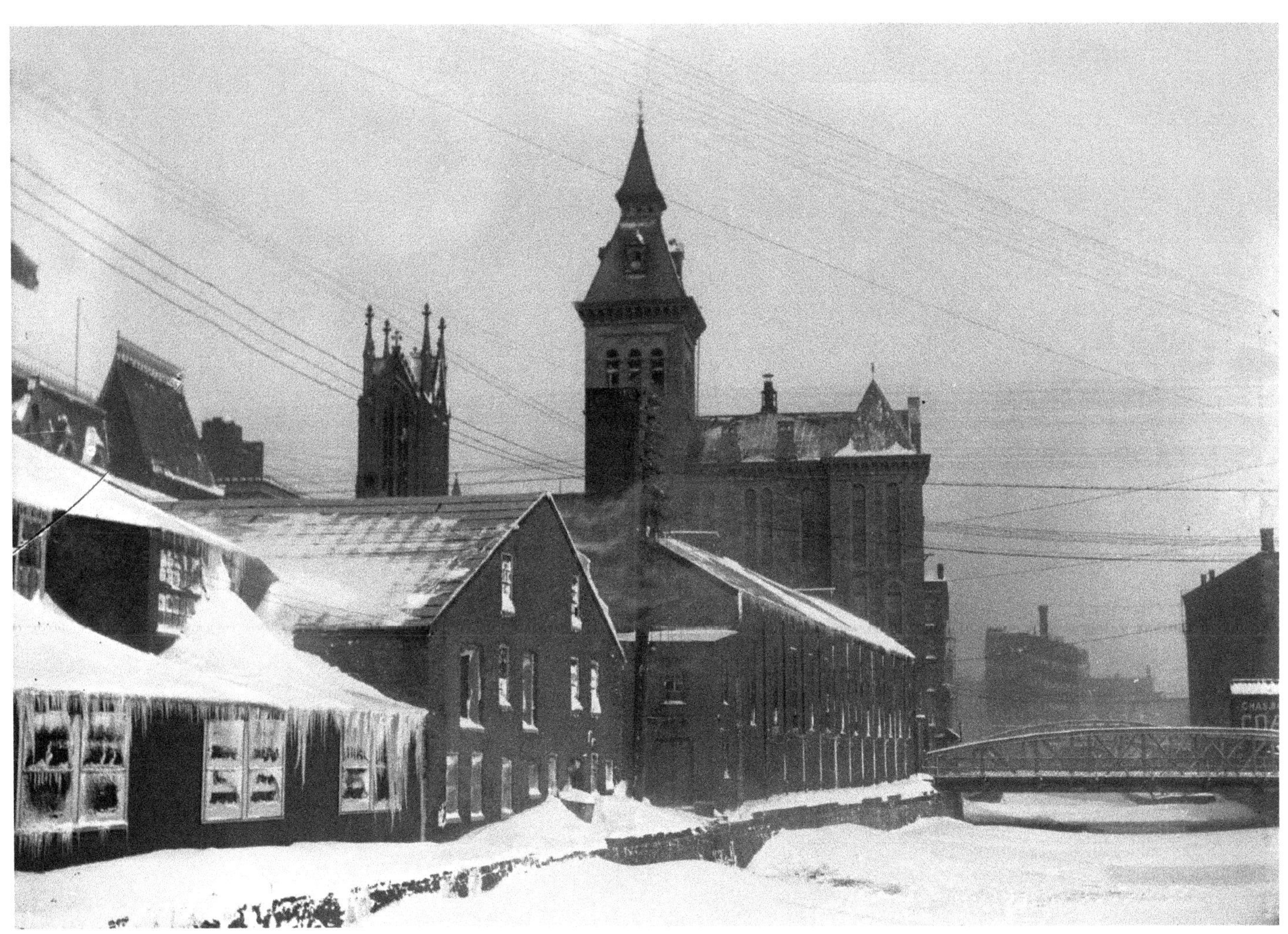

Looking east along the Erie Canal from Plymouth Avenue in winter. Wind-blown snowdrifts pile against the buildings. The pointed bell tower of old City Hall at center and the square steeple of St. Luke's Church at left are visible. The Fitzhugh Street Bridge across the canal was built in 1899 by the Rochester Bridge and Iron Works.

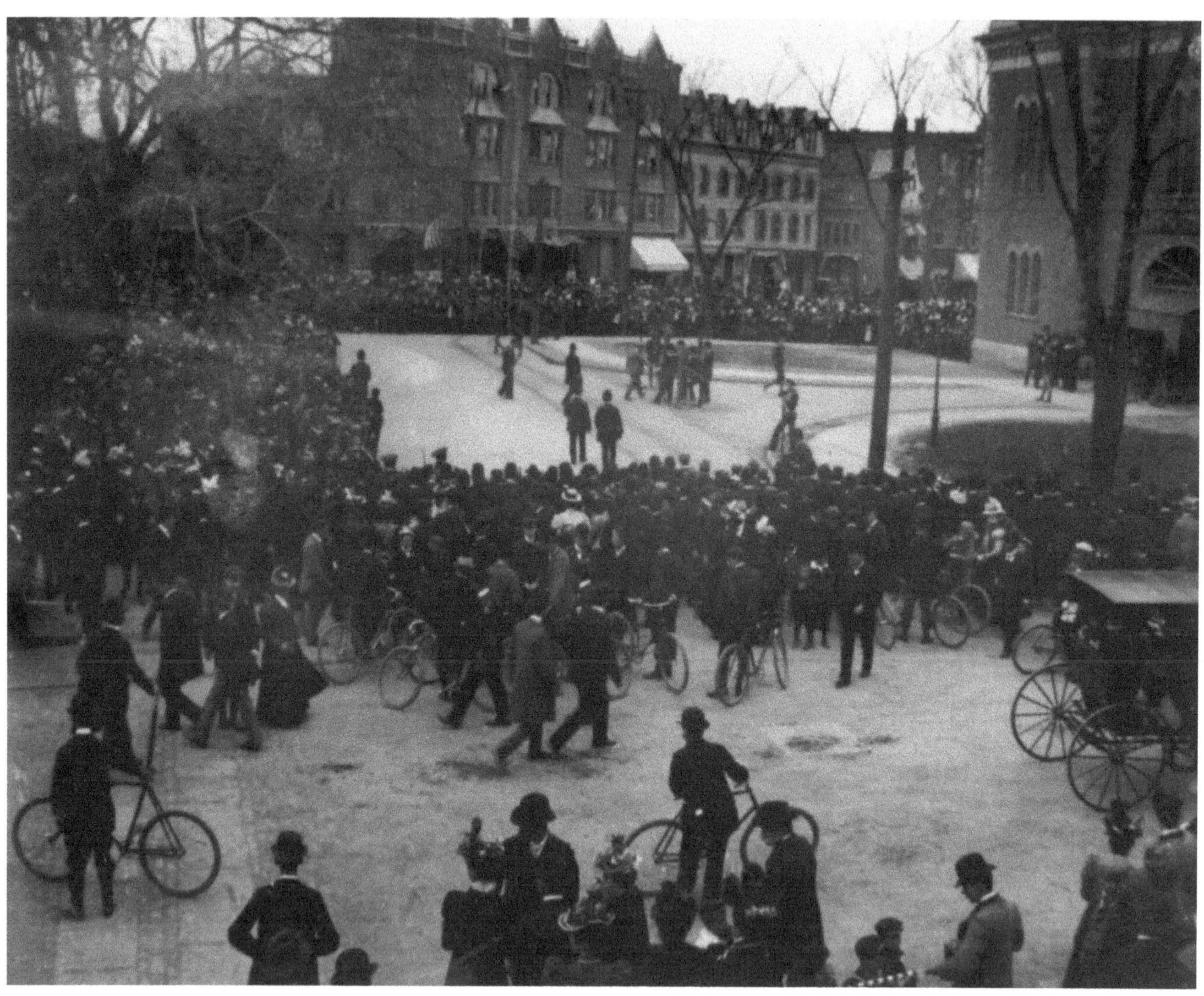

Soldiers leave the Arsenal (now GEVA Theatre) at Washington Square Park for service in the Spanish-American War as a crowd gathers to see them off. (1898)

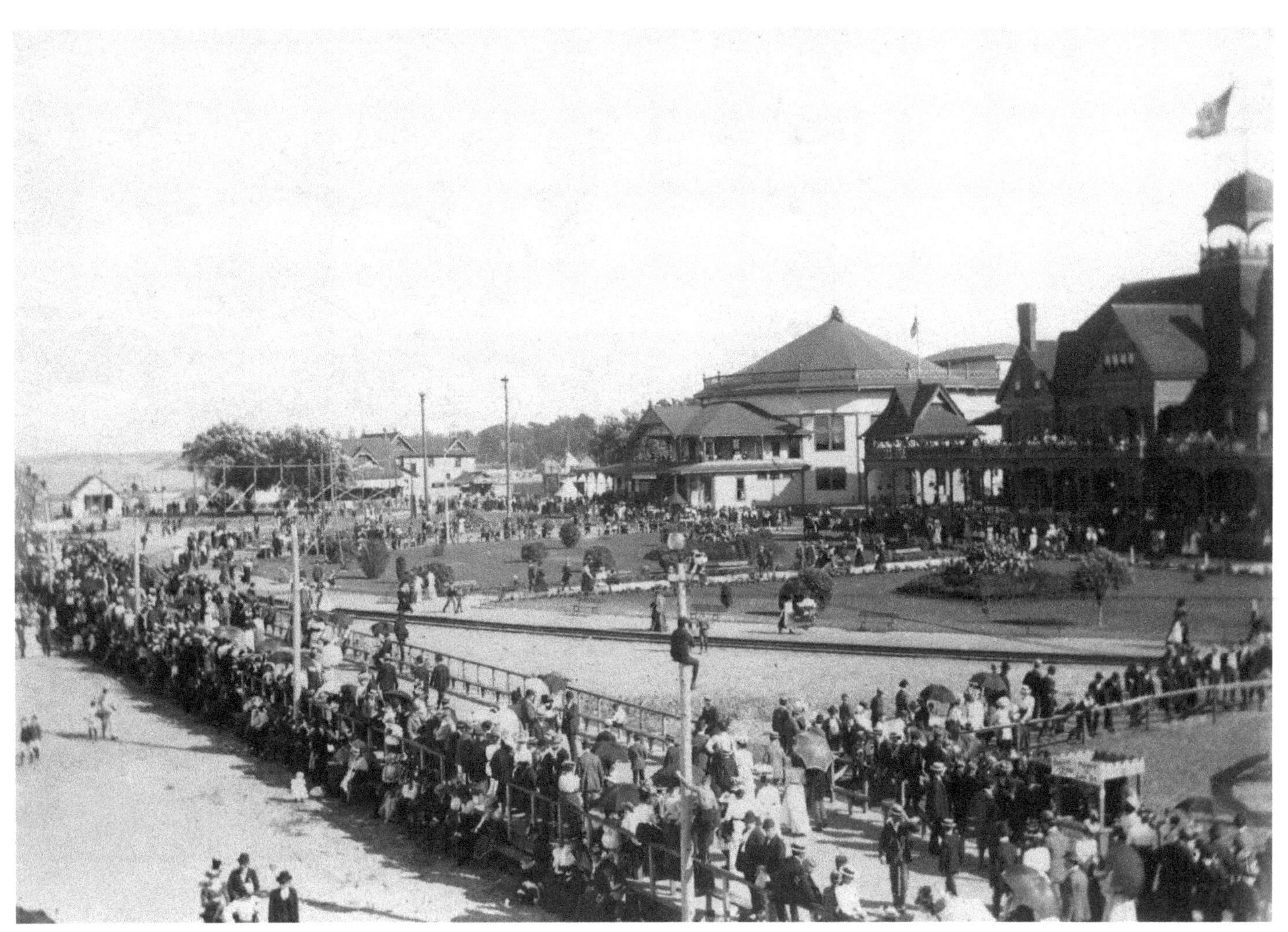

Looking south toward Hotel Ontario and the Auditorium Theatre, the beach can be seen at left. The park is busy with visitors, present to enjoy concerts, exhibitions, rides, fireworks, and refreshments. (1890s)

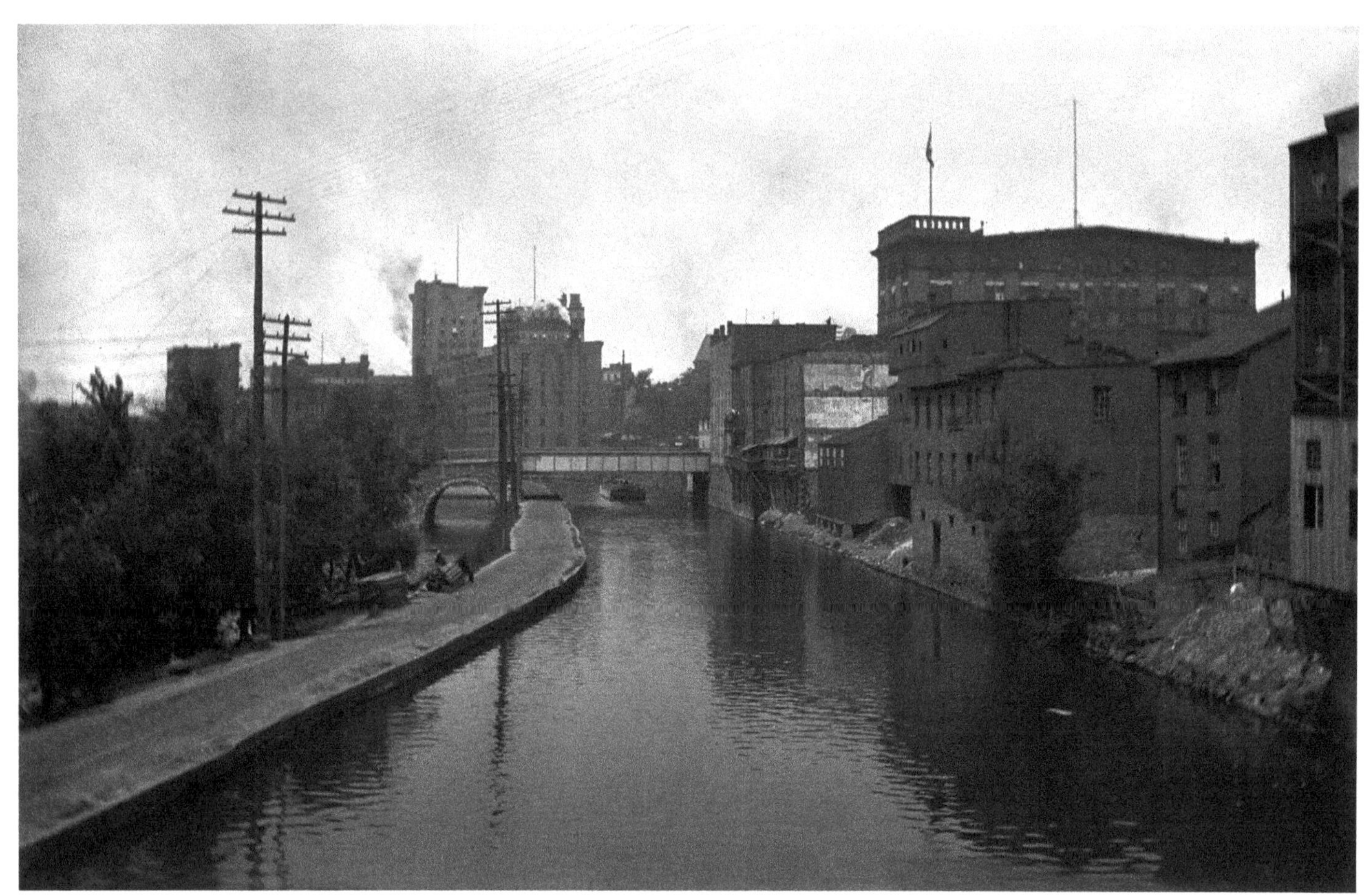

The Erie Canal flows quiet in this 1880s photograph looking north toward Court Street.

Founded by J. Howard Bradstreet and Elden G. Burritt in 1891, their school operated until 1907. Posing for the camera is a Bradstreet hockey team.

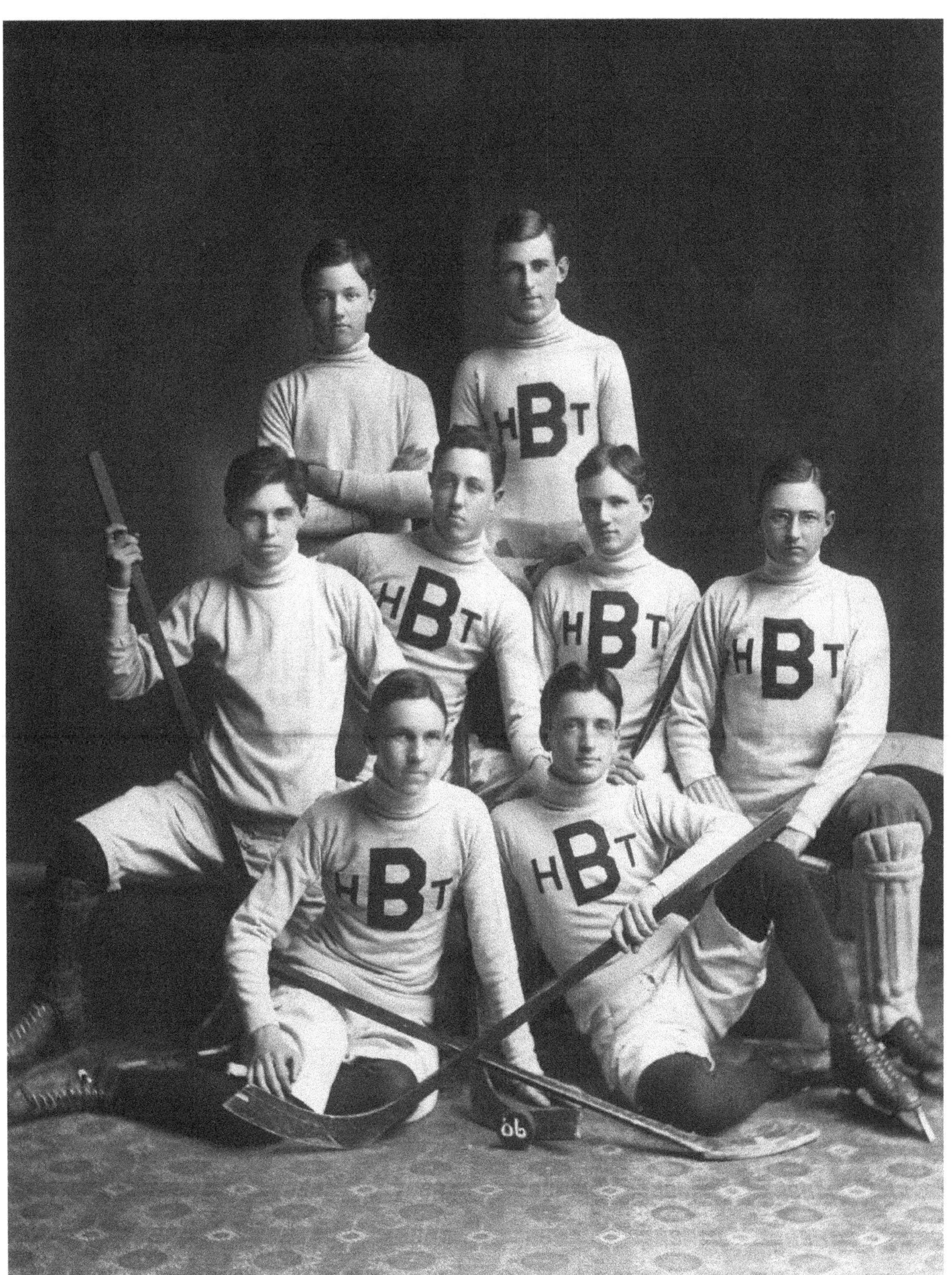

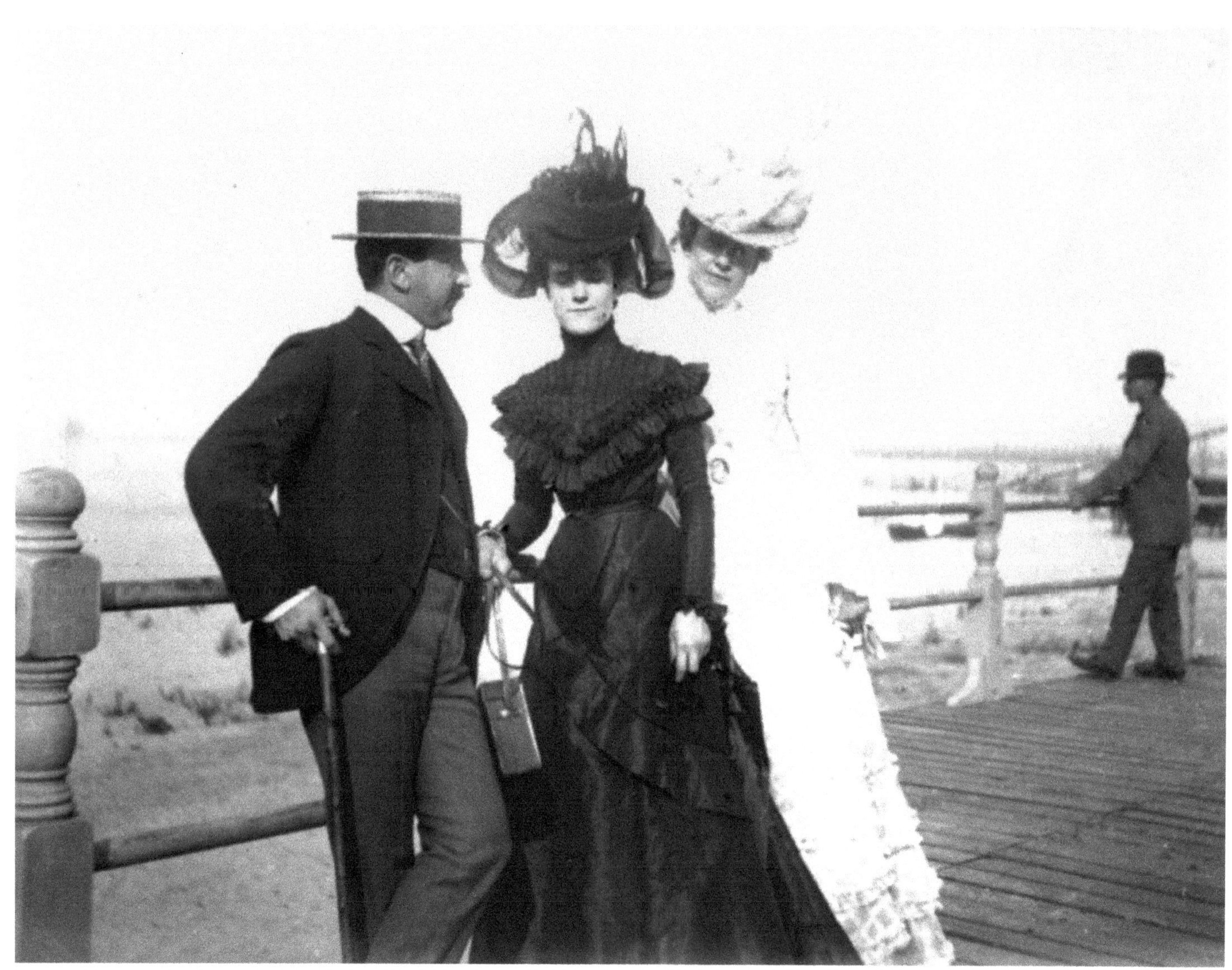

Identified only as Tessie, Amelia, and Fred, these three people enjoy the day on the Charlotte boardwalk at Charlotte Beach on Lake Ontario on July 28, 1899. Until nearly the middle of the twentieth century, people went to the beach in full dress or full-body bathing suits, even in the heat of July. The cooler breezes off the lake gave respite to people from the city. A "fresh air" program brought poor children from the city to the lake in the summer to keep them healthy.

Great Expectations

(1900–1919)

For many people the turn of the century signaled great expectations. While the Millerites took their place on Cobb's Hill awaiting the end of the world, others observed their usual New Year celebration, spending time with family and friends or in small parties at which they toasted the health and wealth of the coming year. On New Year's Day sleighs cut through the snow on city streets as people called upon one another. Holiday dinners evoked conversation as did the newspapers, which recounted the accomplishments of the nineteenth century with great pride and looked to the twentieth century to bring modern scientific advances in medicine, technology, and industry. Periodically an automobile plied city streets, and, as time went by, more people considered replacing their horse and buggy with an automobile. By 1927 the last horse-drawn fire truck was answering its call.

The University of Rochester accepted women as students for the first time in 1900 after Susan B. Anthony, her sister Mary, and others raised more than $100,000 to defray the university's expenses in starting a program for women. Susan passed away in 1906 and her sister three years later. The next generation of women carried the banner for women's rights into the twentieth century and succeeded in winning the right to vote. Anthony also helped to found the Women's Industrial and Educational Union, which helped women to get trained for work, educated, and counseled.

The new flying machines were entertaining people at Genesee Valley Park and landing at Mary Baker's farm field (later called Baker's Field) just outside the city. Testing machines of different shapes and modes of power, pilots were still trying to prove the usefulness of these "contraptions." A test pick-up and airdrop of mailbags from a plane that did not land showed that airmail could be delivered rapidly. Rochester won a contract with the government as an airmail station.

Expectations began to dim as it became clear that the nation would face a world war. City industry tooled up for war production and recruits trained for service overseas.

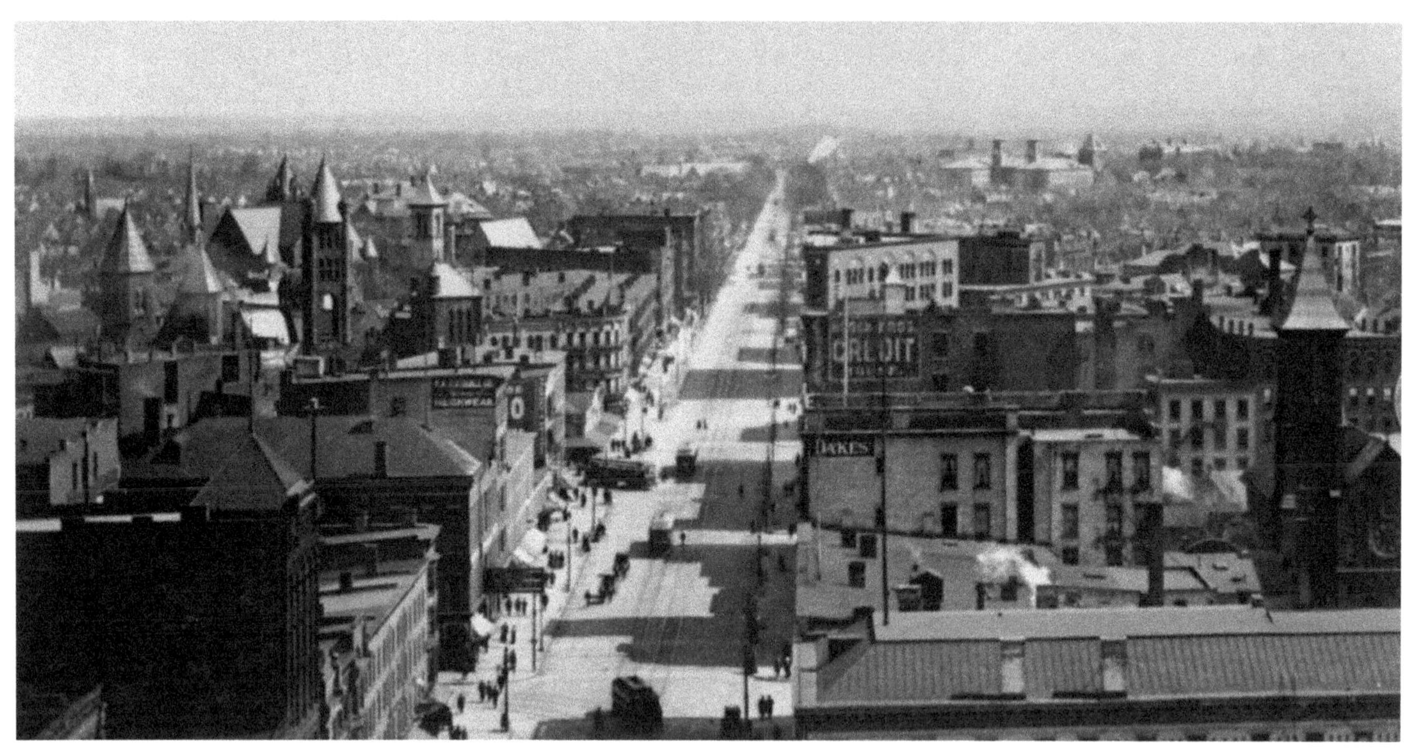

Looking east from the Chamber of Commerce Building, nearly the entire length of Main Street east can be seen in this photograph taken about 1900.

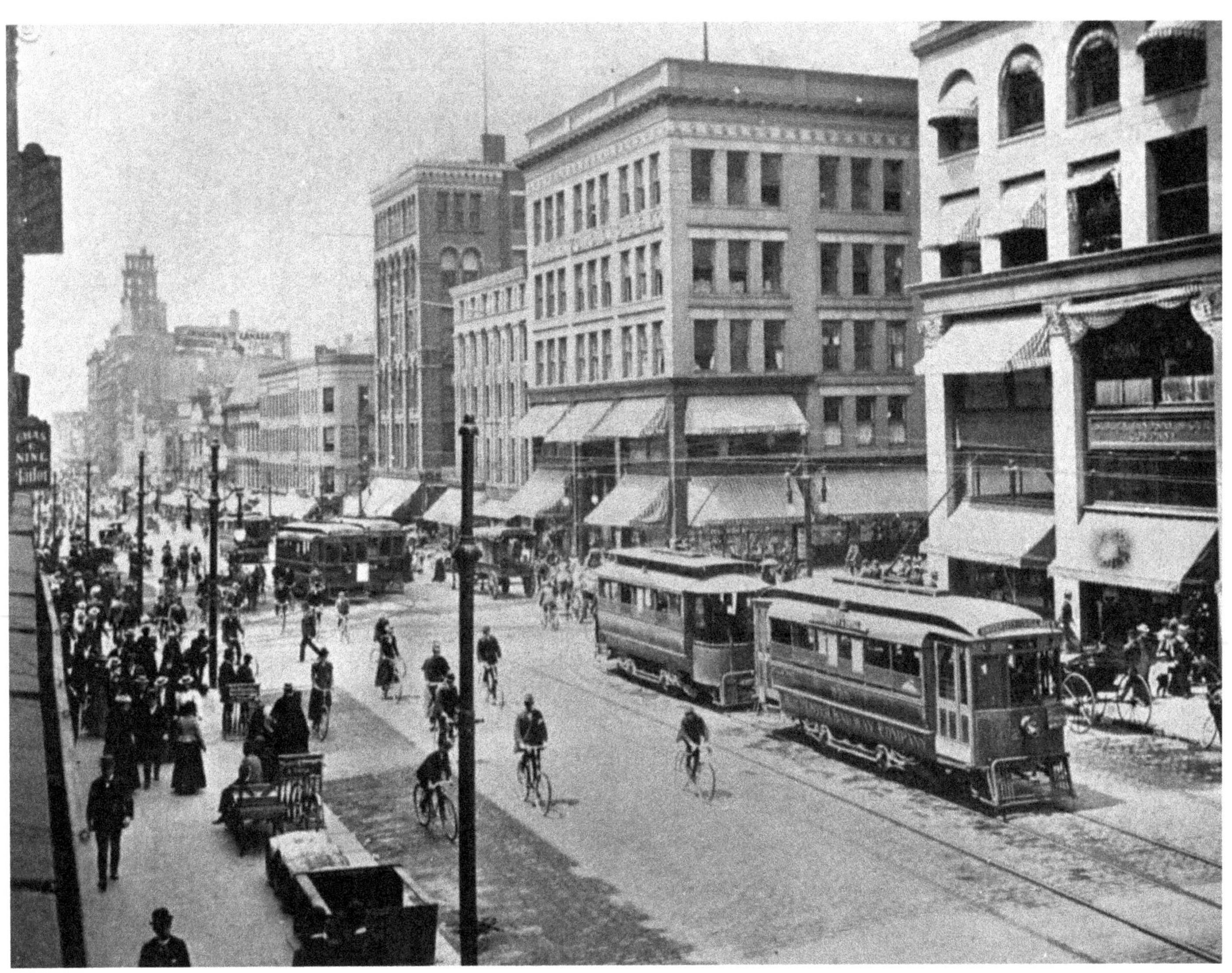

The popularity of bicycles is apparent in this view of East Main Street looking west toward St. Paul Street (1900). The Granite Building is at right and the Burke Building is at center. Electric streetcars reduced the number of wagons crowding city streets. One newspaper complained that the cost of bicycles would keep people from buying them and no one would buy from a businessman who made a sales call on a bicycle.

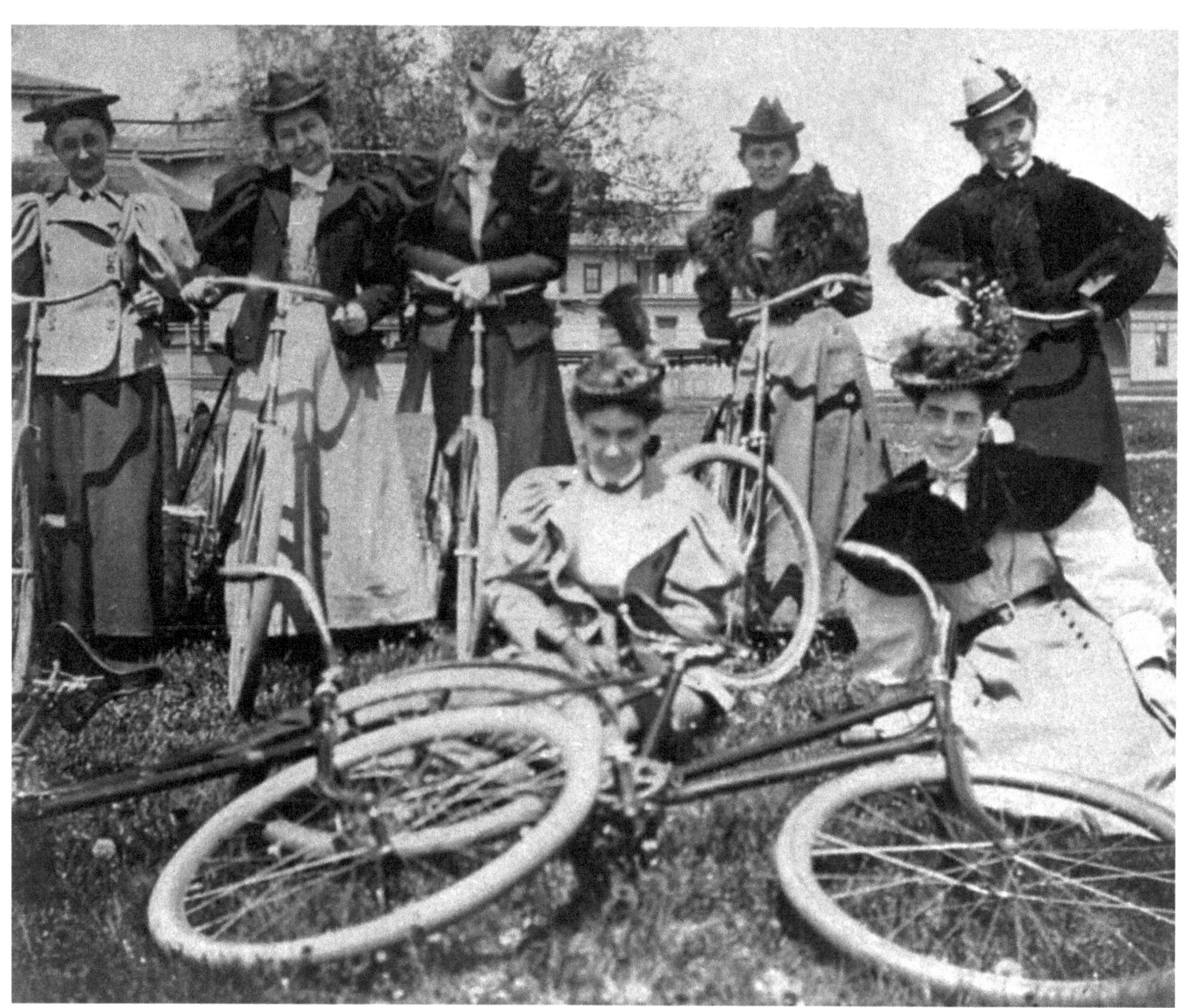

Though the bicycle was predicted to be unsuccessful, by the 1890s there were more than 40,000 in use in Monroe County, and bicycle clubs formed spawning the construction of bicycle paths through Rochester area parks. The bicycle was welcomed by women who enjoyed a newfound freedom of movement.

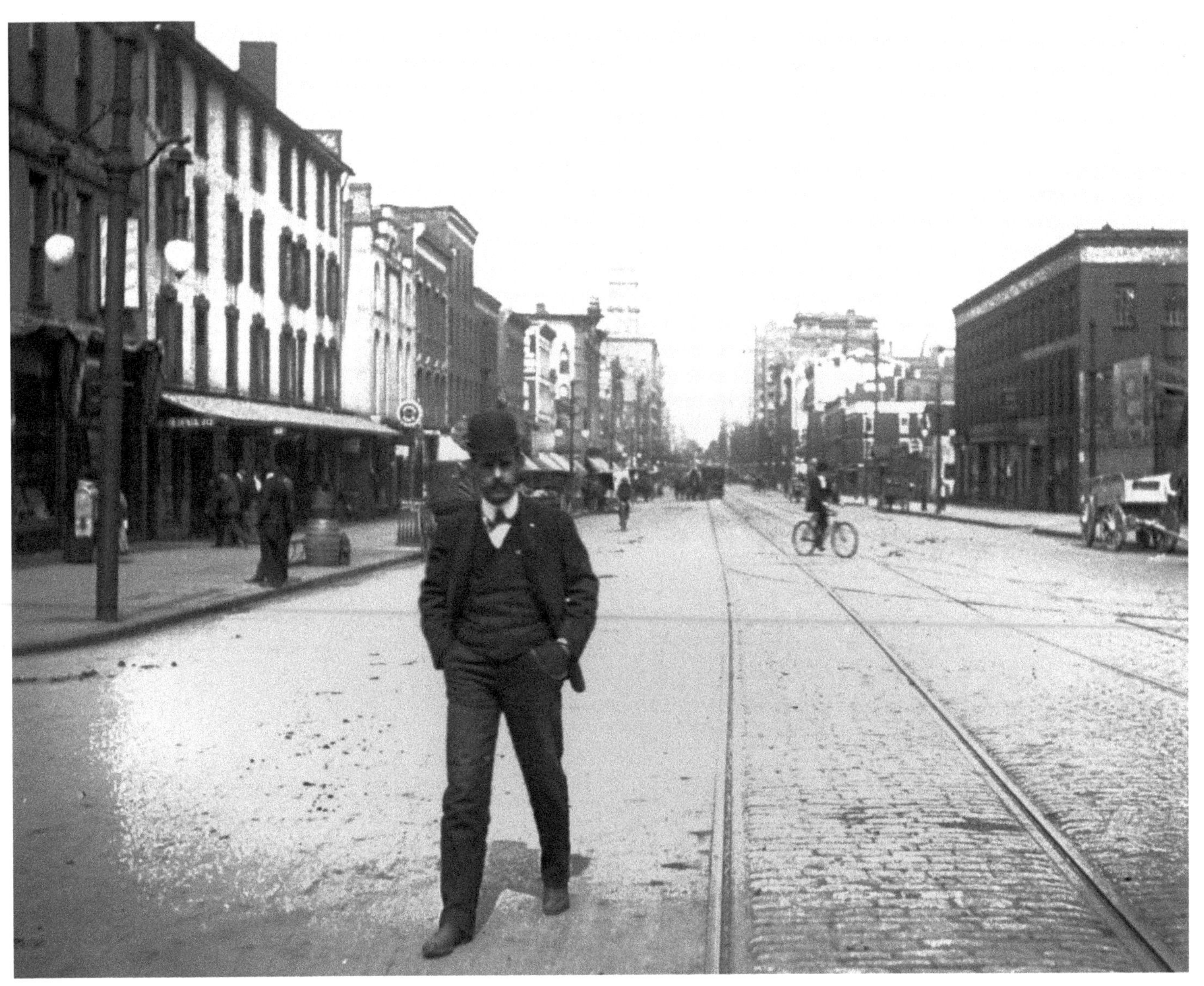

A man dressed in a business suit crosses West Main Street. In this view looking east the length of Main Street, the Powers Building can be seen in the distance.

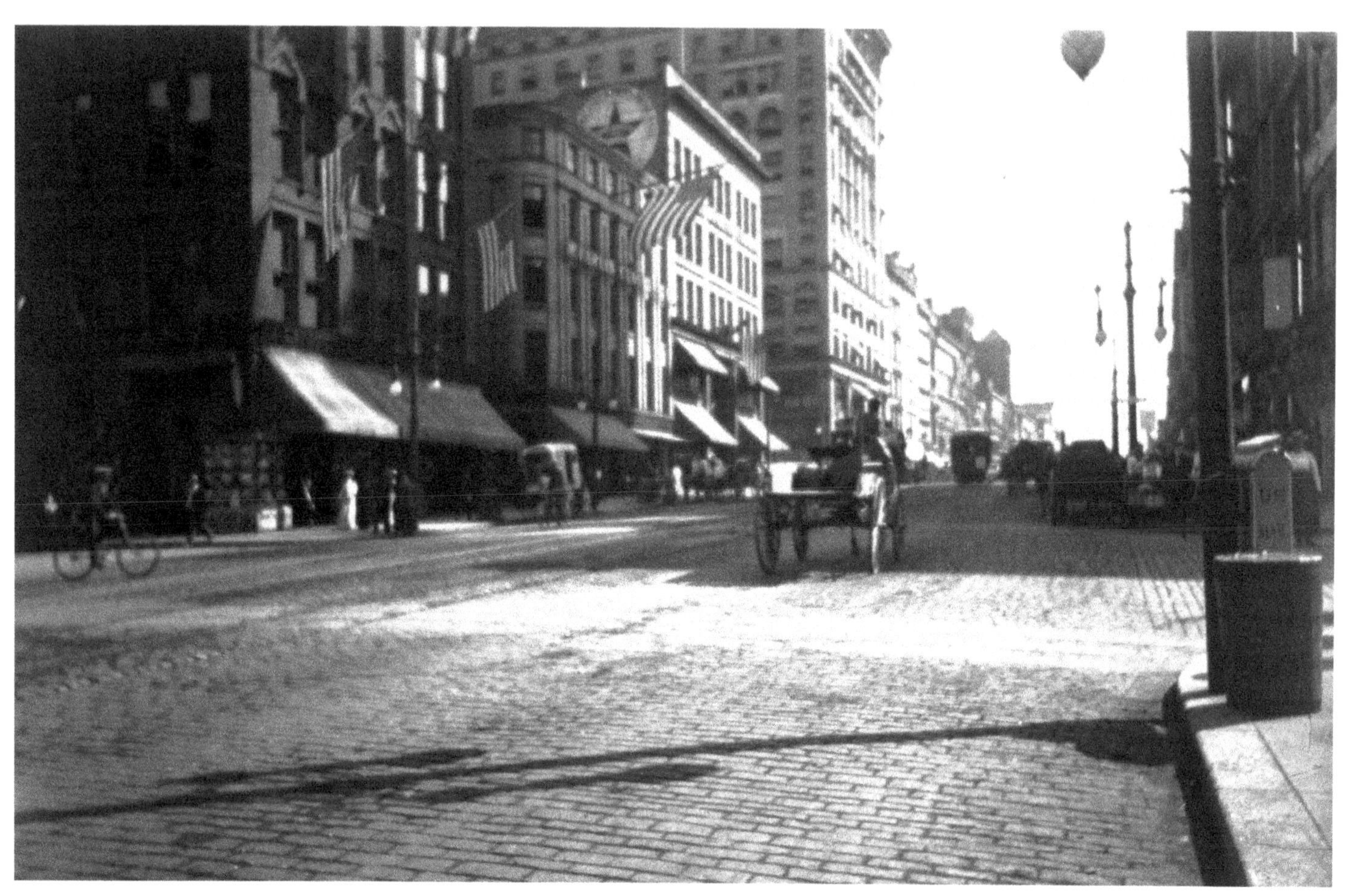

A single horse draws a wagon up Main Street hill heading east past the intersection of Water Street. The Union Clothing Co. and McFarlin Clothing Co. can be seen at left. The Granite Building stands across St. Paul Street.

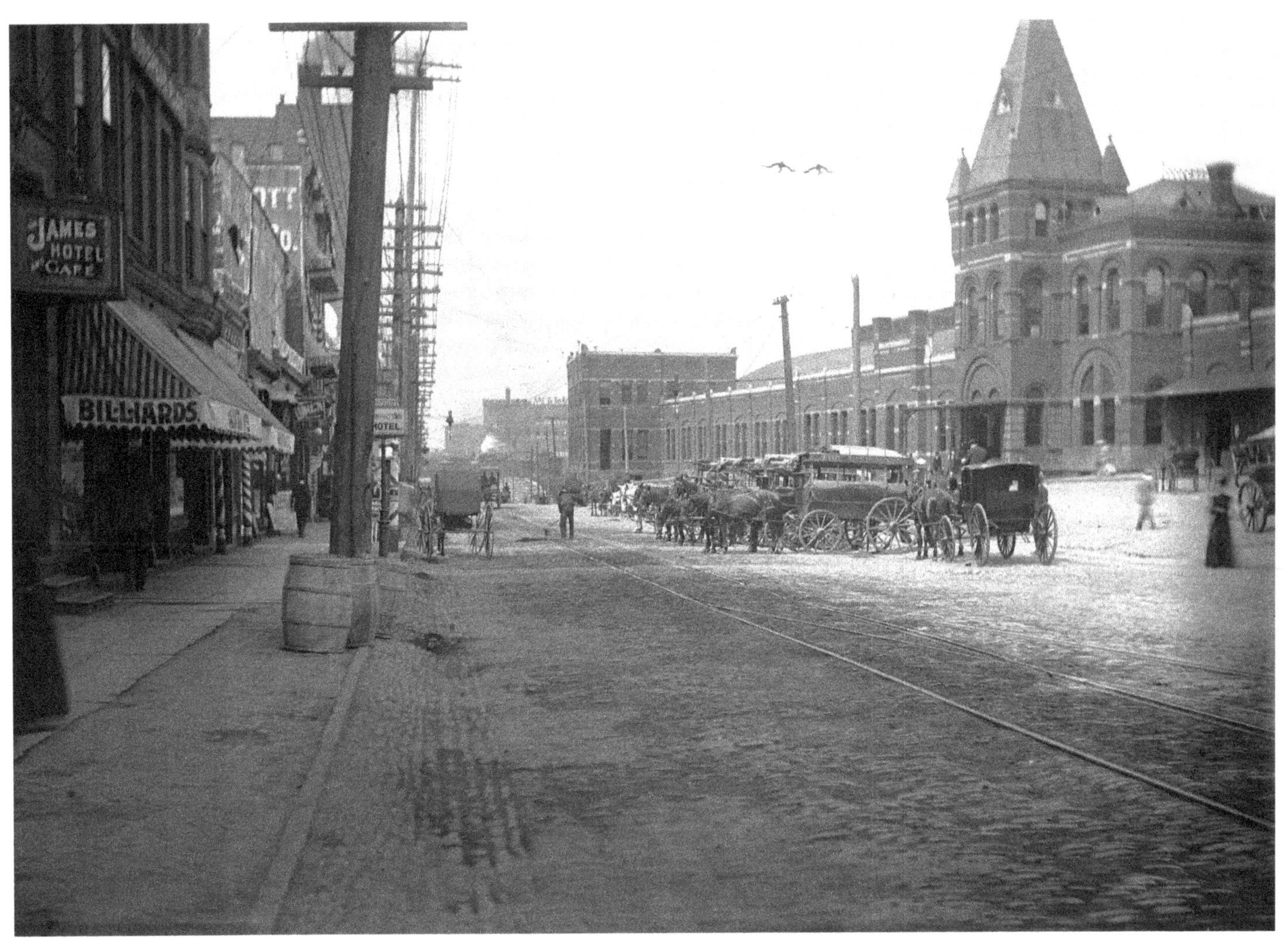

One horse-drawn carriage bears a sign "The Livingston," probably taking the hotel Livingston's guests to and from this New York Central Railroad Station on Central Avenue. Other carriages await in the lot along Central Avenue looking west from North Clinton Avenue. Several hotels, a barber shop, billiards rooms, and other businesses line Central Avenue to serve train passengers.

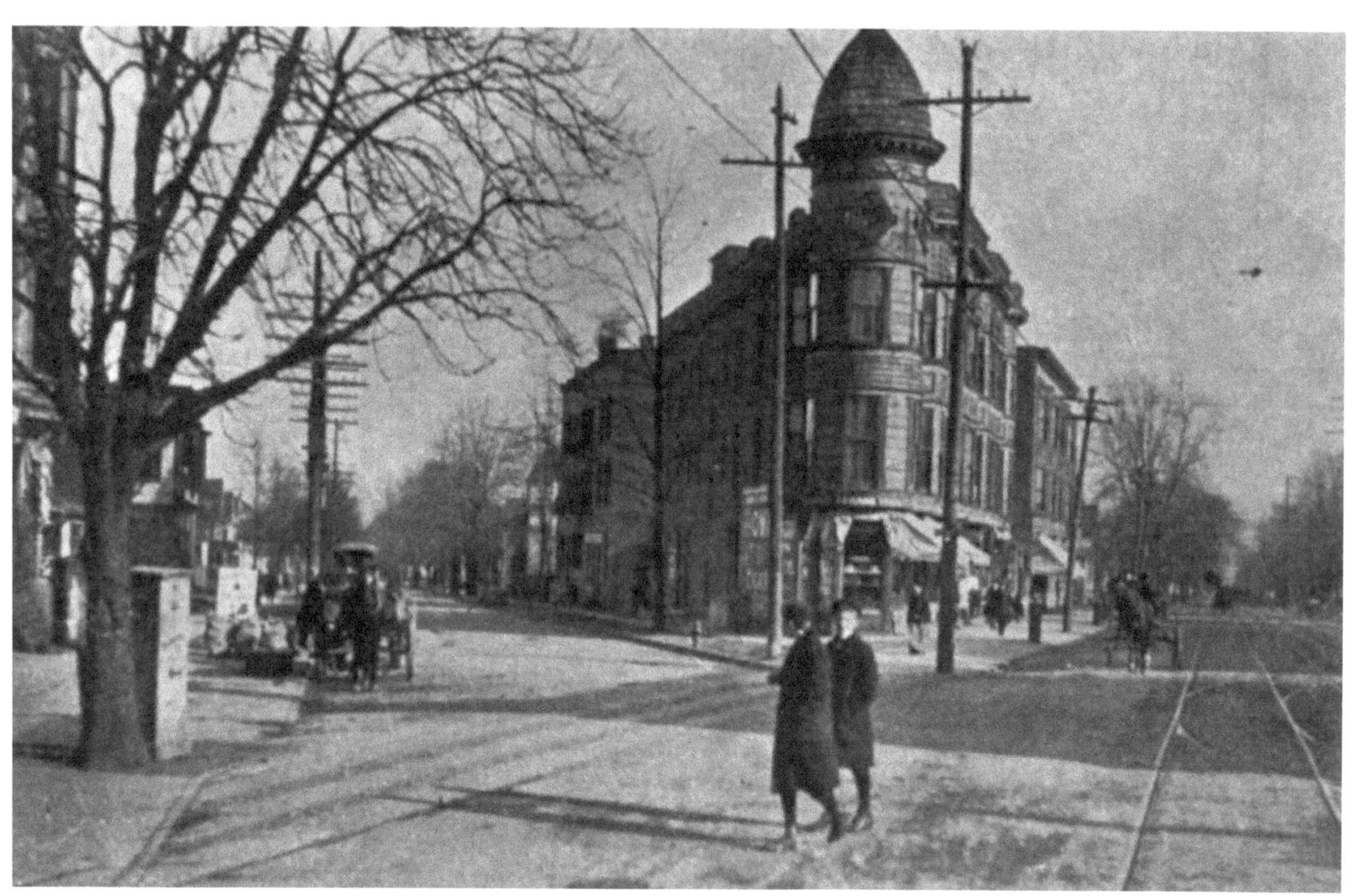

The Kensington Apartment House stands at the intersection of West Avenue and Brown Street, affectionately known as "Bull's Head." Two young boys cross the street as a carriage approaches from West Avenue.

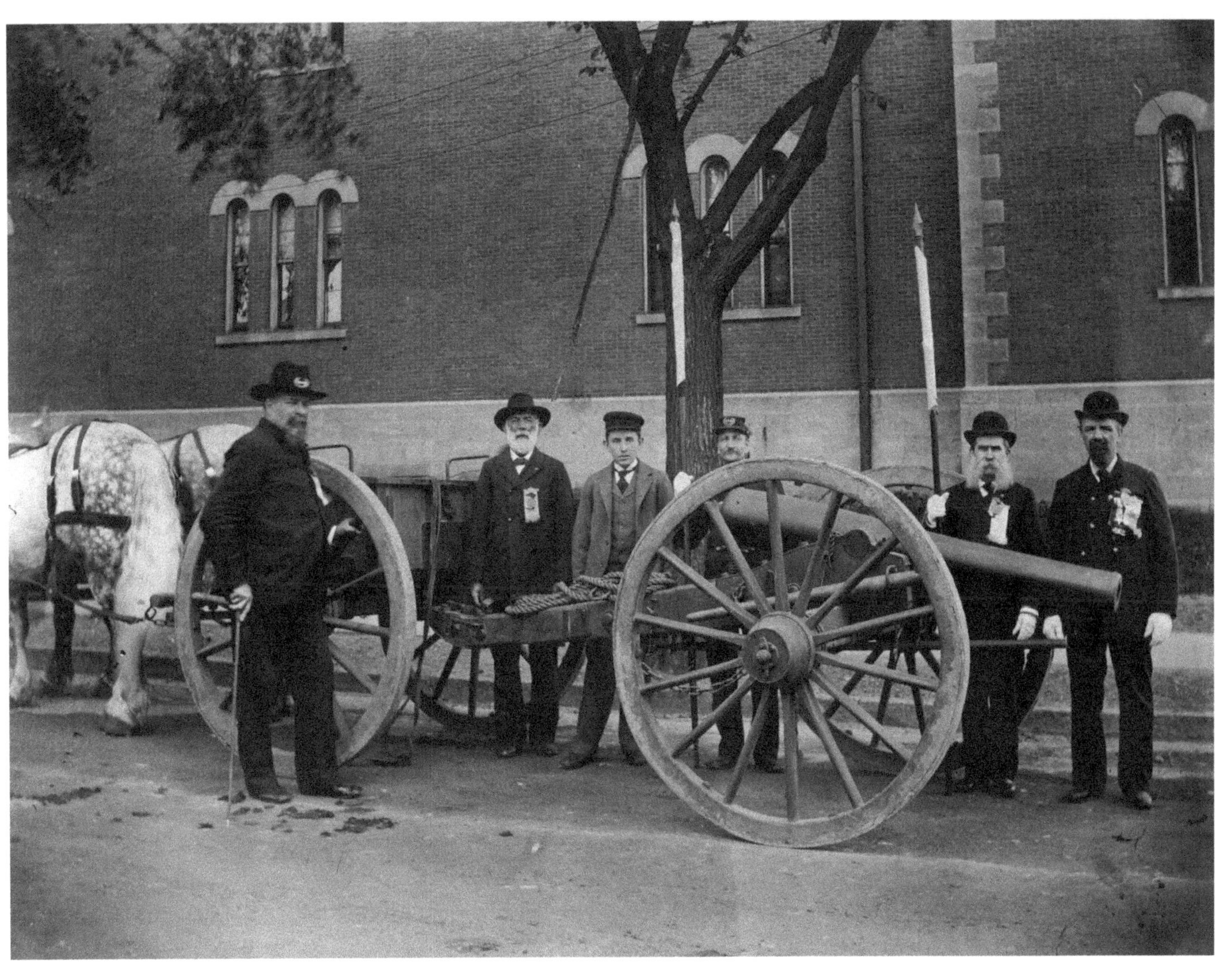

Civil War veterans of the Grand Army of the Republic, probably Reynolds Battery, pose with their horse-drawn cannon around 1900.

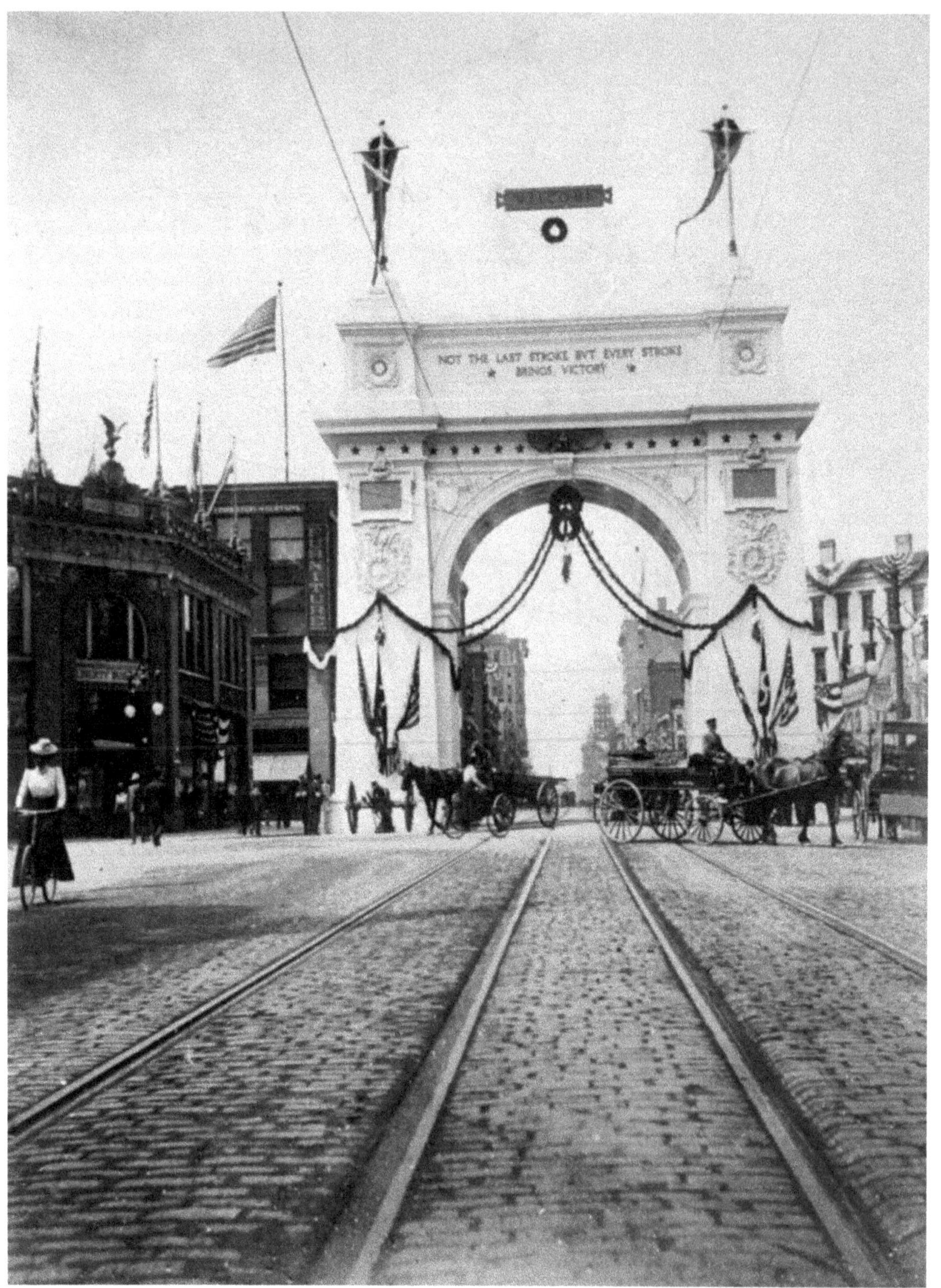

The words "Not The Last Stroke But Every Stroke Brings Victory" are written on the Triumphal Arch built to honor General Elwell Otis on his return from the Spanish-American War about 1900. The arch stood at the corner of East Avenue and Main Street.

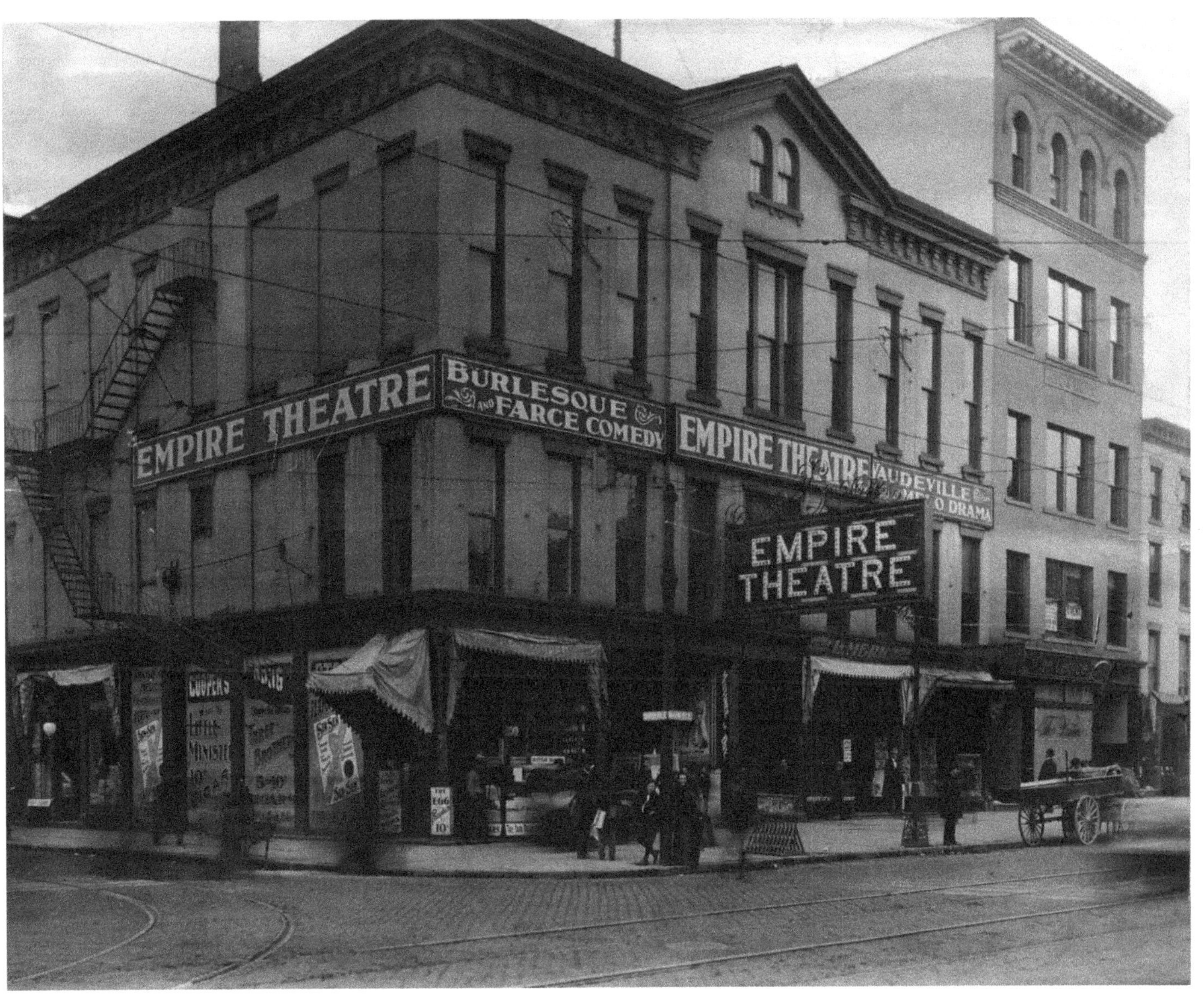

The Empire Theatre stands on the northeast corner of East Main Street and North Clinton Avenue on what became the site of the new Sibley's Store after 1904. Signs on the front upper level advertise burlesque, farce comedy, vaudeville, and melodrama. Cooper's Drug Store occupies the street level.

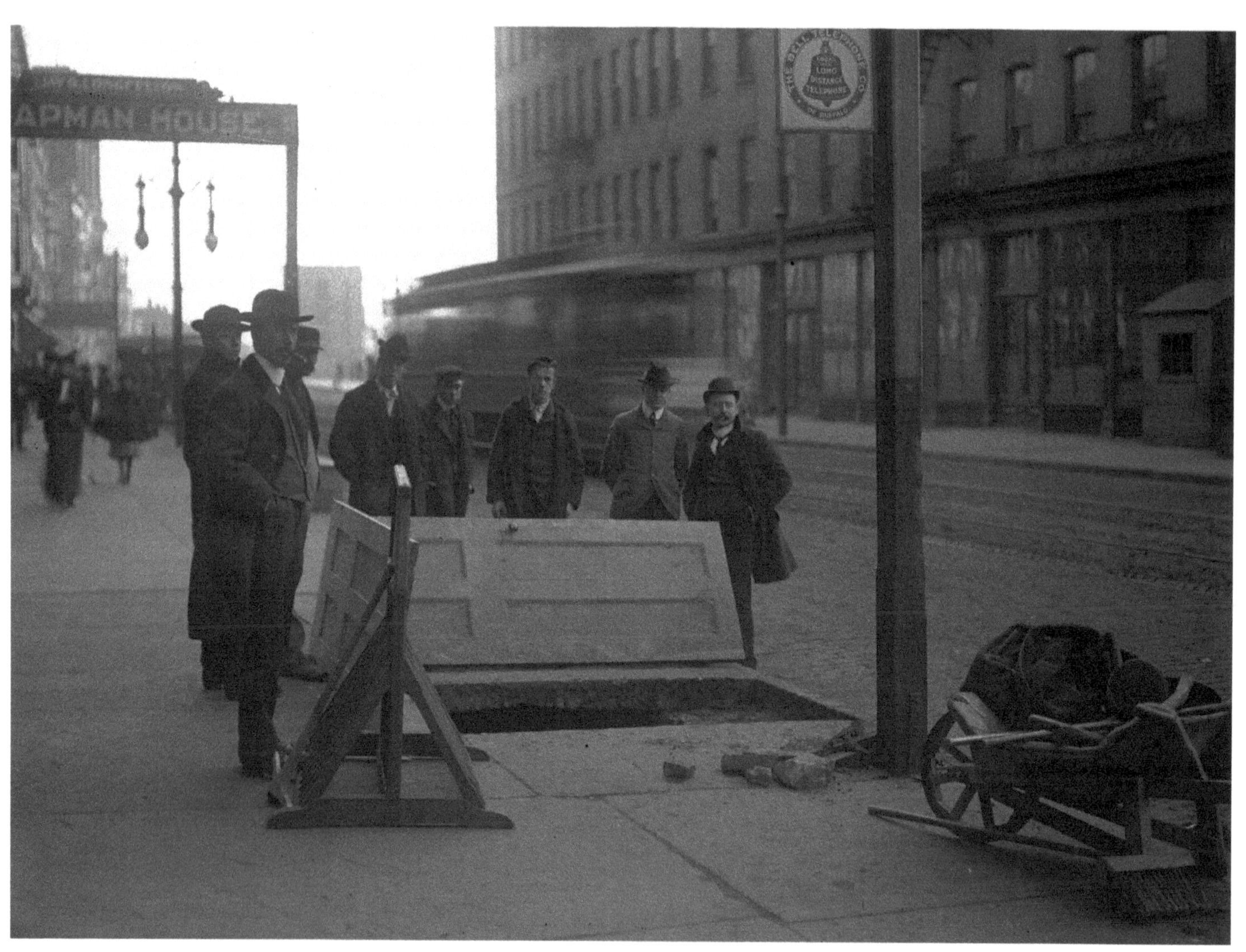

On December 11, 1901, John Hornby of Rhode Island fell into a hole when a section of the sidewalk in front of Chapman House on South Avenue collapsed. Later James Kenney fell into the same hole. Many parts of the city have tunnels for transfer of goods under the street and for delivery to stores. The streetcar is a blur as it passes by on South Avenue.

Three young boys pictured here are infected with smallpox and being cared for at Hope Hospital. By the time the smallpox epidemic ended in 1902, 101 people in the Rochester area had died of the disease. So many people were infected that tents were set up along the river not far from the University of Rochester. In 1903 the temporary hospital and tents were burned to prevent the spread of disease.

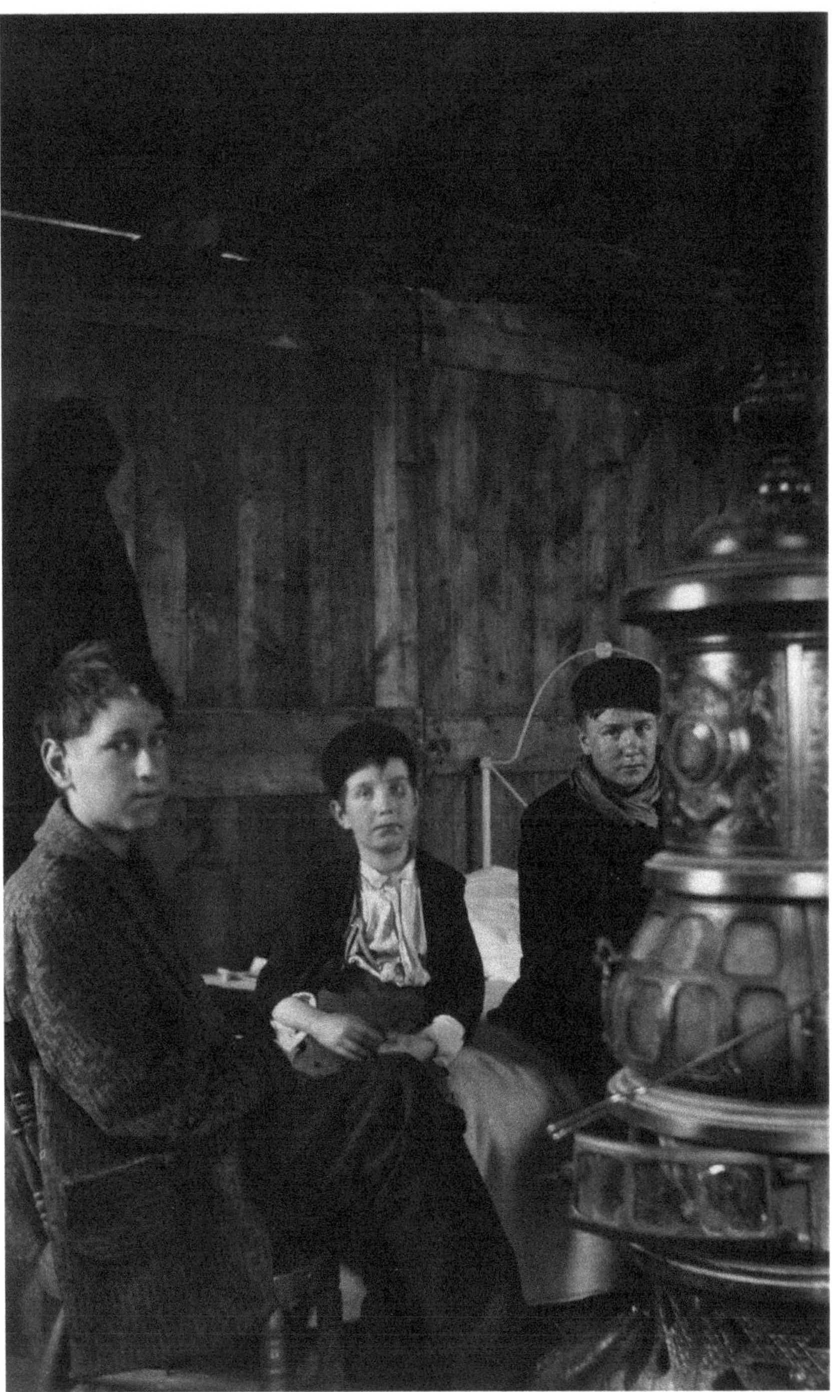

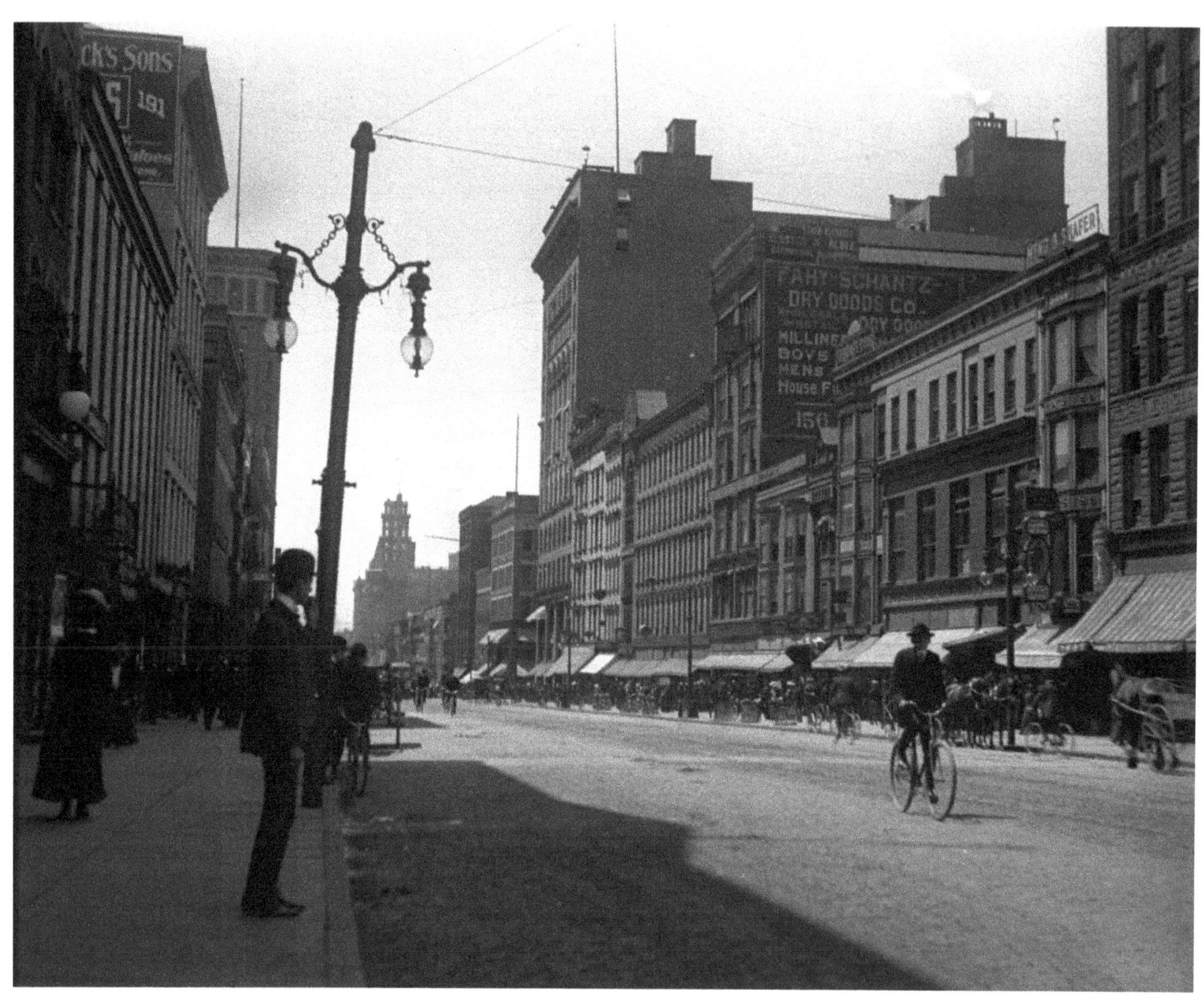

The Granite Building can be seen at center in the distance. Several bicyclists travel along Main Street. Wagons line the north side of the street.

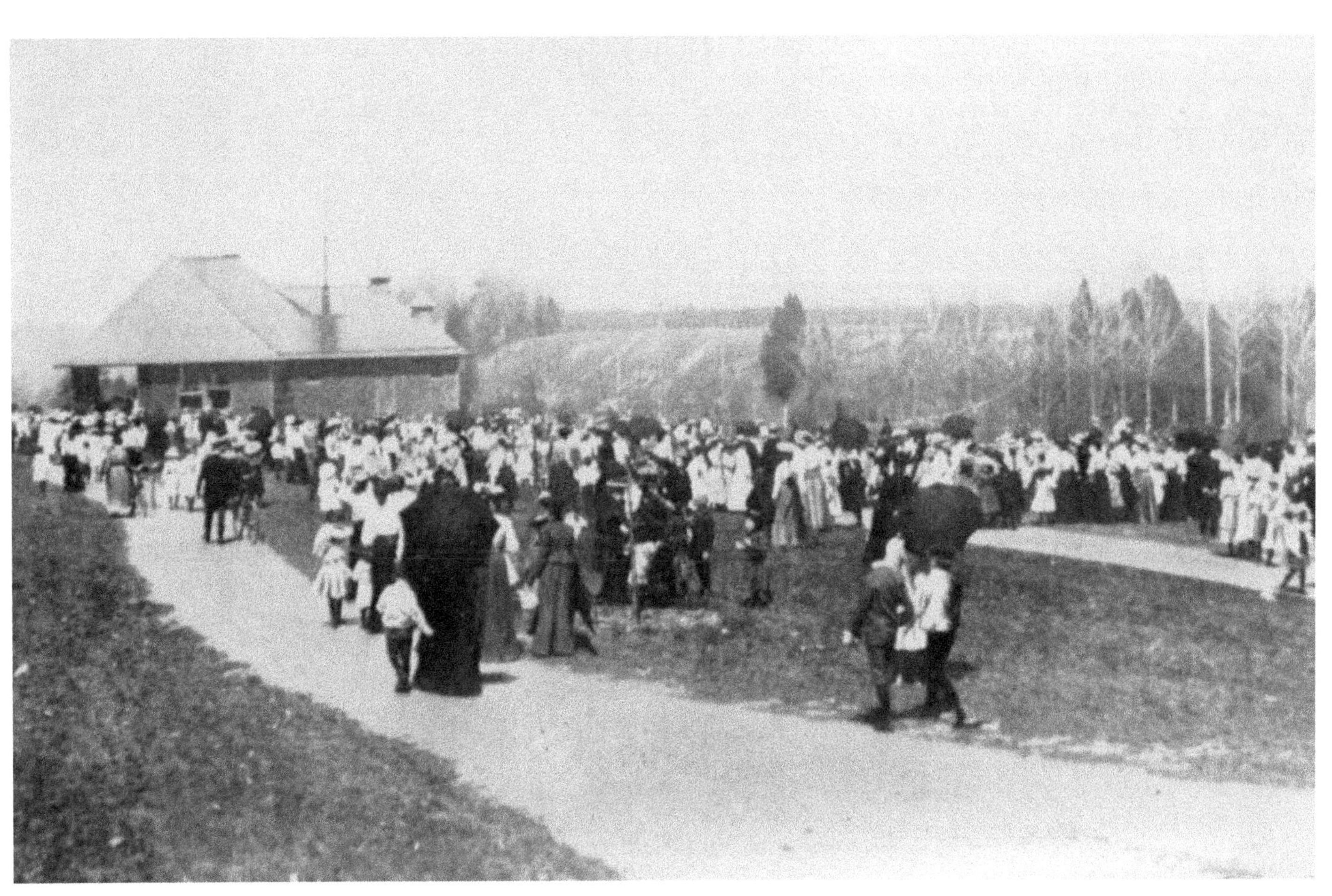

Hundreds of visitors attended the May Day celebration at Seneca Park in 1904. Seneca Park was just over a decade old by this time. Designed by noted landscape architect Frederick Law Olmsted, Seneca Park, overlooking the Genesee River, was a popular destination for area residents.

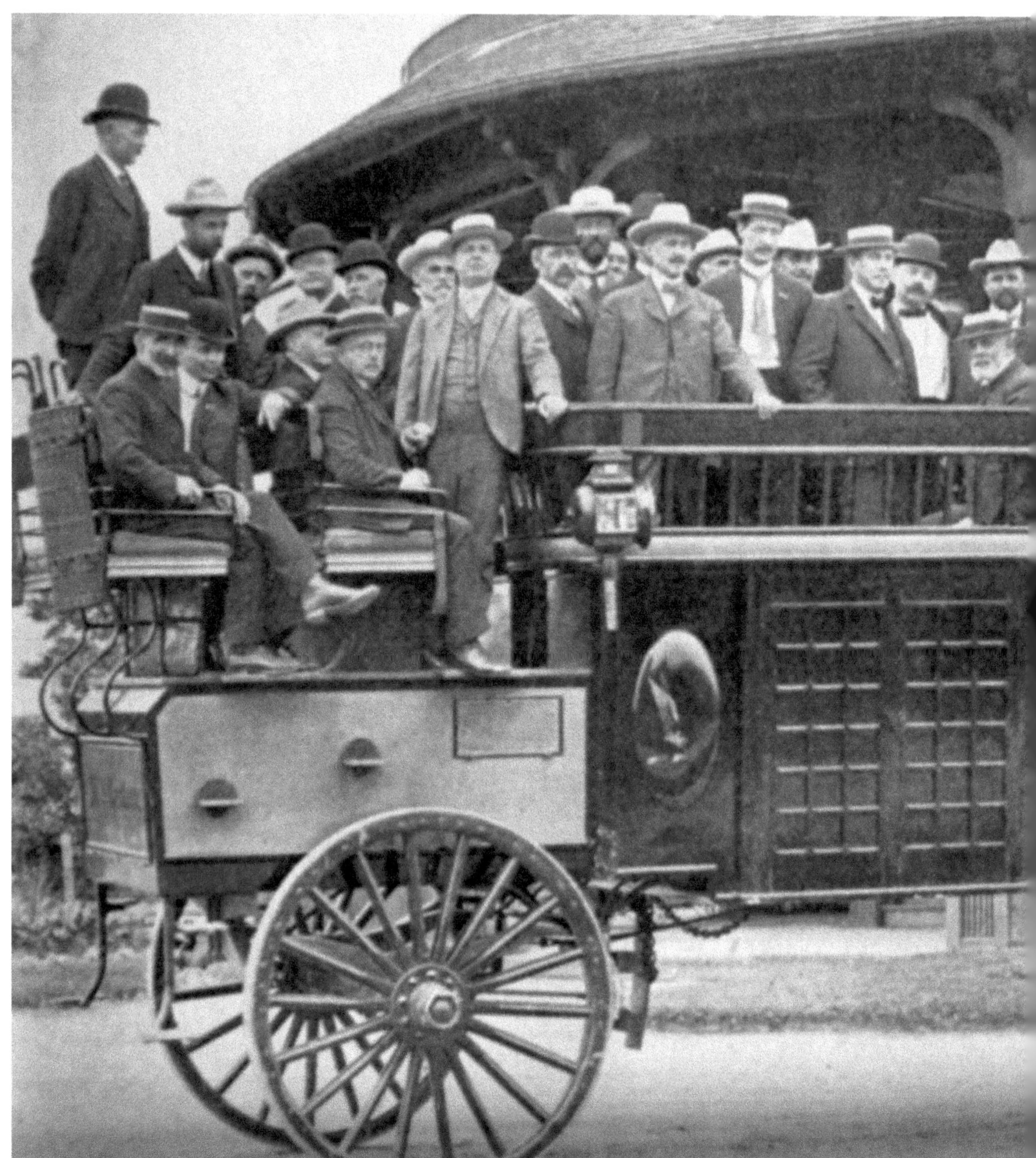

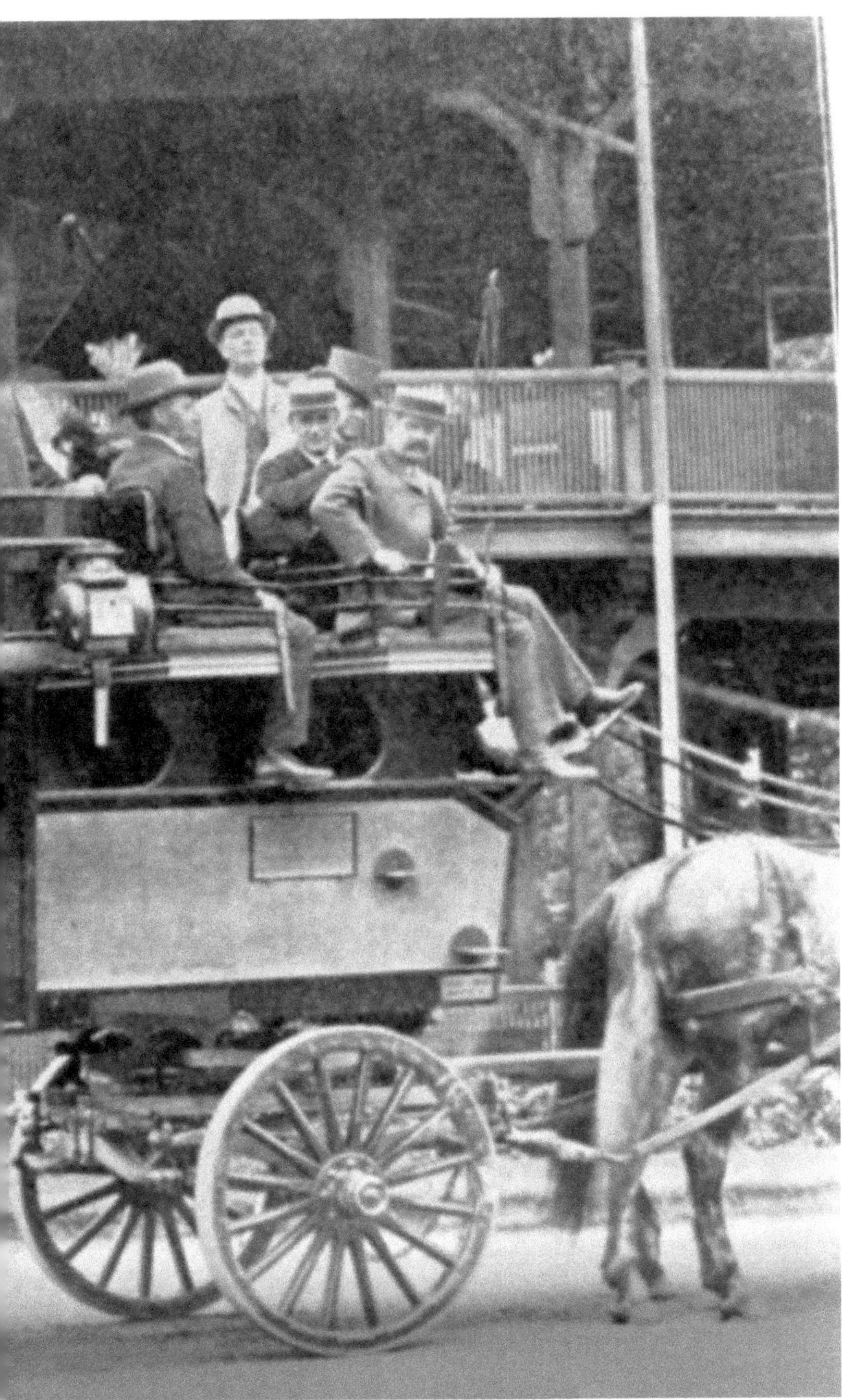

Visiting parks superintendents gather in a large carriage for an outing at Highland Park. The Children's Pavilion, dedicated to the children of Rochester by nurserymen Ellwanger and Barry, is visible in the background. (July 1, 1905)

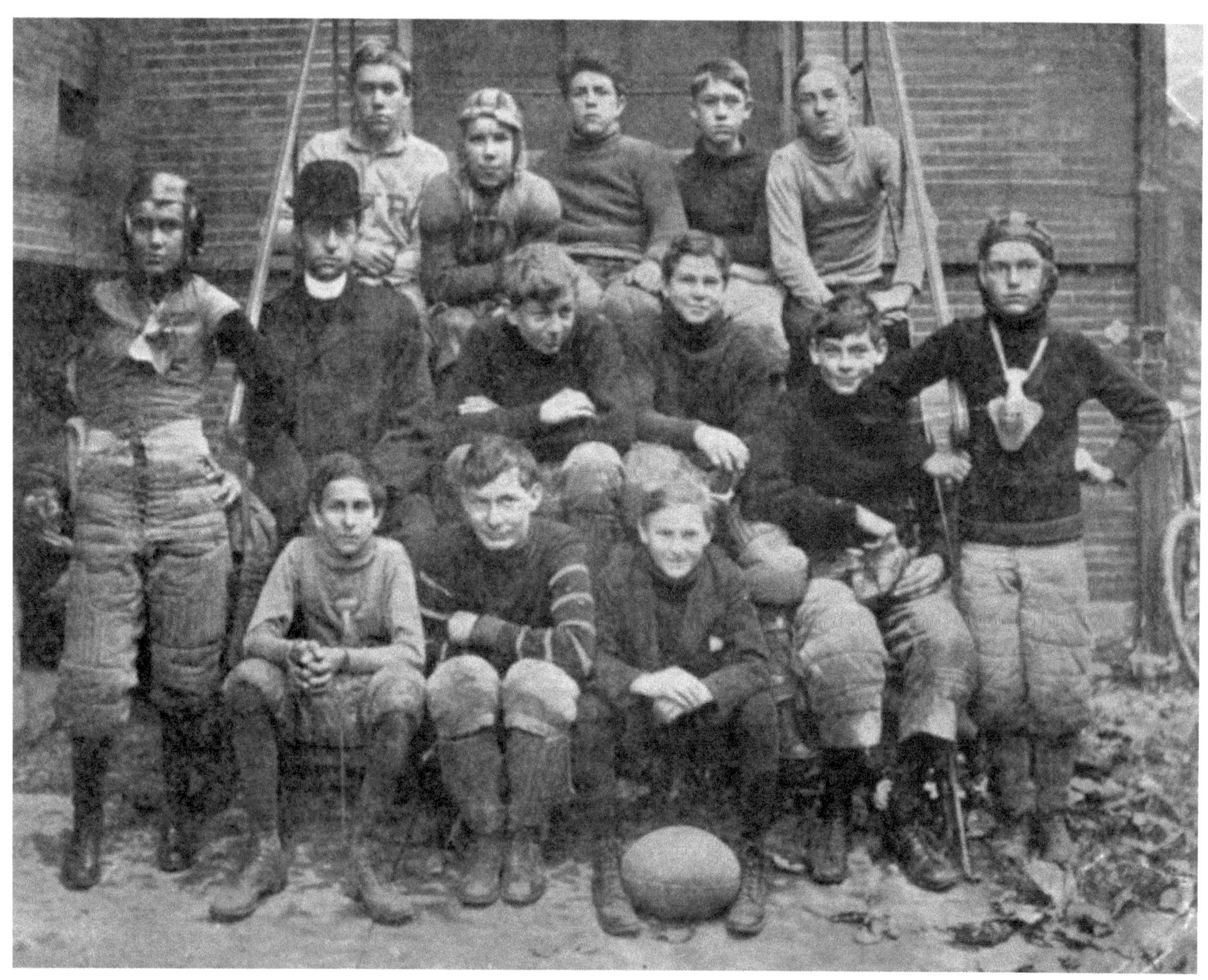

The football team poses with their coach, Wallace H. Watts of St. Paul's Episcopal Church, in this team photograph from the turn of the century.

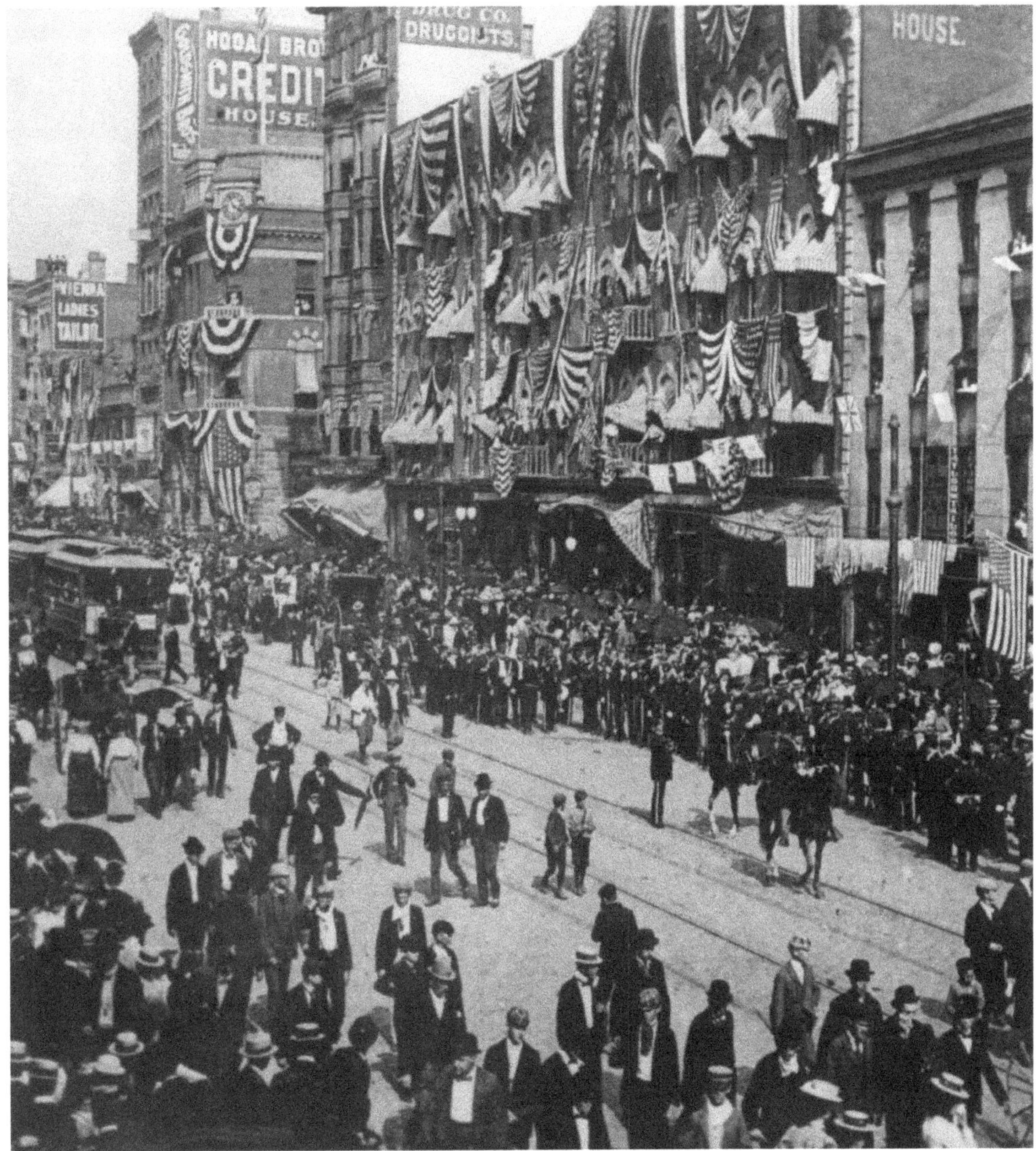

At Main Street near South Clinton Avenue, an early-twentieth-century parade breaks up at the end of the parade route. Flag bunting hangs in celebration from the buildings. Streetcars wait to resume their routine schedule.

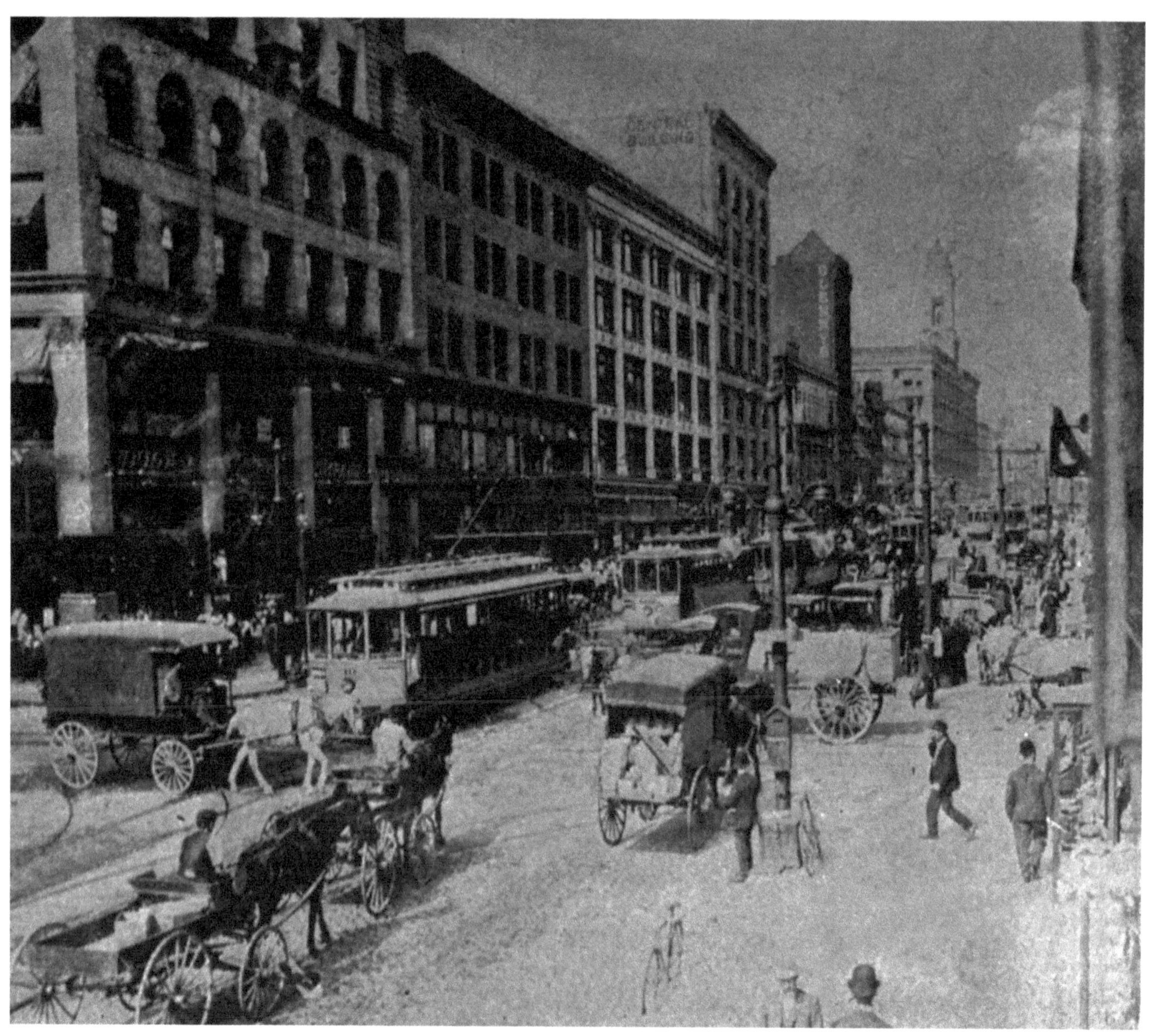

The streets are crowded with electric streetcars, delivery wagons, and pedestrians on this busy July 22, 1906. The photographer is looking east down East Main Street from St. Paul Street. The Granite Building can be seen at left and the Sibley Building at right.

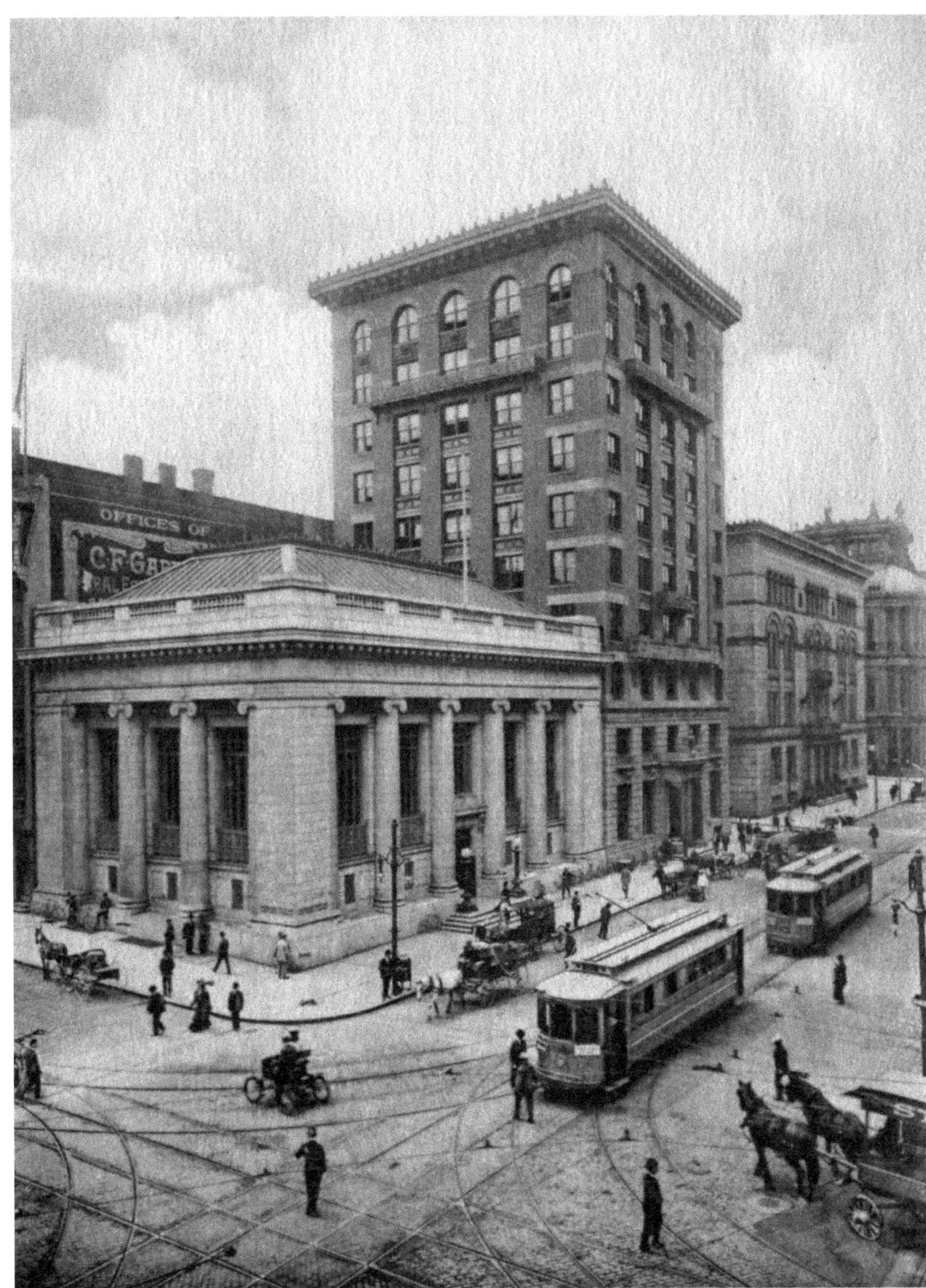

The Four Corners at State and Main streets about 1906 shows the Rochester Trust Company dominating the important cornerstone of downtown commerce. Farther down Main Street, the German Insurance Building, the Monroe County Courthouse, and Rochester Savings Bank can be seen. Surrounded by streetcar tracks, a policeman directs the traffic as two streetcars approach just inches from a pedestrian. A horseless carriage crosses the intersection, foreshadowing the future of the horse-drawn.

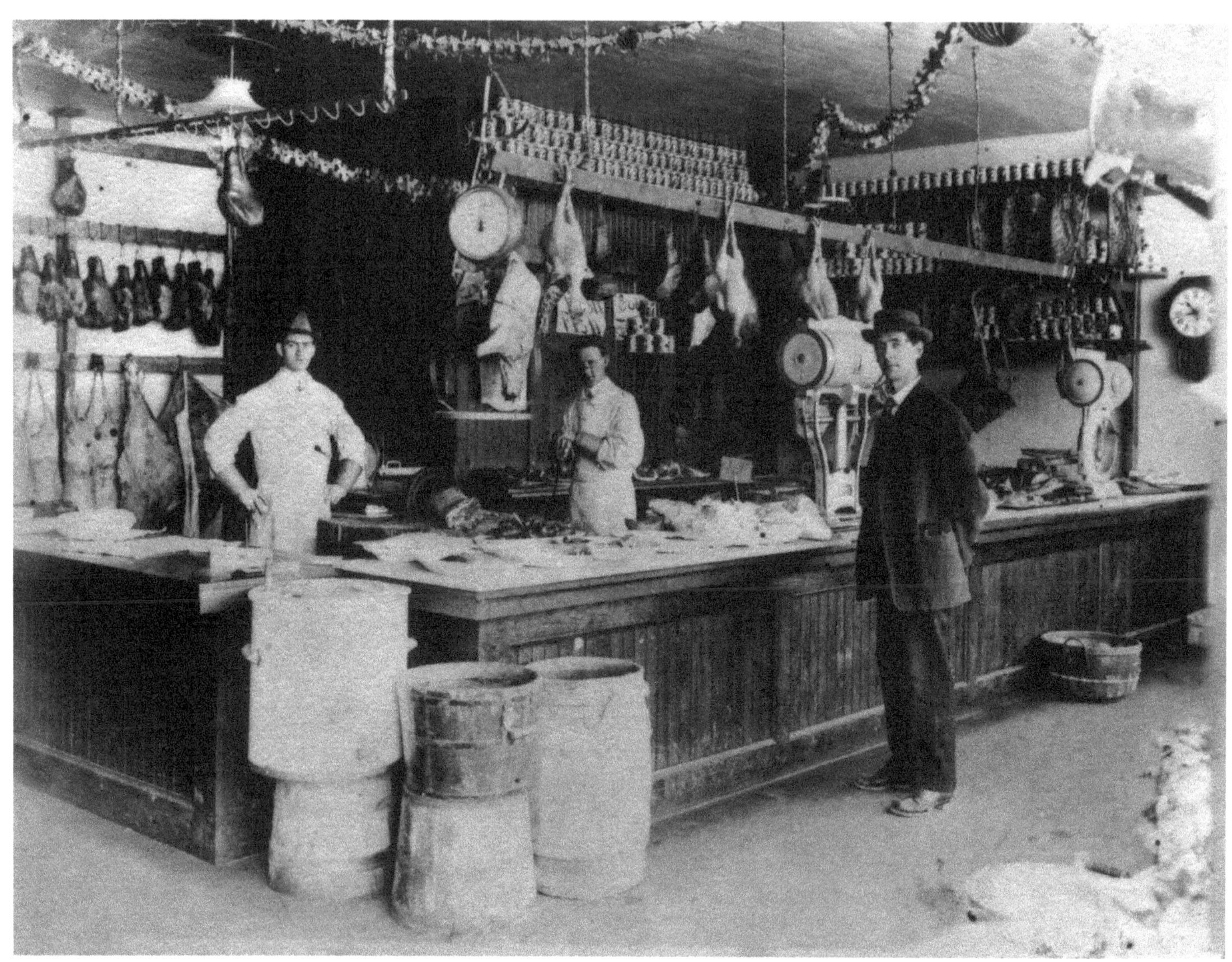

The intersection of Lake Avenue near Ridge Road became known as Wagg's Corners, a landmark to area residents, after Gilbert J. Wagg opened his department store on the east side in 1905. In 1912 he moved the store to the southwest corner. In a fairly new retail concept, the department store offered meats, groceries, dry goods, shoes, hardware, and furniture under one roof. The business operated until 1964 and the building was demolished in 1988.

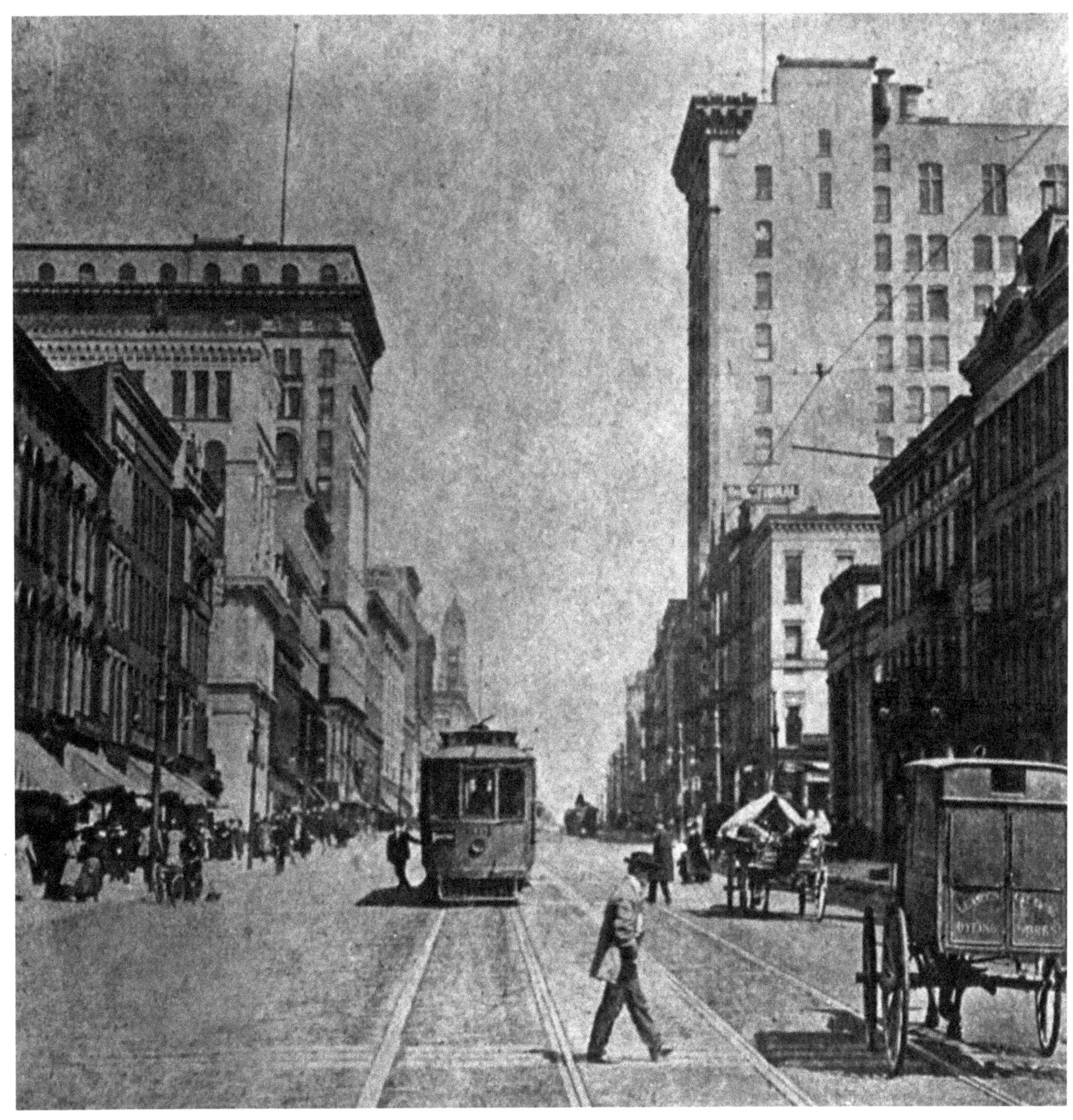

A passenger debarks the streetcar on East Main Street near the Main Street Bridge about 1907. The building at left is the Granite Building. Across the street on the right is the Chamber of Commerce Building.

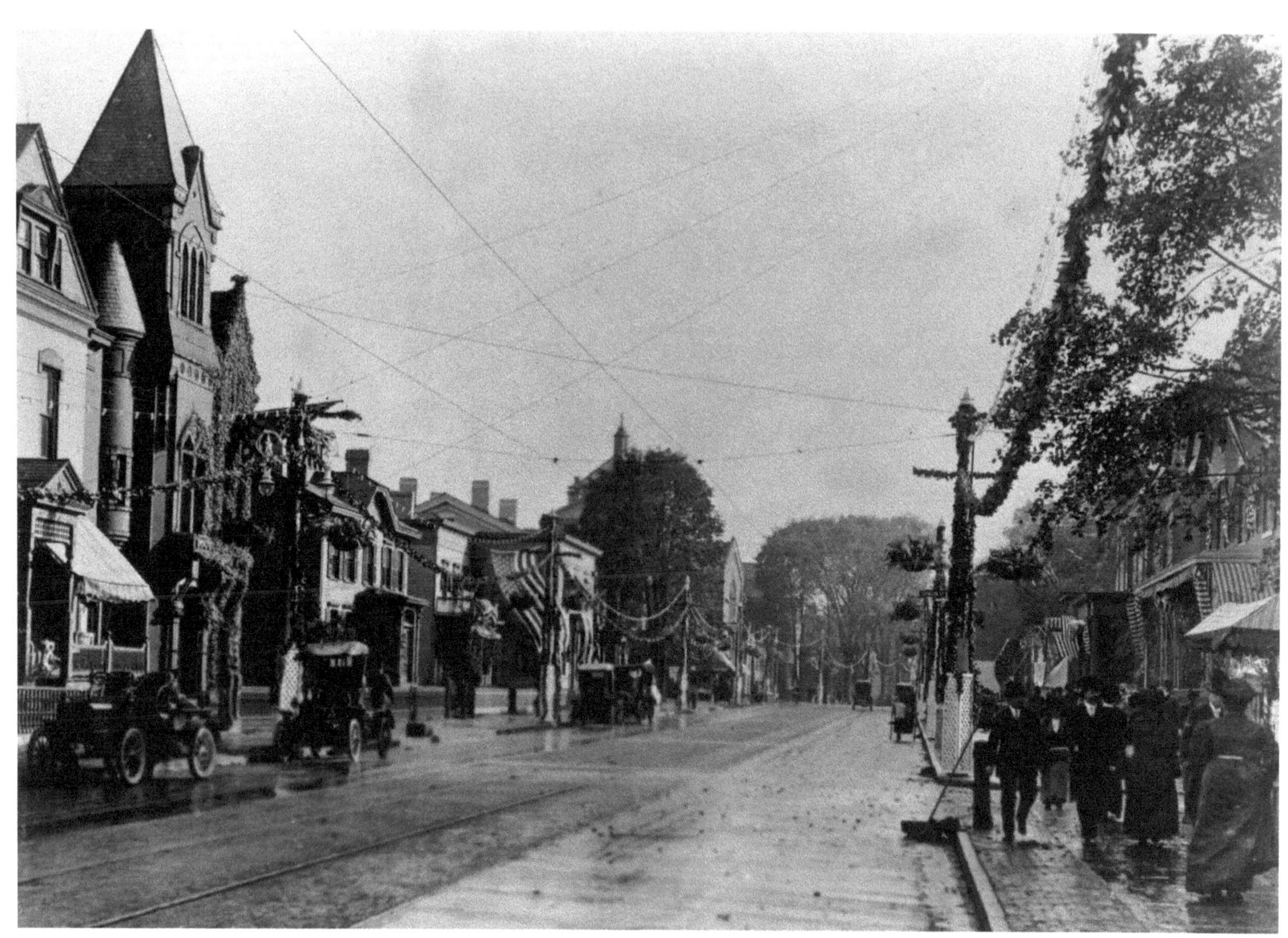

Pedestrians walk along the sidewalk on what appears to be a rainy day in 1909 on South Clinton Avenue between Main and Court streets. Several automobiles are parked across the street.

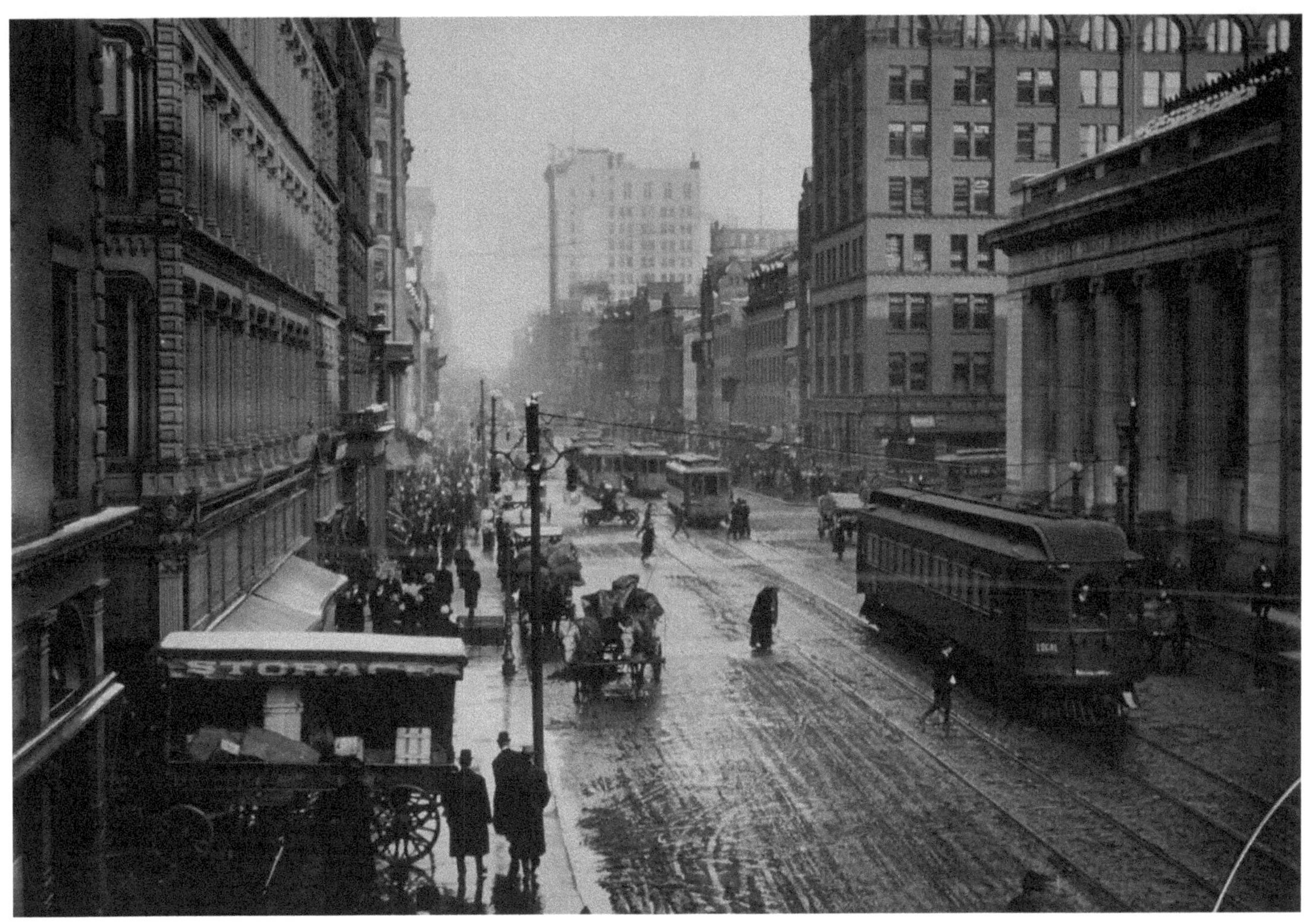

Main Street facing east from the Four Corners in 1910. The Powers Building can be seen on the left and the Rochester Trust and Safe Deposit Company on the right. The rain creates a gloomy mood in the city as the streetcars pass by. Horse-drawn wagons wait at the curb for their drivers.

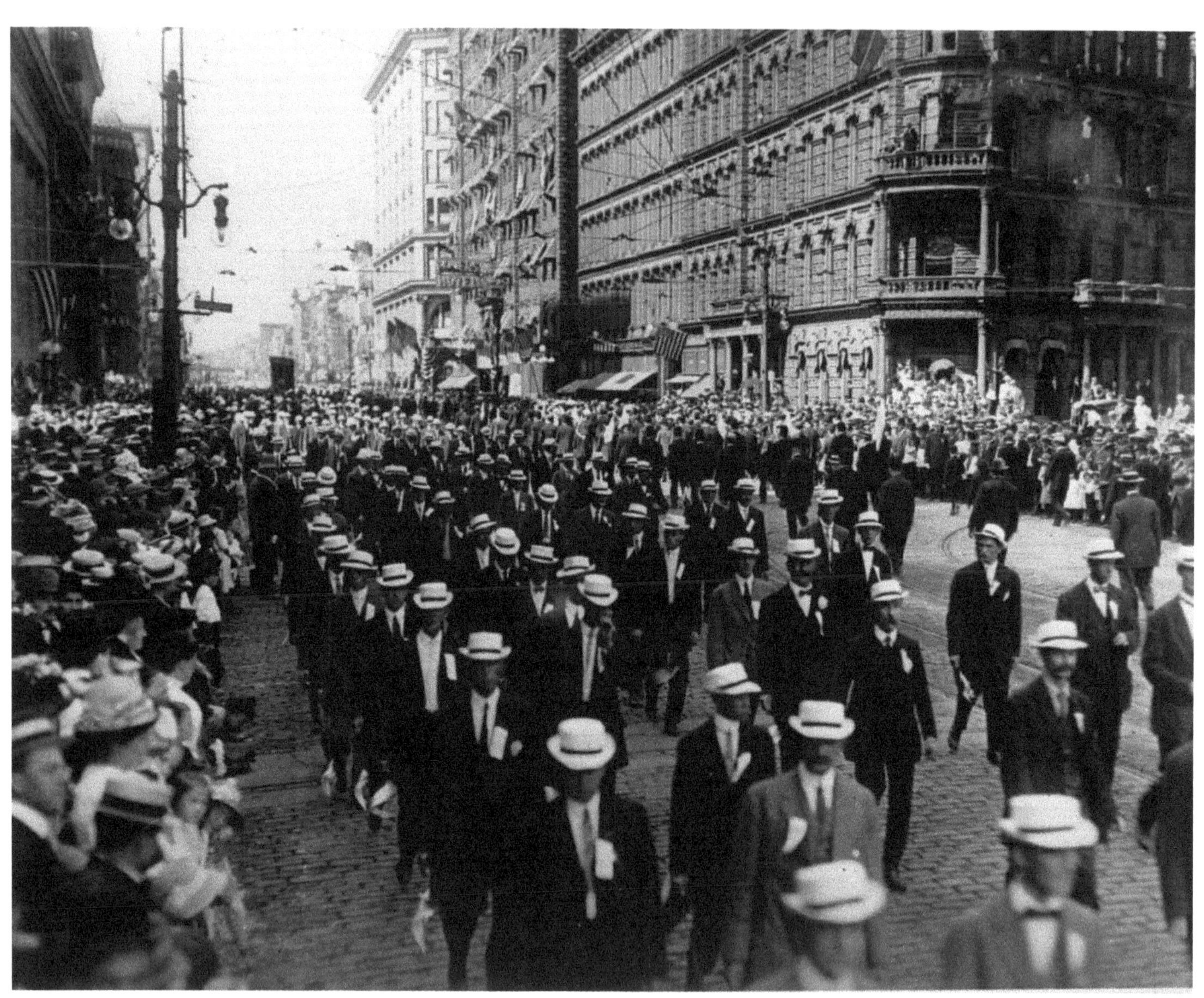

People look out the windows and from the balcony of the Powers Building as hundreds line the streets to watch the Labor Day parade in 1910. Flags fly from the buildings. Labor unions were strong and active in the Rochester area early in the century.

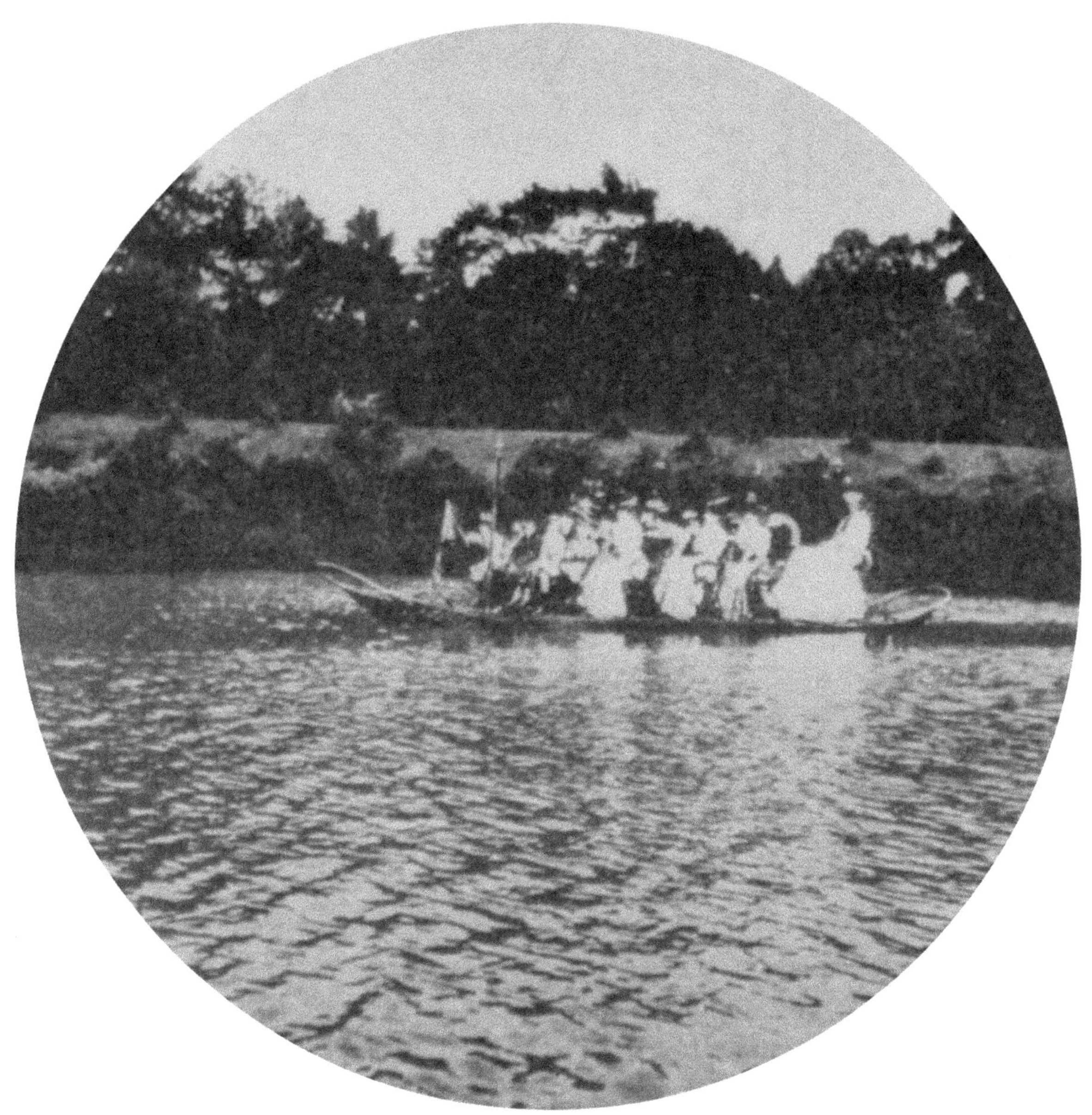

The last swan boat in a Rochester park was at Trout Lake in Seneca Park in 1922. A driver sat in a cast-iron seat in the rear of the boat and pedaled its passengers around the lake. The boats are similar to those still in use in Boston.

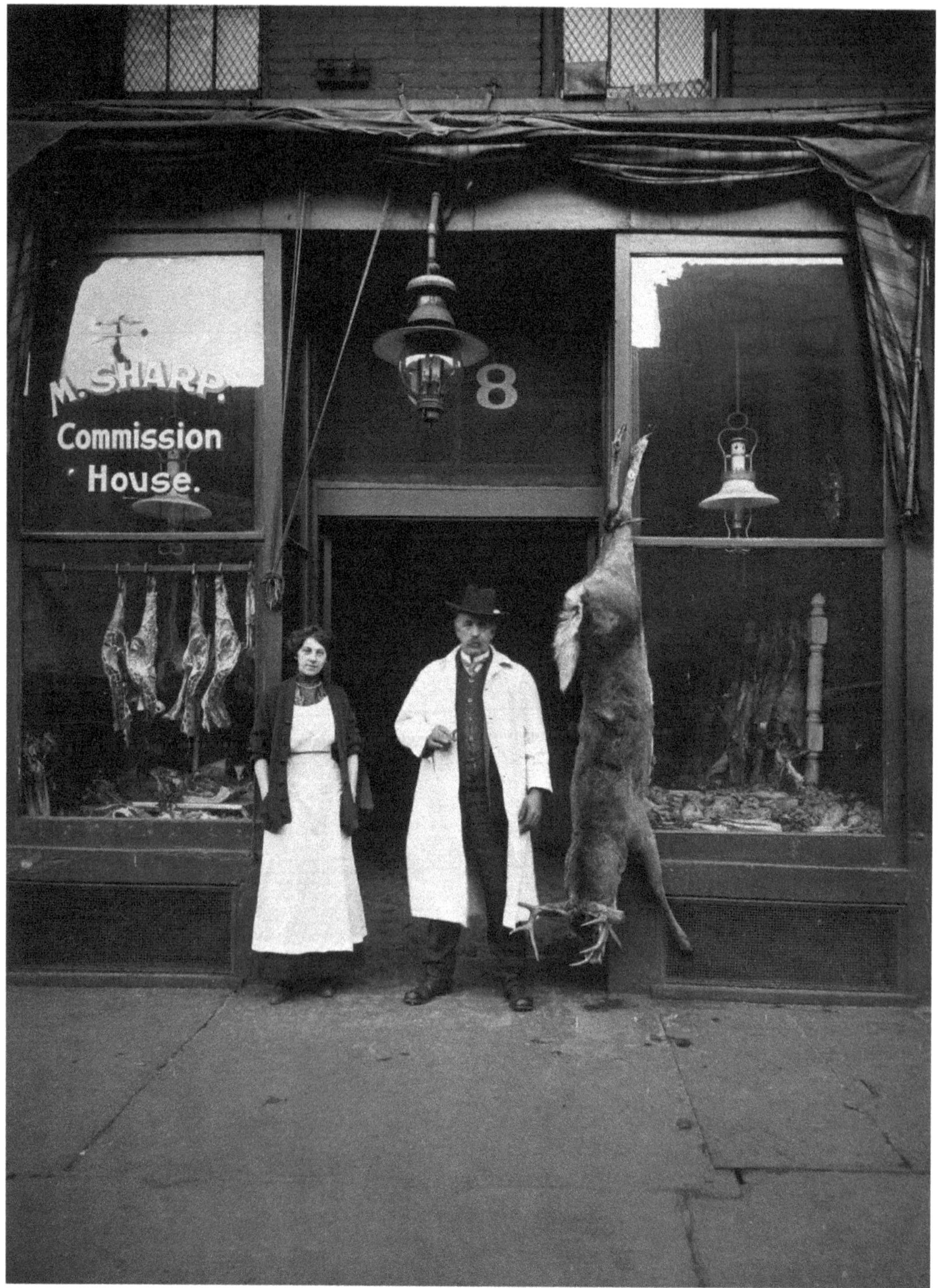

Mr. and Mrs. Moses Sharp stand in front of their commission house on Front Street about 1910. Farmers and hunters brought game and farm animals to Sharp's Commission House for processing and sale on commission. On Saturdays Sharp sold meat at retail.

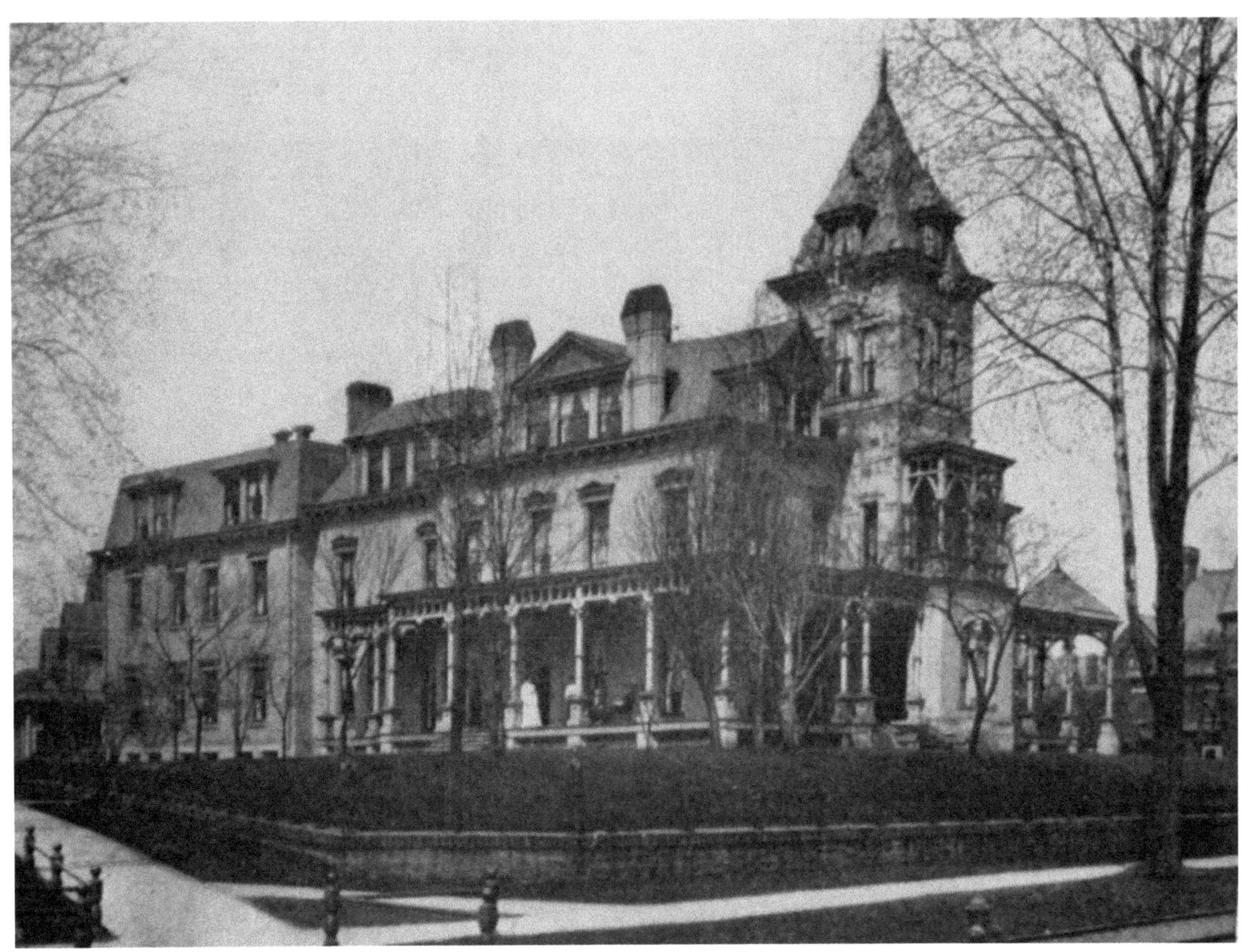

The private surgical Lee Hospital on the northwest corner of Lake and Jones avenues was opened by surgeon John Mallory Lee in 1898. Medical and obstetrical cases were accepted later and nurse's training offered. The hospital was in service until 1928.

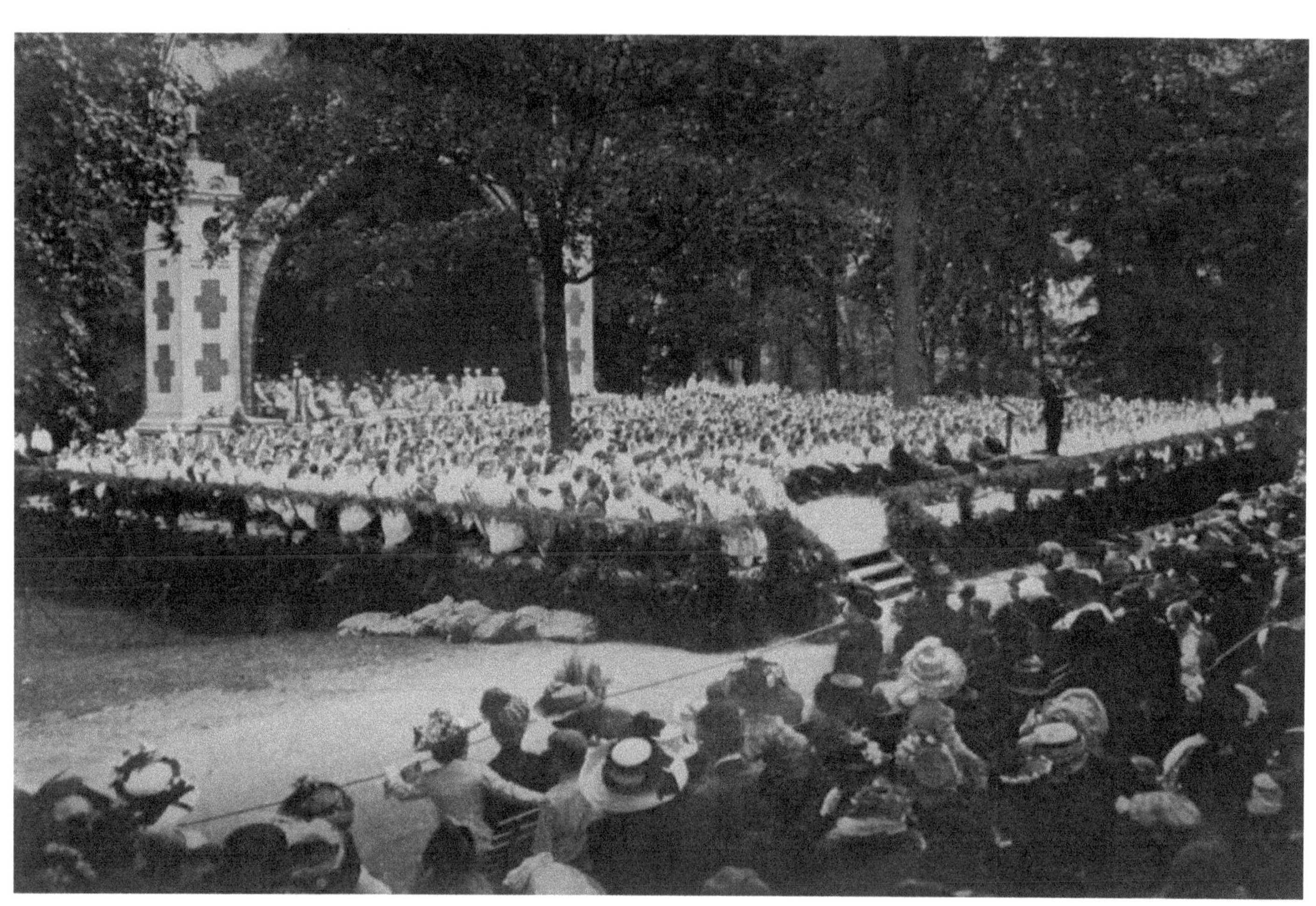

A crowd gathers in 1911 for ceremonies and performances at the dedication of the bandstand at Genesee Valley Park.

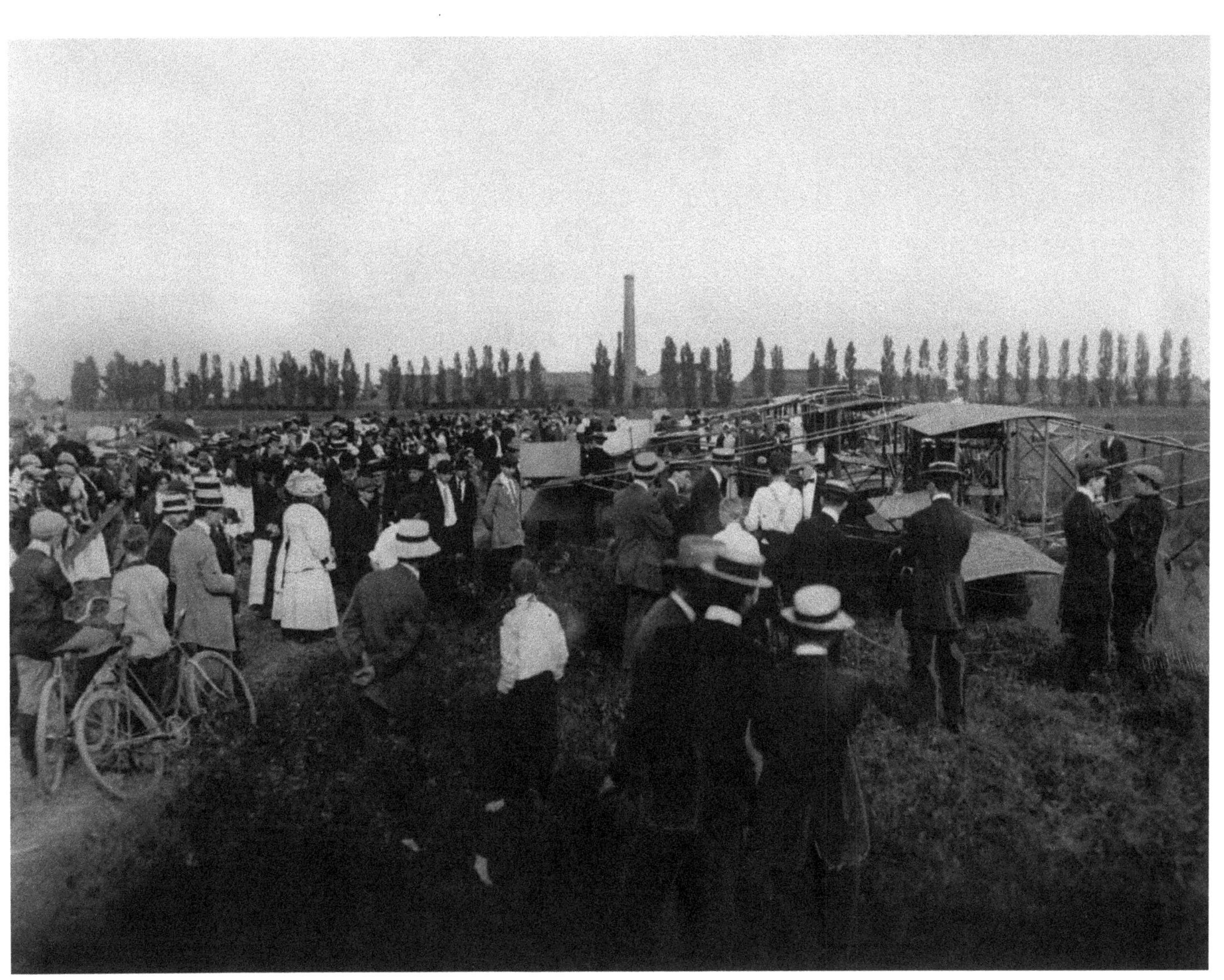

John Frisbie prepares a second test flight the year of his death. Frisbie was one of several aviation pioneers in the Rochester area. (1911)

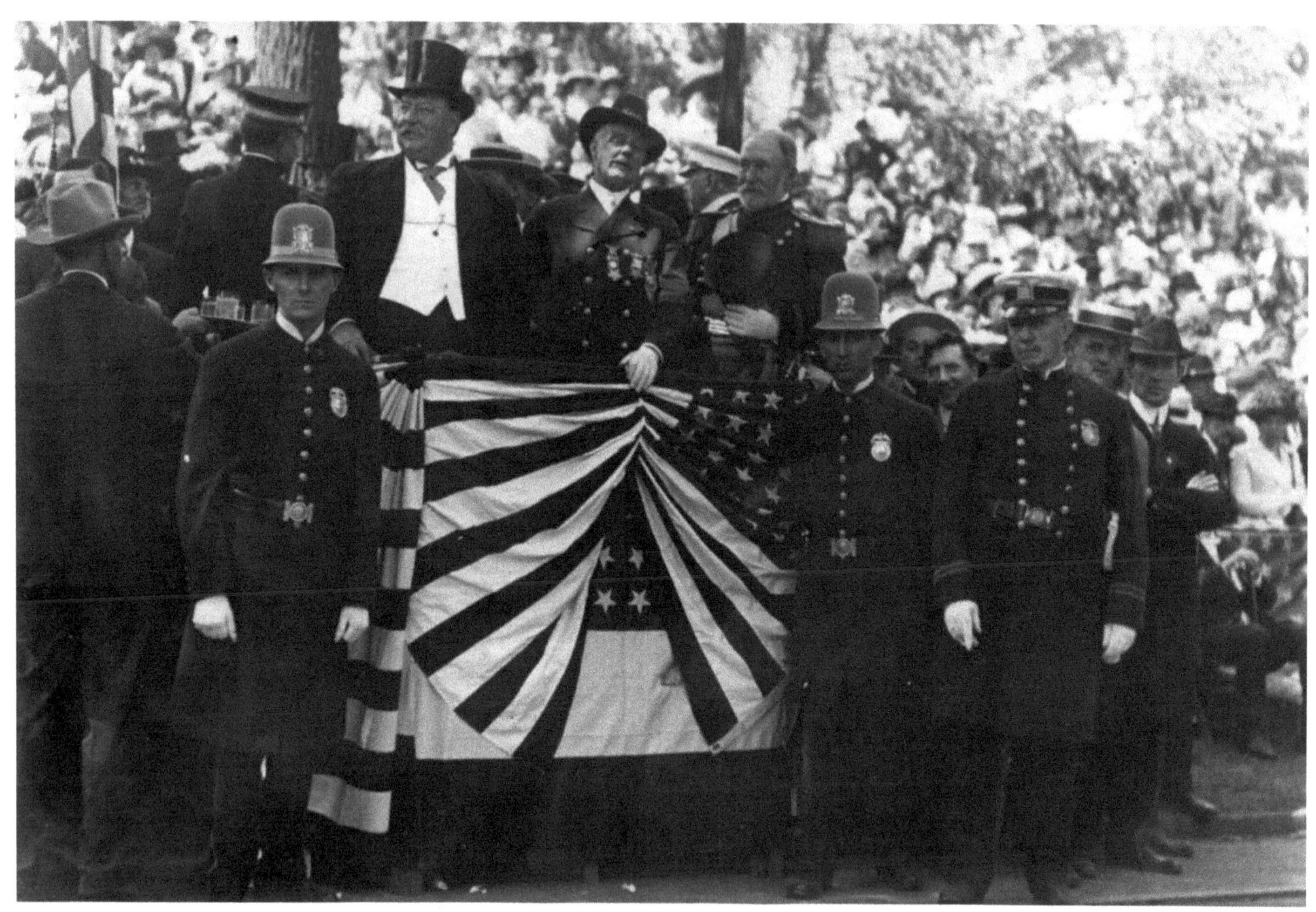

Wearing a top hat, president William Howard Taft looks down from the review stand on the Grand Army of the Republic parade on the south side of the Soldiers and Sailors Monument at Washington Square Park. Hundreds crowded the park and viewed the parade in August 1911.

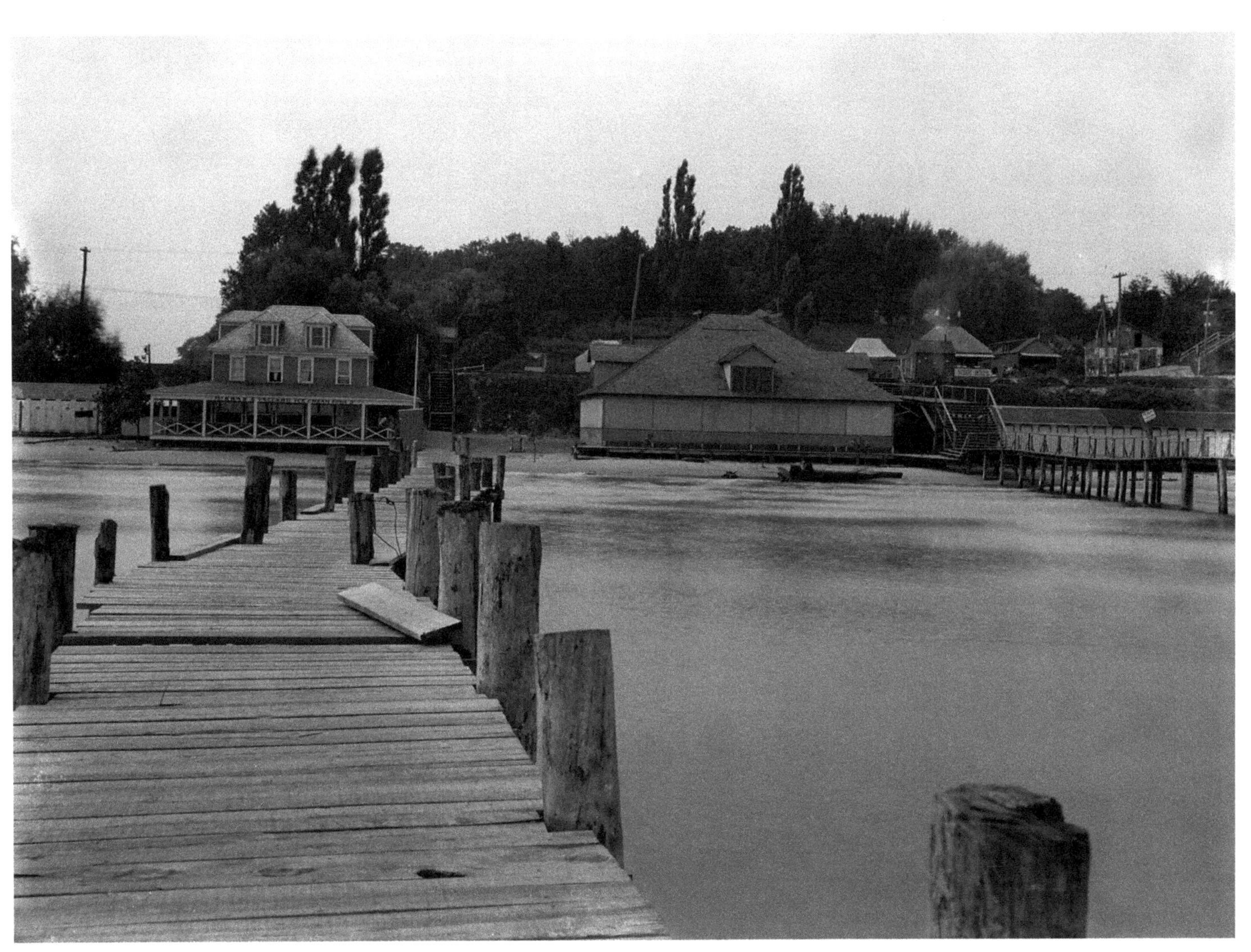

Looking south from the Steamboat Pier at the Pier Hotel (left) in Sea Breeze.

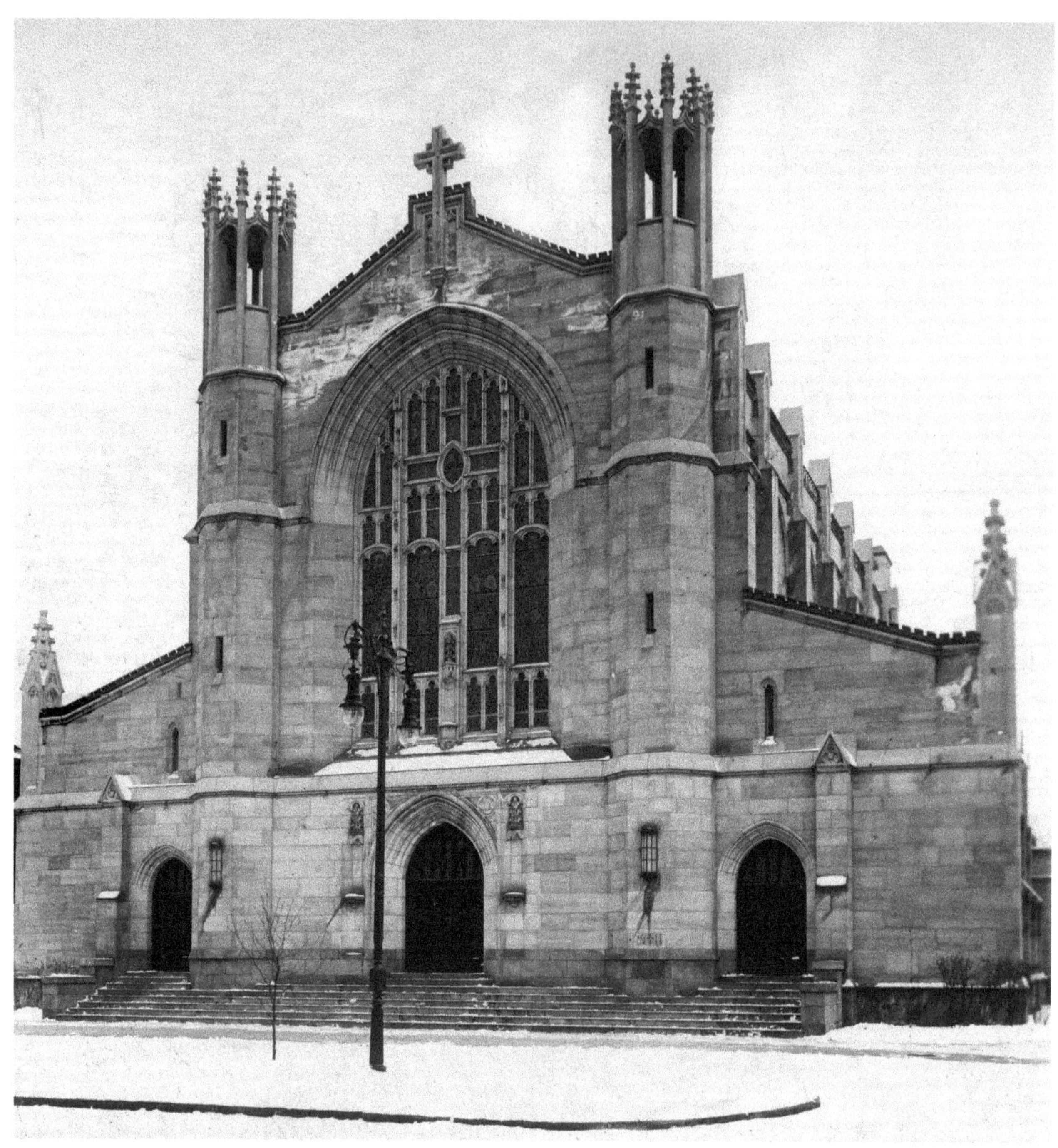

The Church of the Blessed Sacrament, designed by Gordon and Madden, was dedicated in 1912 on Oxford Street near Monroe Avenue. The church replaced an earlier church on the same site.

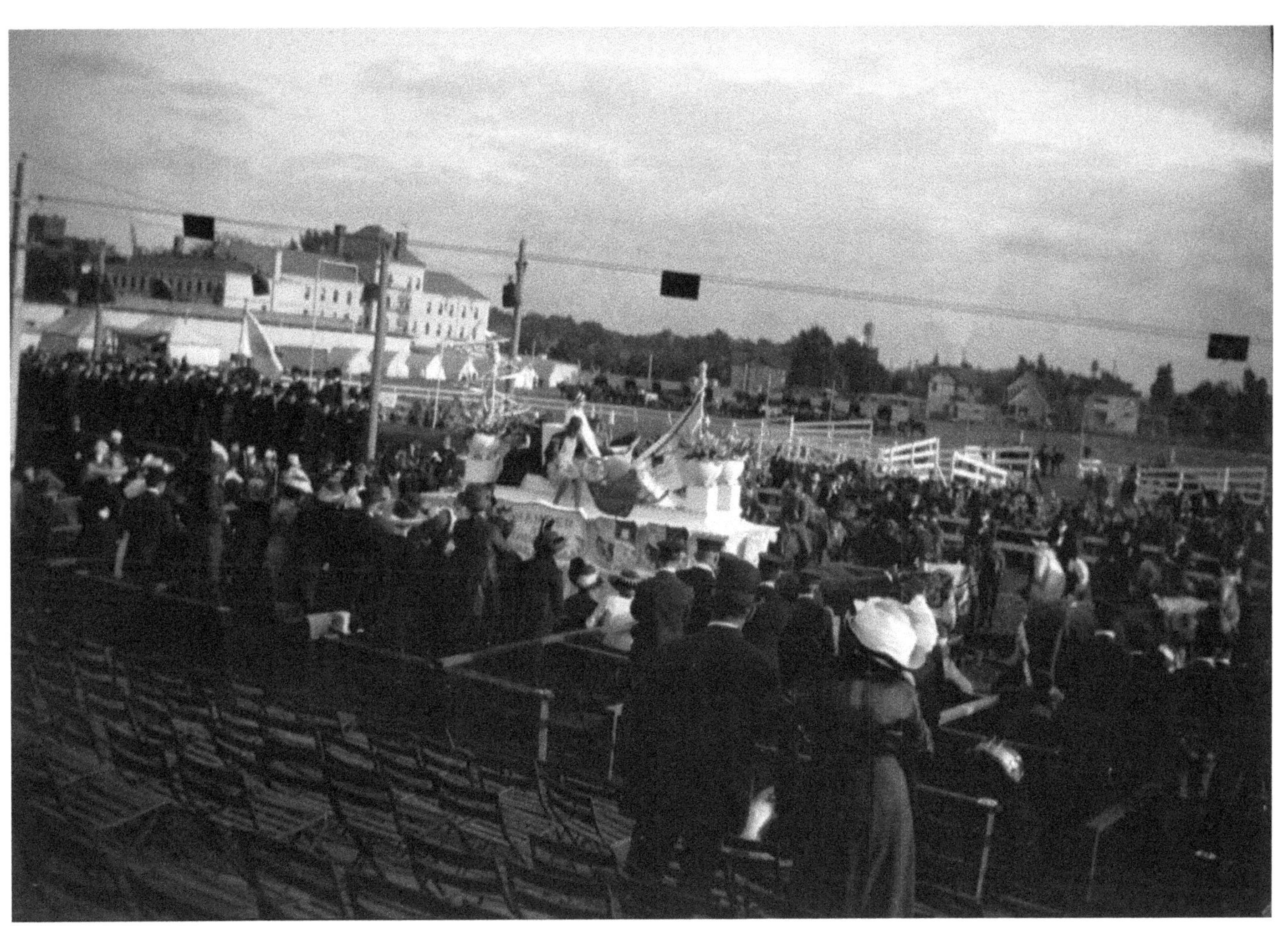

In 1912 a crowd watches as a float passes Exposition Park (later Edgerton Park) during the centennial celebration of the settlement of the One Hundred Acre Tract, the nucleus of today's Rochester.

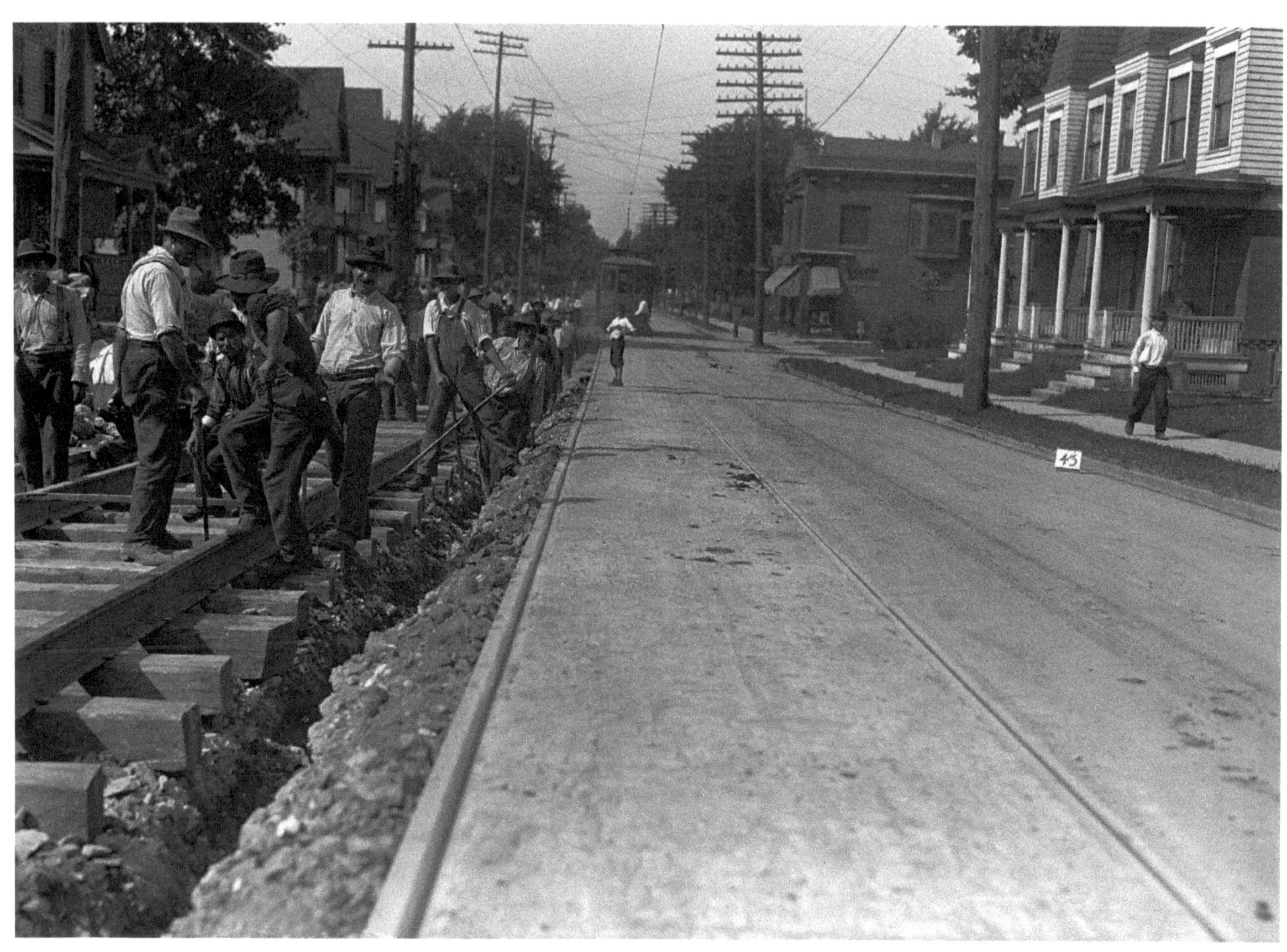

Laborers work to lay streetcar tracks along Dewey Avenue from Ravine Avenue. In the distance a streetcar crosses near Glendale Park. (August 1913)

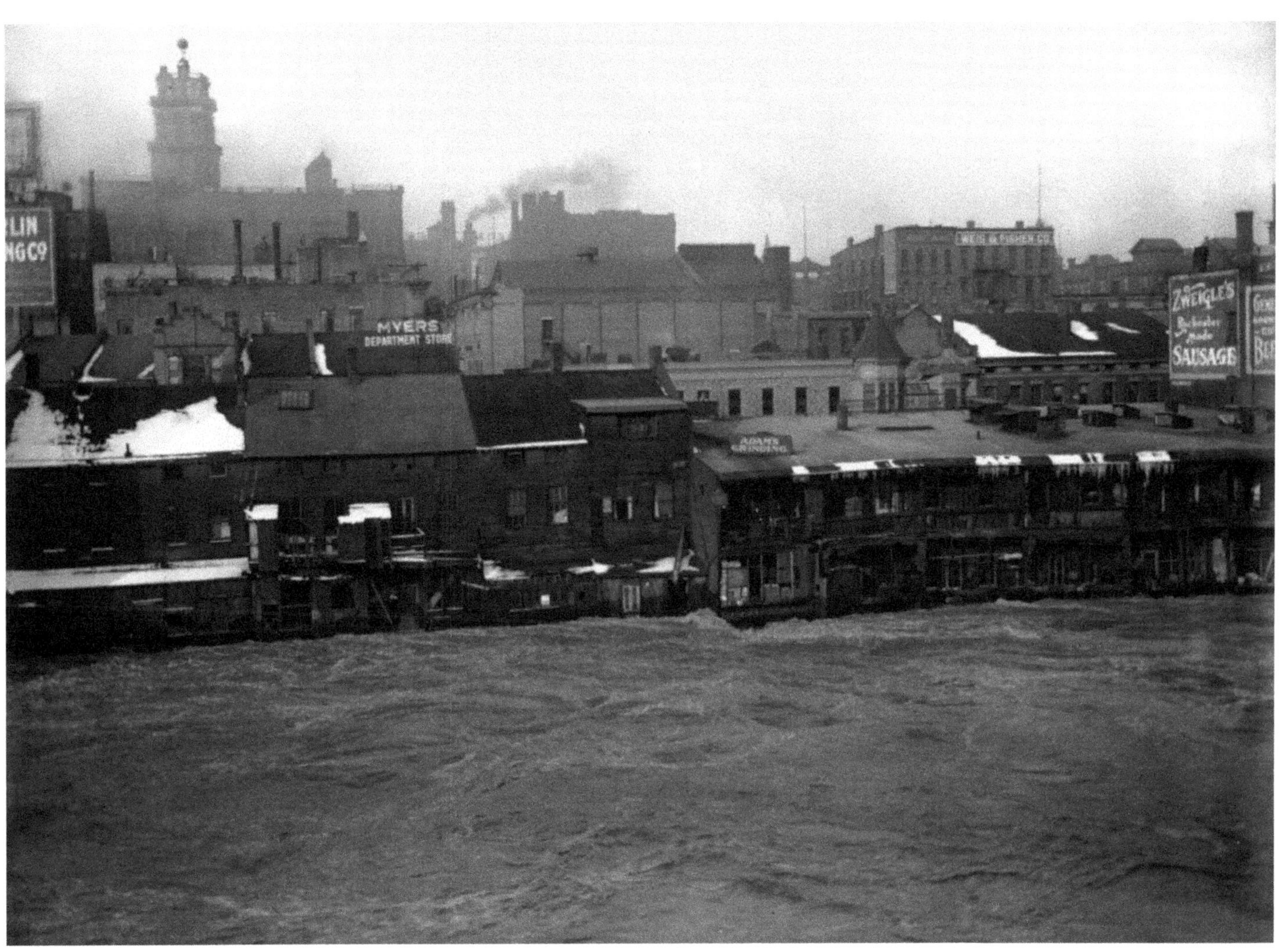

Probably during the flood of March 28, 1913, this photograph shows the backside of Front Street businesses enduring the dangerous river waters threatening the foundations of buildings. Myer's Department Store, Charles Adam (a grinder), Zweigle's (a sausage maker and saloon), and the Weis and Fisher Company are visible from 27 to 52 Front Street.

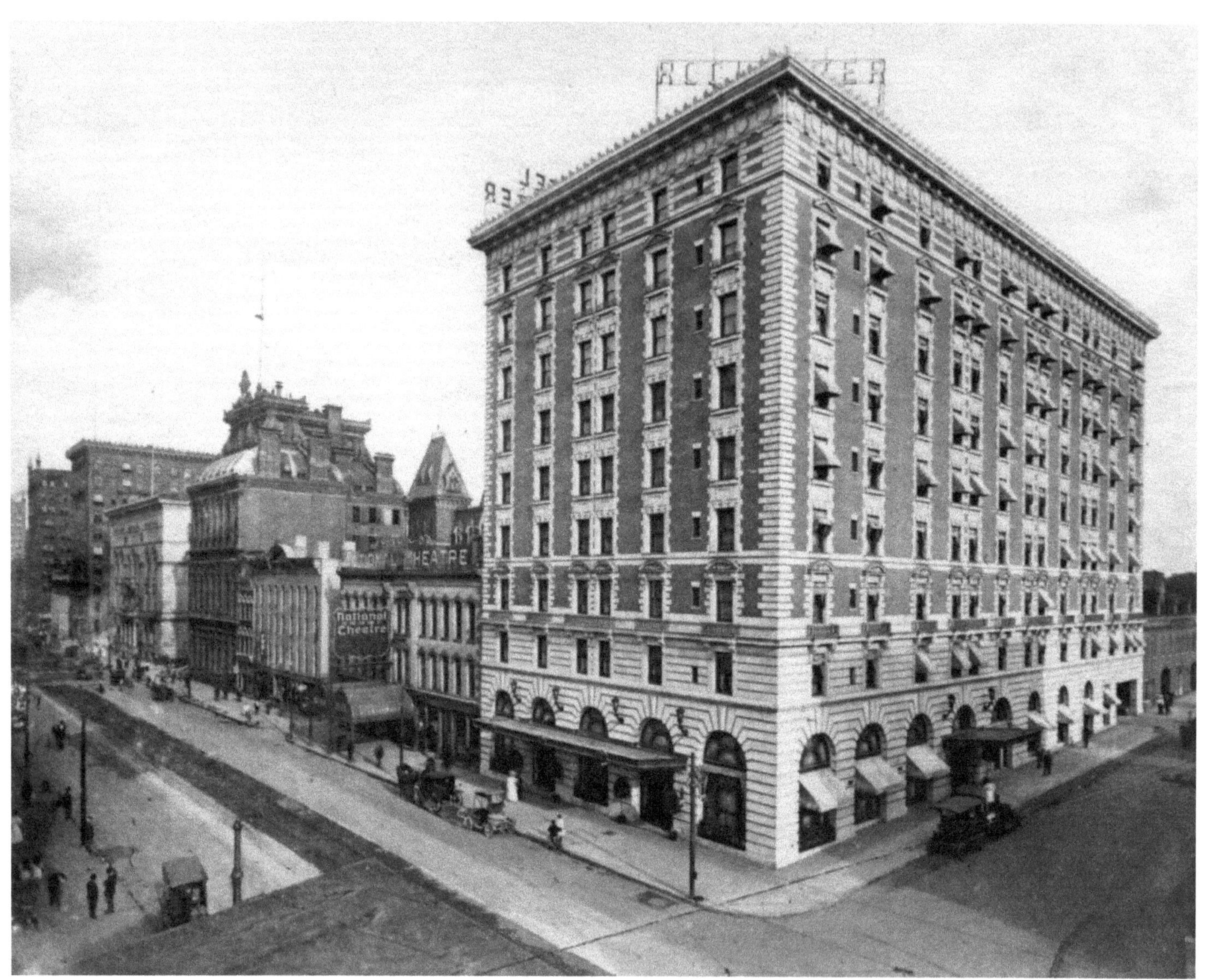

The 300-room fireproof Hotel Rochester was built by Walter B. Duffy on the southeast corner of West Main Street and Plymouth Avenue in 1908. Designed by architects Charles F. Crandall and John F. Strobel, the eight-story building was a hotel until 1957, when it became dormitories for students at Rochester Institute of Technology (RIT). The ten-foot-wide main entrance on West Main Street was bordered by an ornamental cast-iron marquee. The women's entrance was on Plymouth Avenue. The hotel offered a ladies reception room and parlor, billiards room, and a men's cafe.

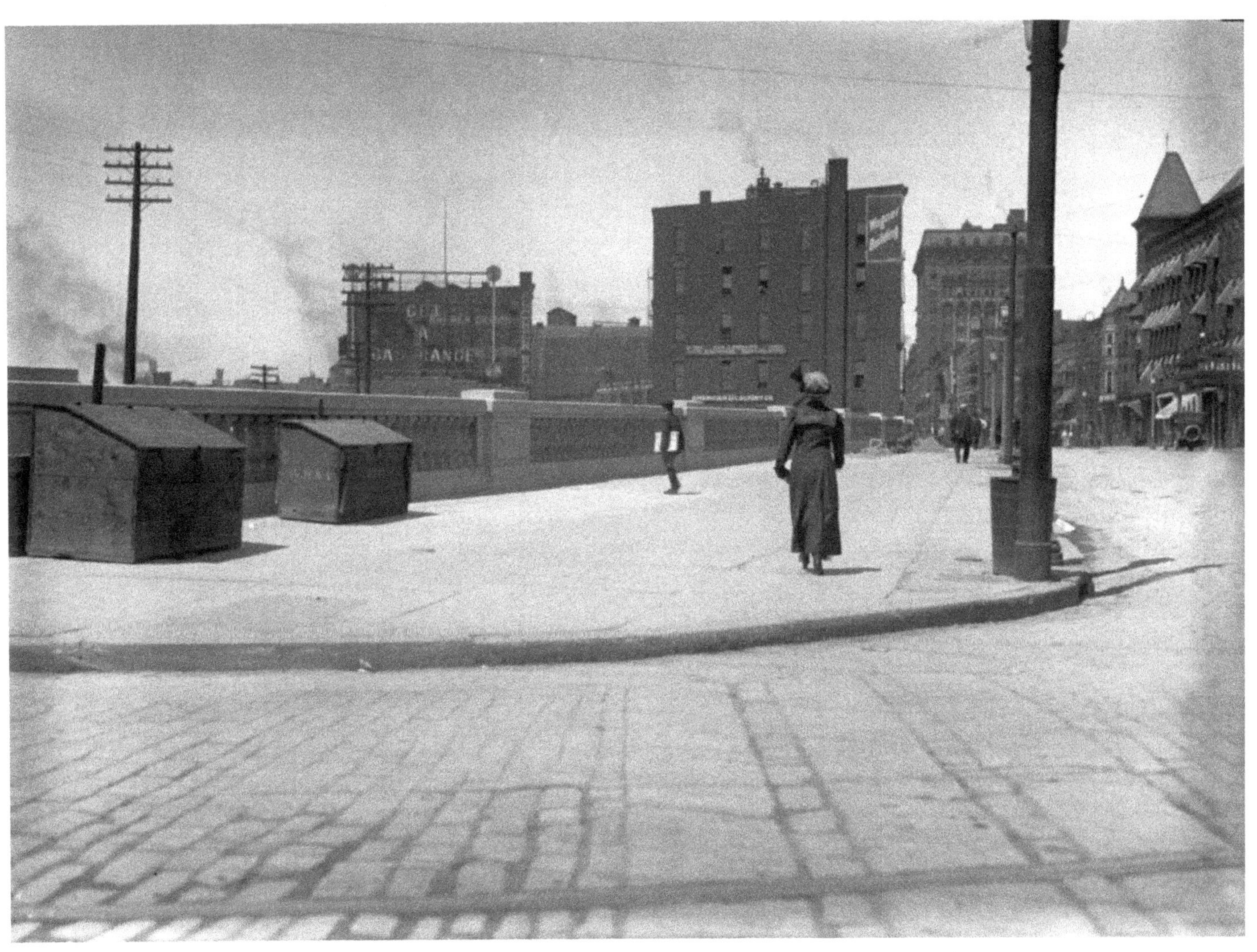

Looking north along South Avenue from Court Street at what became the site of the Rochester Public Library in the Rundel Memorial Building. The Wagner Building at 77 South Avenue is visible in the distance at center. The Rochester Gas and Electric Company sign reads "Get a Gas Range." The Genesee River and Erie Canal are to the left, the new Osburn Hotel to the right.

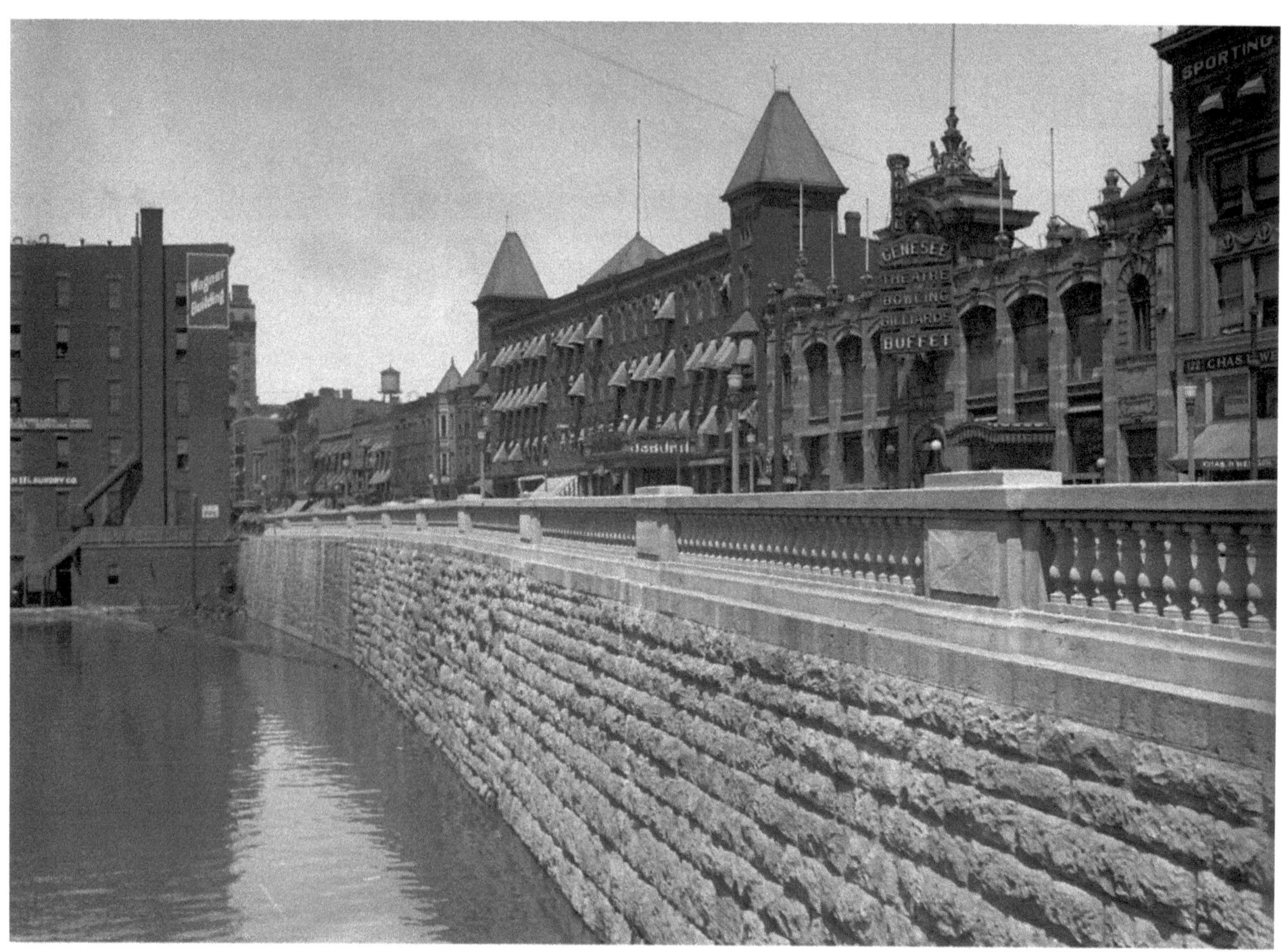

The stone wall of the Erie Canal below South Avenue. When the canal was emptied at the end of the season in 1919, subway tracks were run through its bed. In 1936 the Rundel Memorial Building housing the Rochester Public Library was built over it, supported by steel beams and accessible from South Avenue. The Osburn Hotel, on the site of today's library addition, is more visible in this view. (ca. 1914)

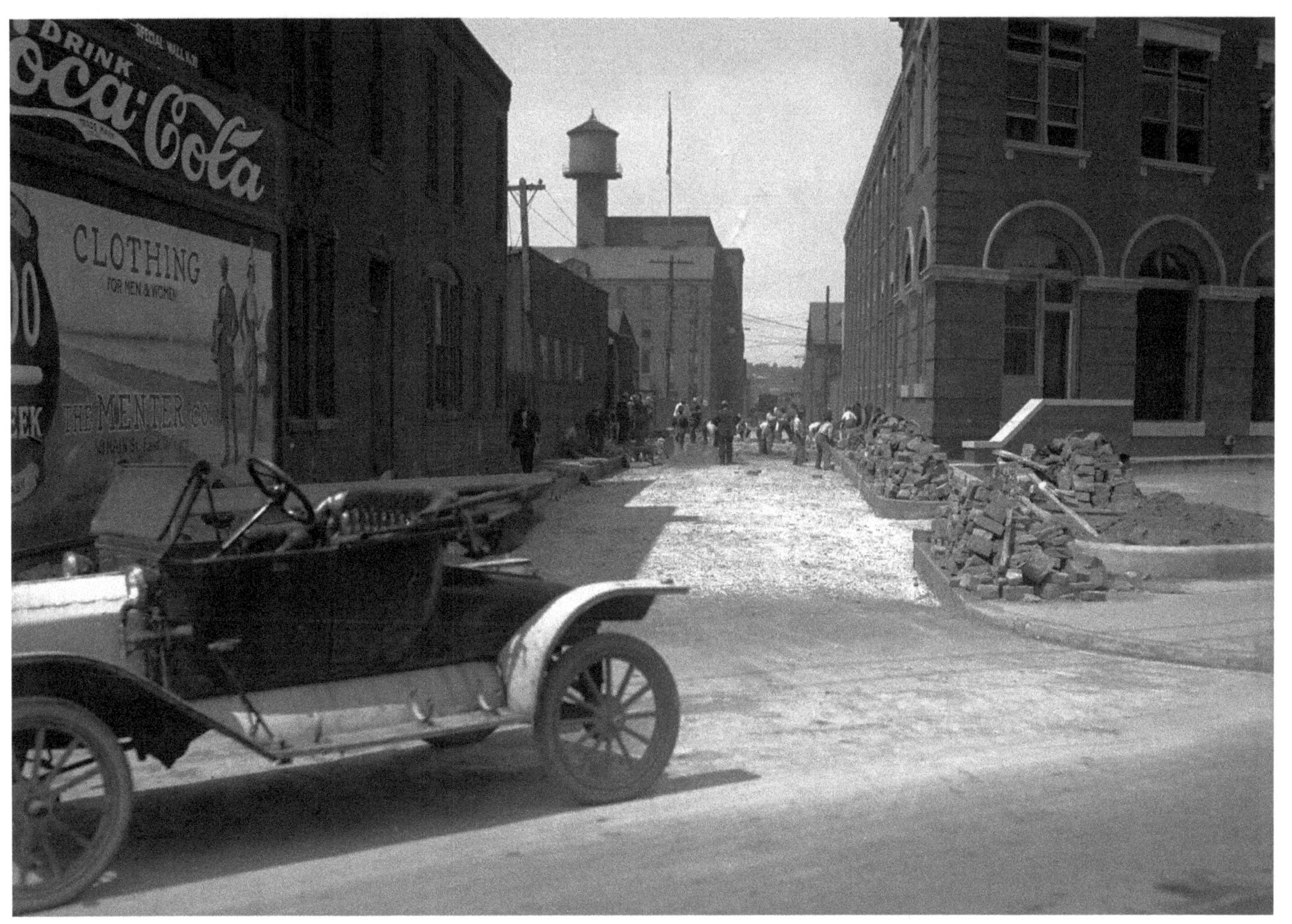

Street-paving bricks lie in piles for laborers working on Curtice Street near St. Paul Street. A city engineer car parked at the intersection may indicate a job inspection or supervision. The Bartholomay Brewing Company building is on the right. (June 1914)

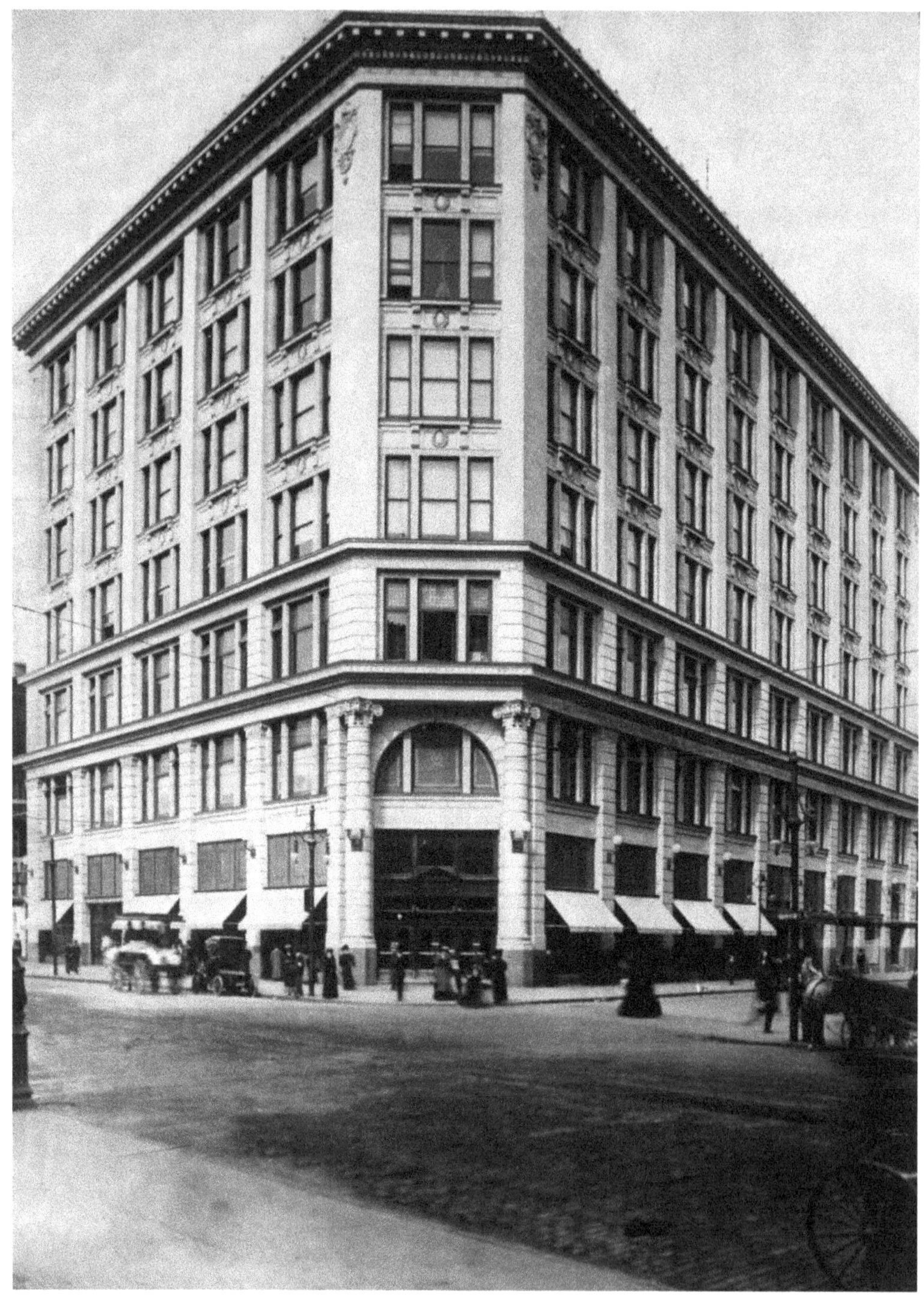

The Duffy-Powers Building at West Main and Fitzhugh streets was the largest retail dry goods store between New York City and Chicago. Founded in 1907 as Duffy-McInnerney Company it became Duffy-Powers in 1911. The store went bankrupt during the Depression in 1932. The city took over the vacant building and opened the Civic Exhibits Building in 1940. Three years later the Navy manufactured war materiel here. In 1961 Rochester Institute of Technology took up residence. (ca. 1910–1915)

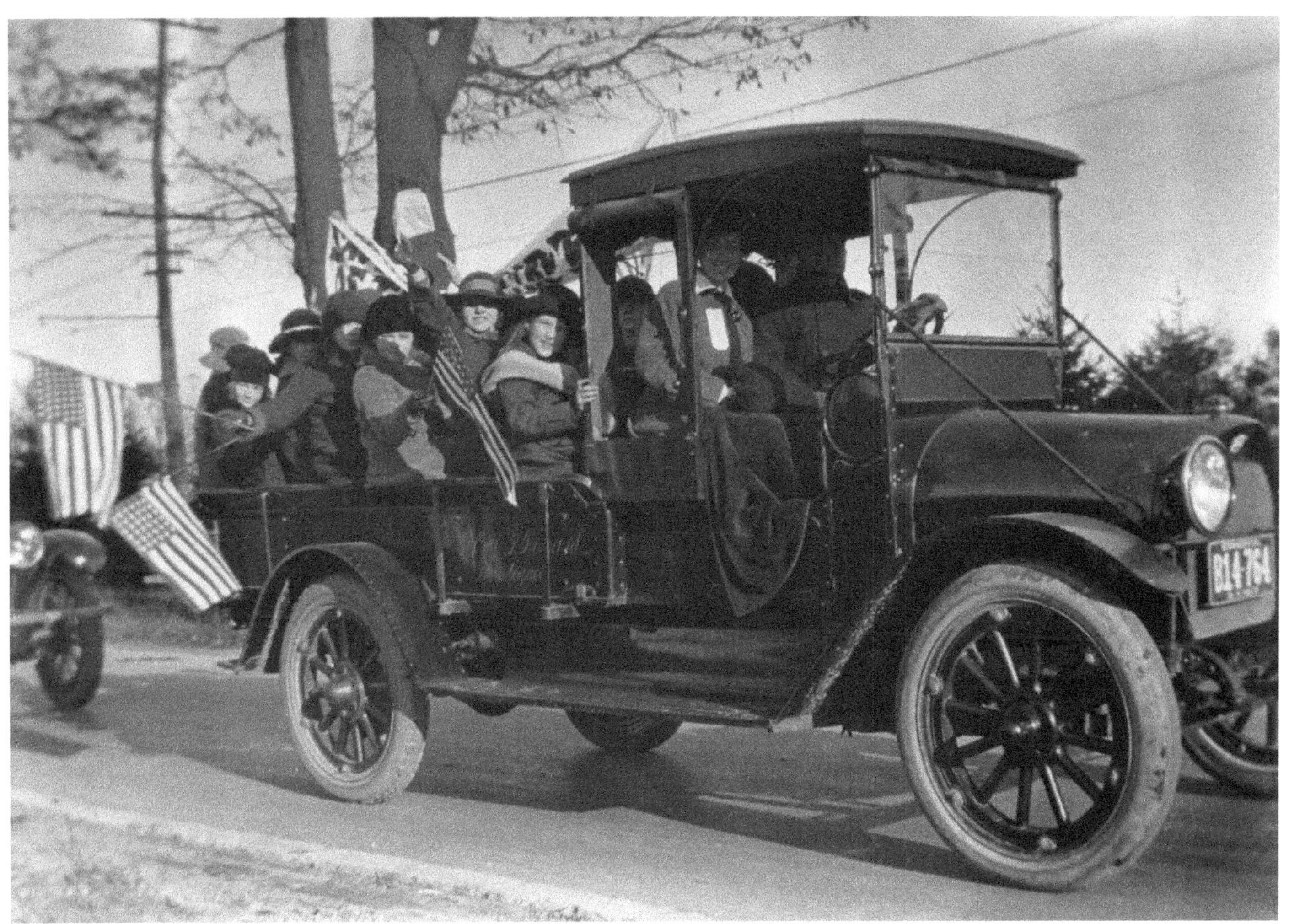

Principal Maude West led students from the Irondequoit Union Free School in support of Prohibition in November 1915. They participated in a flag-waving Prohibition parade. Here they are seen in a truck crossing Titus Avenue in Irondequoit. Maude West is seated next to the driver. She became Irondequoit's first town historian in 1922 when the New York State Education Law first required every town and village to appoint a historian.

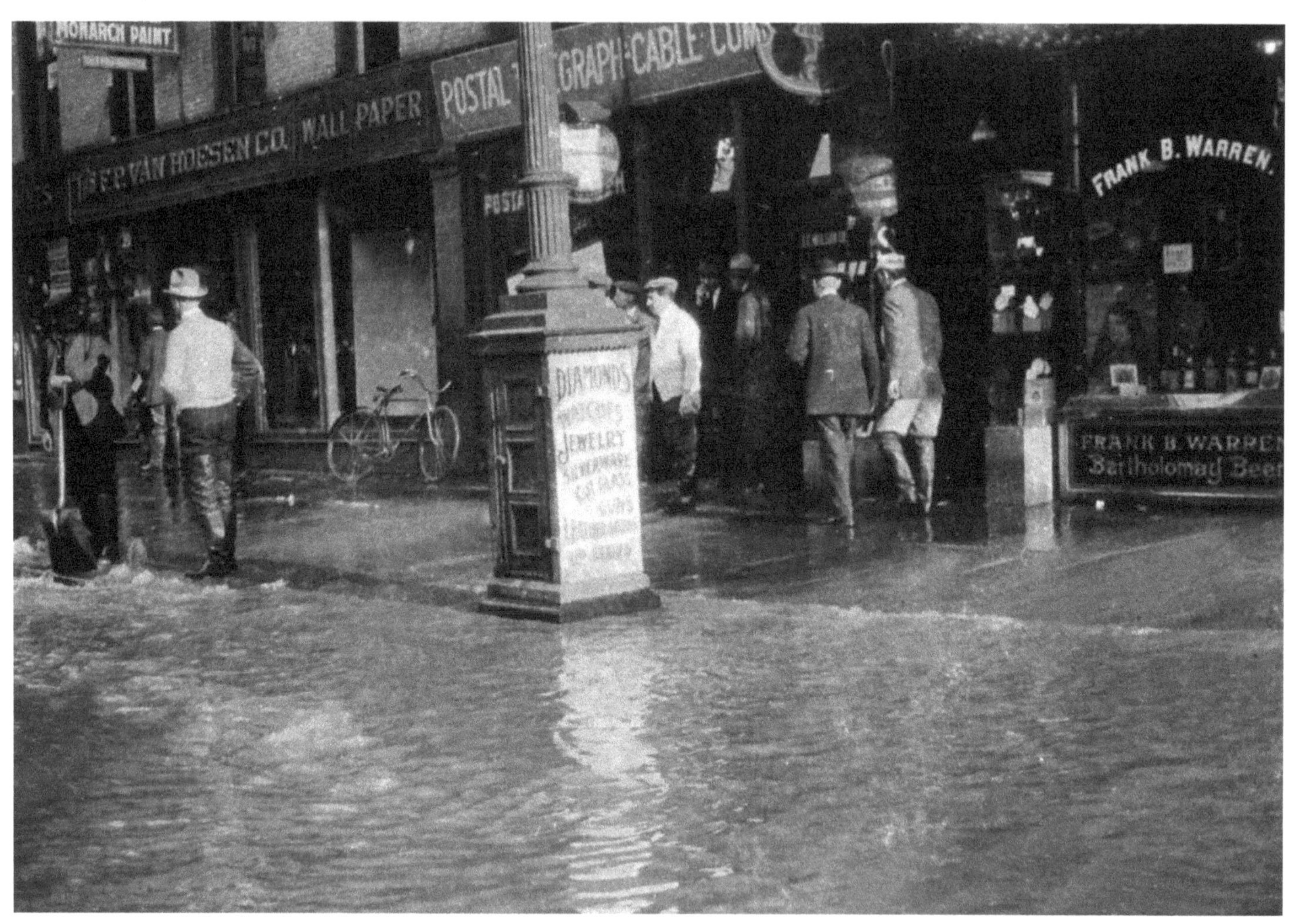

Most likely sewers and retaining walls built in response to earlier floods prevented the flood of March-April 1916 from becoming more damaging. Spring snowmelts brought unusually high water levels to the city as seen here on Exchange Street downtown. Though a current can be seen in the floodwaters, business continues.

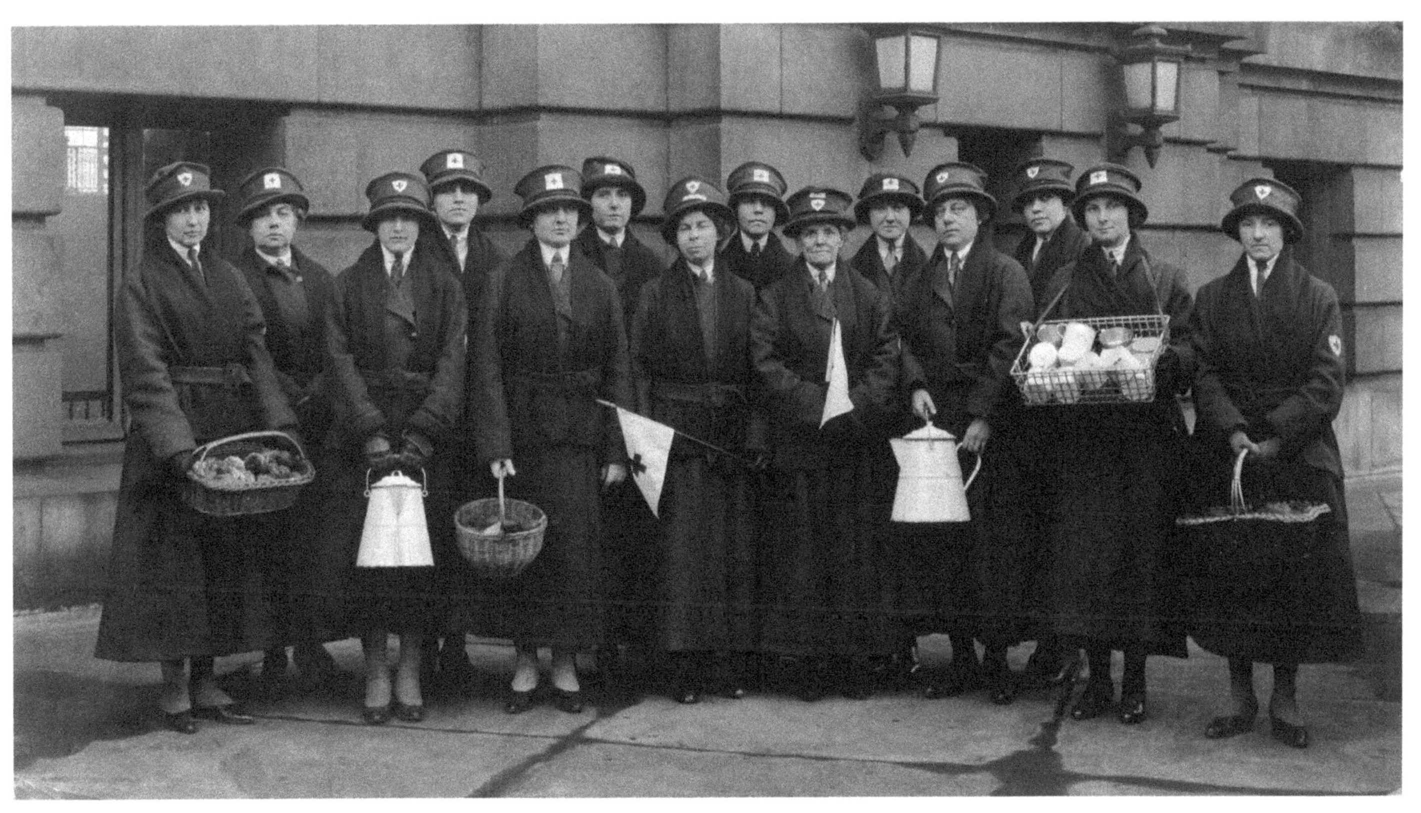

Organized in 1903, the Rochester Chapter of the American Red Cross established a canteen at the New York Central Railroad Station during World War I to offer refreshments and friendship to soldiers passing through Rochester. This group photograph of Red Cross canteen workers was taken sometime during World War I.

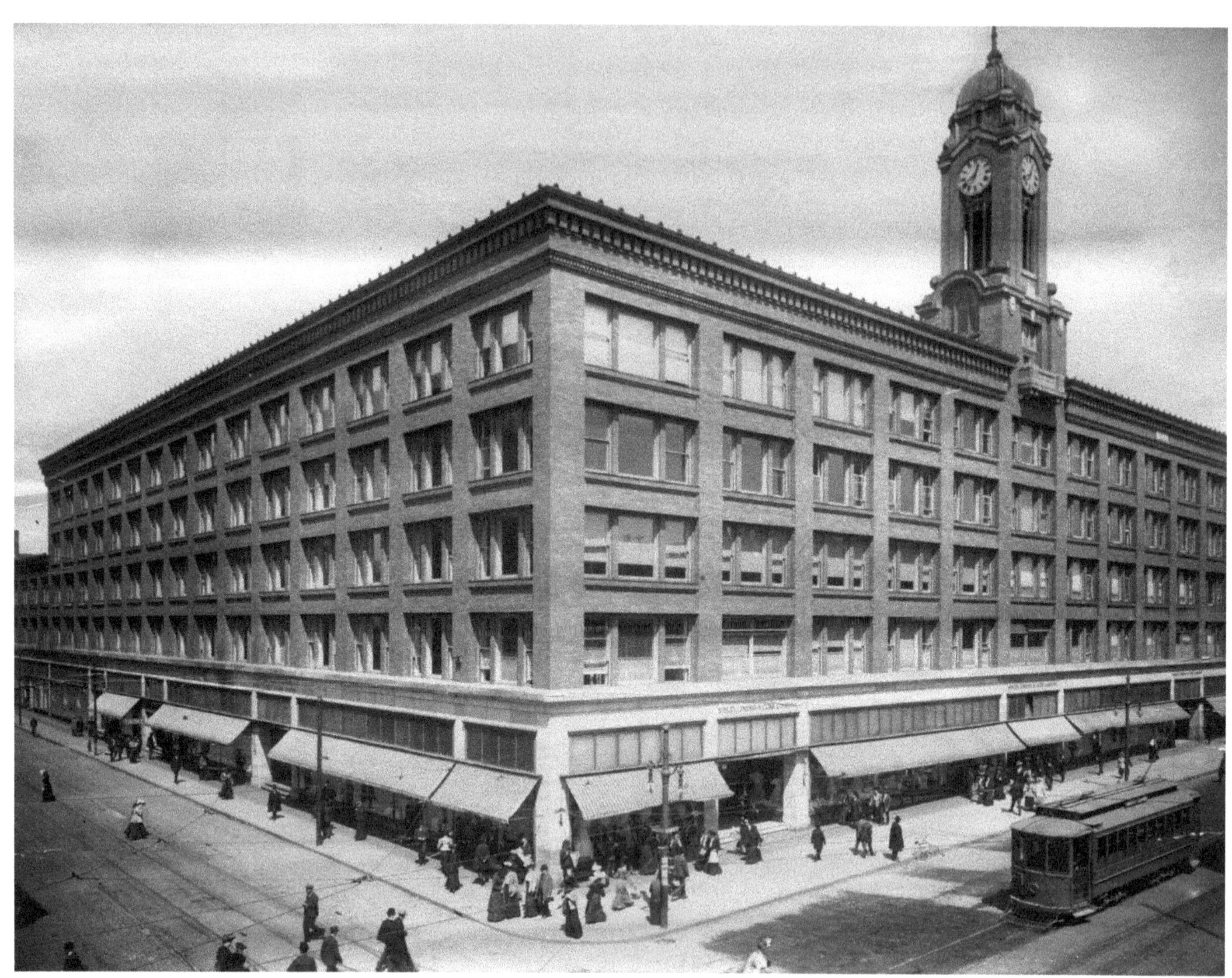

Looking northeast from the southwest corner of Main and Clinton streets at the Sibley Department Store. The local landmark Sibley clock tower is visible above the store in this 1916 photograph.

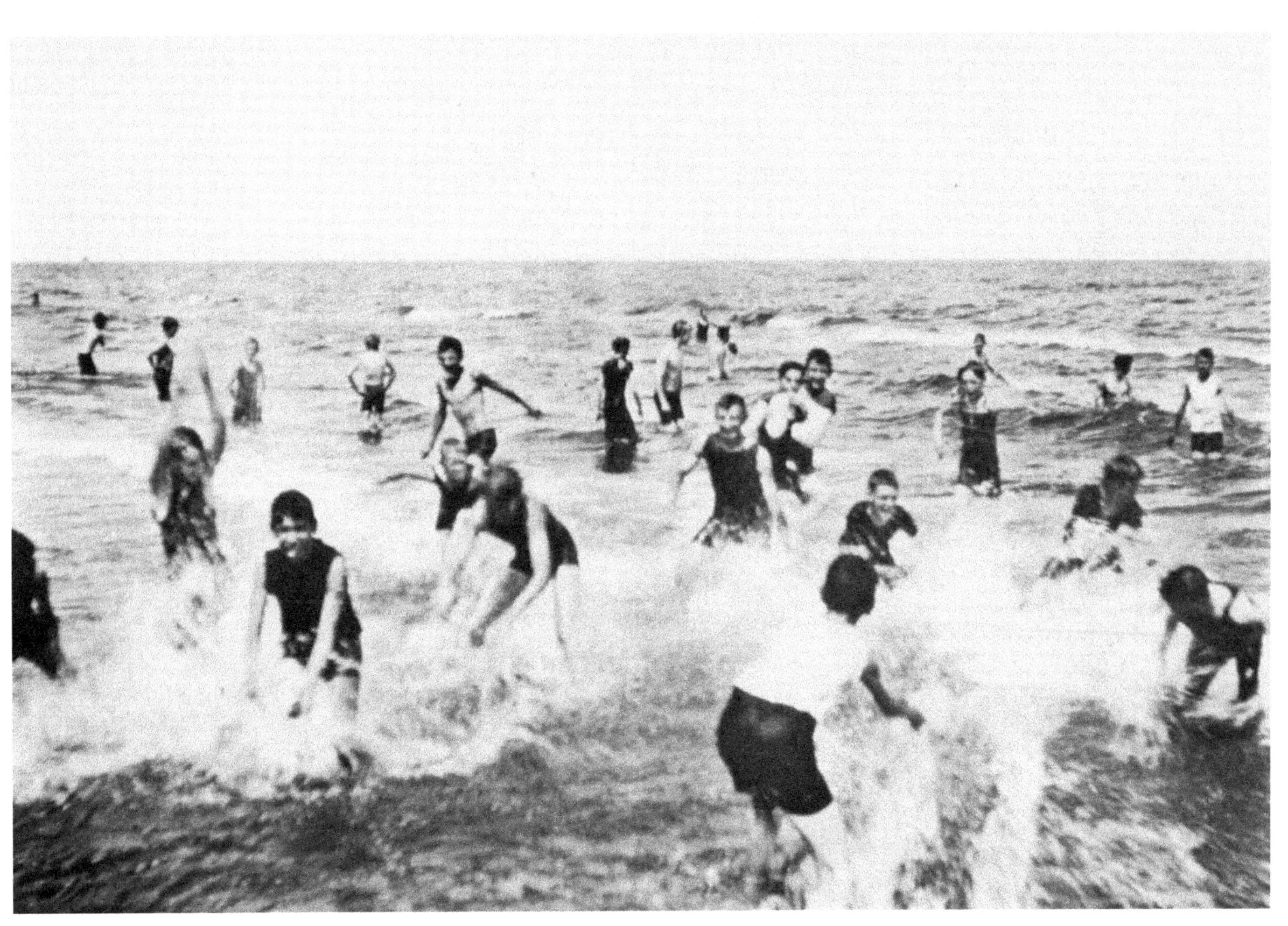

A group of Boy Scouts in 1916 joins in swimming at Durand-Eastman Park as part of a summer playground program that included games, cooking, and other outdoor skills necessary to a young man.

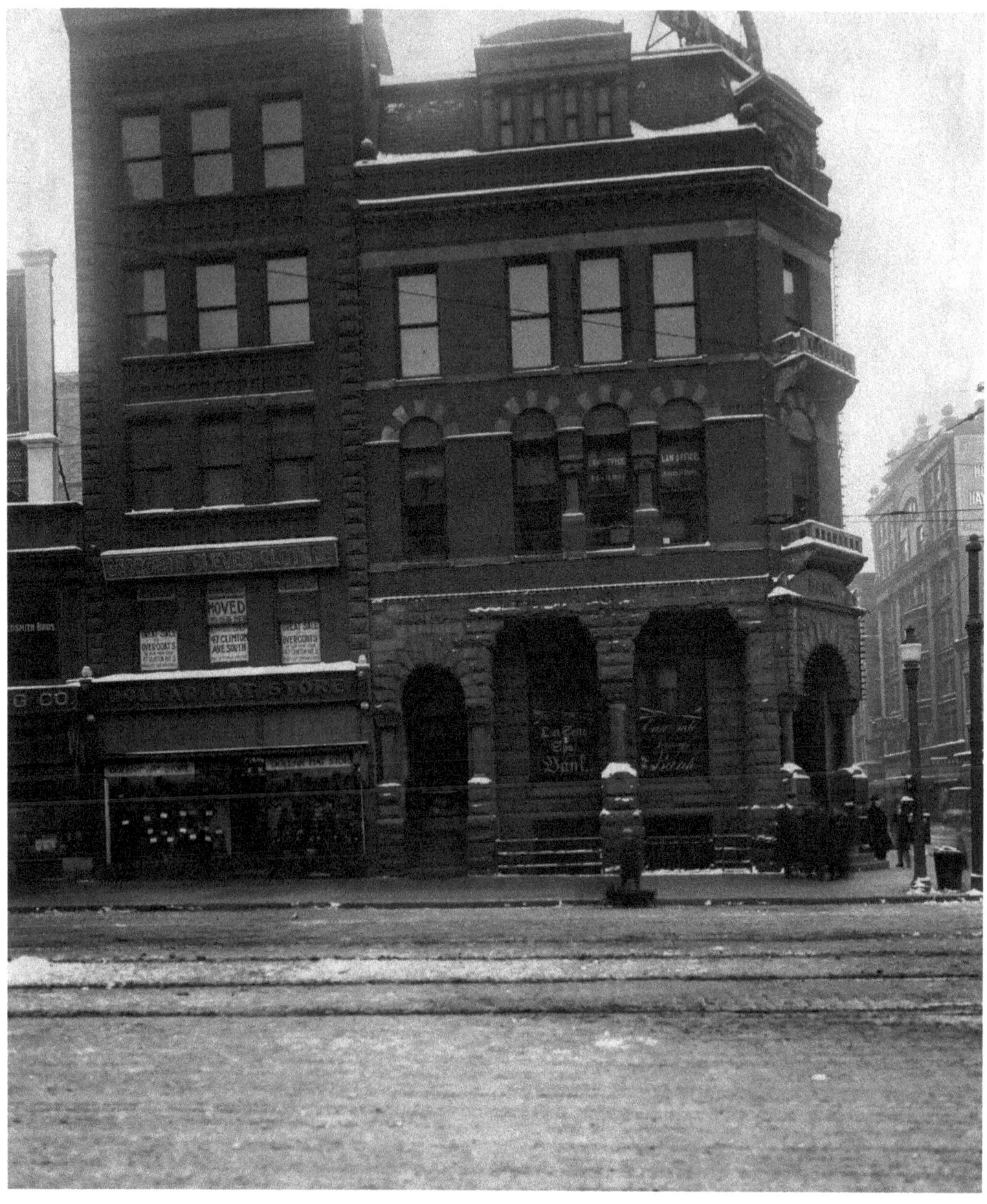

The East Side Savings Bank on the southeast corner of East Main Street and South Clinton Avenue about 1916. The building was designed by Warner and Brockett and built in 1885. It was razed in the late 1950s to make way for the Community Savings Bank that opened on that site in 1958.

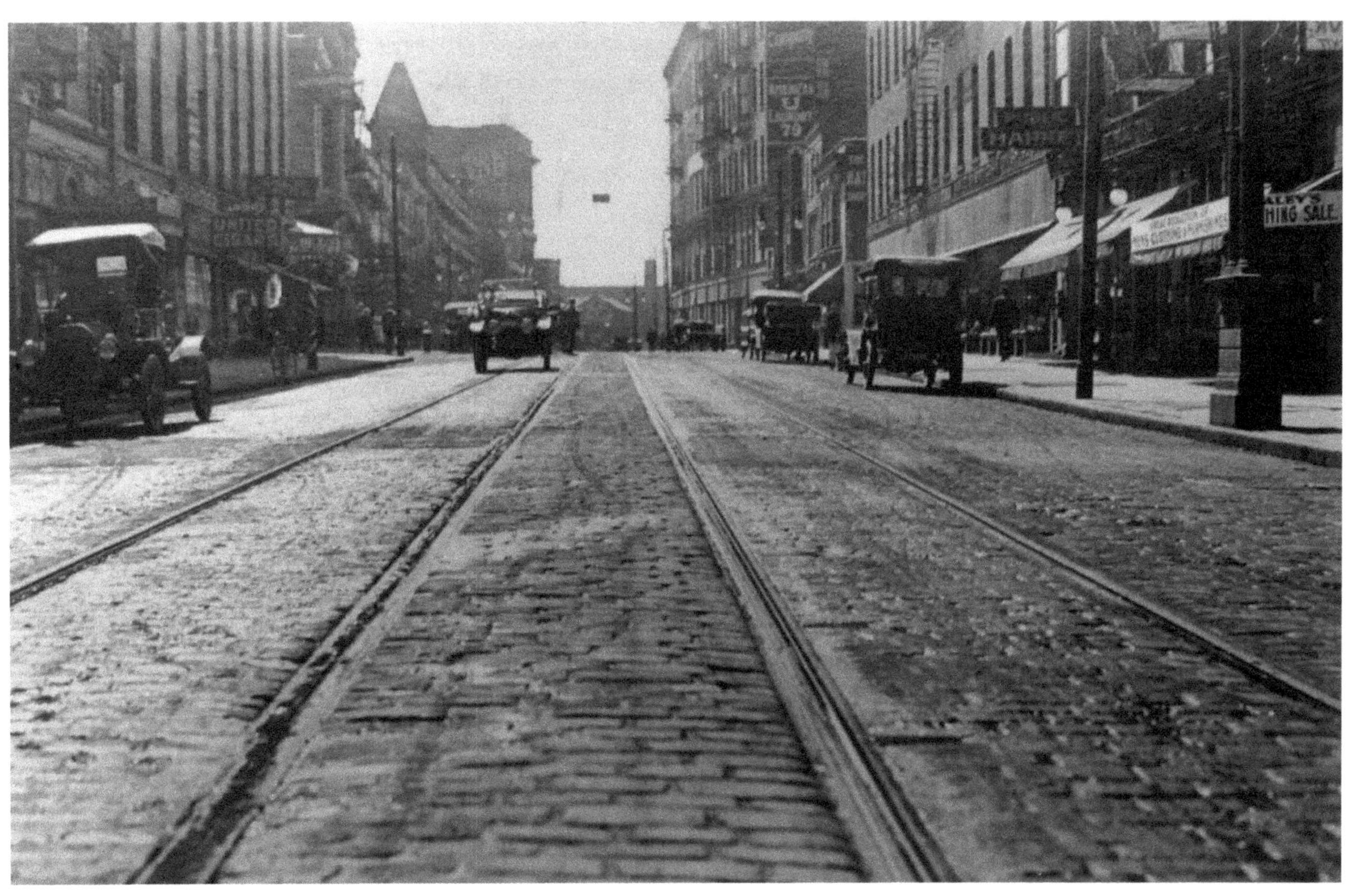

Looking south on South Avenue from near Main Street. In the distance is the tower of the Osburn Hotel on the site of today's new library downtown. No streetcars are visible though two sets of tracks run the length of the street. Early cars seem to have replaced horse-drawn vehicles in this 1917 photograph.

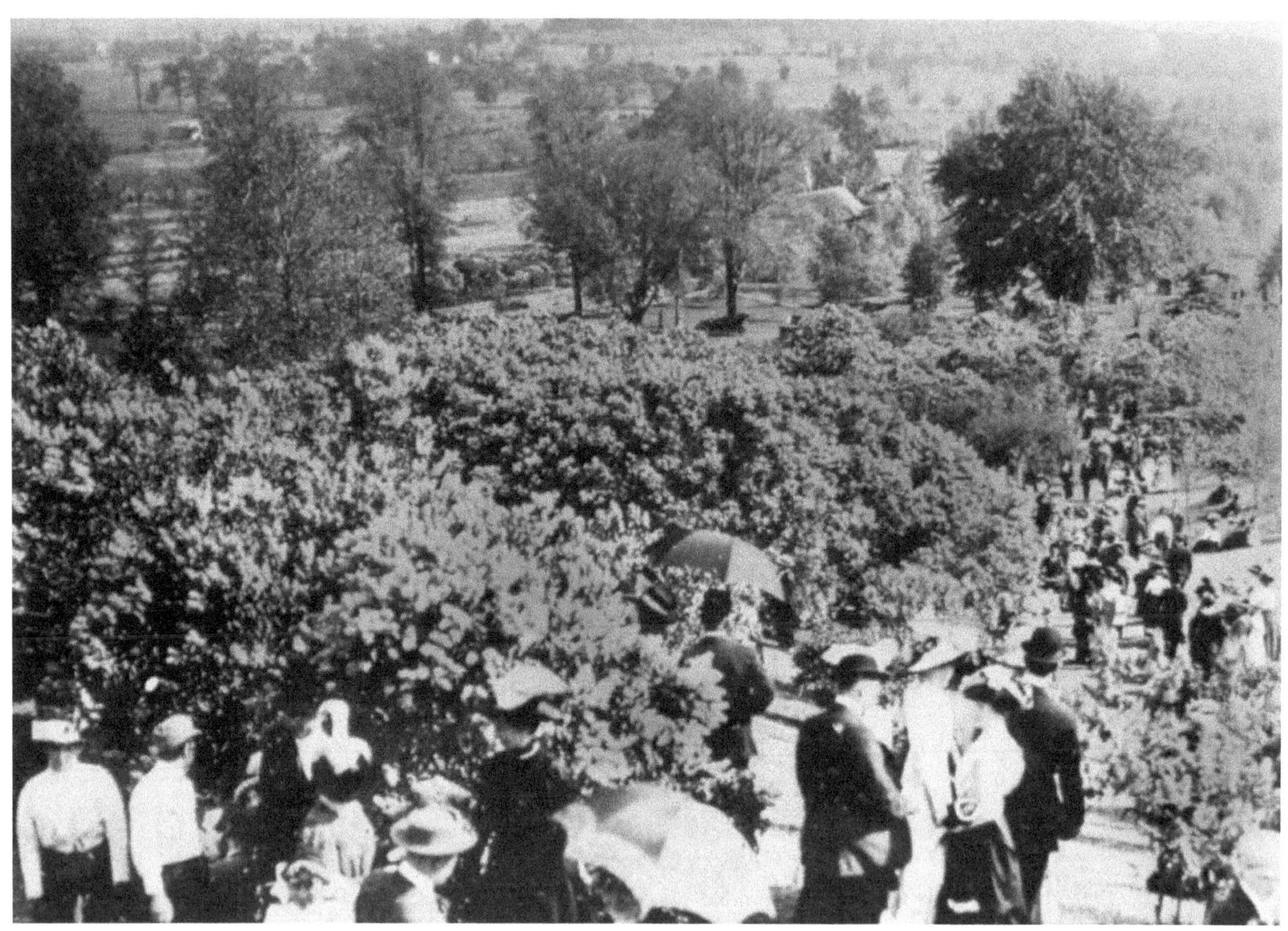

Over time lilacs in May became synonymous with Rochester in the spring. The first Lilac Sunday was held in Highland Park in 1905, growing in popularity to become a weeklong festival. In 1978 it became a ten-day event. Part of the reason for lengthening the festival was the difficulty of predicting when the lilacs would bloom. The festival was so popular that groups from out of state booked buses and hotels a year in advance.

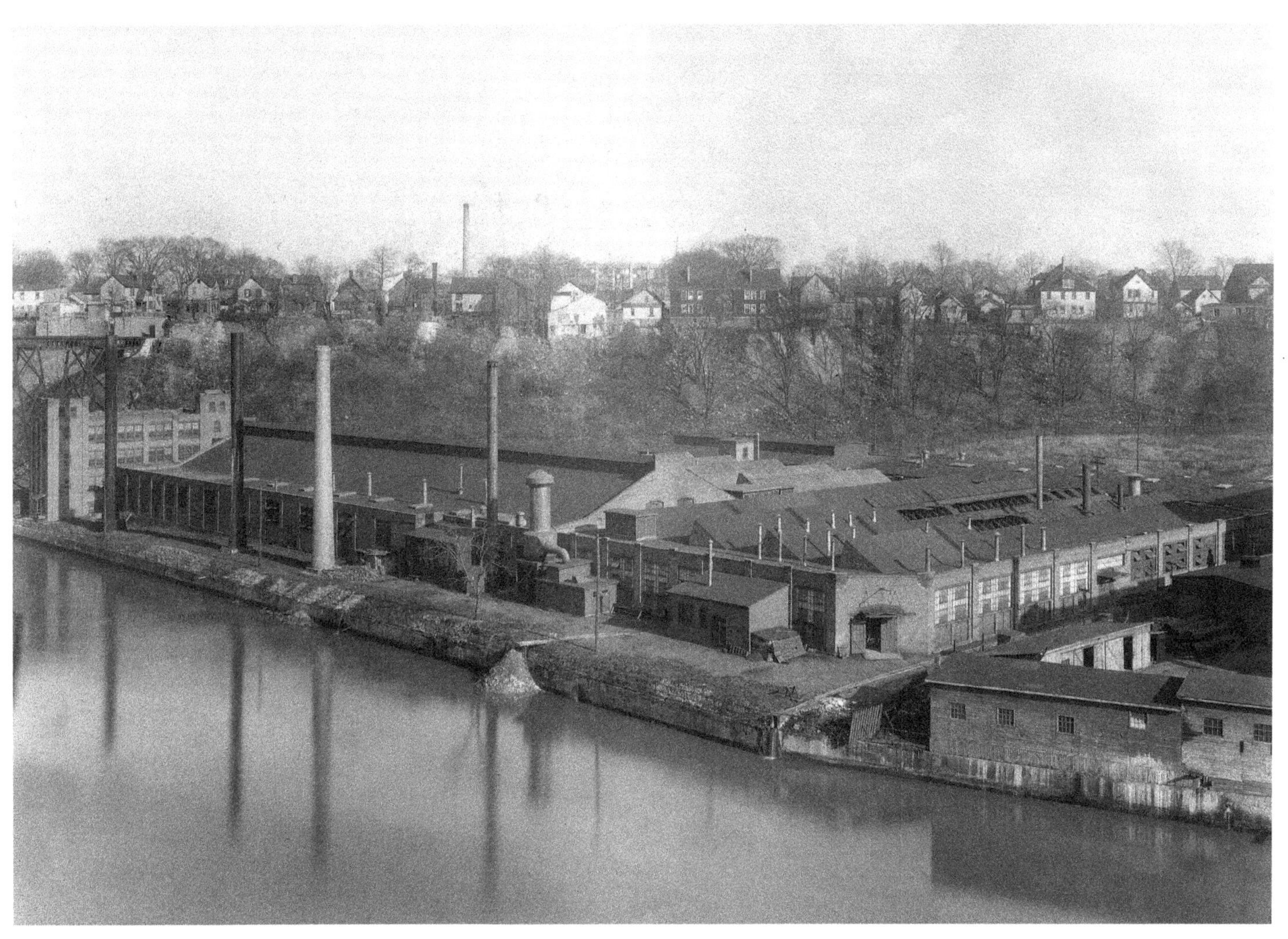

Just north of the Bausch Bridge on the east side of the Genesee River, this Bausch and Lomb Glass Plant produced eye-glass products. During World War I the plant produced optical glass for the military.

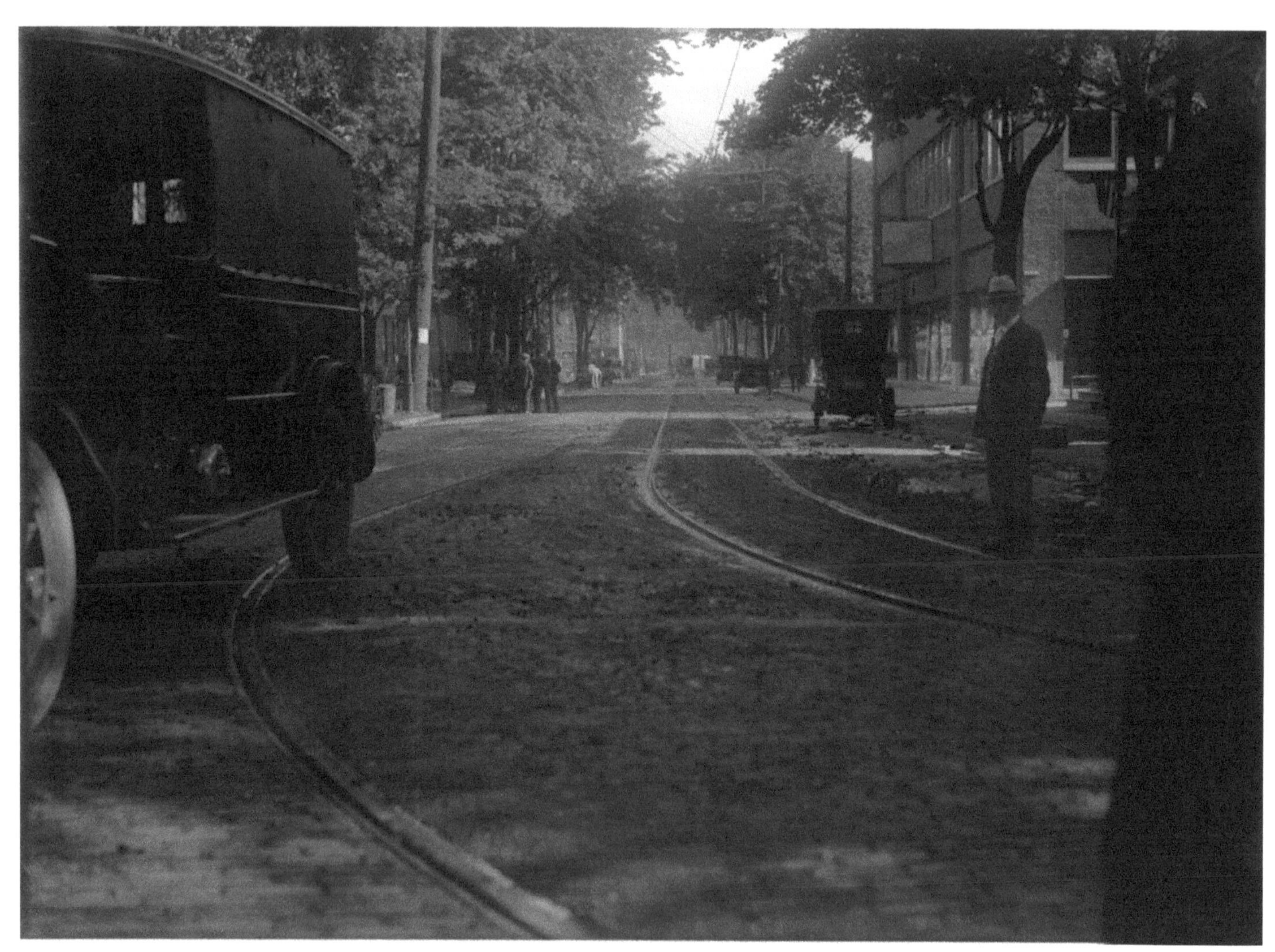

A van is parked unsafely on the streetcar tracks on south Union Street near Gardiner Park. The tracks ran on Union Street between Gardiner Park and Court Street. The building on the right is the Overland-Rochester Company.

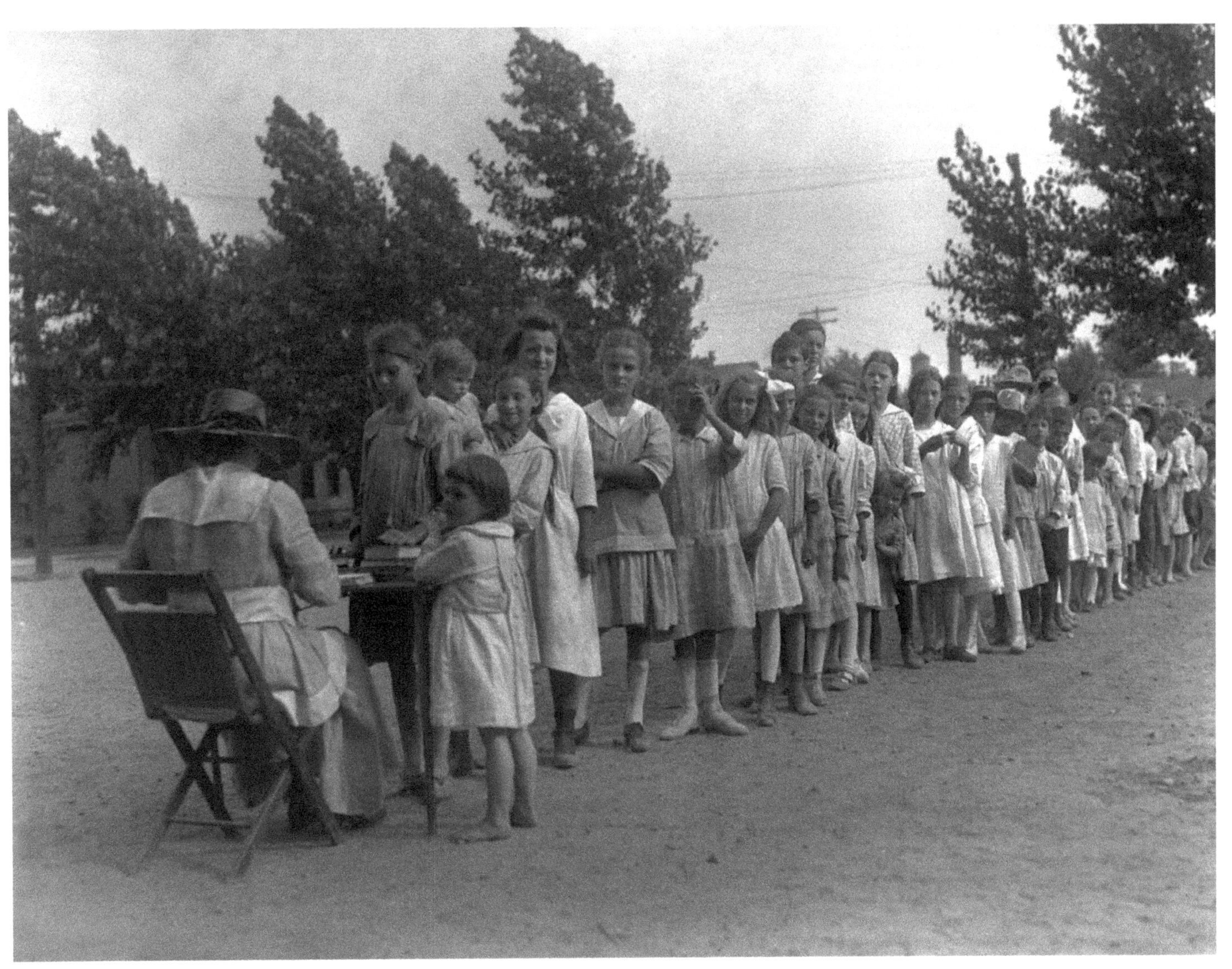

The Rochester Parks Department worked with the library to bring books to children to check out to encourage reading. In 1917 children line up in the playground of School No. 36 as the librarian checks out the books. Story hours also were held in the city's playgrounds.

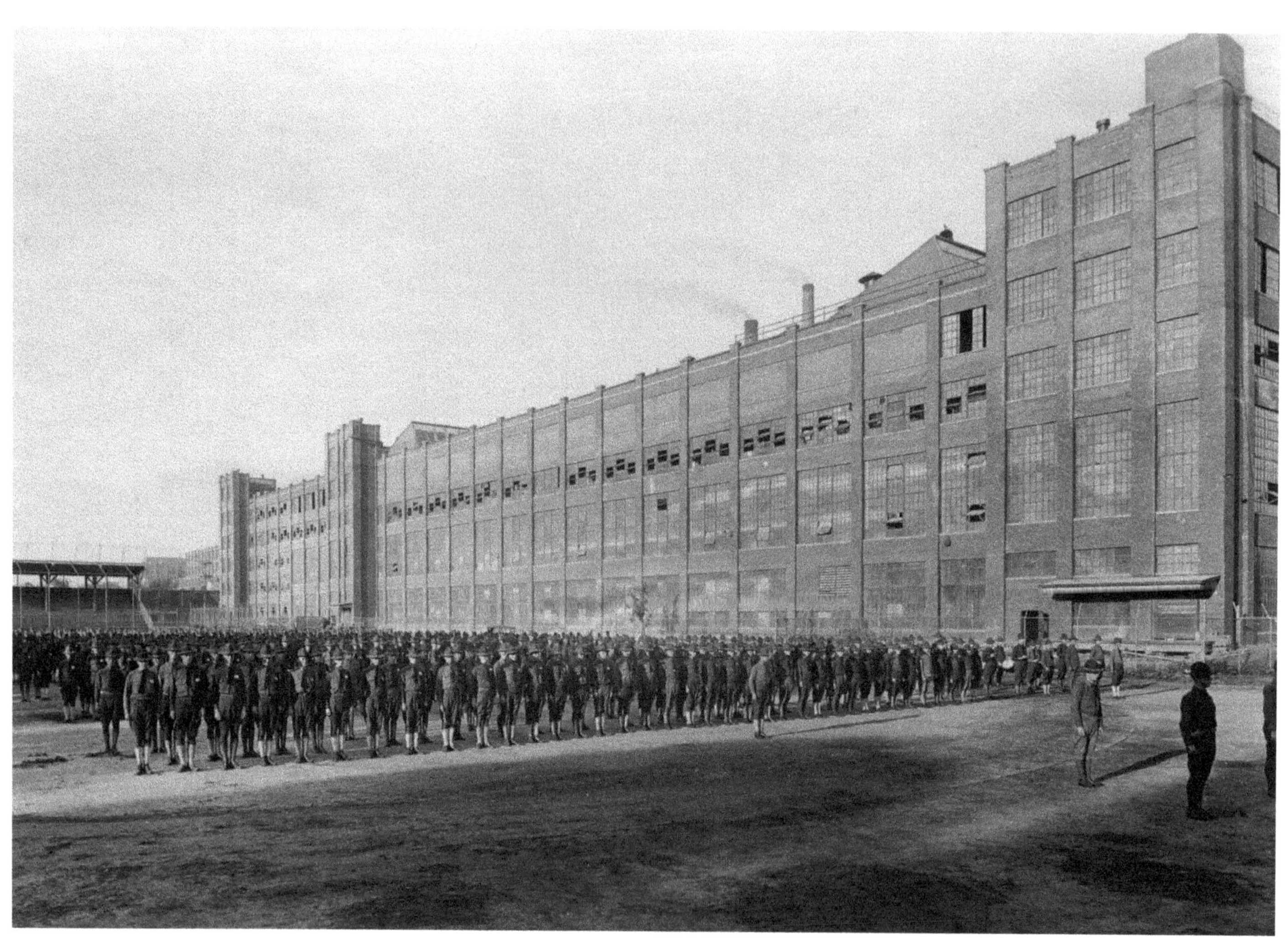

Students in the U.S. School of Aerial Photography at Kodak Park learned photography and camera repair from March to December 1918. More than 2,000 servicemen were taught aerial reconnaissance, but World War I ended before they were assigned to combat units.

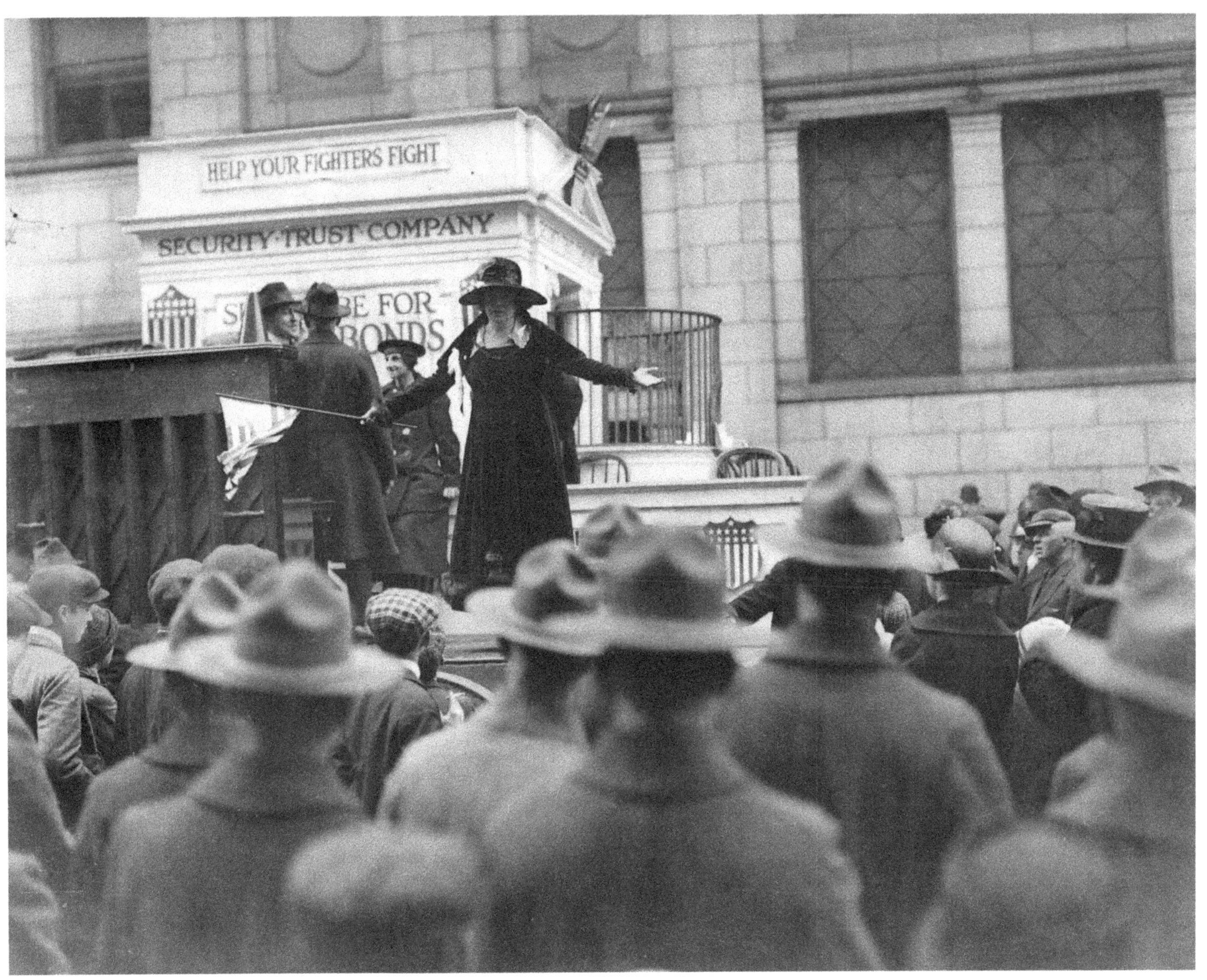

At a rally to sell war bonds during World War I, Bertha Eldridge challenges the crowd to do their patriotic duty and buy the bonds. She and other women worked as Minute Women until the war ended.

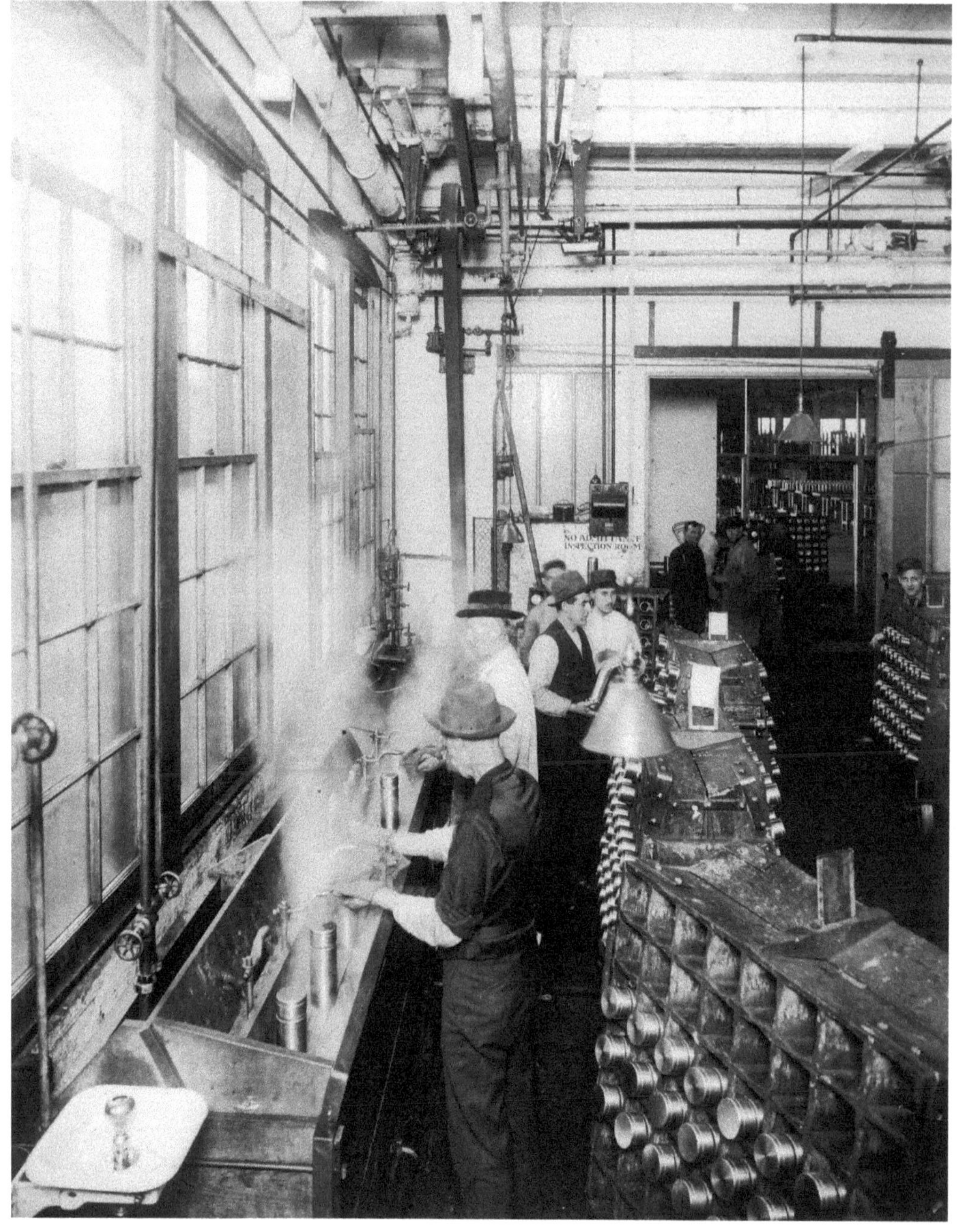

Employees at T. H. Symington Company work to manufacture up to 15,000 shell casings and sockets a day; first for the British during World War I, then for the United States when it entered the war.

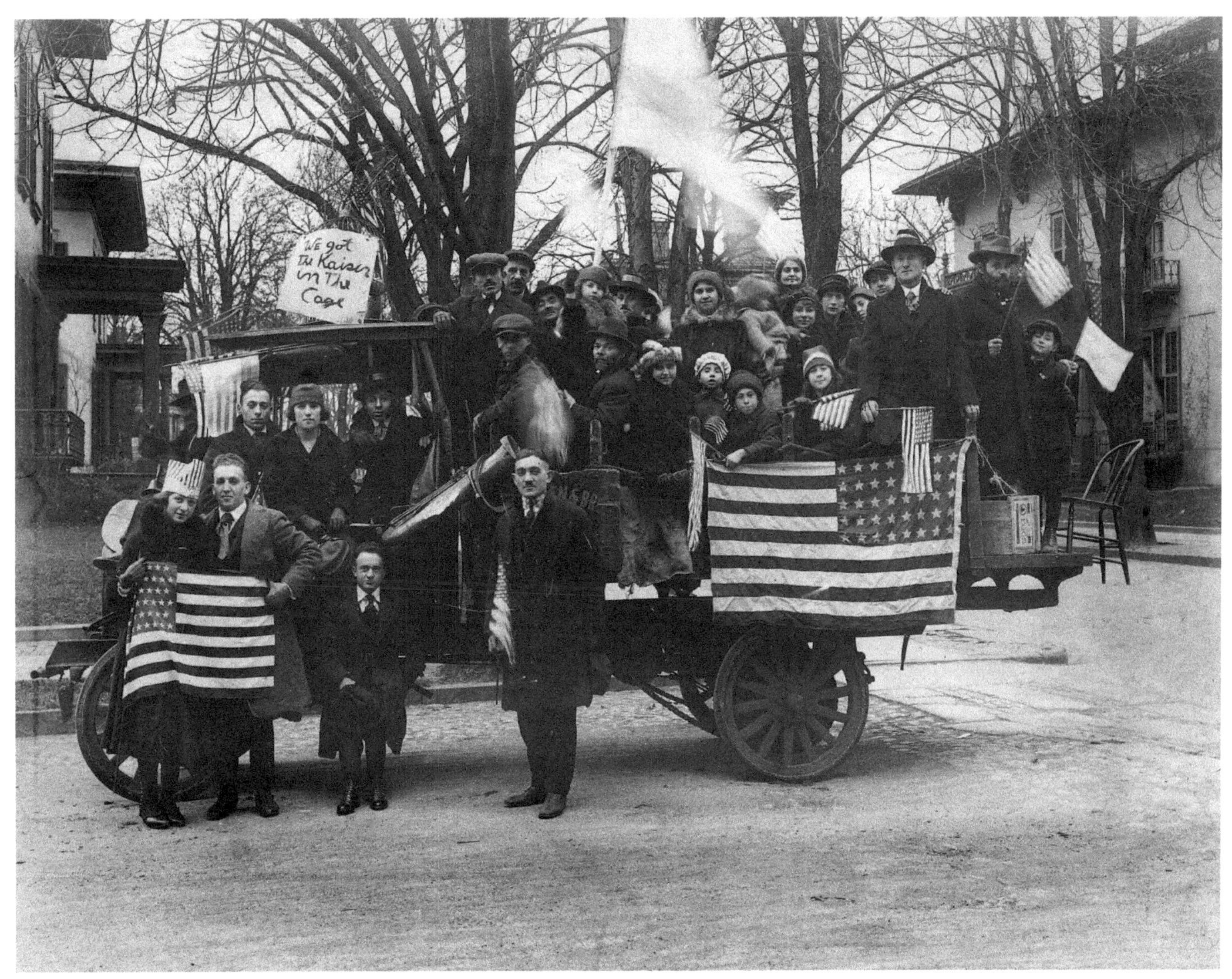

Celebrating Armistice Day, a group of patriotic people crowd a flag-draped truck to travel through the city's streets celebrating the end of World War I. The sign in the front reads, "We got the Kaiser in the Cage."

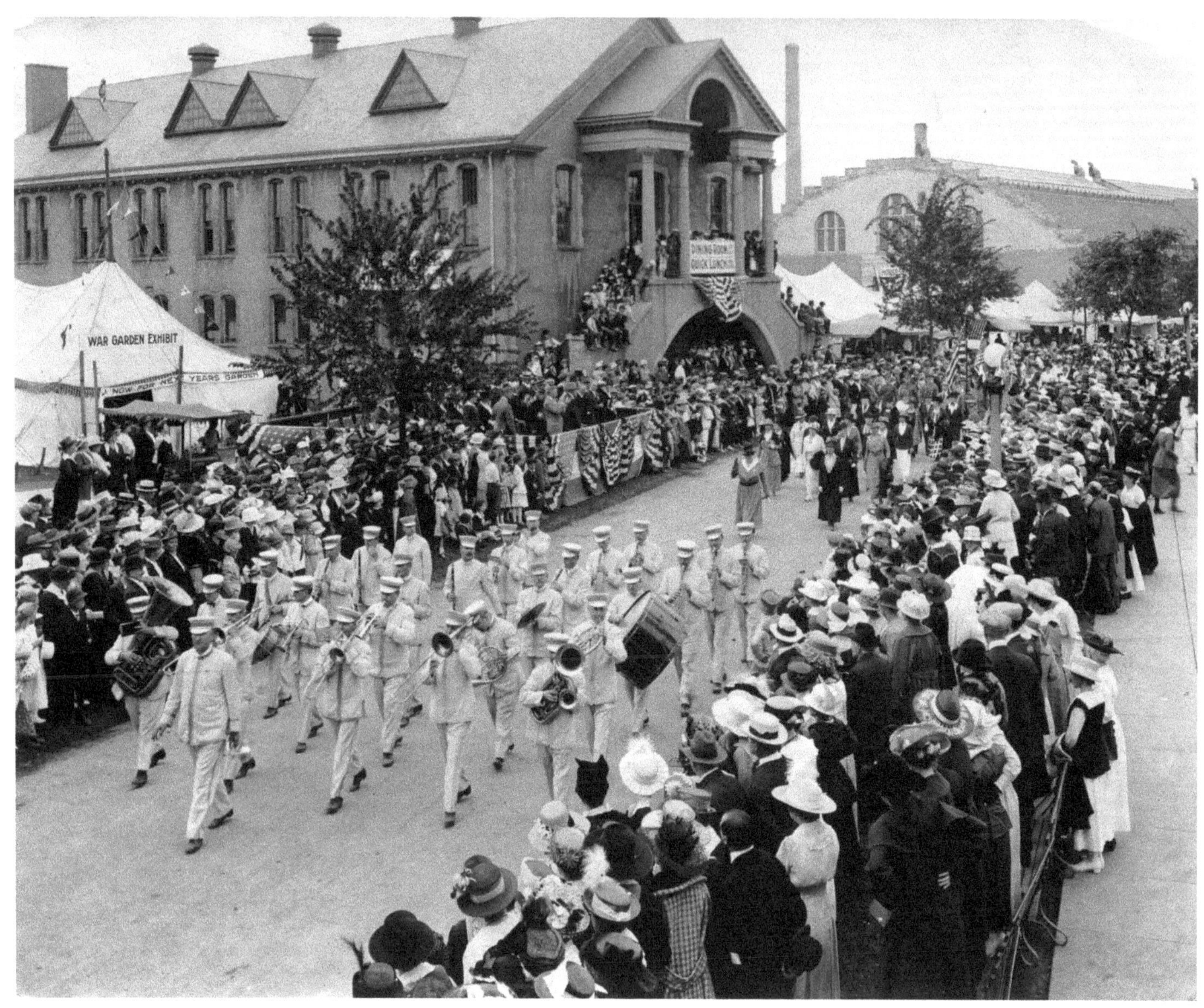

About 6,000 mothers of military personnel in World War I were honored at Exposition Park with a medal. If a mother lost a son, her medal bore the gold star that represented their loss. Gold Star mothers displayed a gold star in the windows of their homes. Sadly, some mothers displayed more than one star.

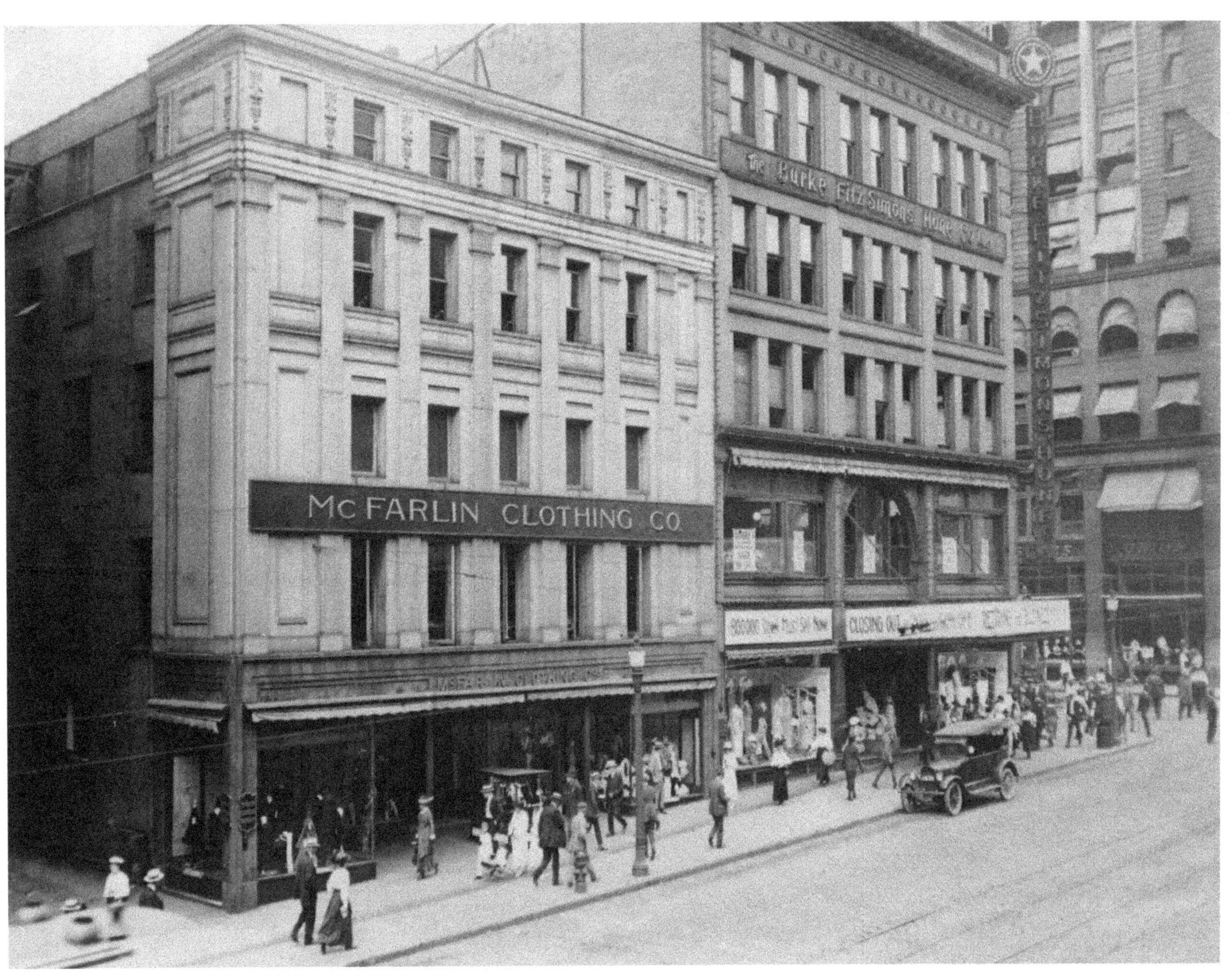

Often referred to as the Burke Building, Burke, Fitzsimons, Hone and Co. opened in 1849 and remained in business until 1919. Burke stands next door to McFarlin's Clothing Company at 110-116 Main Street. Francis M. McFarlin opened his clothing store in 1860 and remained in business at various locations until 1983.

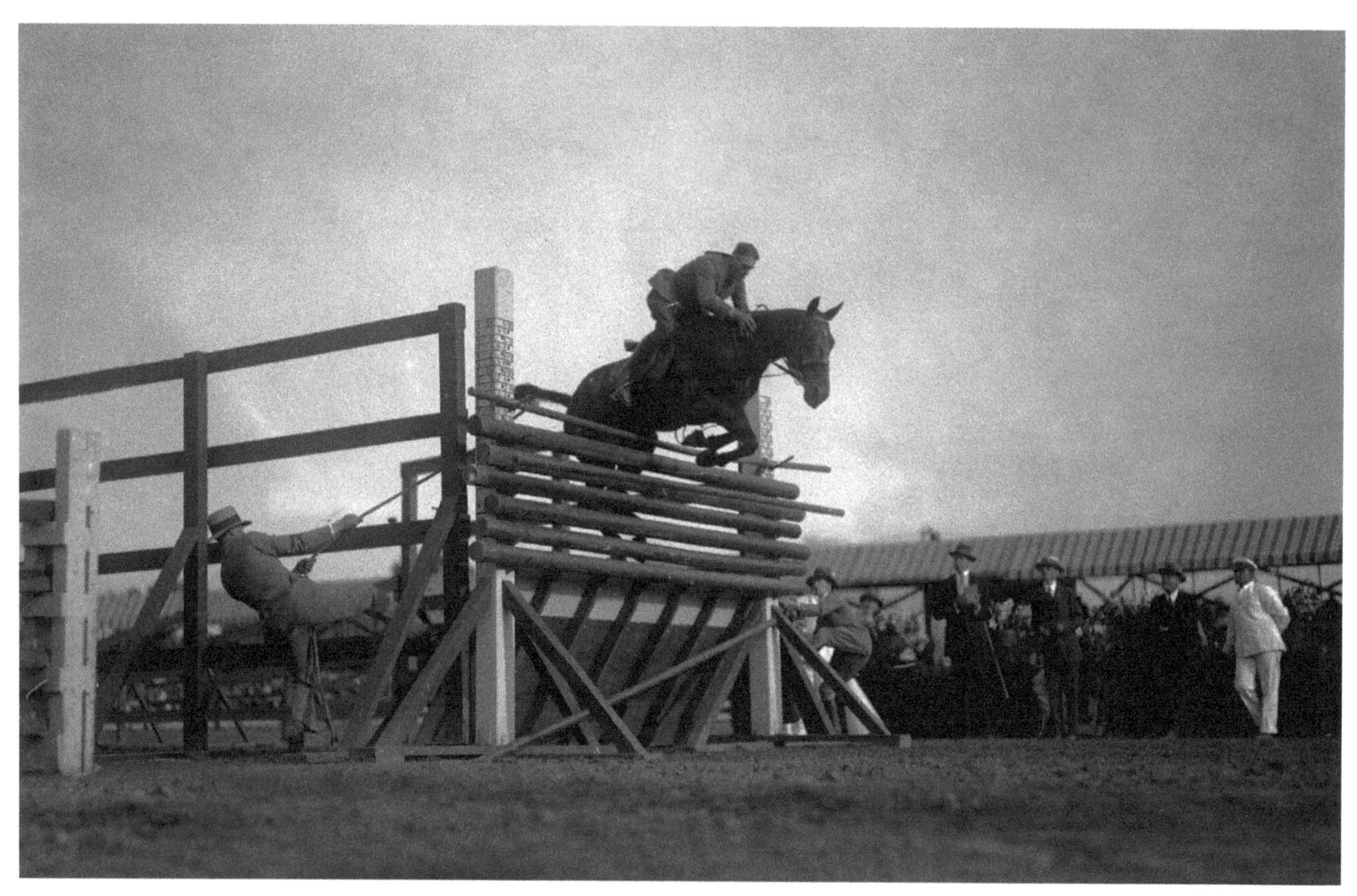

A rider successfully completes a difficult jump as his horse clears a 7-foot-4-inch rail. Men hold the rail in place as judges look on in the horse-jumping competition at the Rochester Exposition. (September 3, 1919)

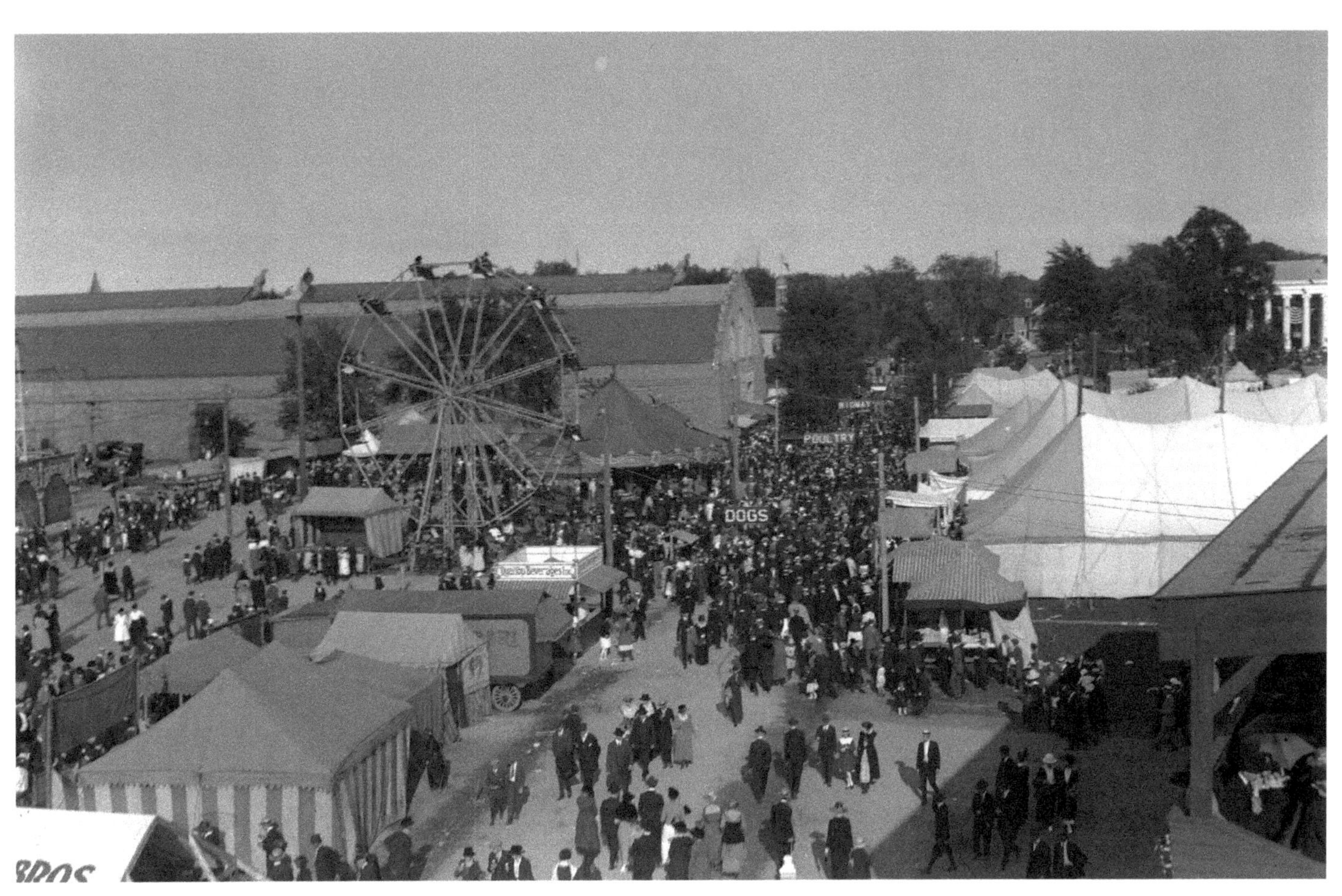

The Rochester Exposition of 1919 attracted hundreds of people to exhibition tents, food stands, and a variety of entertainment. The Ferris wheel in the background was certainly one of the most popular attractions. (September 3, 1919)

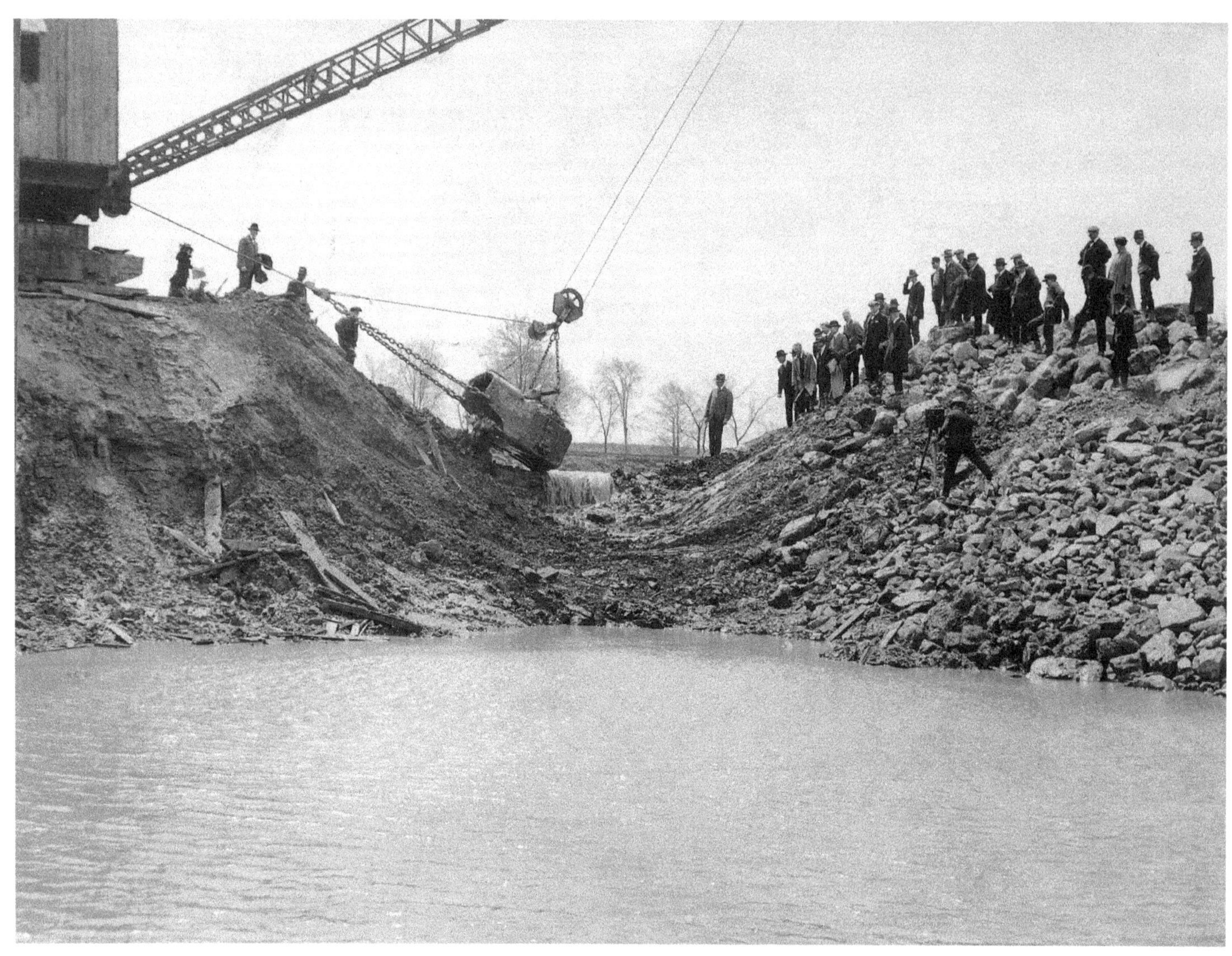

Construction laborers work on the New York State Barge Canal in the early 1900s. The Erie Canal was moved from downtown Rochester in 1918–1919 to the Genesee Valley Park, where it crossed the Genesee River at grade level rather than over an aqueduct as it had downtown. The section of the Genesee River from the canal crossing to the Court Street Dam became a part of the canal system.

Rochester Rises to the Challenge

(1920–1939)

Not even the stock market crash of October 1929 diminished the usual optimism of Rochester businessmen. In wake of the growing prosperity of the 1920s, there was no immediate clue to the Depression that was about to grip the world. Only a month after the crash, Roger Balsam addressed the Chamber of Commerce saying, "The worst is over." Estimates of unemployed workers ranged from 10,000 to 24,000 by the new year. The city council established an employment bureau in response to swelling public welfare rolls.

By spring several thousand unemployed workers were demonstrating in Washington. In a single year the city's welfare cost jumped 44 percent to one and a half million dollars.

In 1931 New York State Industrial Commissioner Frances Perkins chose Rochester as the site of the first statewide employment office. The city's government became leaner as employees not only received no raises, but began to weather severe cuts in needed equipment and staffing. City Manager Stephen B. Story suffered a $5,000 cut in salary in late 1930, just a year after the crash. Rochester began to give greater ear to Socialist Milwaukee Mayor Daniel W. Hoan. The city assigned 250 acres of land to be divided into gardens for about 2,000 families.

As the early years of the depression advanced, city officials realized the taxes they anticipated from the 1929 real estate tax assessment were not going to materialize—the unemployed were unable to pay expected taxes.

The election of New York Governor Franklin Delano Roosevelt to the presidency marked the beginning of a different approach to solving the crisis. A number of WPA construction projects in the city were started, providing jobs to many workers. Marion Folsom, treasurer of Eastman Kodak and president of the Council of Social Agencies, pushed a plan for unemployment insurance. He was appointed by Roosevelt to a committee in Washington, D.C., to design such a national plan that is today the federal Social Security system.

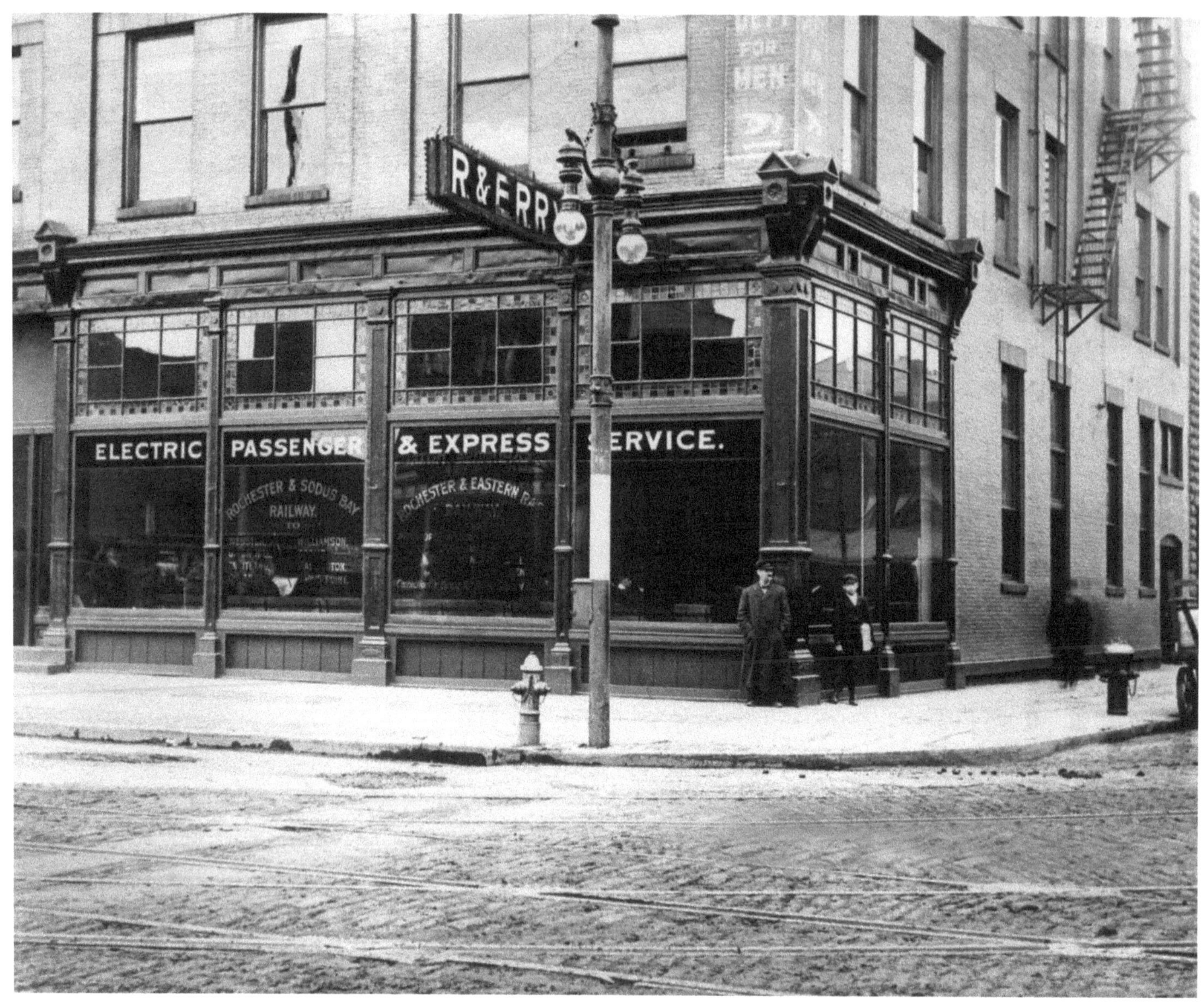

Before World War II mass transportation was important in local travel. On the northeast corner of Court and Exchange streets, the Rochester and Eastern Rapid Railway and the Rochester and Sodus Bay Railway operated out of this Electric Passenger and Express Service building until 1927. The building was demolished in 1951 to make way for the Rochester War Memorial.

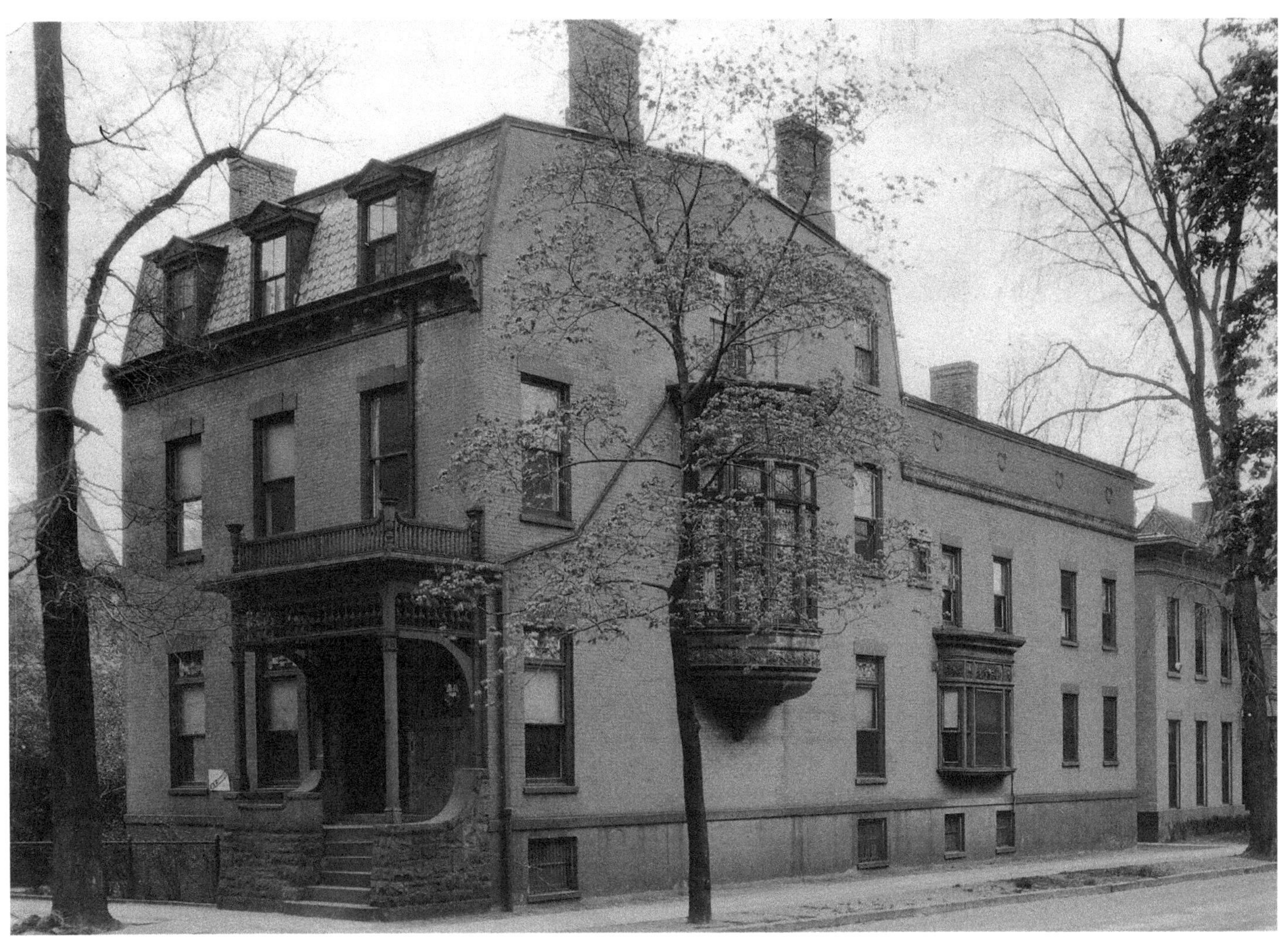

Architect Daniel Loomis designed this house on the southeast corner of Spring and South Washington streets for Thomas Hart Rochester, son of the city's founder, Colonel Nathaniel Rochester. Thomas was the 6th mayor of Rochester. Mary Bliss later ran a school in the house before it became a dormitory and fraternity house for Mechanics Institute, predecessor of today's Rochester Institute of Technology. In 1921, about the time this photograph was taken, the Locust Club purchased the house.

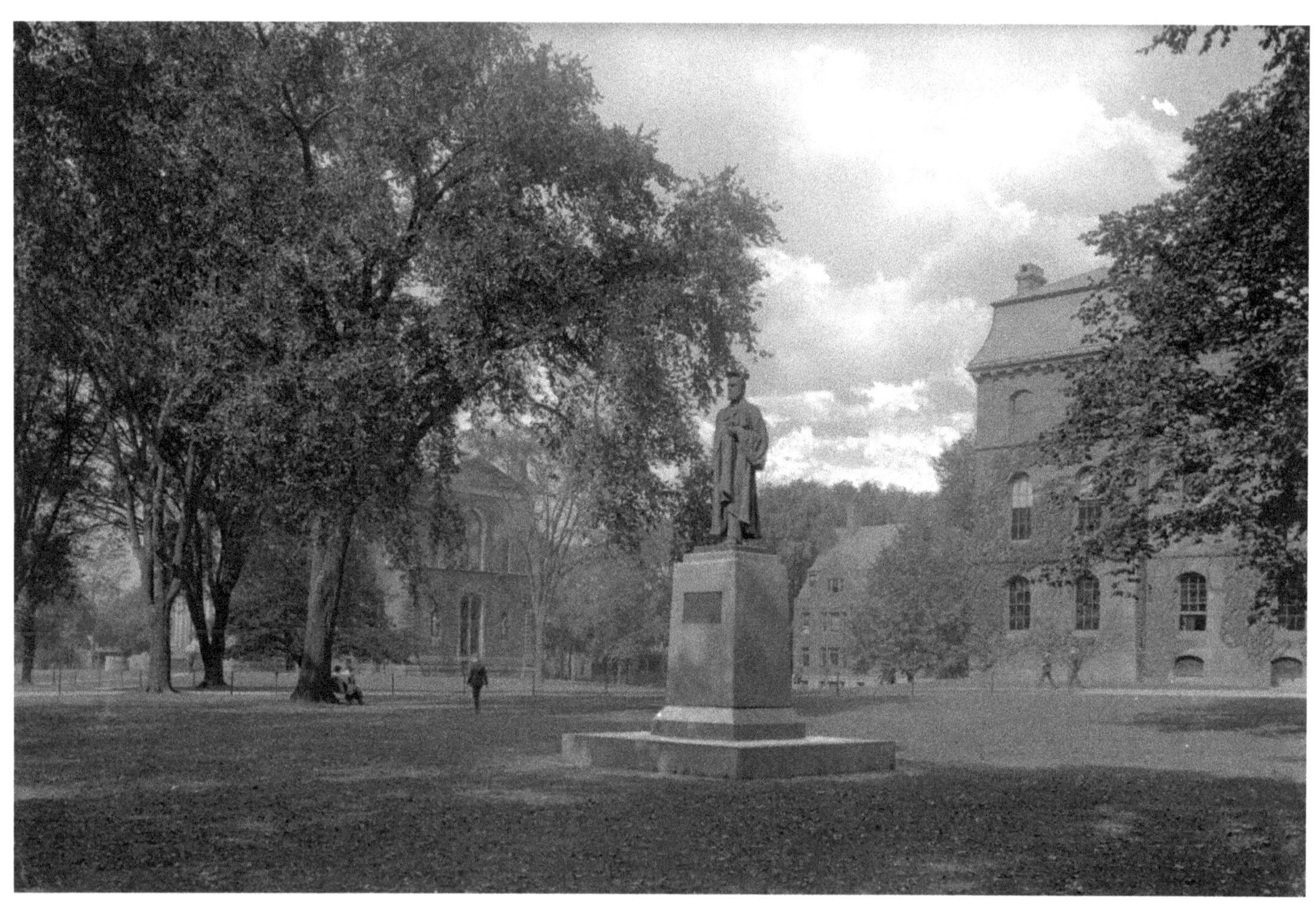

The statue of the University of Rochester's first president, Martin Brewer Anderson, stands on the Prince Street campus. The statue was created by J. Guernsey Mitchell, who also created the statue of Mercury that stands today on the Rochester skyline. The statue of Anderson was later moved to the university's River Street campus. This Prince Street site became the women's campus. To the left is the Sibley Building. On the right is Anderson Hall.

Across Broad Street from Fitzhugh Street, old City Hall was used from 1875 to 1978, when city officials moved to the old Federal Building at Church and Fitzhugh streets. In the foreground is George Higgins's business, where automobiles were rebuilt or repaired. Higgins set up his business as a carriage repair shop, but as many other mechanics like him discovered, it was necessary to change with the times in order to stay in business.

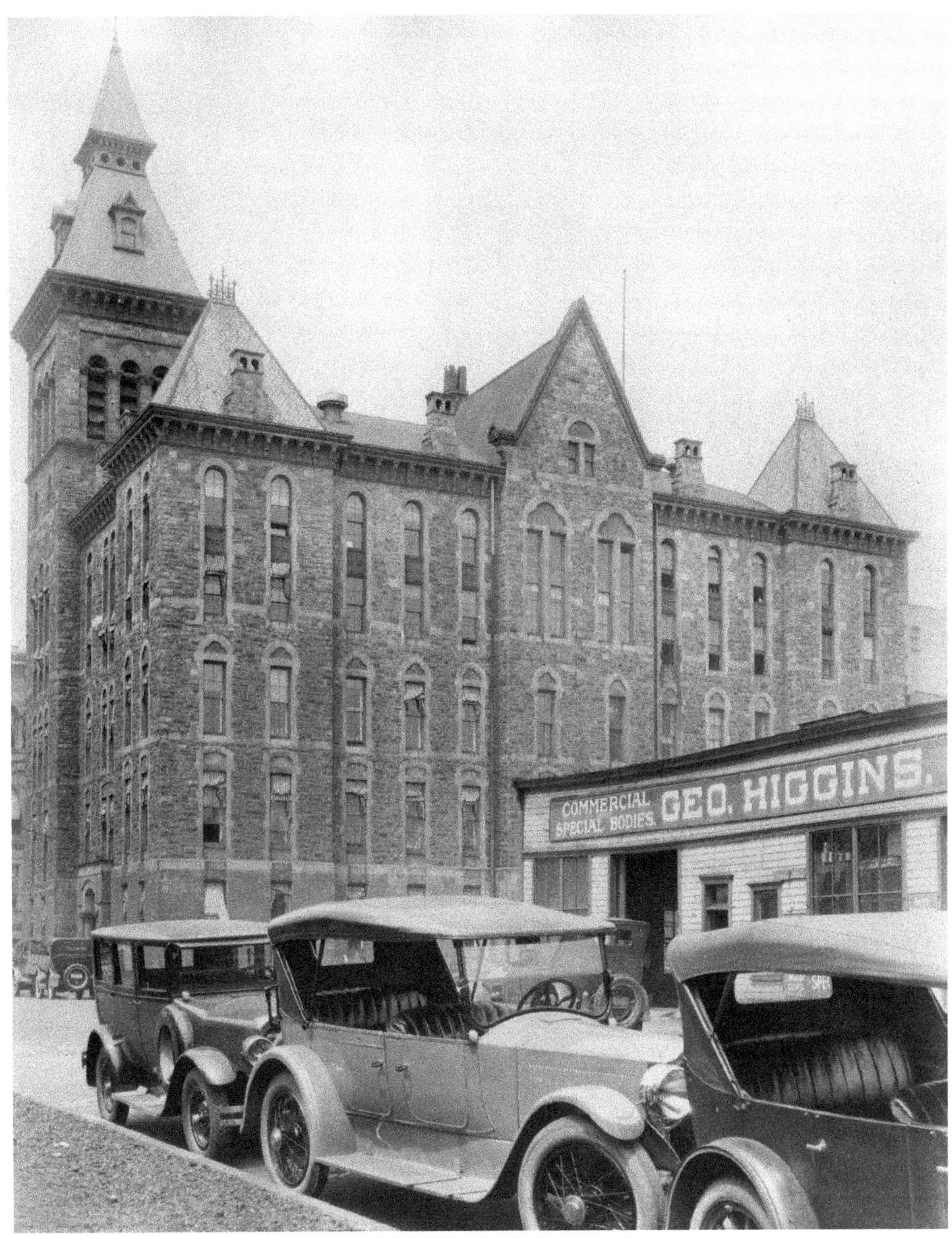

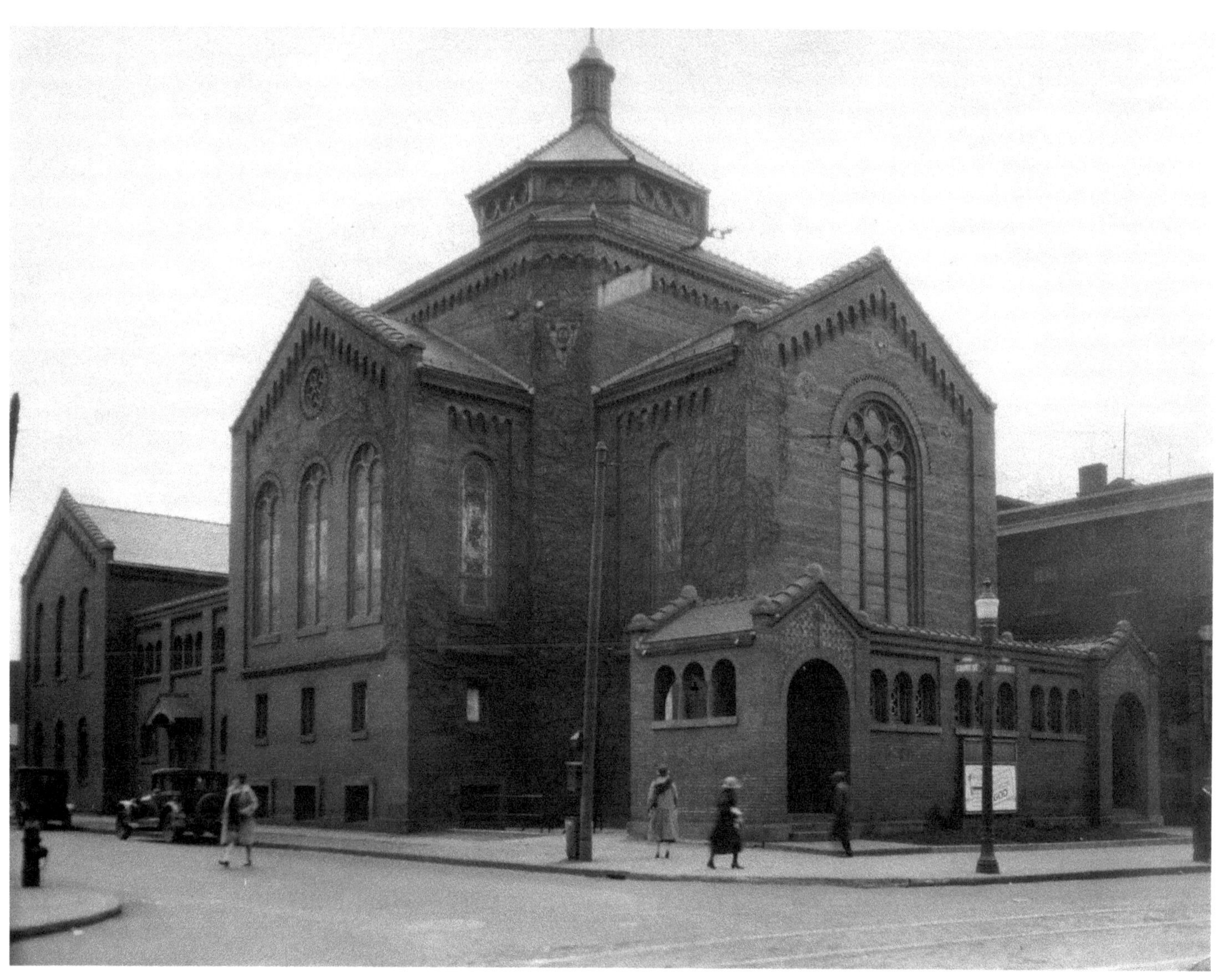

Architect Claude Bragdon designed the First Universalist Church at Court Street and Clinton Avenue near Washington Square Park in 1908. It replaced the church that was razed to make way for the nearby Seneca Hotel.

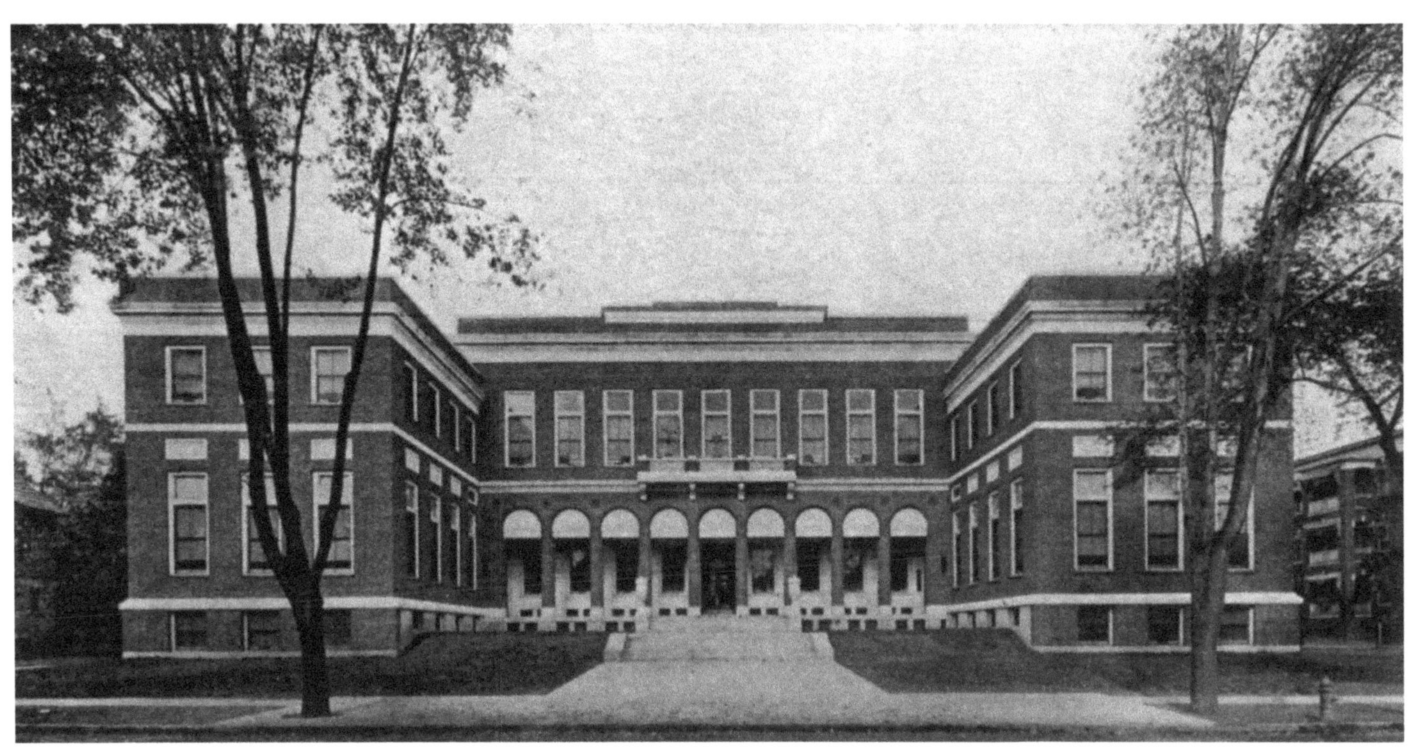

Opened in 1917, the Rochester Dental Dispensary was started by Kodak founder George Eastman to serve the dental needs of Rochester's children, and later on, adults as well. Eastman later opened similar dispensaries in other parts of the world. The building still stands today. (ca. 1920)

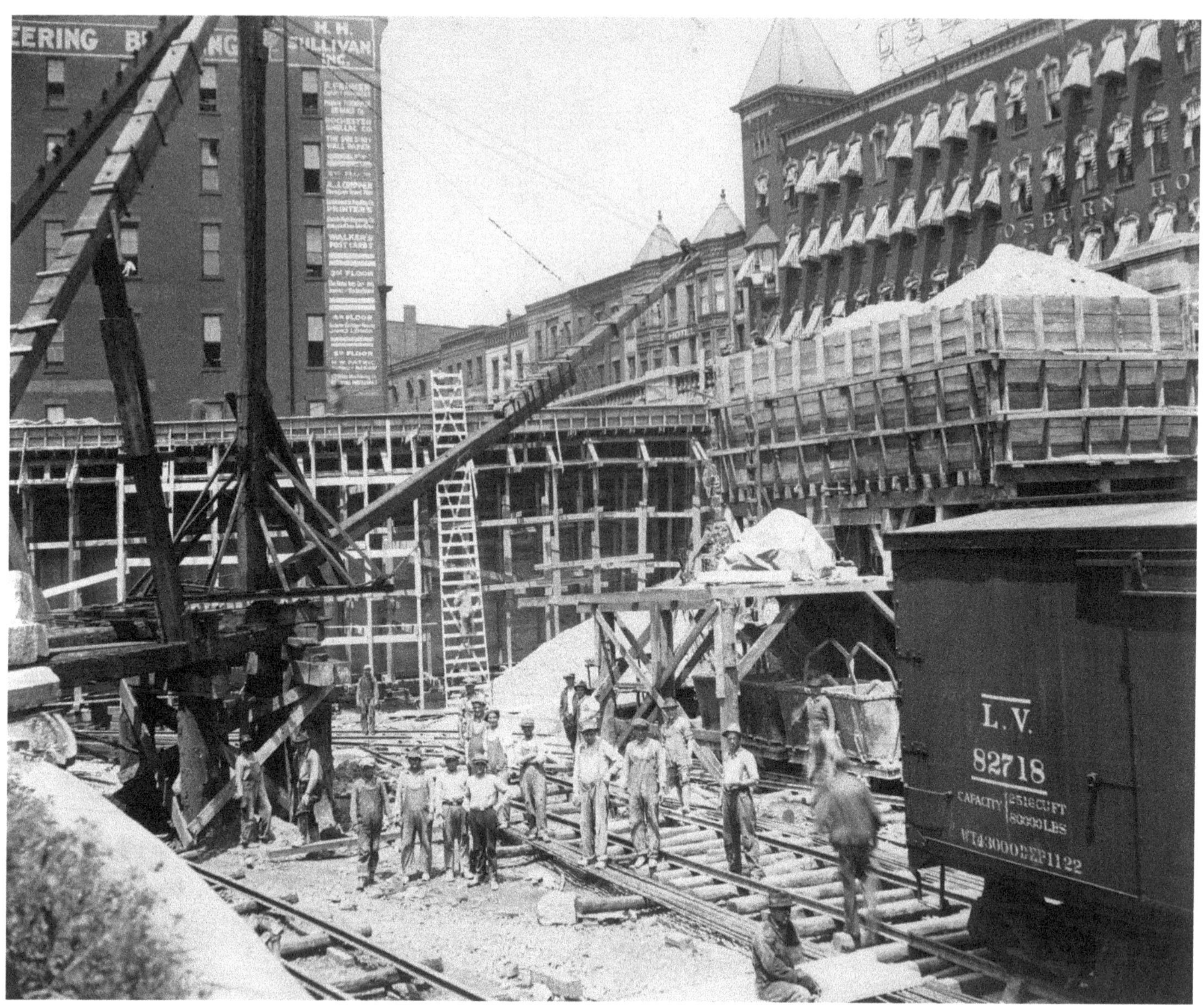

In the early 1920s laborers work on the subway at the east end of the Broad Street Bridge. The subway ran through the old Erie Canal bed after the canal was relocated to the Genesee Valley Park on the south border of the city. A road deck was built over the old canal bed so that automobiles could travel above the new subway. In 1956, the subway was abandoned, and today numerous plans propose various uses for it.

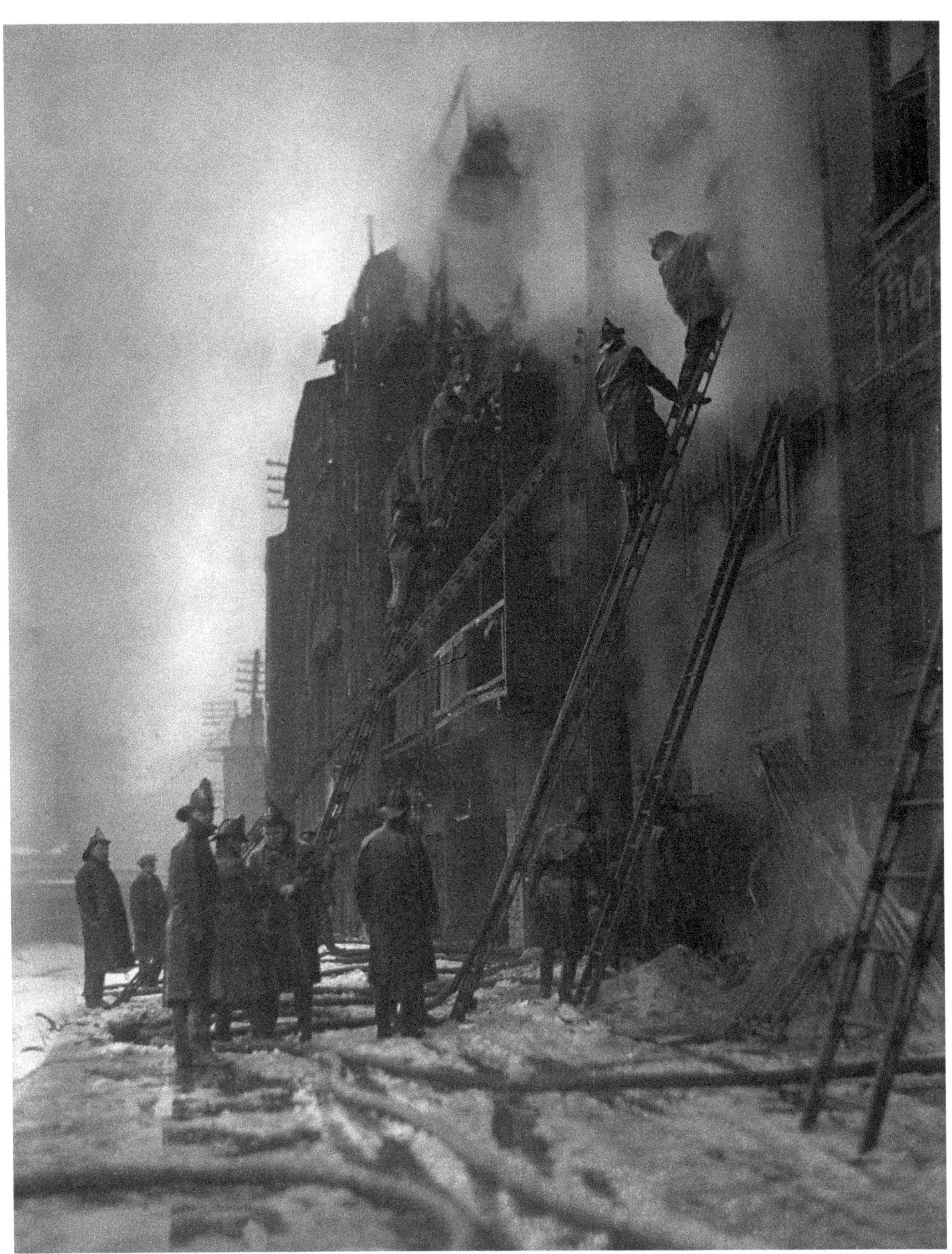

Six firemen were injured fighting the fire at the Lawless Paper Company on North Water Street in April of 1924.

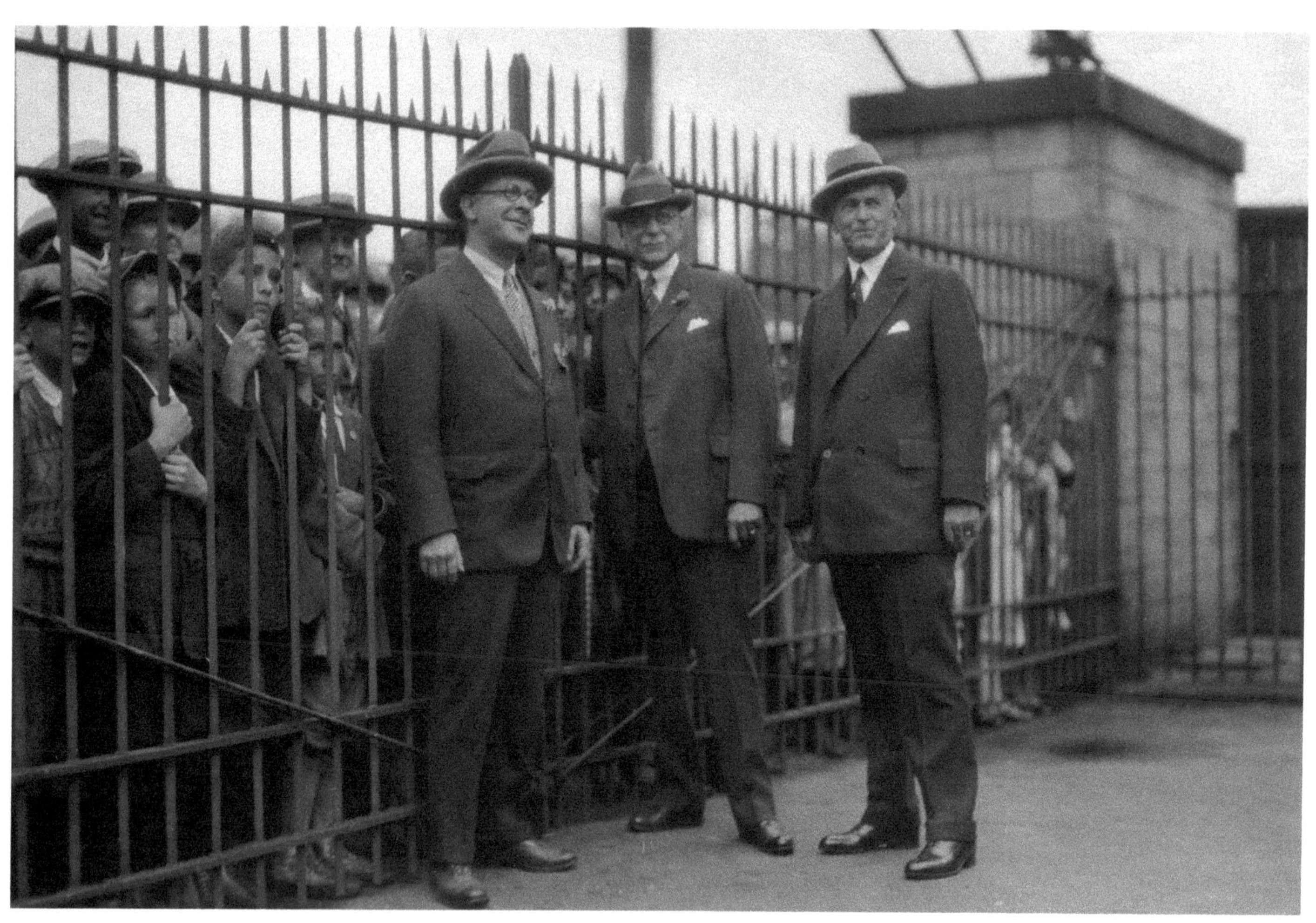

Crowds wait to enter as Exposition Park General Manager Edgar Edwards and Mayor Clarence Van Zandt open the gate to officially kick off the 1925 Rochester Exposition.

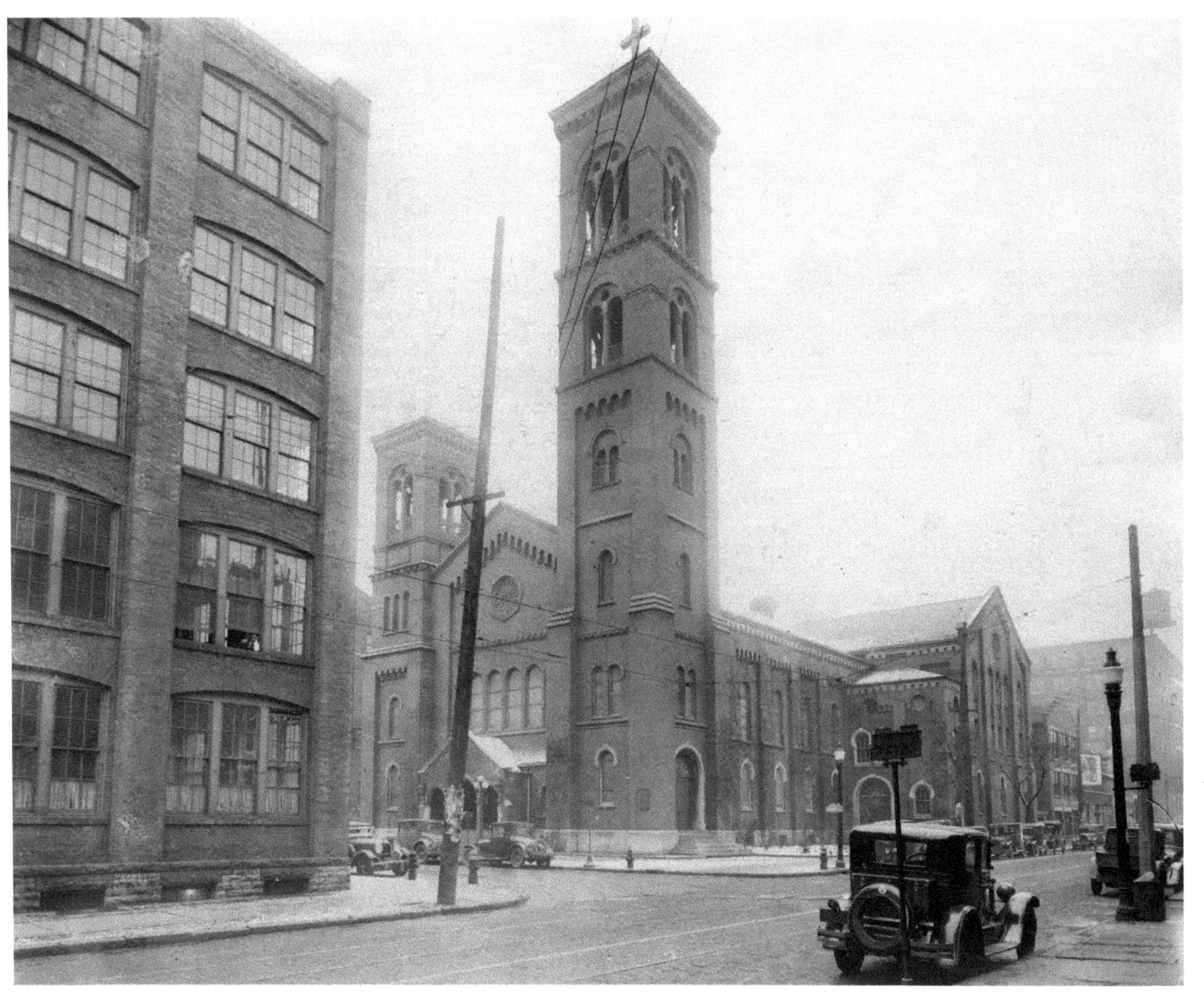

In this view looking southwest across Allen and Fitzhugh streets, the Brick Presbyterian Church is visible as it appeared around 1904. The north tower, with its ten-foot illuminated Roman Cross, replaced the Gothic steeples on top of the church destroyed by fire in 1903.

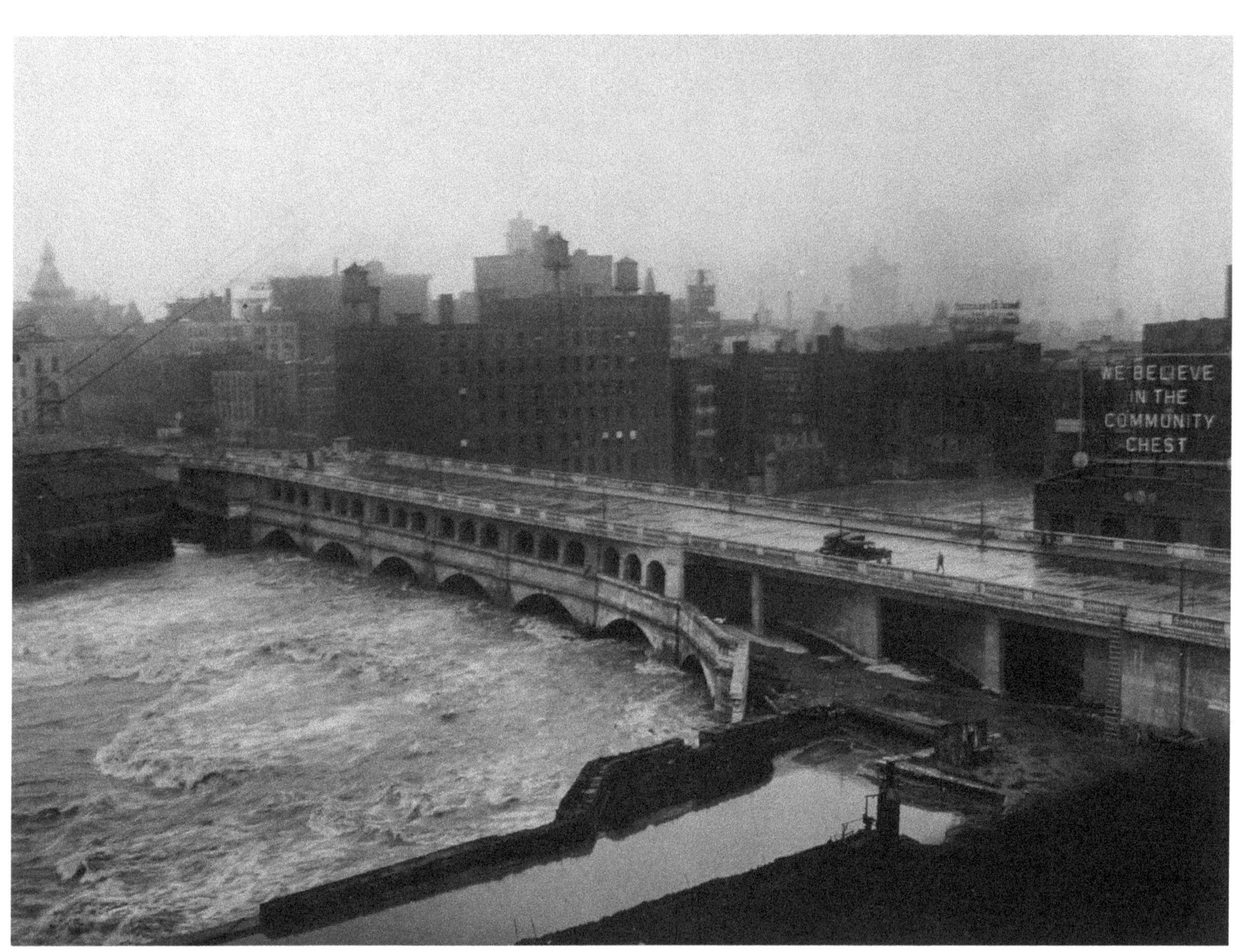

On this gloomy, rainy day in downtown Rochester, the stencil on the side of the building along the Broad Street Bridge declares, "We believe in the Community Chest" (predecessor of the United Way charity). It appears construction on the east side of the subway is still under way.

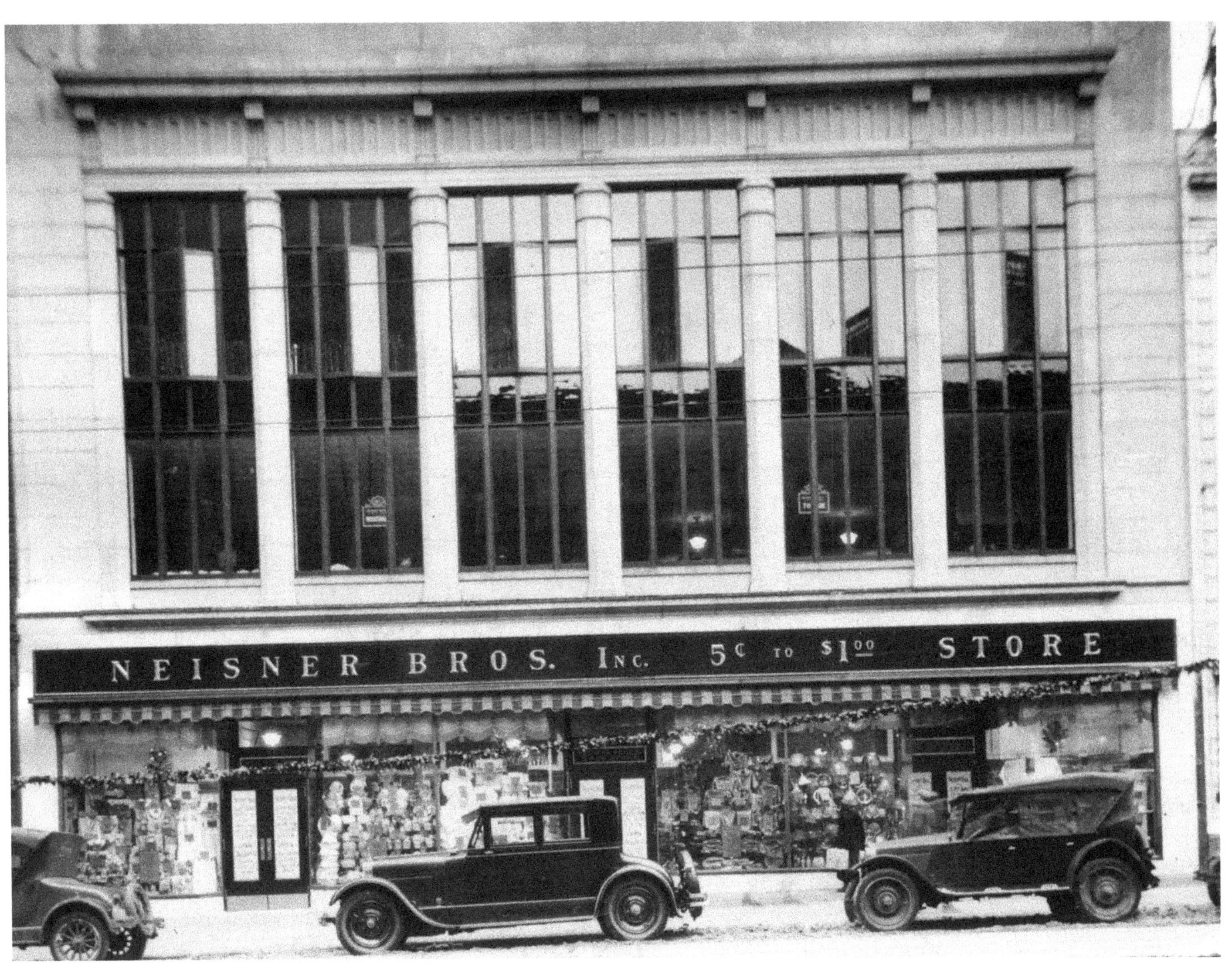

Abraham H. and Joseph M. Neisner started this discount variety store in 1911 in Rochester and franchised it four decades later in more than one hundred locations in the United States. Neisner's merged with Ames in 1978 and was bought out by McCrory's in 1980.

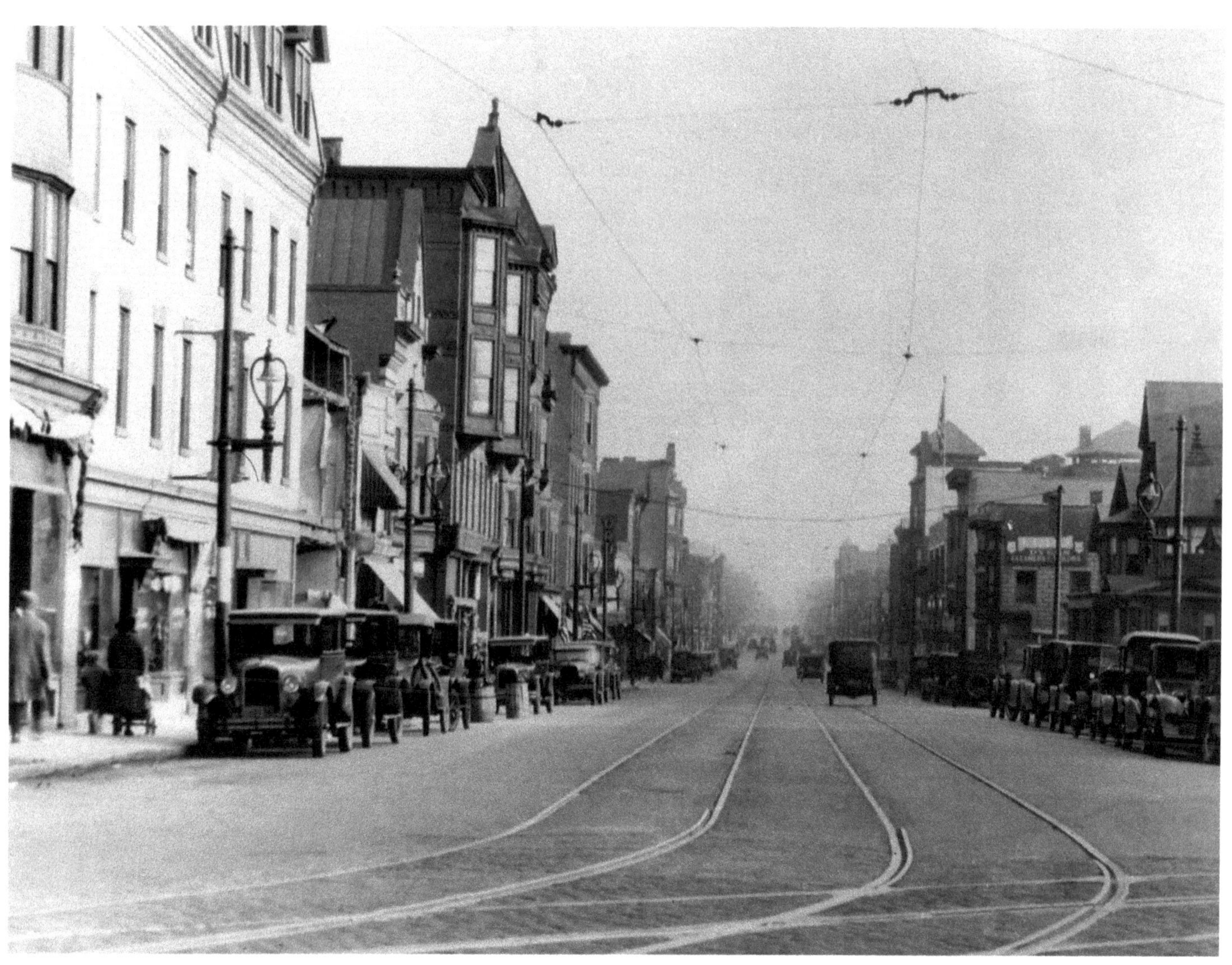

Looking southeast from the corner of South Clinton and Monroe avenues in the early 1920s.

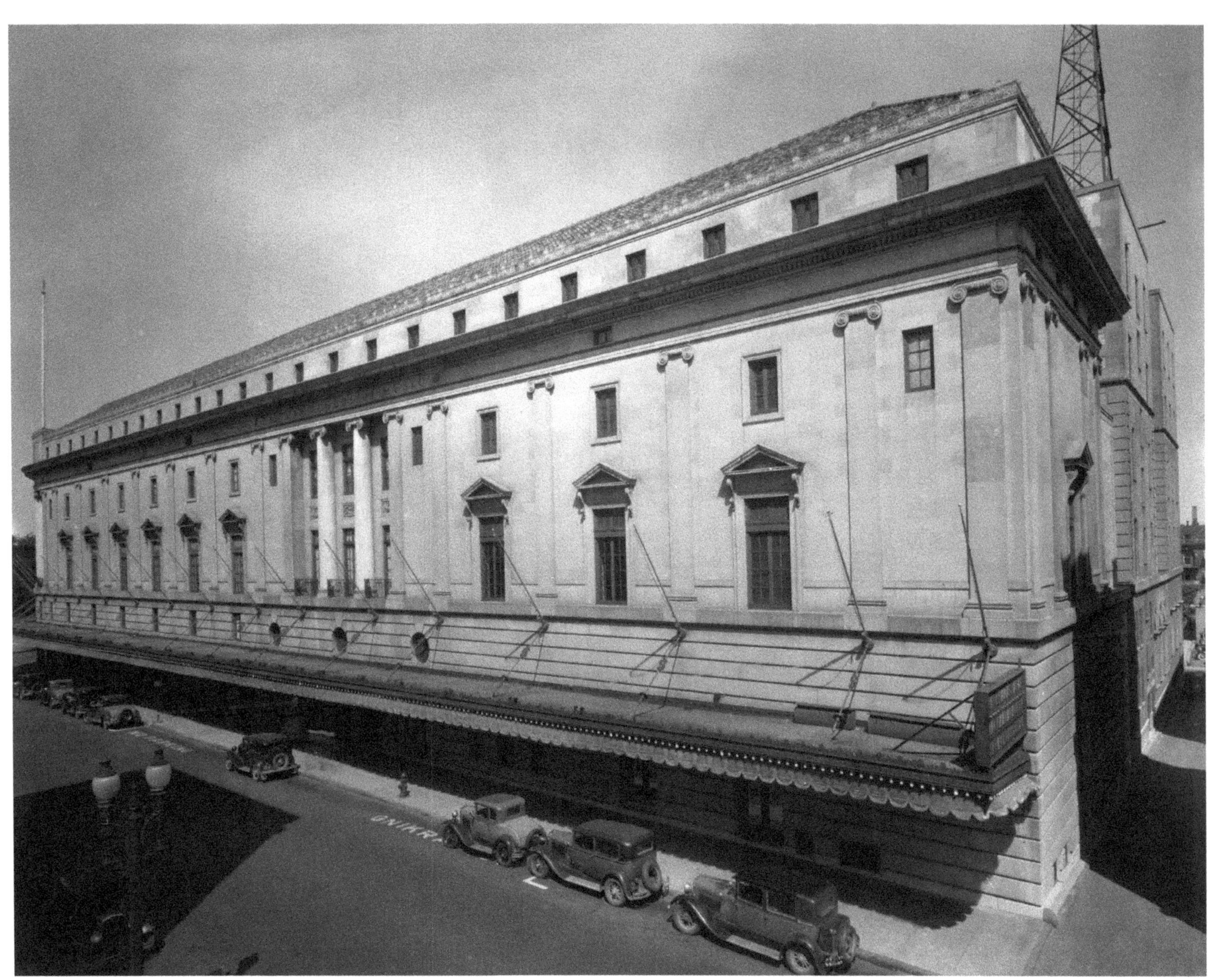

The Eastman School of Music, part of the University of Rochester, opened with the Eastman Theatre in 1921 on Gibbs Street at Main. The Eastman School often broadcast from WHAM Radio, whose tower can be seen in the background.

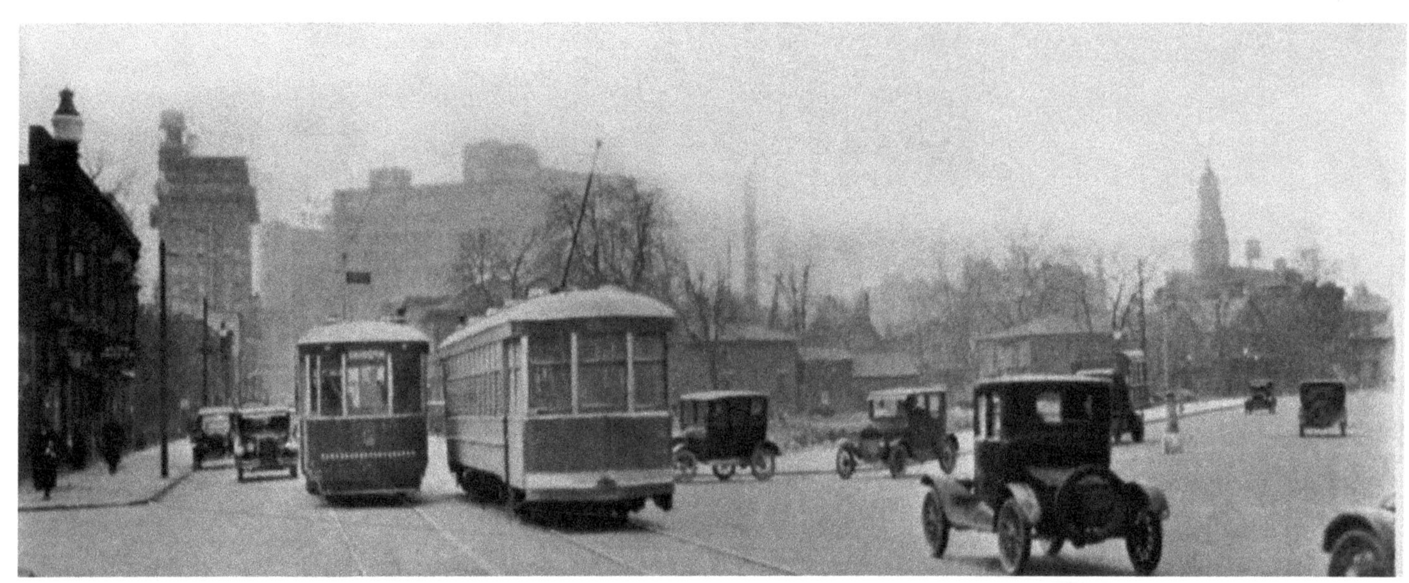

Streetcars and early automobiles pass through the intersection of Main and North streets around 1928.

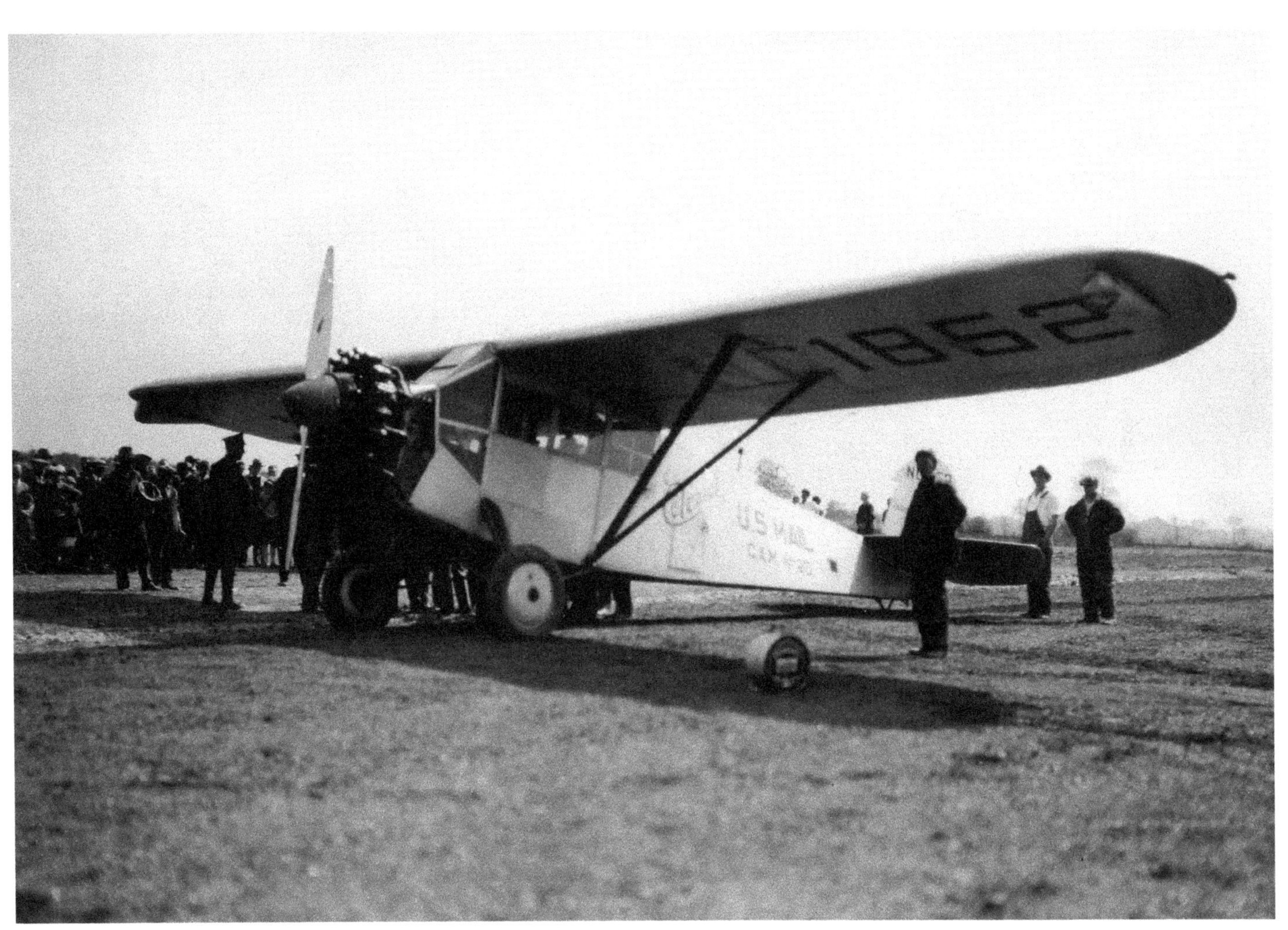

The first airmail was picked up in Rochester on June 1, 1928, after a test run. Early Rochester aviators demonstrated the usefulness of airplanes in the first two decades of the twentieth century. Regular passenger service was not far behind.

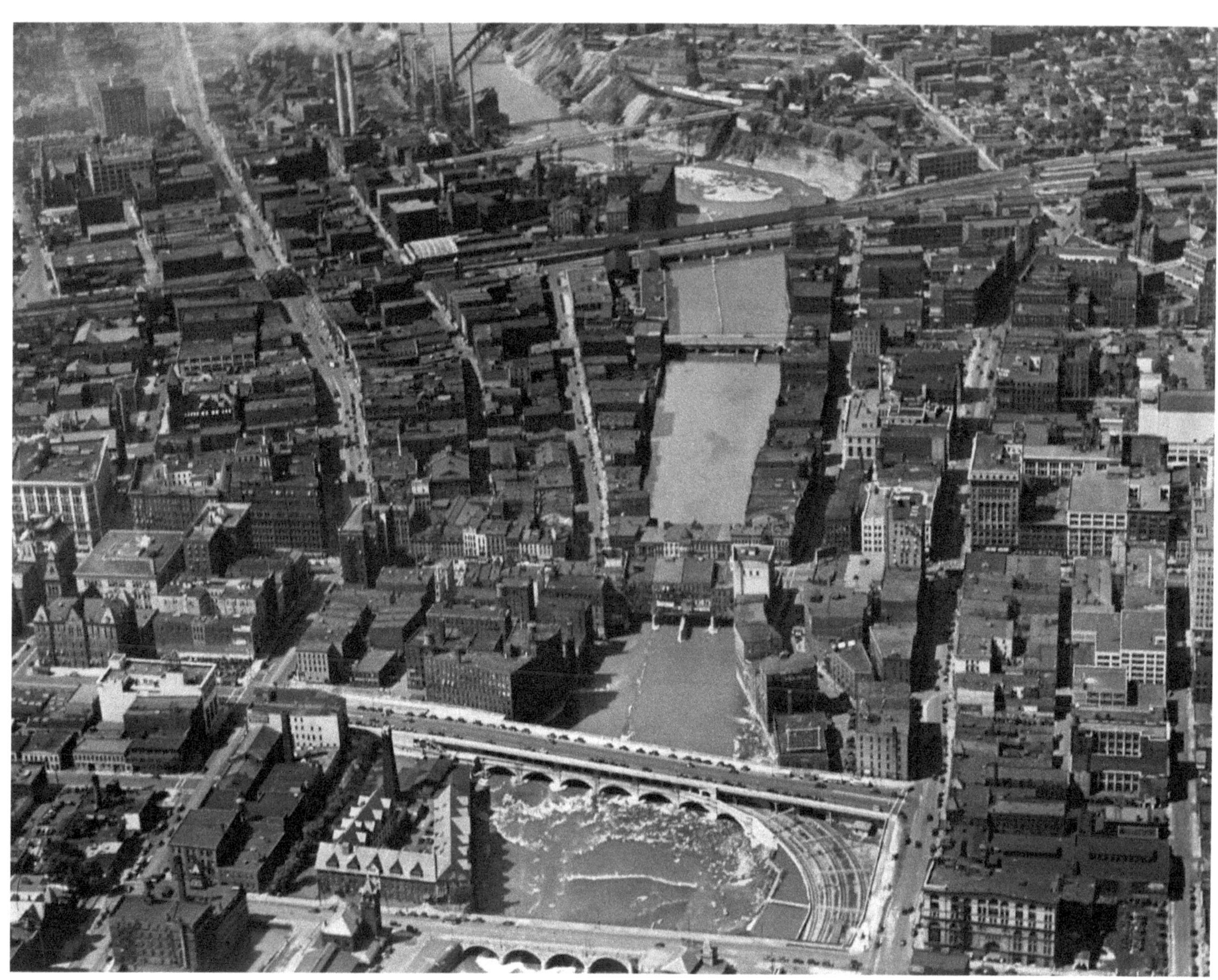

Cars had been passing over the Broad Street Bridge for less than a decade when this aerial photograph was taken over the Genesee River (ca. 1929). North of the Court Street Bridge (at bottom) are the Broad Street Bridge, the built-over Main Street Bridge, the New York Central Railroad Bridge, the Platt Street Bridge (today Pont de Rennes pedestrian bridge), and the RG&E footbridge near their old power-generating plant.

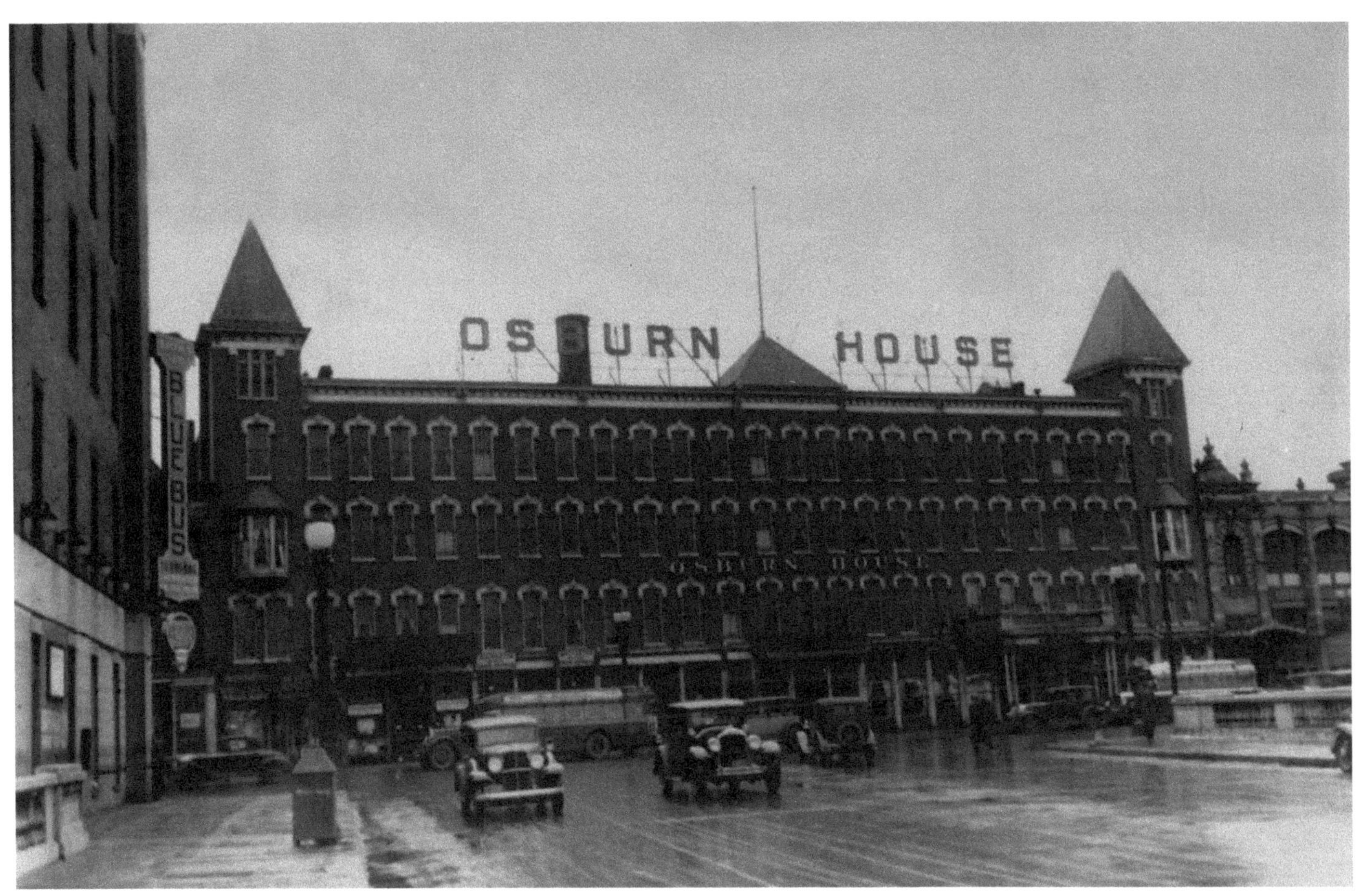

After its last season downtown in 1918, the Erie Canal was rerouted to cross the Genesee River at grade level south of the city in Genesee Valley Park. The old aqueduct was revamped for vehicular traffic and a subway was run along the old canal bed underneath the street. In the image, the Osburn Hotel stands where today Broad Street is extended. To the left is the Blue Bus Lines Terminal.

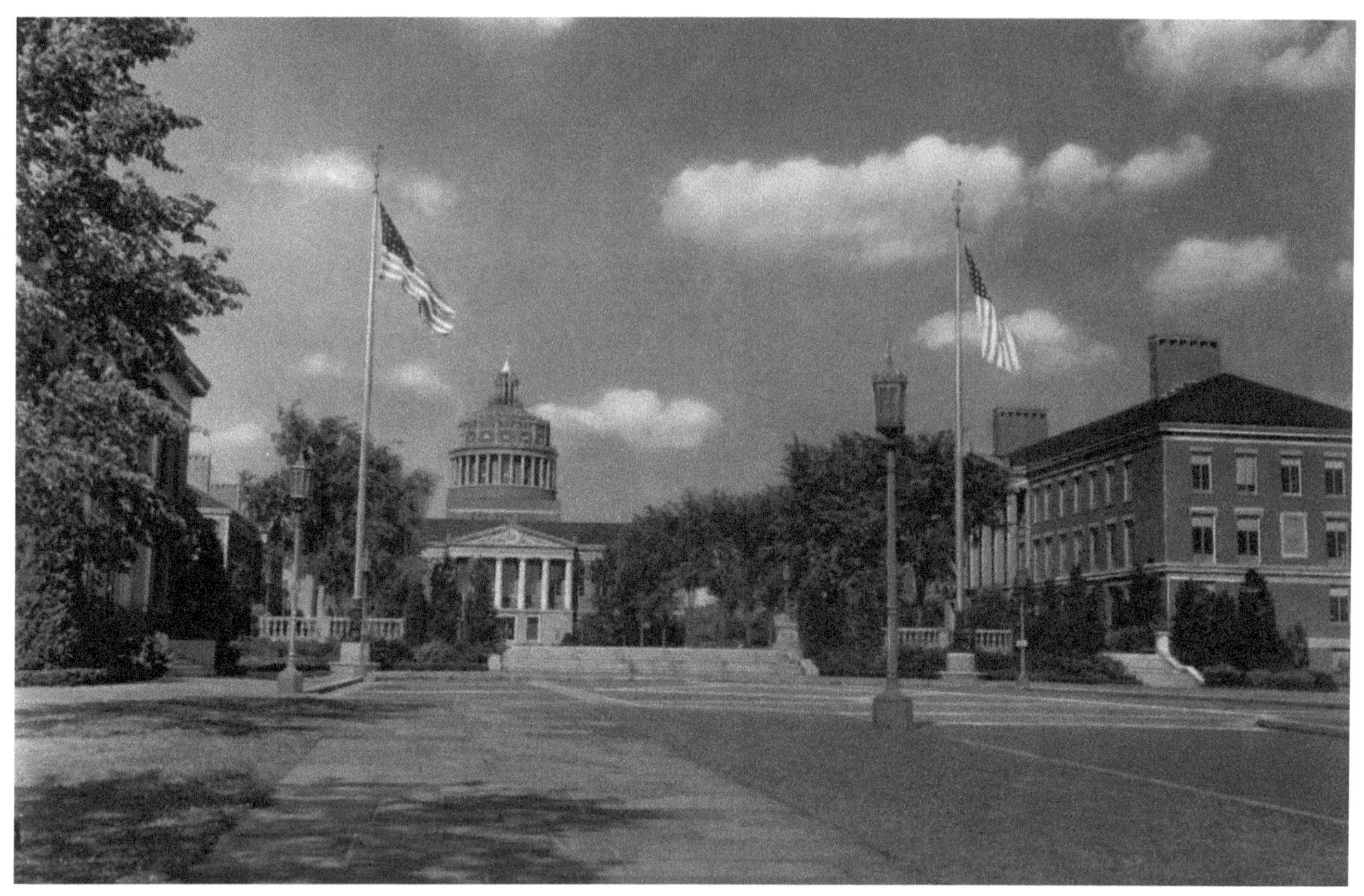

Founded in 1854, the University of Rochester began in downtown Rochester and later built a beautiful campus centered on Prince Street. The university moved in 1930 to the River Campus. The building with the dome in the center background is Rush Rhees Library, named for the man who served as president from 1900 to 1935. He persuaded Kodak founder George Eastman to donate millions of dollars to the university.

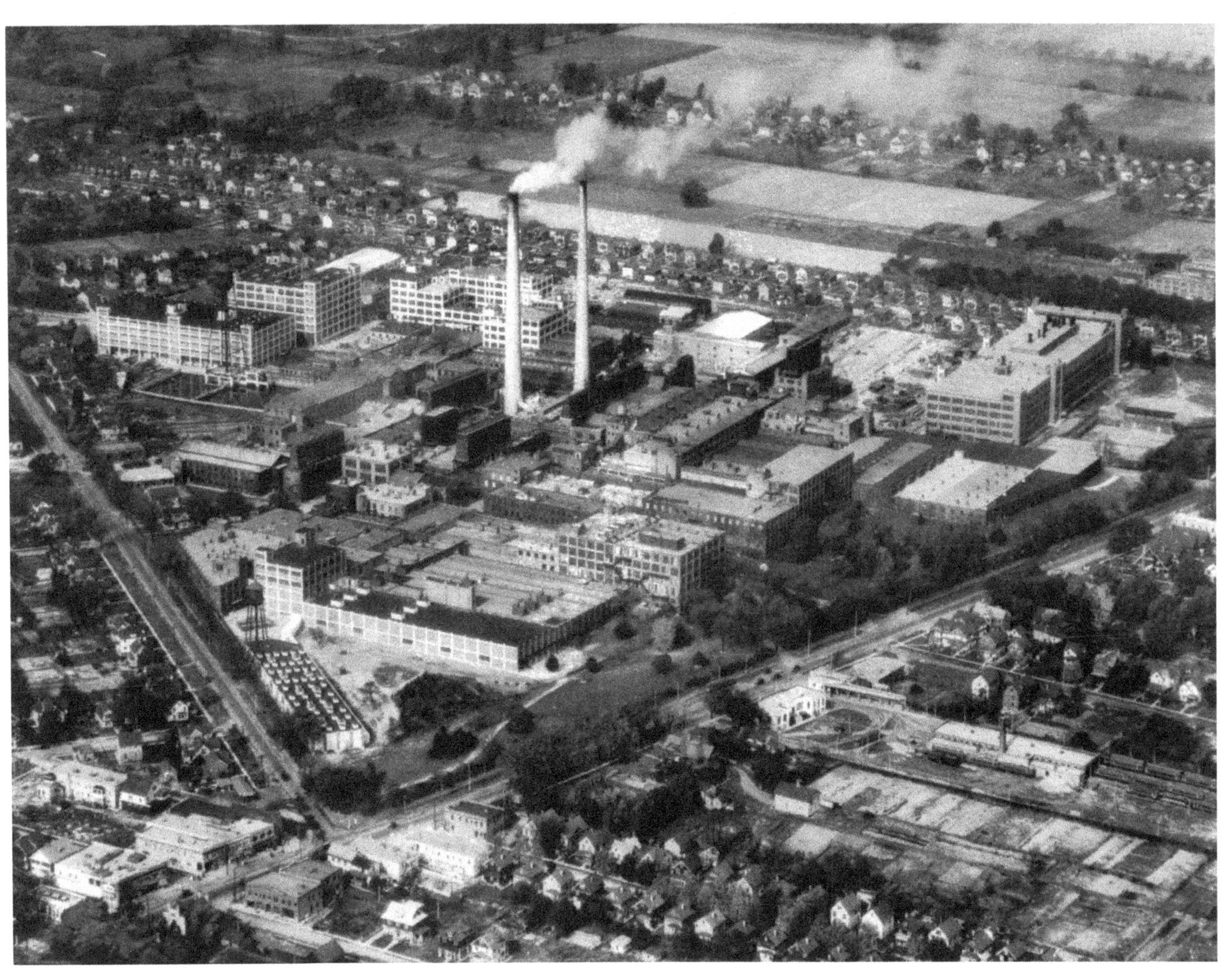

This aerial view of the city around Kodak Park shows the intersection of Lake Avenue on the right and Ridge Road on the left. At the time, Kodak was the chief employer in the Rochester area. Few people had not worked for Kodak or were not related to someone who did.

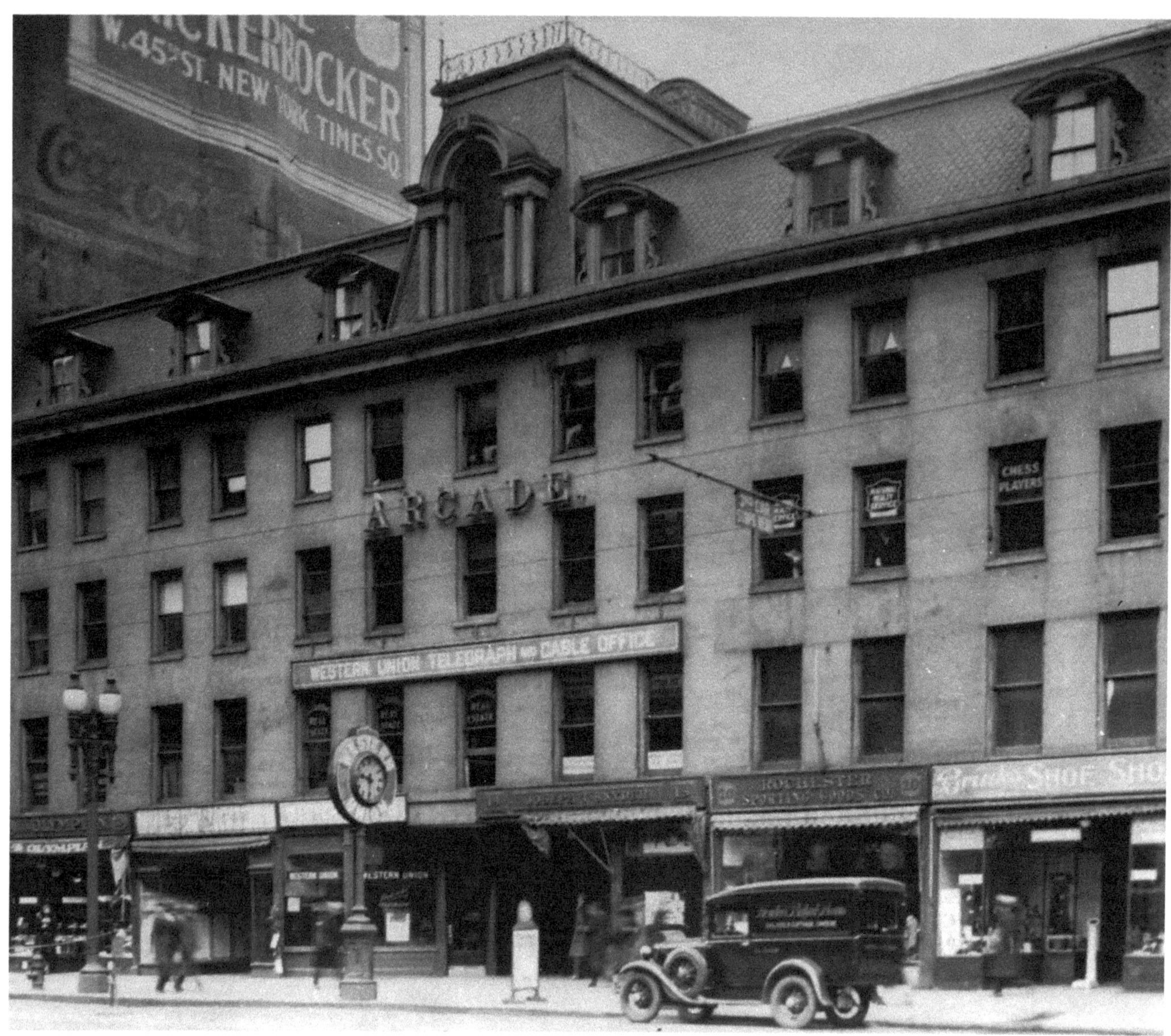

The first Reynolds Arcade was built by Abelard Reynolds in 1828. It was at the time the largest commercial building west of the Hudson River. It housed the first post office, Western Union Telegraph, Dewey Book Store, and the infant Bausch and Lomb Company. Many abolitionists and temperance advocates raised money there among the many businesses. This building was demolished in 1932 to make way for the art deco building by the same name that now stands on the site.

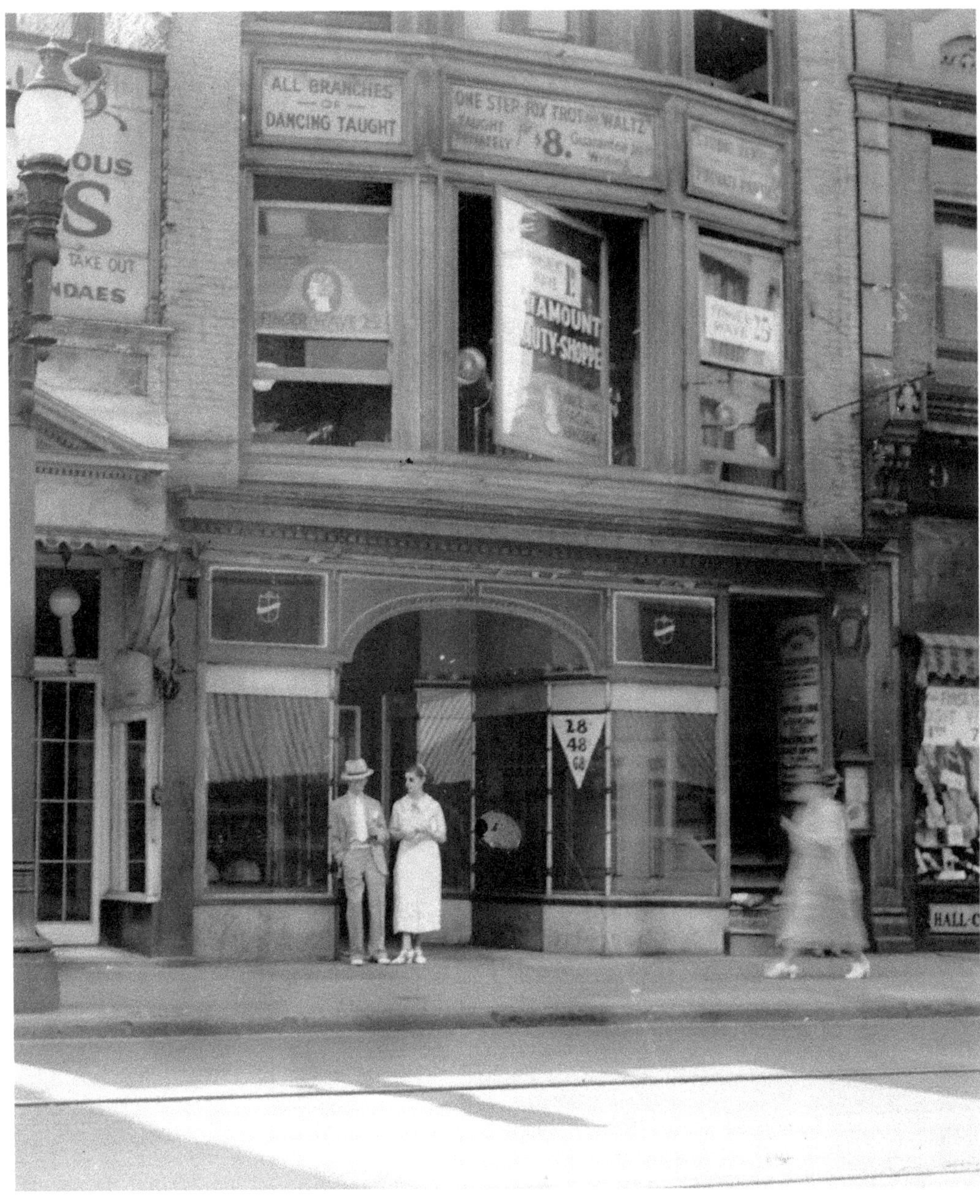

About 1935 a man and woman stand in front of No. 7 Clinton Avenue, where there was a beauty shop, a dance studio, and Hall-Covell men's furnishings. Clinton Avenue was also known at the time for its wonderful cinema theaters.

Known popularly as the Rochester Free Academy, this building on South Fitzhugh Street was first used as Rochester's first public high school in 1874. From 1905 to 1926, it housed city offices as the Municipal Building. The Rochester City School District began to use it after 1926. It stands next to the pioneer St. Luke and St. Simon Cyrene Episcopal Church (once St. Luke's Episcopal Church).

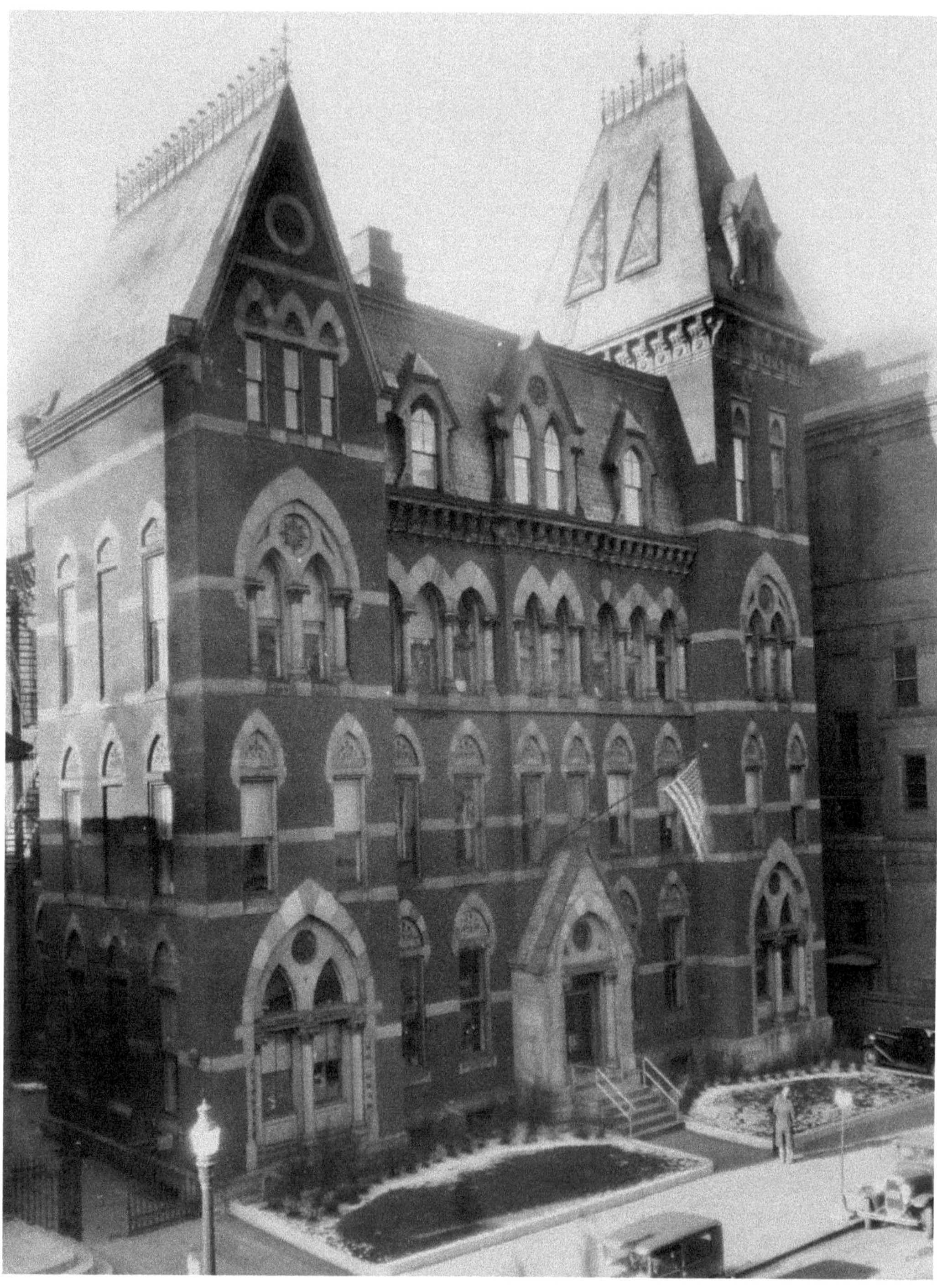

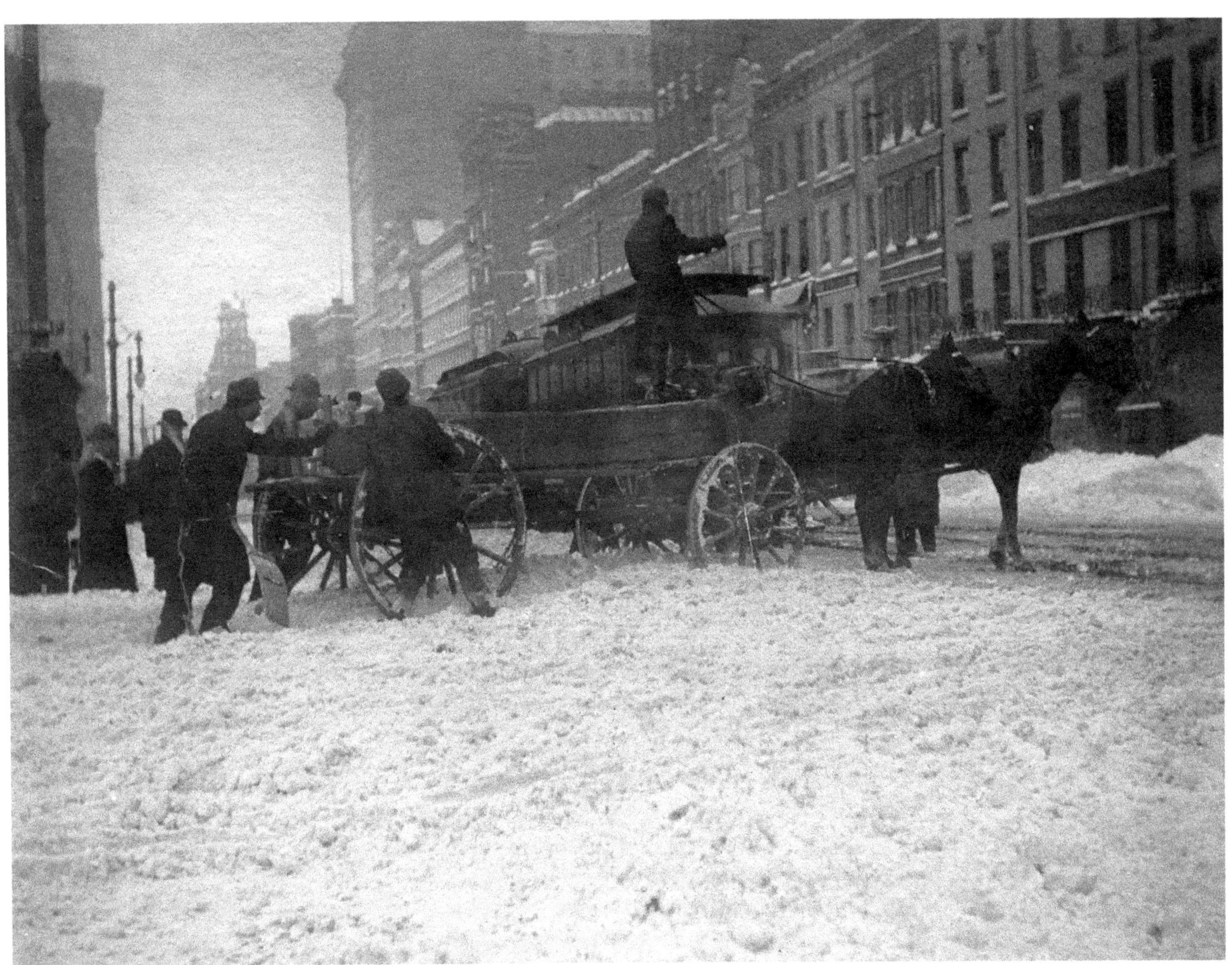

In the mid-1930s, men struggle to remove snow from downtown streets. Snowstorms were dreaded before the advent of powerful equipment to clear emergency paths for fire and ambulance vehicles. Excess snow was dumped over the bridges into the Genesee River. Some days the city was nearly brought to a stand-still. People today who complain about the inconvenience and damage wrought by snowstorms may have little idea what residents went through a century ago.

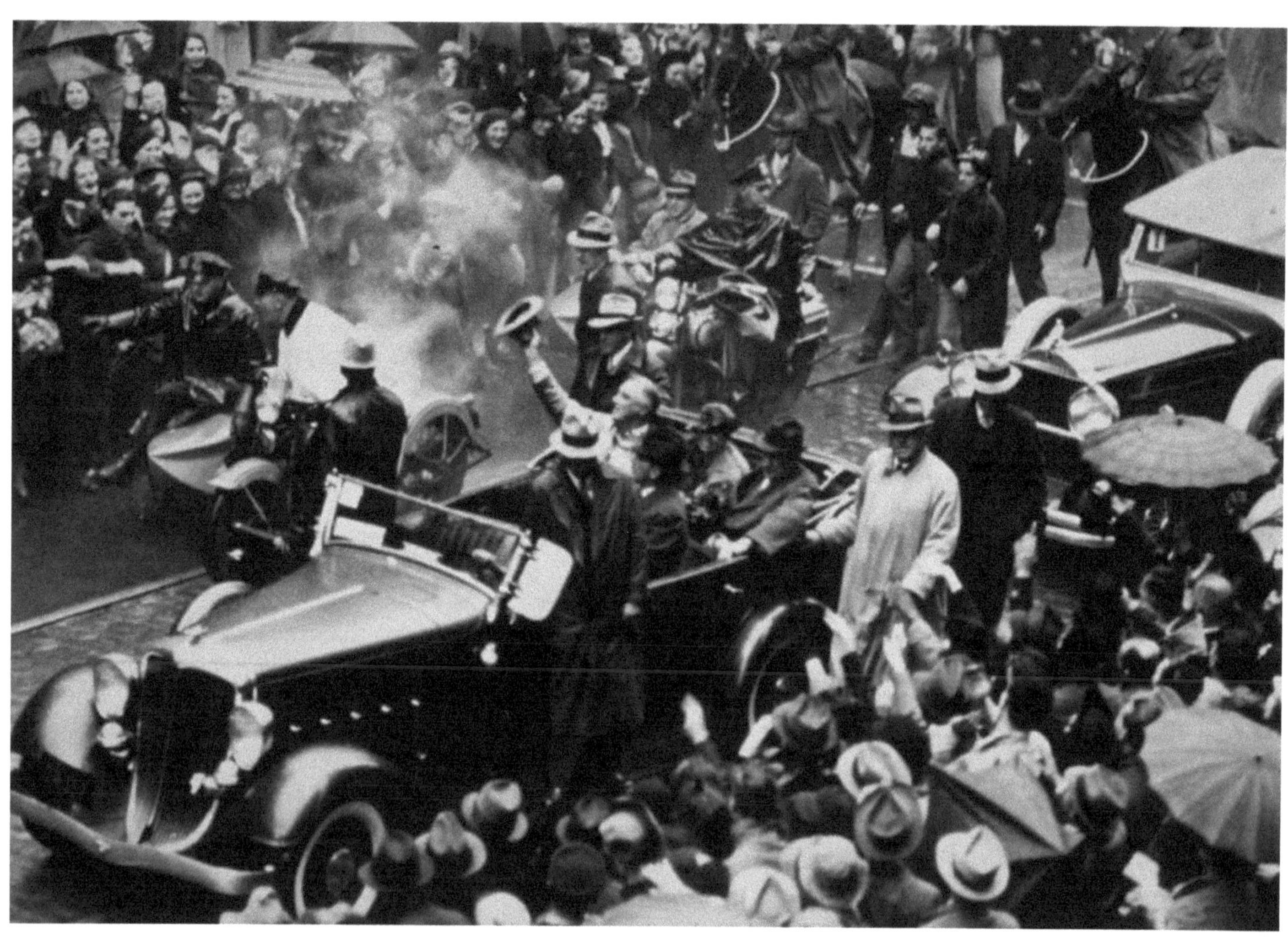

Secret Servicemen and patrolmen on motorcycles or horses flank the motorcade of President Franklin Delano Roosevelt and First Lady Eleanor Roosevelt in an October 1936 visit to Rochester. Despite a light rain, crowds turned out to greet the president, who was leading them through the Great Depression.

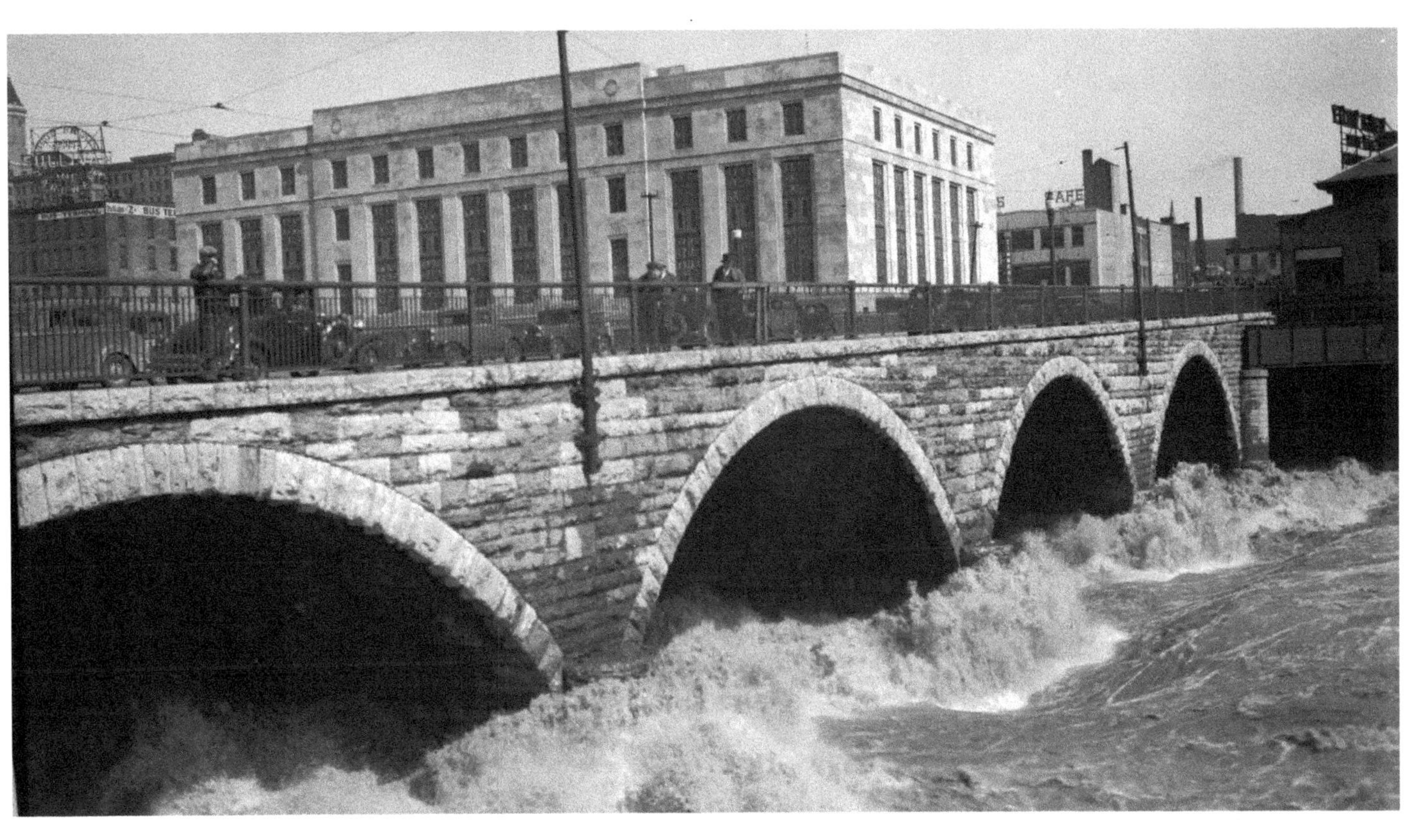

Pedestrians cross the Genesee River over the Court Street Bridge as water rushes against the supports. The Rochester Public Library in the Rundel Memorial Building stands (in the background) on metal supports above what was once the subway system, anchoring the south end of downtown.

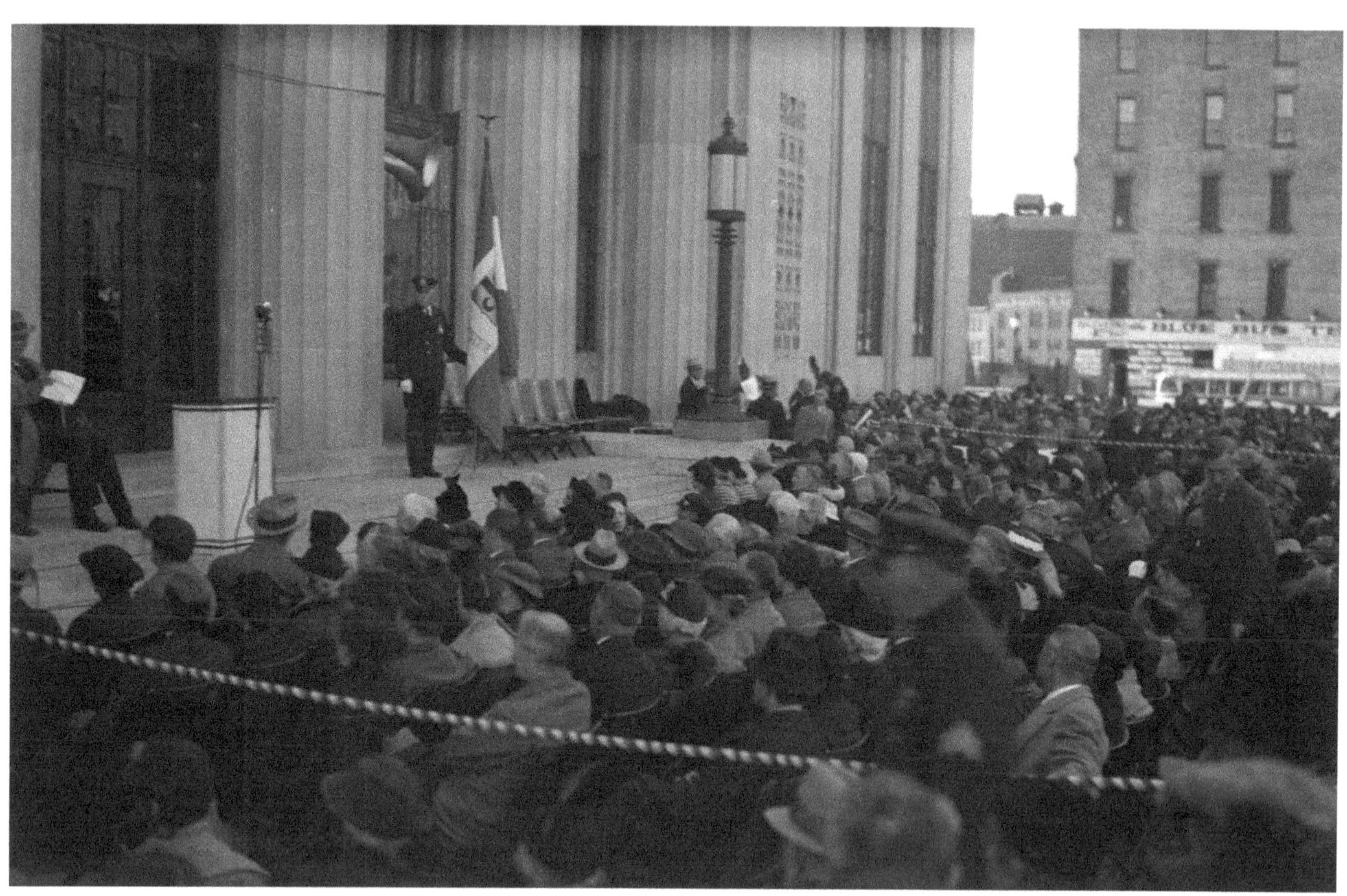

On October 4, 1936, the long awaited Rochester Public Library was dedicated in the Rundel Memorial Building at South Avenue between Broad and Court streets. The library system was unusual in that it had branch libraries long before it had this central library. Many people who had either lost their employment or needed to retrain for other jobs, trained themselves through the library's facilities.

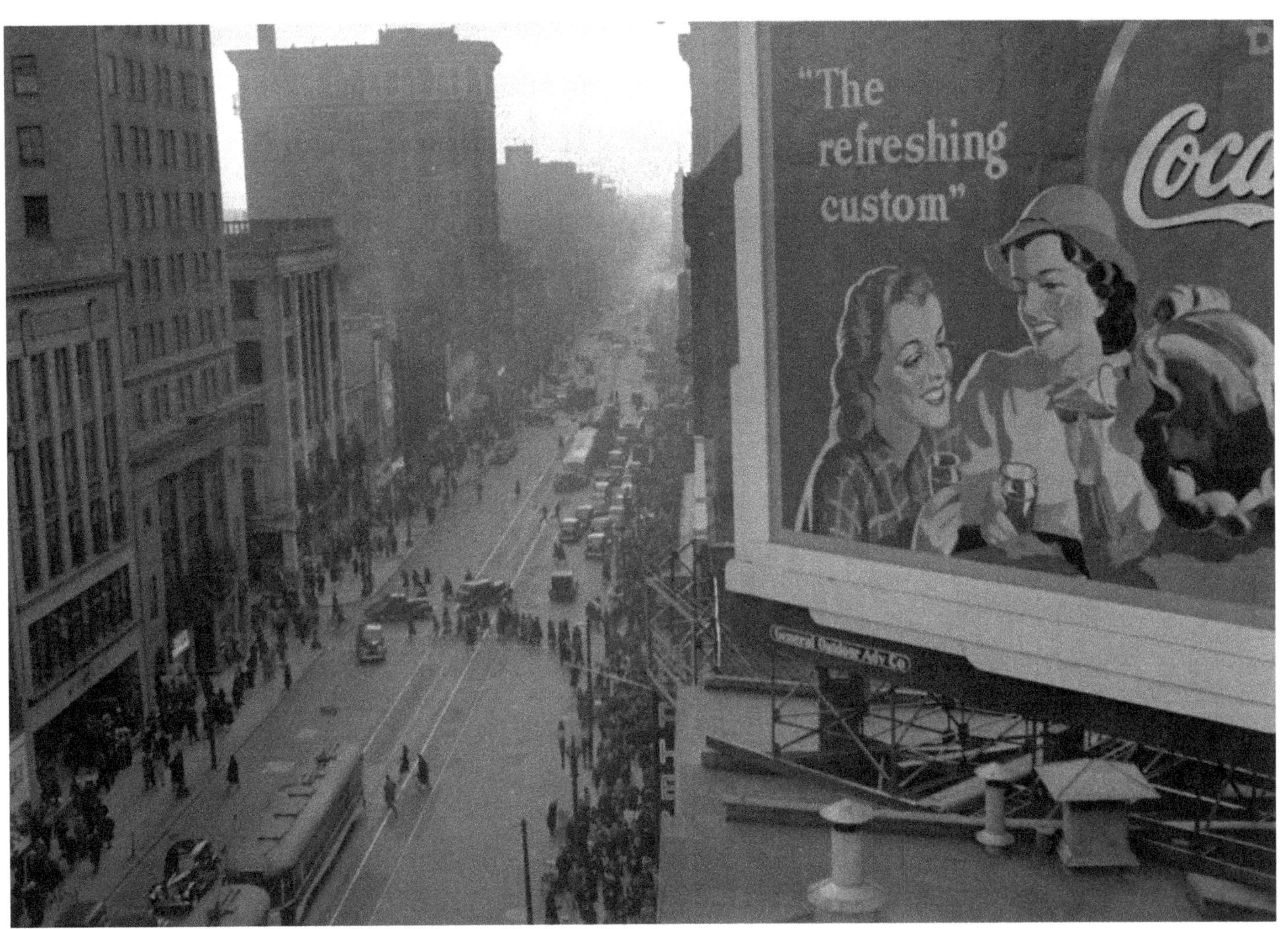

In this view looking west down East Main Street from the Sibley Building in the late 1930s, a large Coca Cola billboard establishes that the soft drink has become "the refreshing custom" in American life. On the street, pedestrians are busy shopping and running errands among the streetcars and automobiles. The Lincoln Alliance Bank Building stands tall on the left. The next building is the National Clothing Company. The farthest building is the Commerce Building, also known as the Keeler Building.

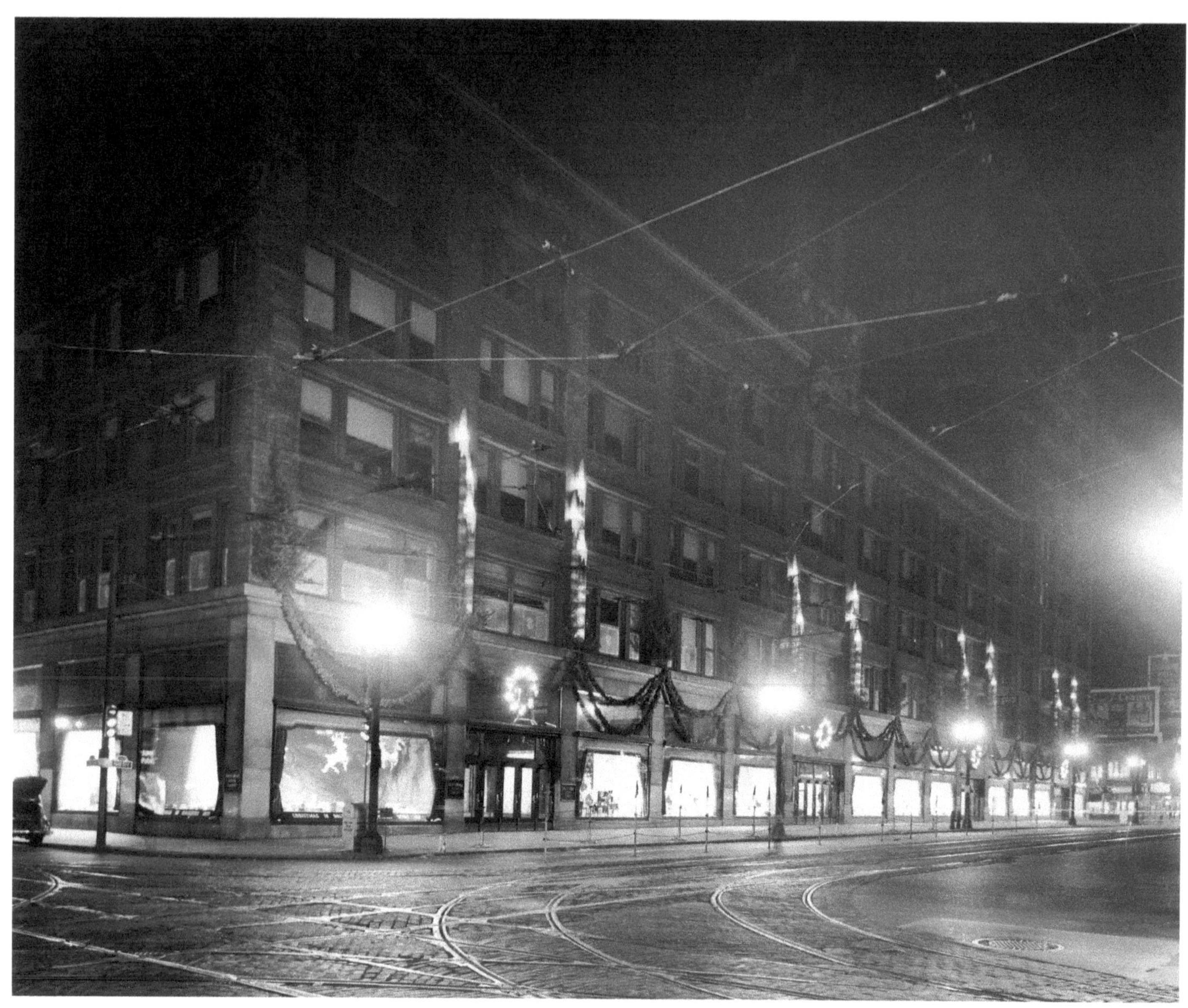

The Sibley, Lindsay and Curr Department Store at night around Christmas 1939, showing Christmas a century earlier in the window displays. The store was a success from its beginning in 1868. The store expanded downtown and in 1893 moved into the Granite Building, where it remained until the great Sibley fire of 1904 gutted the building. The business then moved to a new location on Main Street between Clinton and North streets, pulling the hub of downtown farther east.

United to Win the War

(1940–1949)

Since the mid-1930s when Hitler overran one country after another, Rochester citizens had watched with great interest. After Japan's unprovoked surprise attack on Pearl Harbor on December 7, 1941, America's military response was swift and the draft that followed quickly filled the quota.

Some local companies retooled to produce war materiel and added more shifts. As the war progressed, production in some factories went forward twenty-four hours a day, seven days a week. The draft and enlistments created a manpower shortage. Women and minorities were encouraged by factories to apply. Women began to wear blue jeans to work and rode bicycles to save on rationed gas. Posters calling on women to show their patriotism by working, portrayed women like "Rosie the Riveter." Workplaces set up drop-off daycare to reduce employee absence.

Kodak showed its support of embattled England by keeping its plant there at Harrow, calling on American company employees to take in children of the English workers. About 156 children came to Rochester between autumn of 1940 and the end of the war.

As supplies of materials like metal and paper fell short, scrap drives were launched. Schoolchildren pulling their wagons collected scrap. Bond drives were held and rationing of gas, butter, some meats, even tires and machine parts, was gladly endured by citizens eager to show their patriotism.

High school students as well as Italian and German POWs harvested the orchards and fields in the surrounding area. Migrant workers, who in previous years harvested in the area, took jobs in factories vacated by "workers turned soldier."

Rationing, long work hours, and the long years of war finally gave way to incremental victories—then VE and VJ days. Celebrations erupted spontaneously in the streets as the news of victory was learned. Plans in Rochester were made to house returning soldiers, some in the vacated POW barracks at Cobb's Hill Park. Veterans' educational benefits allowed former soldiers in record numbers to earn a college degree or get skilled training. Though building materials remained in short supply for a few years following the war, new housing was built in the suburbs, forecasting the changes and growth to come in the decade of the baby boomers.

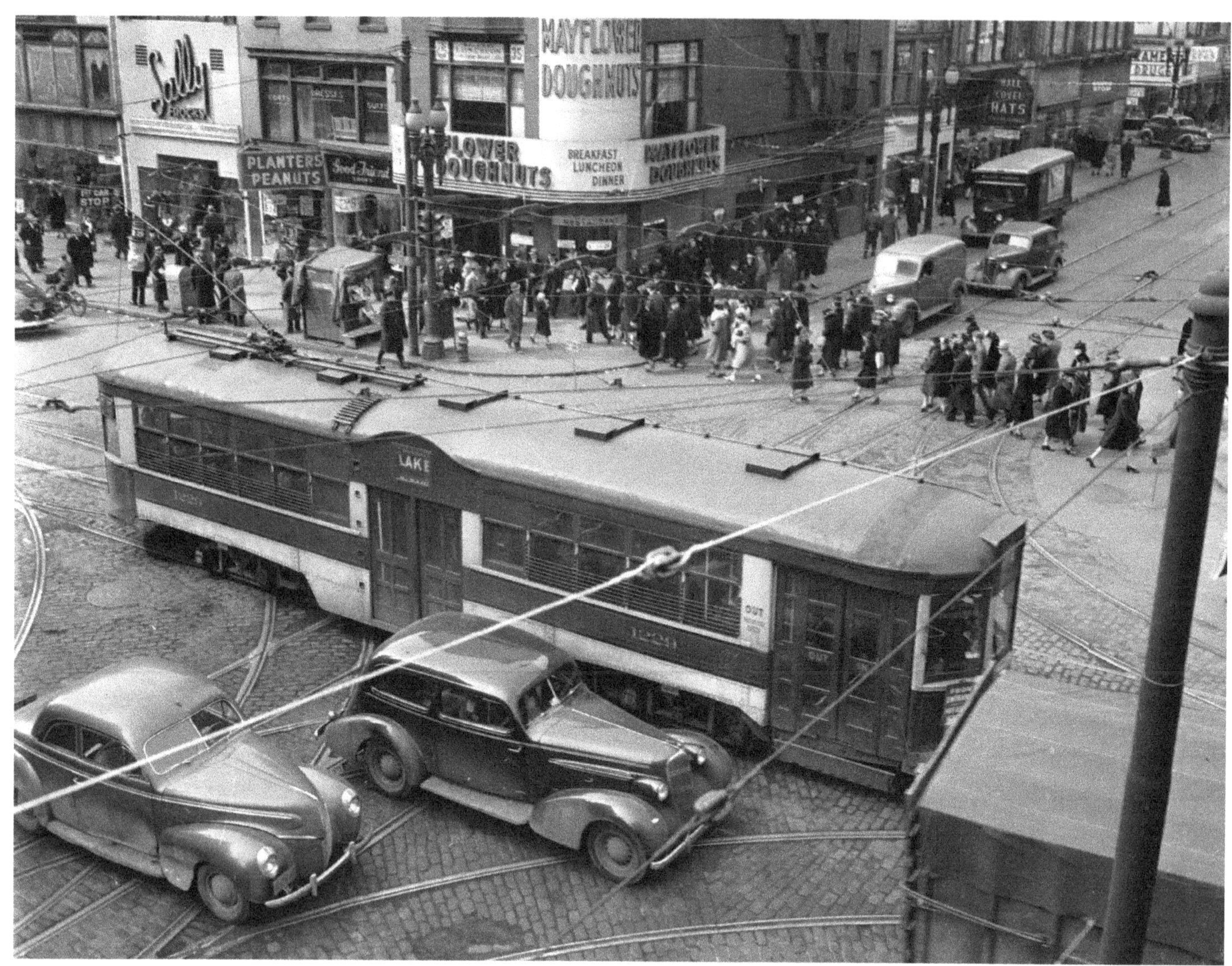

On the brink of World War II, the streets of downtown Rochester at the intersection of Main Street and South Clinton Avenue are busy with shoppers, cars, delivery trucks, and streetcars. Tracks crisscrossing around the cobbled roads point up continuing reliance on the streetcar.

Several people look at the photographer as they board the streetcar on East Main Street about 1941. The driver must watch carefully for anyone in the roadway. The sign near the door says, "Front entrance—Pay as you enter." Neisner Brothers Dime Store and Stephen's Women's Clothing are visible at right.

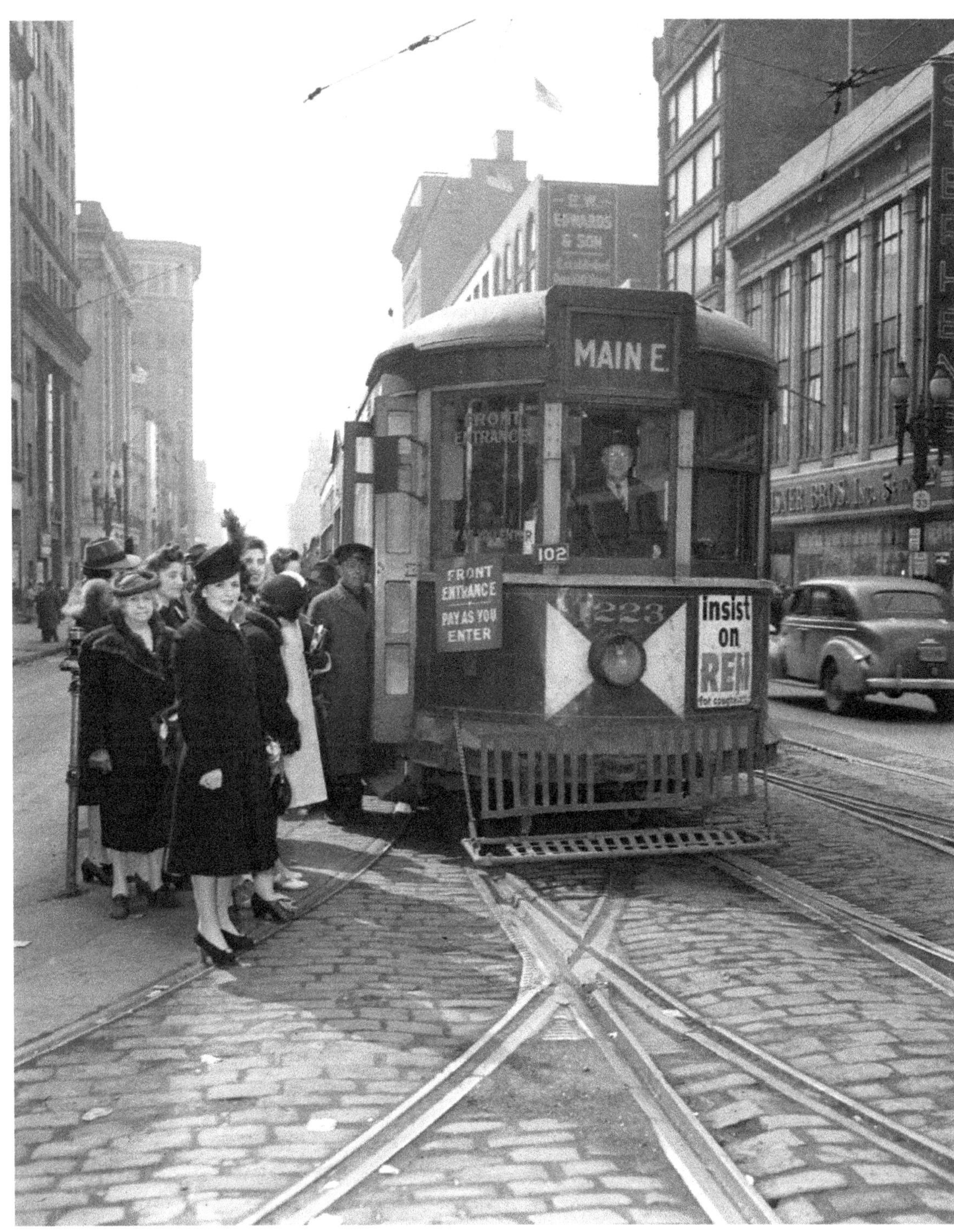

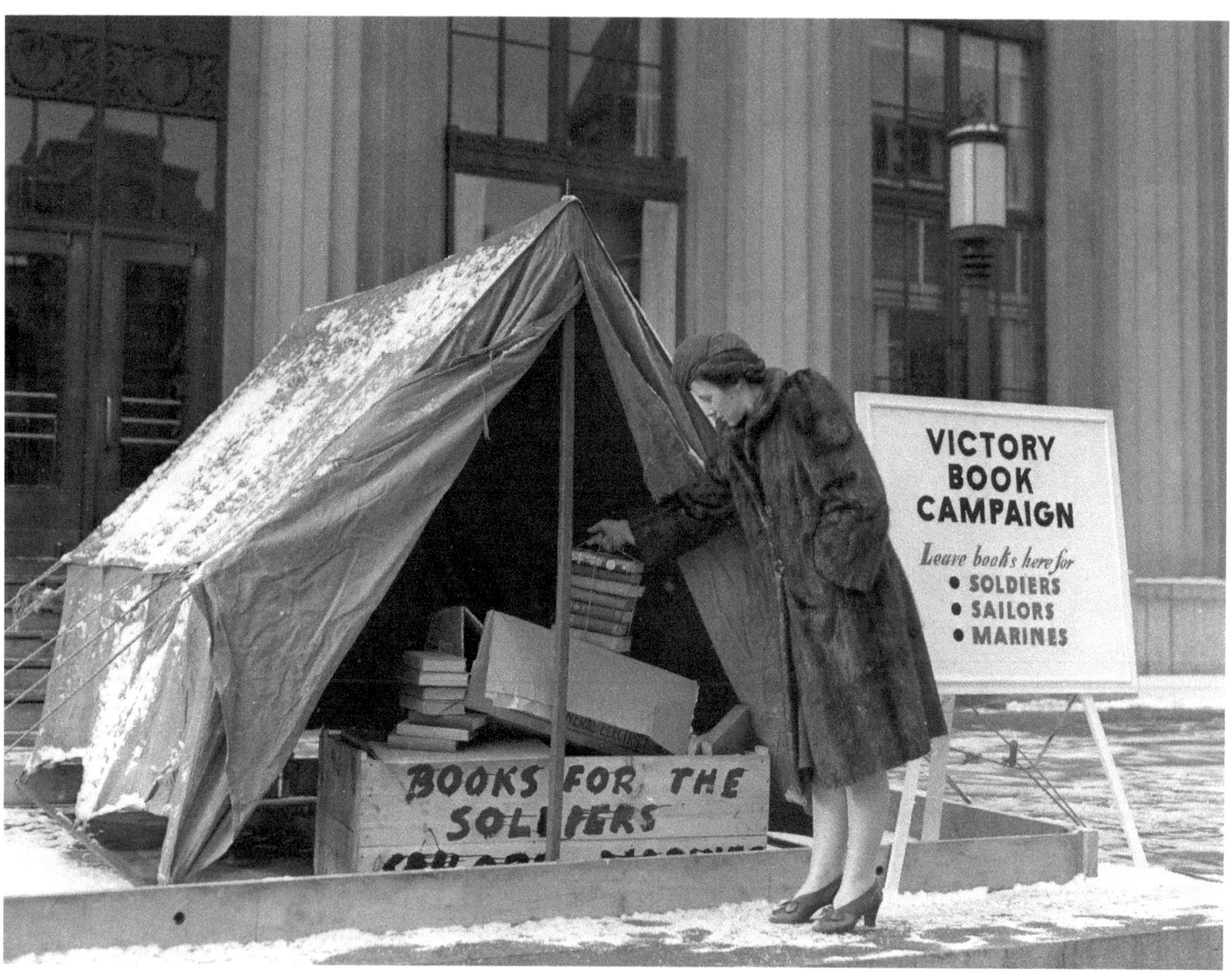

Mrs. Robert McGlashan places her donated books into the tent set up for the "Victory Book Campaign." Similar drop-off points were set up at libraries throughout the area. Between January 12 and 24, 1942, the joint effort of the American Library Association, American Red Cross, and the United Service Organization sought to collect ten million books. Three million were reportedly gathered. People continued to donate after the campaign ended.

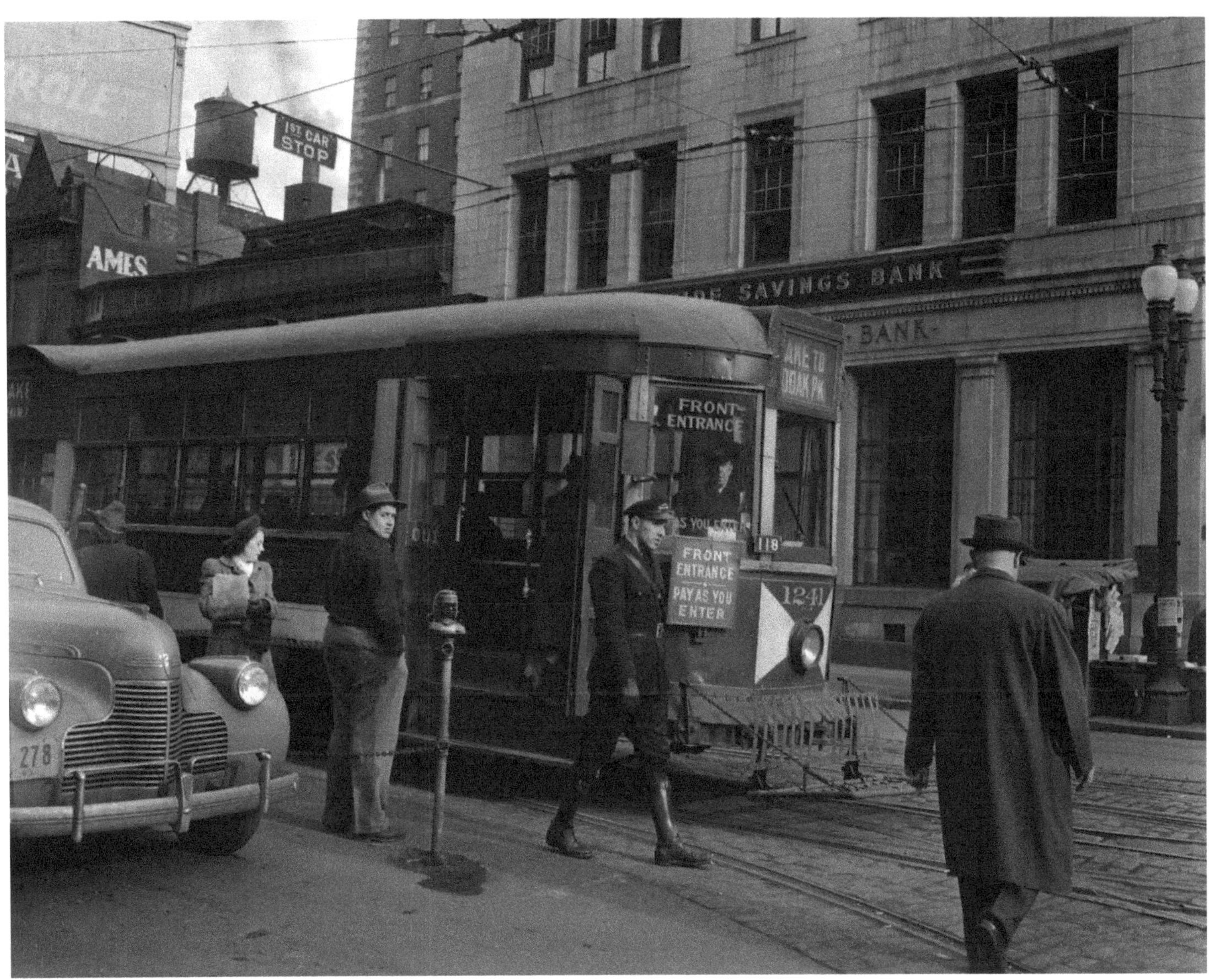

A motorcycle policeman strides past a streetcar on East Main Street near Clinton Avenue. The Monroe Savings Bank is seen across the street. Streetcar drivers had to be very alert to pedestrians such as the man crossing the street in the foreground. Passengers boarded in the street and were sometimes struck by the streetcar or other vehicles as they crossed to the sidewalk.

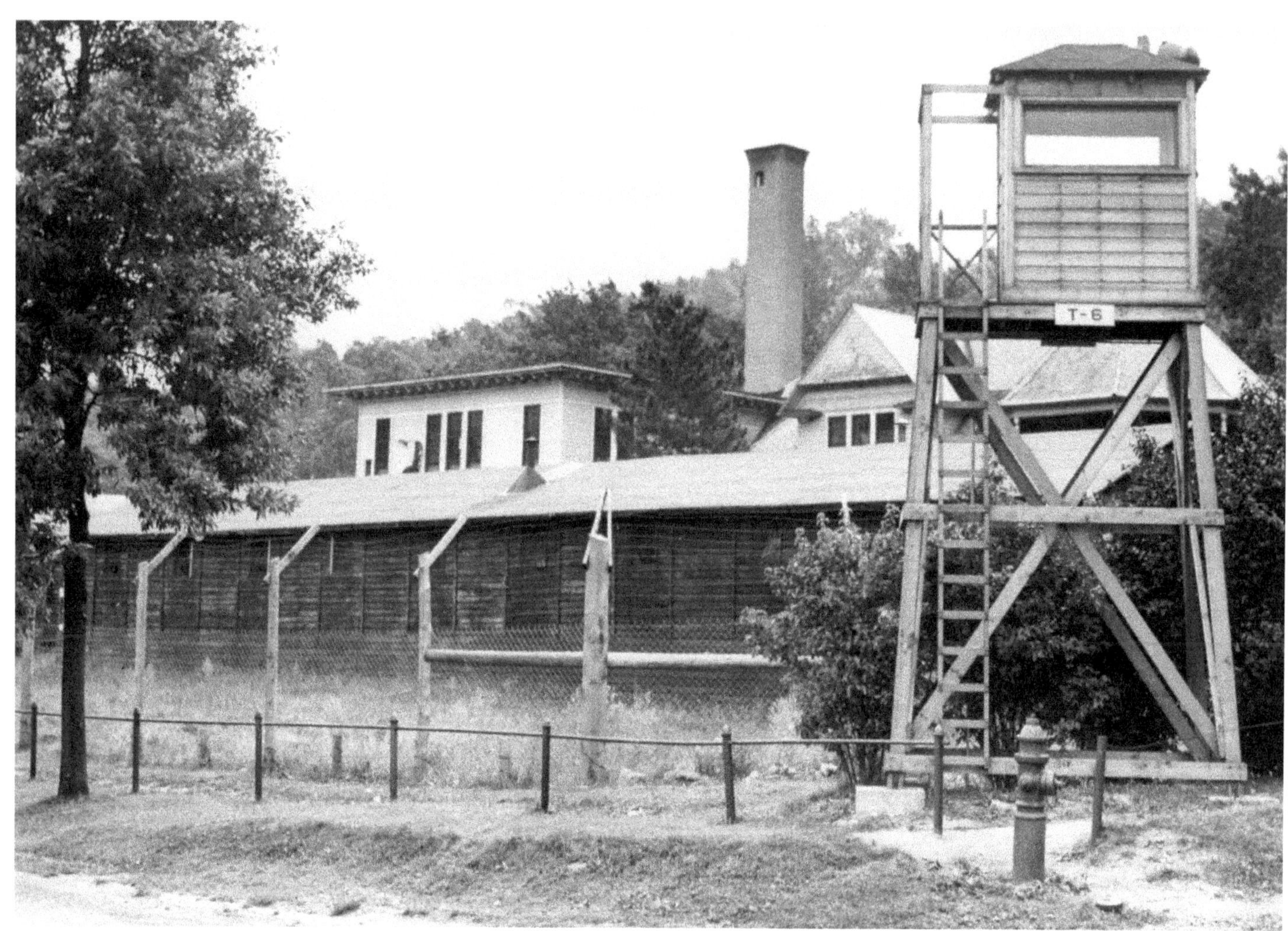

The Prisoner of War camp at Cobb's Hill was one of three in western New York including those at Hamlin and Romulus. At Christmas the German prisoners of war sang Christmas carols with Americans of German ancestry on the other side of the fence. Germans took part in work in the area including farming and snow removal.

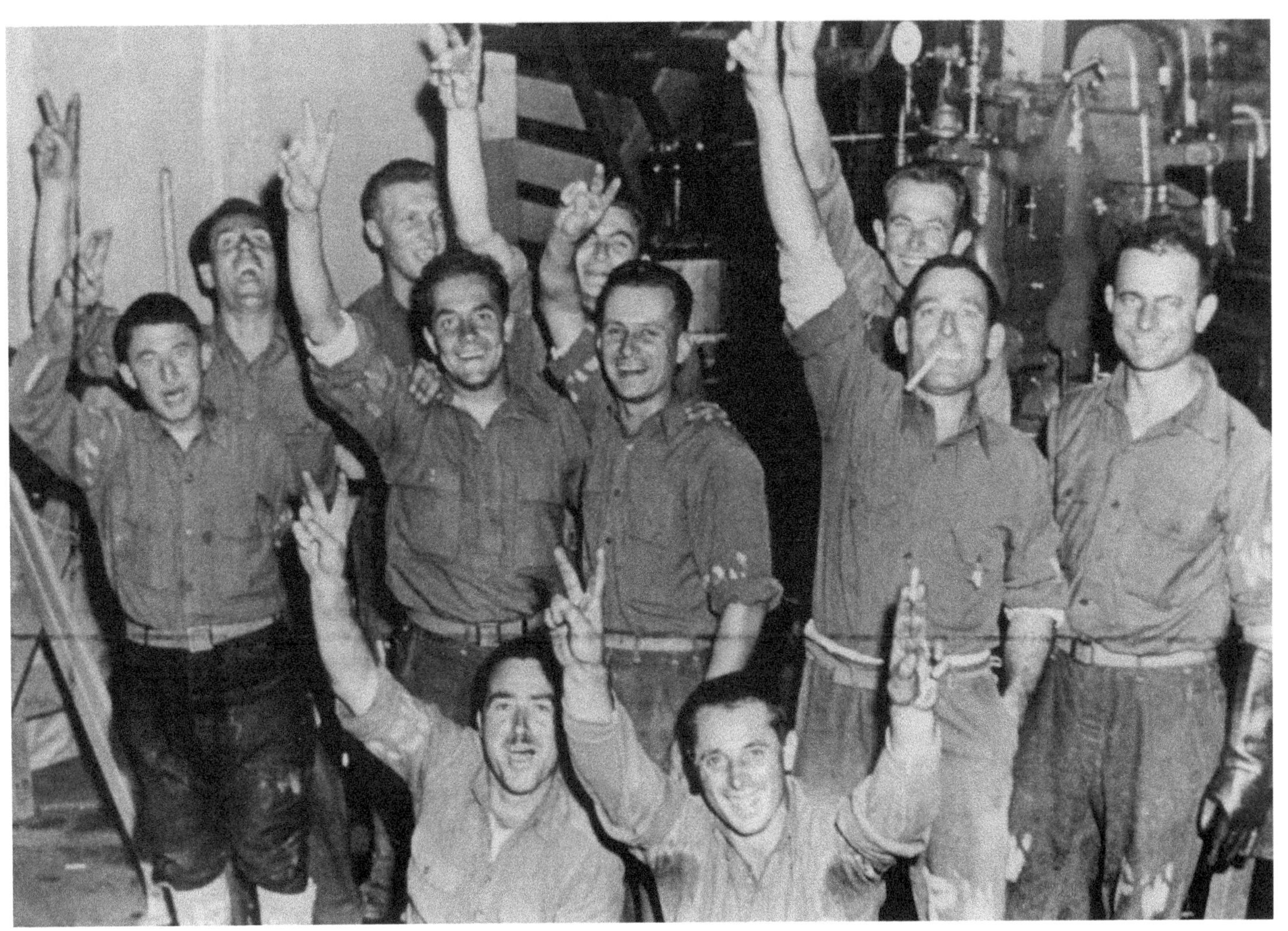

German prisoners of war detained at Cobb's Hill in Rochester in 1944 raise the sign of victory as they hope for the end to World War II.

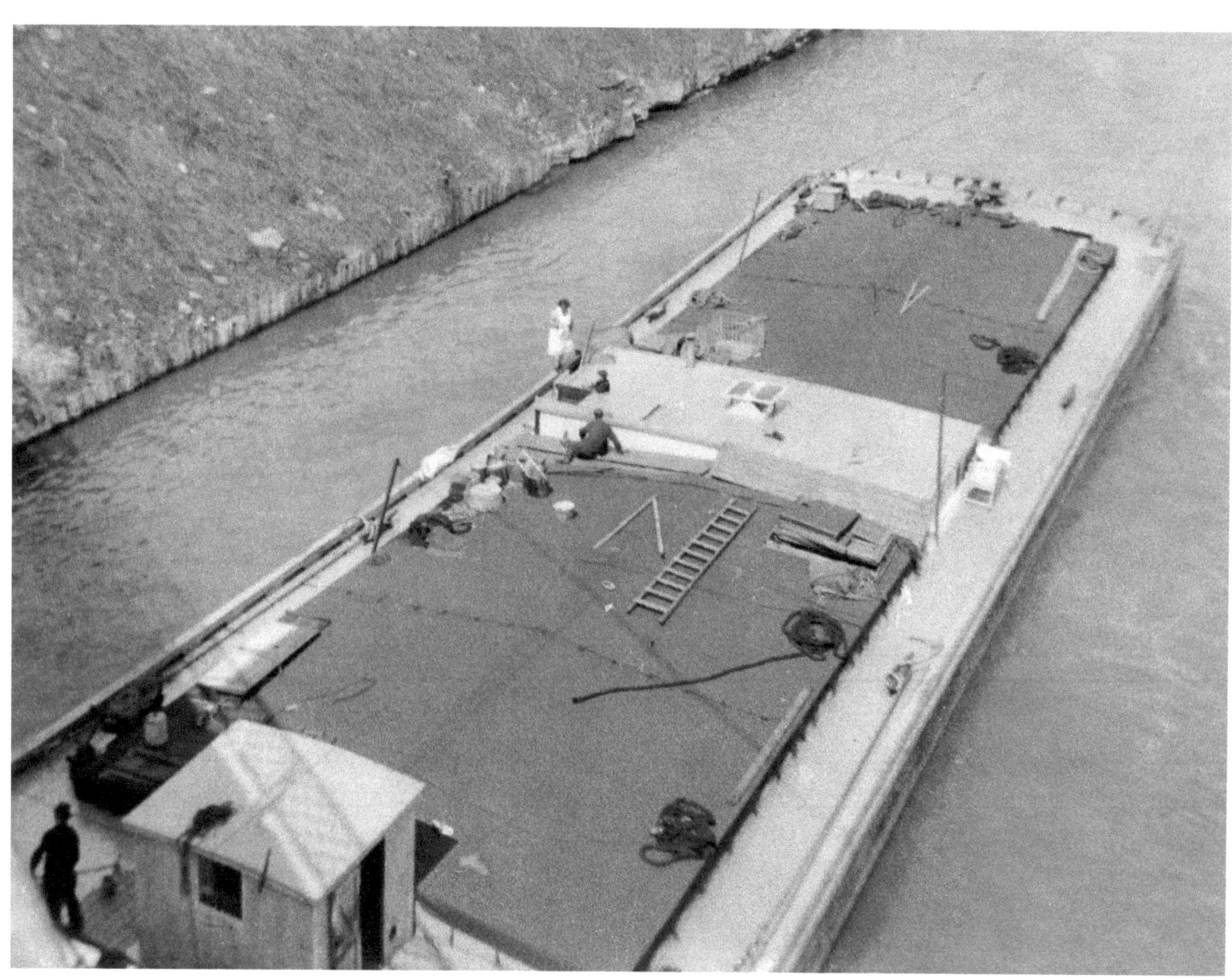

In 1943 a barge passes along on the New York State Barge Canal at an unnamed location. The canal played an important role in transporting war materials cheaply when the war demanded fuel conservation and rationing.

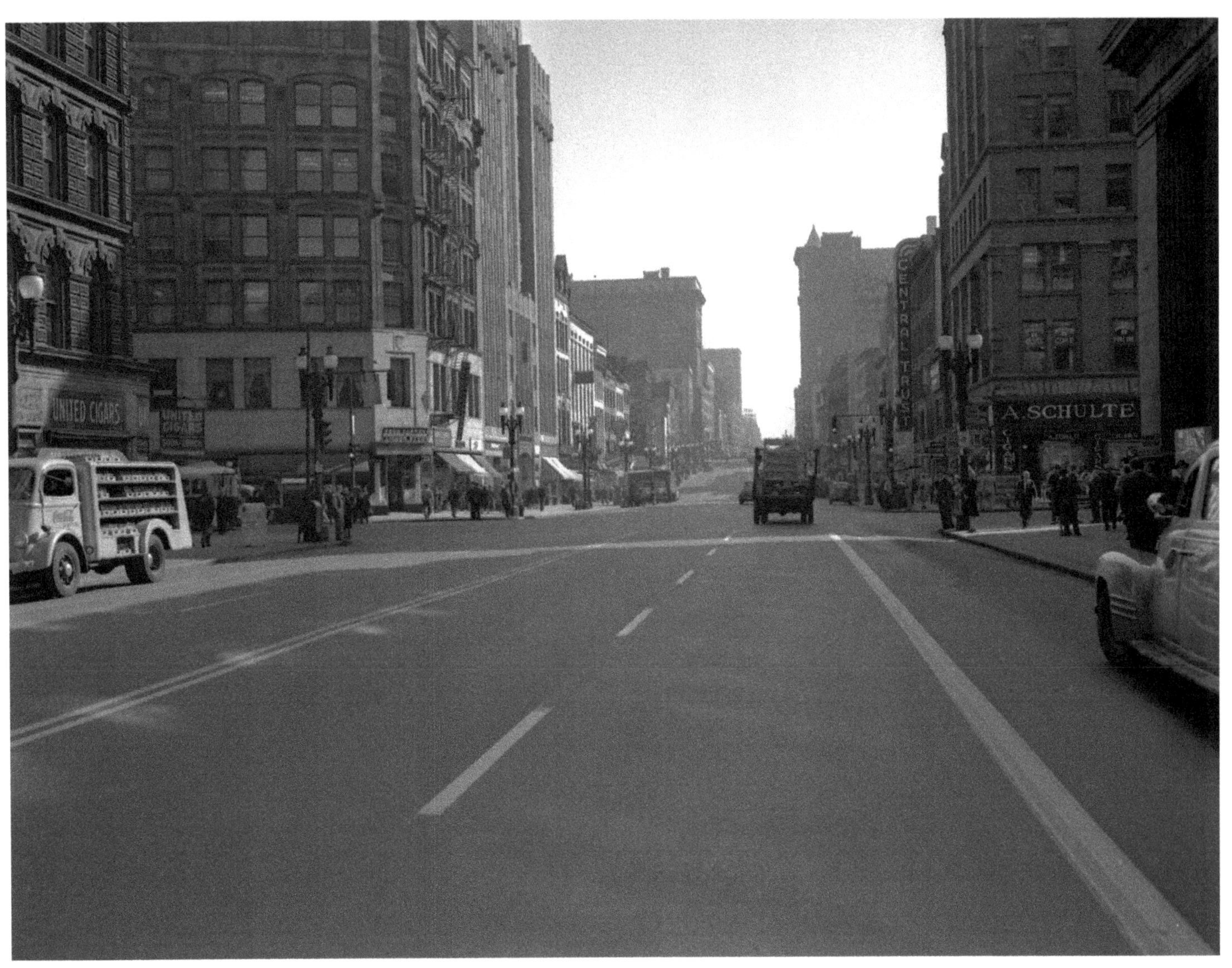

Looking east down Main Street from the Four Corners intersection of Main and State streets. The corner of the Powers Building is visible at left and the Wilder Building is diagonally across the street. The Elwood Building, across Main Street from the Wilder Building, is left of center. (September 13, 1946)

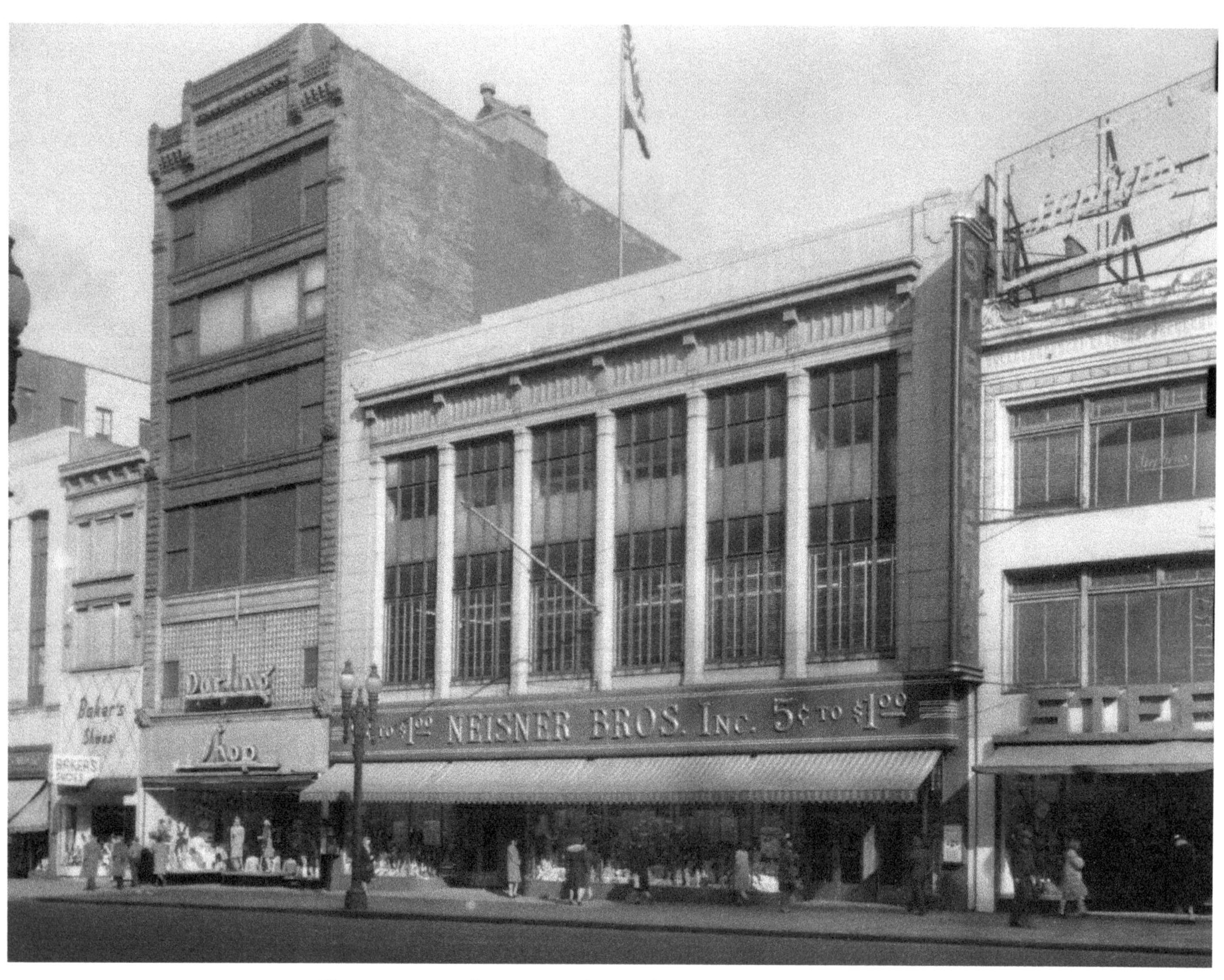

Shoppers gaze in the store windows and make purchases along East Main Street in the years after World War II. Along the street from the left are Baker's Shoes, the Darling Shop (women's clothing), Neisner Brothers Five Cents to a Dollar, and a glimpse of Stephen's Women's Clothing Store.

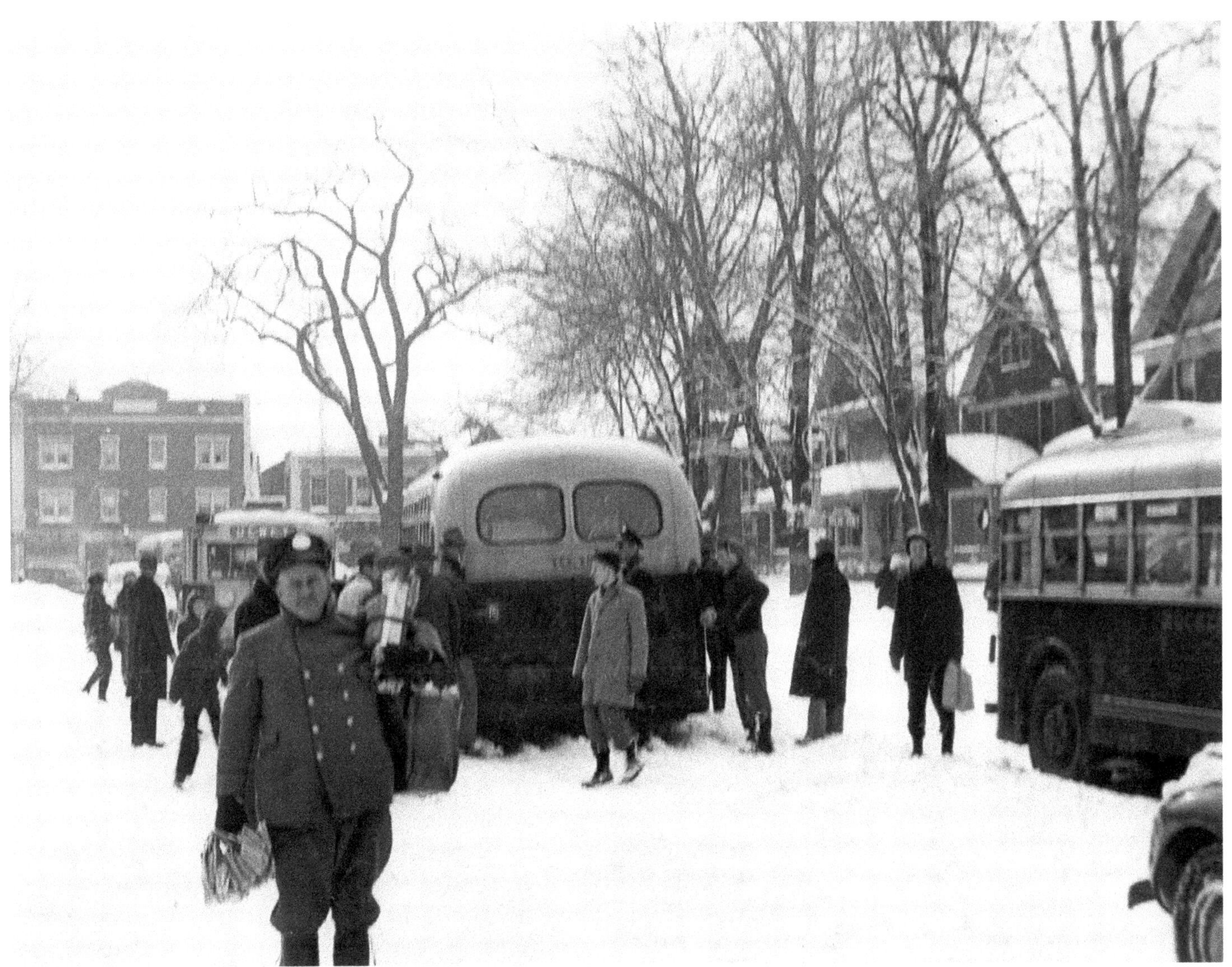

Mail carrier William Ball looks at the photographer capturing an image of a snowstorm about 1945 along Dewey Avenue. Students are near the Rochester City School District school buses. Snowstorms were an inconvenience to the schools, which had hundreds of students to deliver. Sometimes school was canceled to give the plows free access to the streets and to protect students who walked and could not be seen behind the mounds of snow piled at street corners.

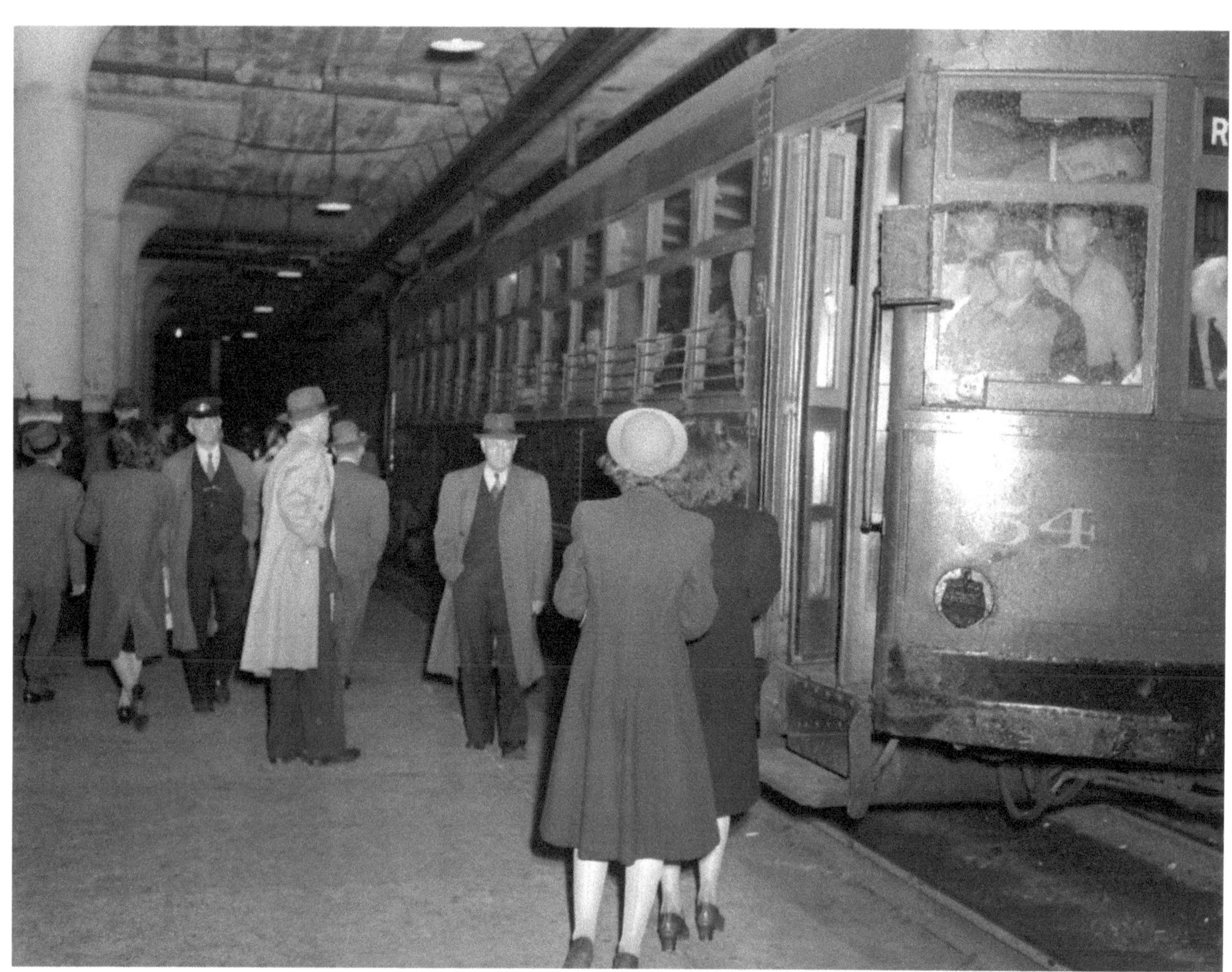

Two women prepare to board the city subway at Exchange and Broad streets as passengers prepare to step off at the City Hall station on October 22, 1945.

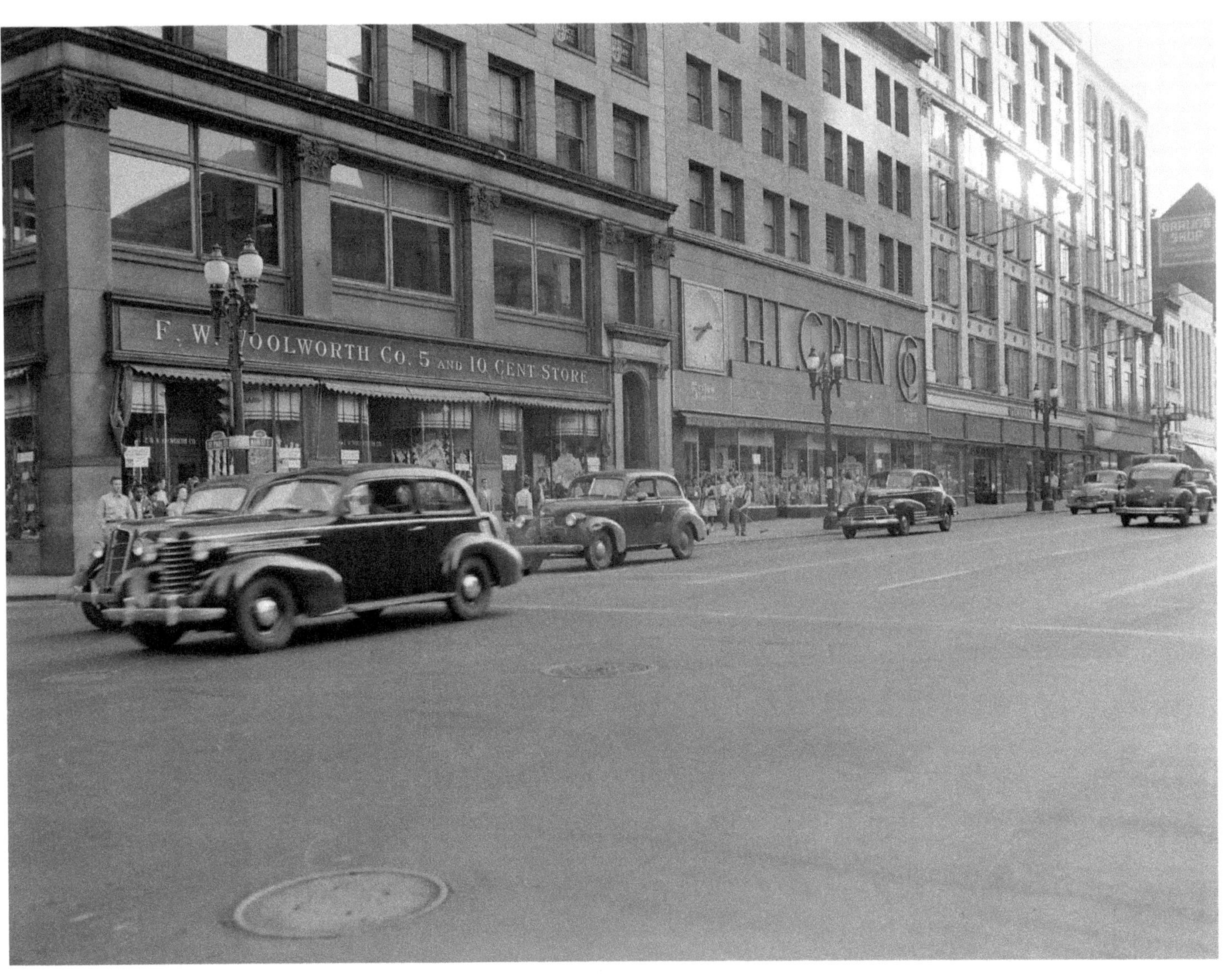

East Main Street near St. Paul Street is busy with shoppers on October 6, 1947. F. W. Woolworth stands on the corner of Clinton and Main in the Granite Building that once housed the old Sibley, Lindsay and Curr Store before it burned in 1904. At right is the H. L. Green Five and Dime Store. Edwards and Son Department Store is next door.

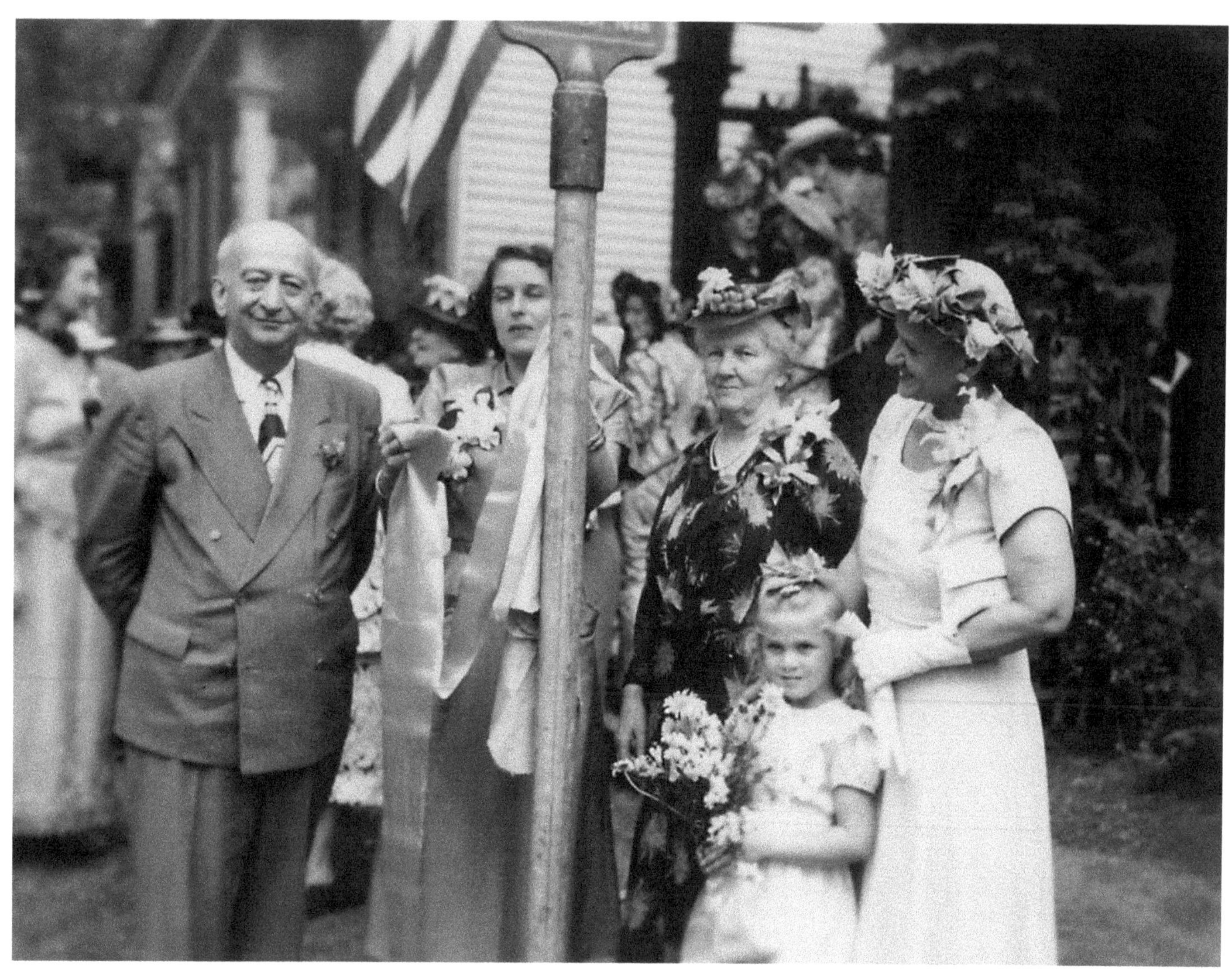

On the centennial of Susan B. Anthony's arrival in Rochester, a memorial marker was erected at her house at 17 Madison Street. Shown from left to right are Mayor Samuel Dicker, Susan B. Anthony III, Martha Howard, and Caroline Gannett. Anthony shared the home with her sister, Mary, until their deaths in 1906 and 1909, respectively. The Rochester Federation of Women's Clubs purchased the home for the Susan B. Anthony Memorial and it is today a museum.

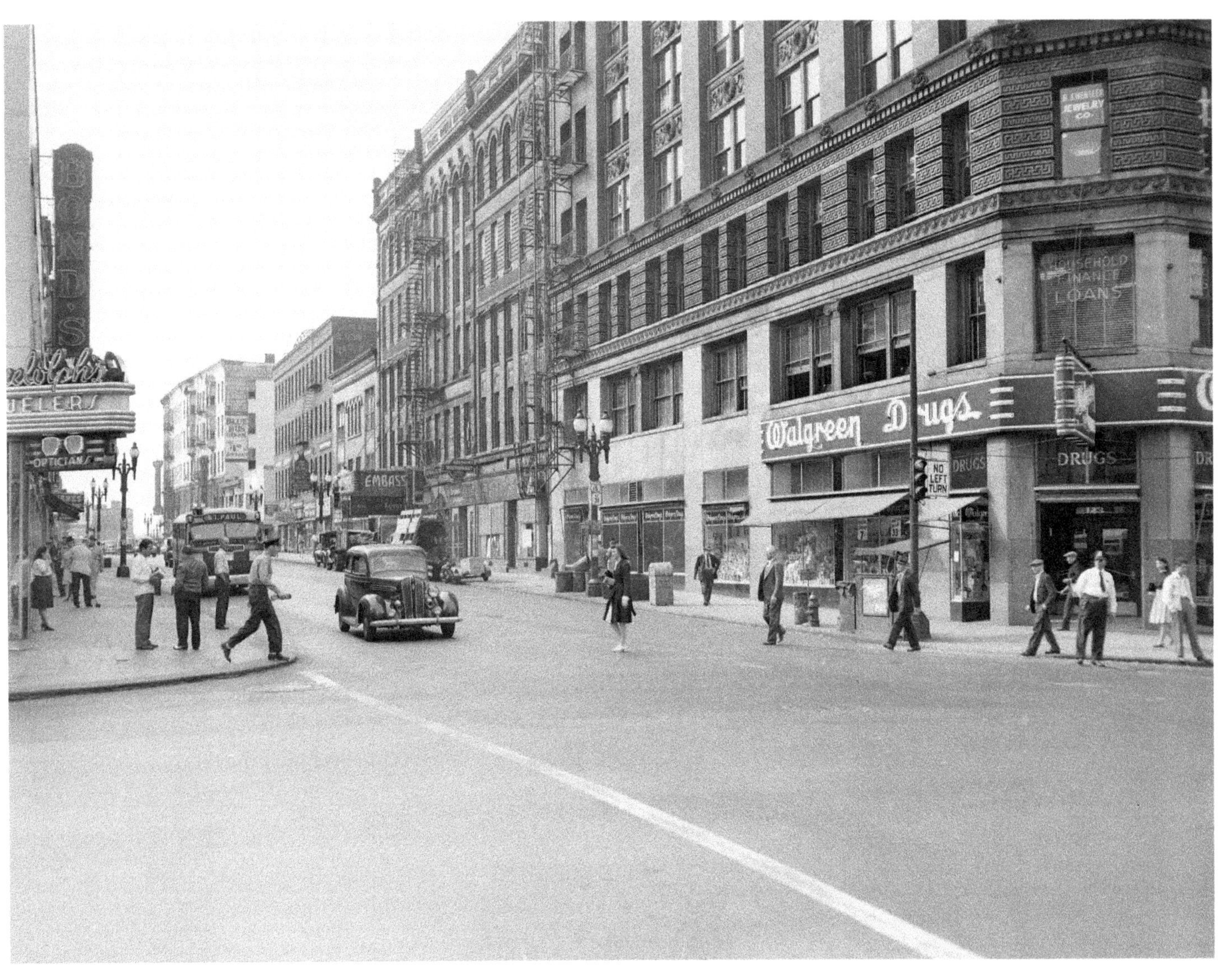

On South Avenue from East Main Street are, at left, Rudolph's Jewelers and Opticians and the South Avenue entrance to Bond Clothing. At right is the Main Street entrance to Walgreen Drugs. The Embassy Theatre and Georgia's Restaurant are farther down South Avenue.

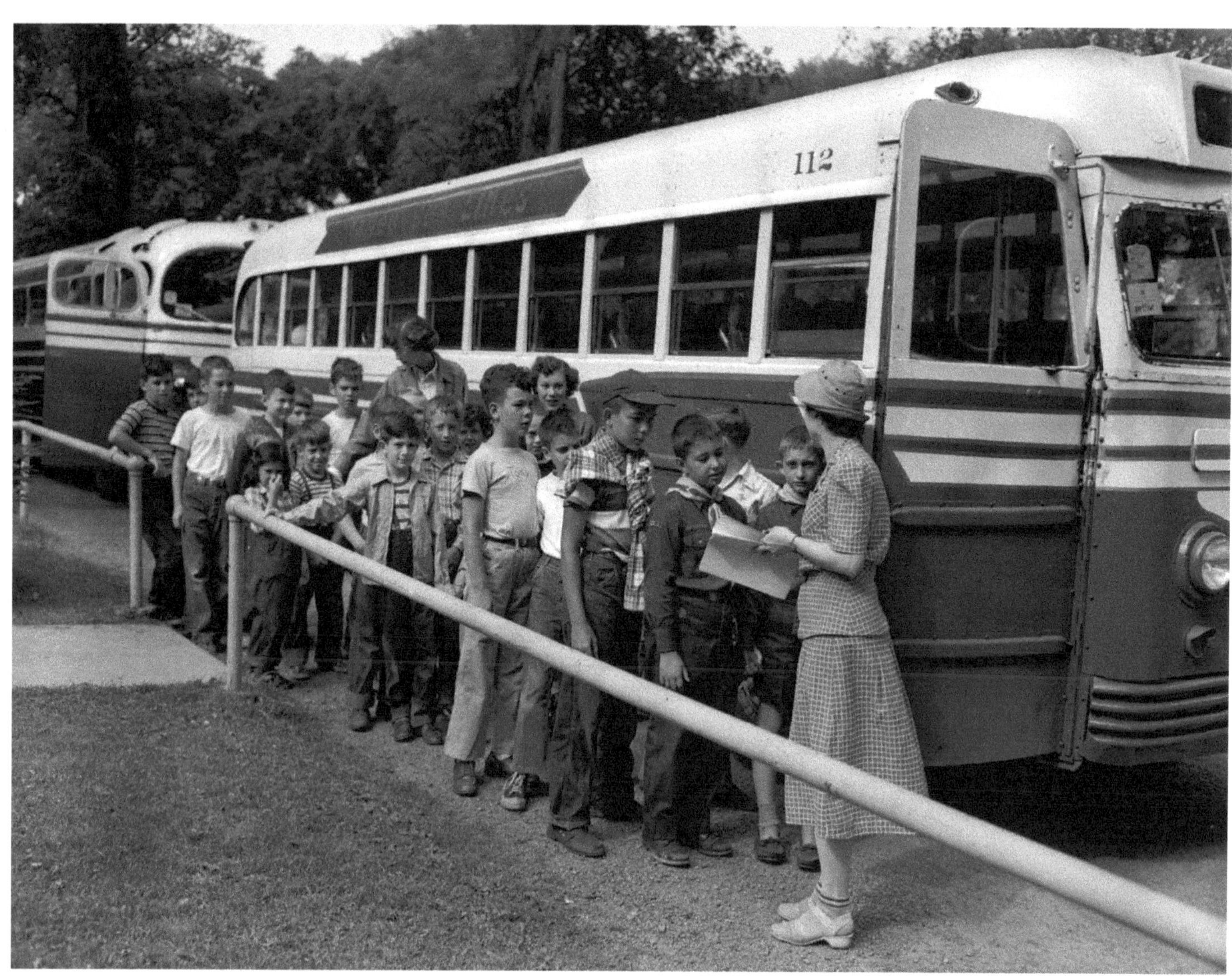

The Rochester Museum of Arts and Sciences (today Rochester Museum and Science Center) chartered buses to send as many as sixty children between the ages of 6 and 16 on nature hikes over a six-week period in the summer of 1949. City schools worked with the Parent and Teacher Association to sponsor the children for the day trips. Here, Marion Peake, head of the school service at the museum, helps children board the bus on July 6.

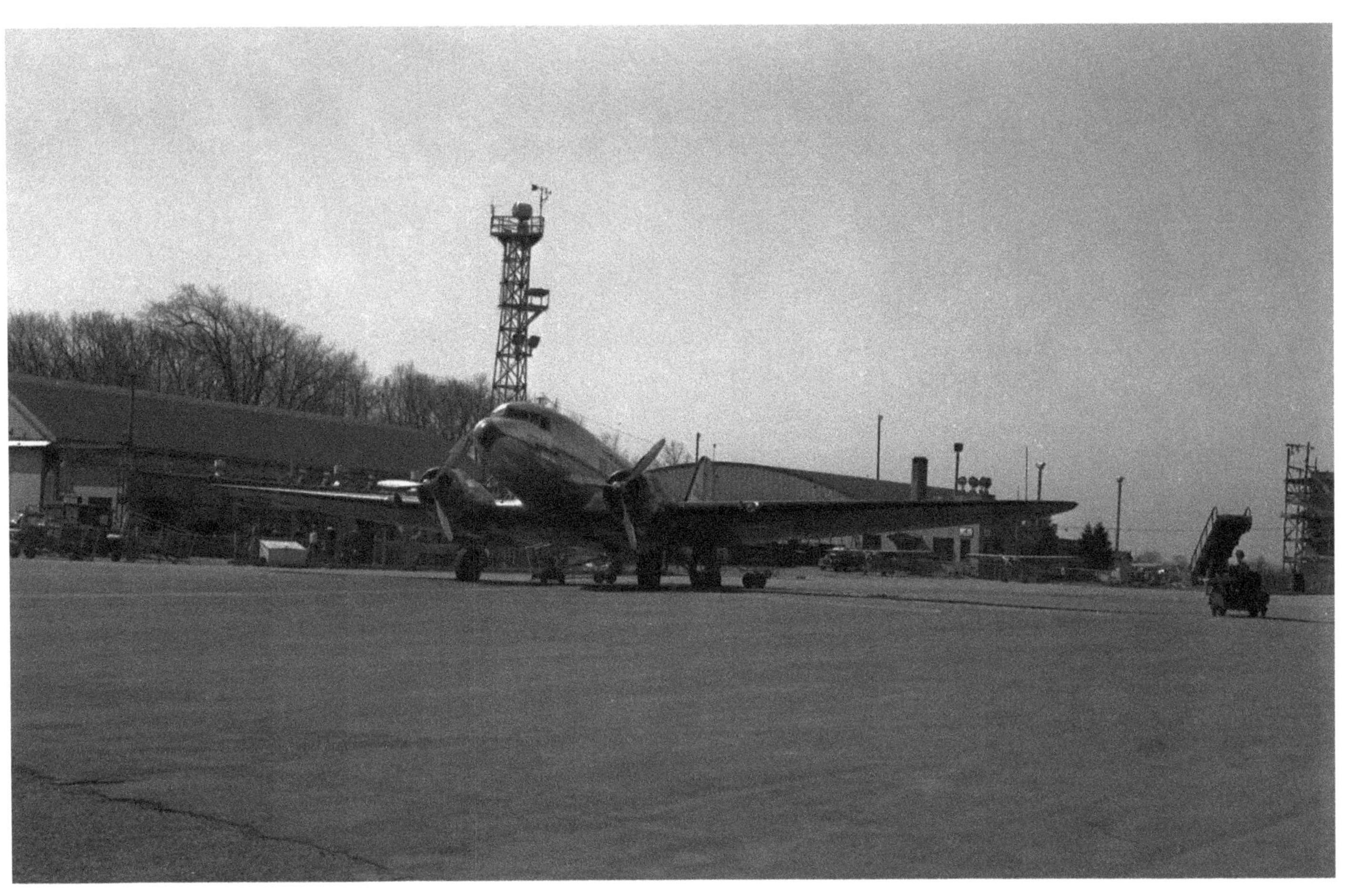

On March 24, 1948, a passenger plane sits outside the terminal at the Rochester Municipal Airport on Scottsville Road. Since before the Wright brothers made the first flight at Kitty Hawk, North Carolina, Rochester had aviation pioneers. With the advent of powered flight, pastures became airfields and soon commercial airports were constructed. Today several airline companies fly jets from the Rochester International Airport.

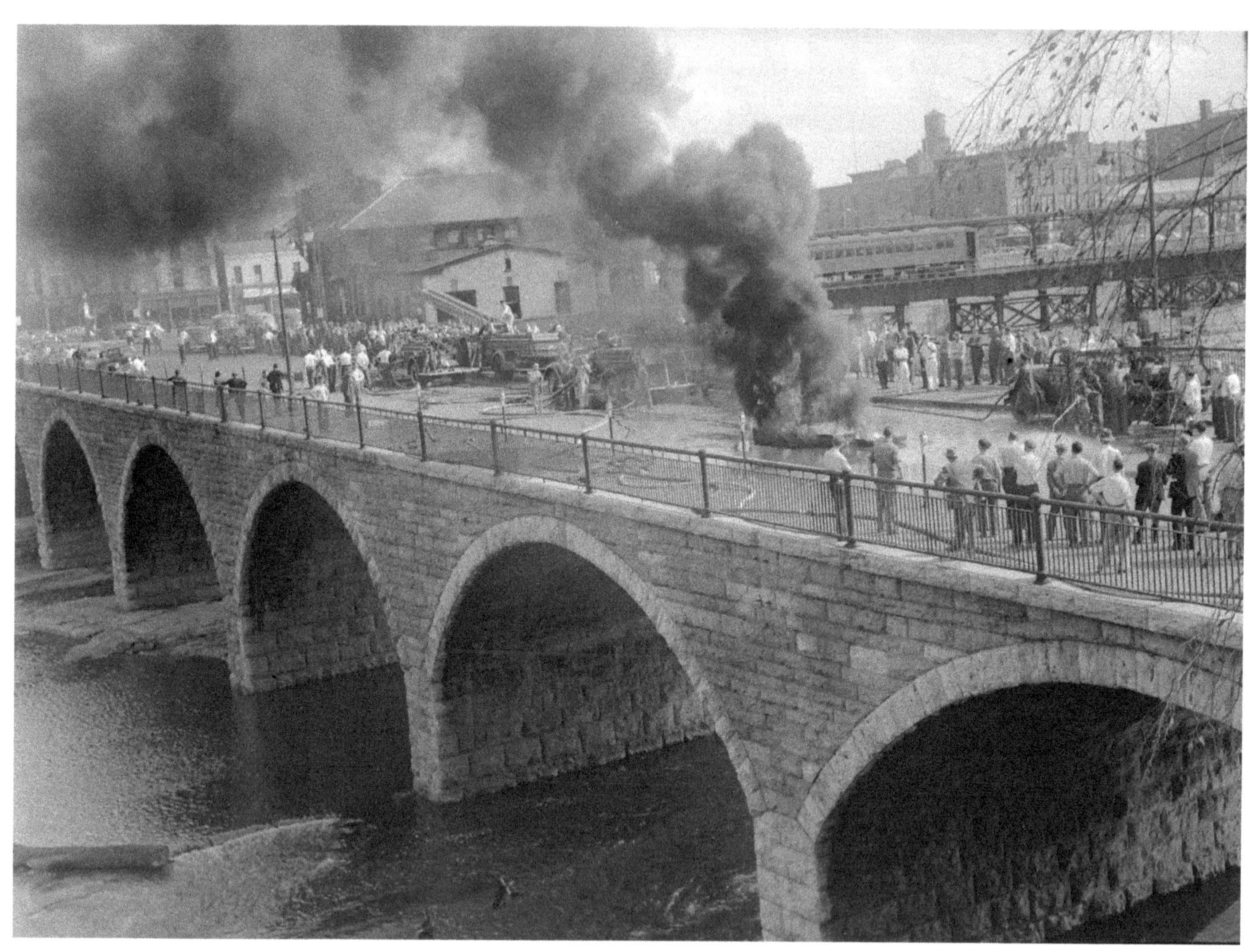

On October 3, 1949, the Rochester Fire Department demonstrated their fire trucks and hoses on the Court Street Bridge during Fire Prevention Week. The Lehigh Valley Railroad Station and a passenger train are visible in the background.

Growth and Change

(1950–1970s)

Housing developments began to spring up in the suburbs to accommodate the returning veterans. Stimulated by postwar industrial growth in Monroe County, new housing construction grew by 40 percent between 1959 and 1965. In need of additional space, expanding factories moved to the suburbs and workers followed. Main roads were widened as traffic increased between the city and suburbs, and mass transportation declined as more families purchased an automobile.

The migration of blacks from the South to the city during the war continued into the 1950s. In the city, however, the population was declining even as the county population climbed. A growing restlessness in the black community festered, little noticed by government or corporate leaders until rioting occurred in 1964. Urban planners, considering the needs of the new arrivals, initiated an urban renewal plan that would continue into the next decade. Old, dilapidated houses were demolished to make way for public housing in the northeast section of the city.

Eastman Kodak's continued growth made it one of Rochester's largest employers. The growth of Xerox was phenomenal after the invention of the copier by Chester Carlson. The number of workers grew from 4,000 in 1960 to 11,300 just four years later. General Dynamics, General Motors, Delco, and Rochester Products employed thousands more.

Urban renewal brought great changes to Rochester's skyline. The musical international doll clock in the midtown mall became an immediate attraction. The War Memorial dramatically changed the historic corner. Other older buildings were demolished in Corn Hill to make way for the Hall of Justice and Public Safety Building at Civic Center Plaza. The New York Central Railroad Station, designed by architect Claude Bragdon, was demolished much to the alarm of city preservationists. Century-old buildings along Front Street and the Main Street Bridge were also demolished, a disheartening experience for those who remember shopping visits to the area.

In 1965 a new Liberty Pole was erected on the traditional historic site of earlier liberty poles. Each year the new pole is decorated for Christmas with lights that stream up its metal cables. Like poles before it, it became a landmark and gathering place for public celebration, protest, and small public markets.

By the close of the 1970s, the skyline of Rochester stood modernized, and the area was a cultural and business center to both city and suburban residents. But many more changes were to come.

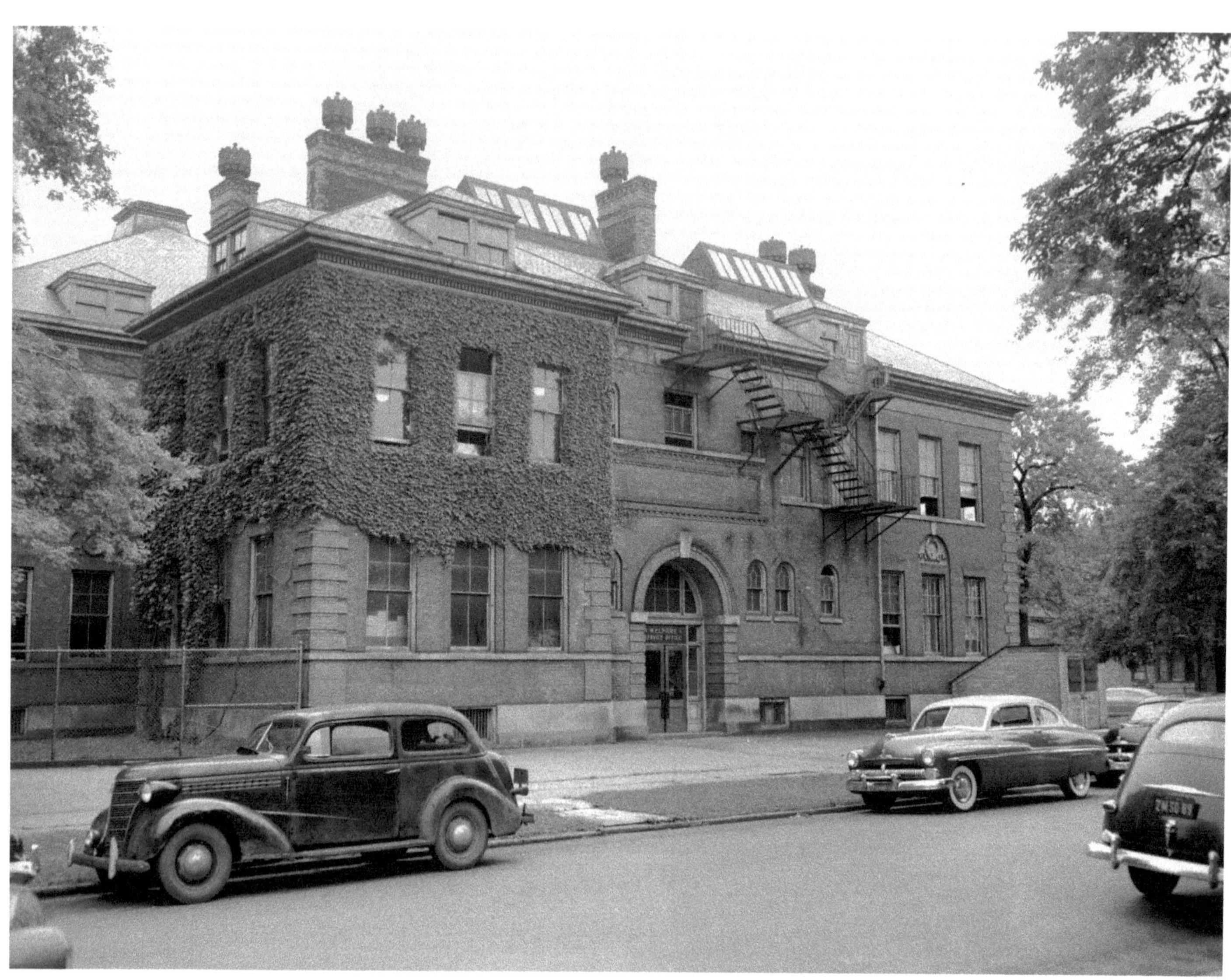

By August 29, 1950, when this photograph was taken, the old General Wadsworth School No. 12 was being used as Rochester's Department of Public Welfare. Built on Clinton Avenue between Marshal and Howell streets in 1899, the school was used for the WPA (Works Progress Administration) headquarters during the Depression and as the center for the Monroe County Rationing Board during World War II.

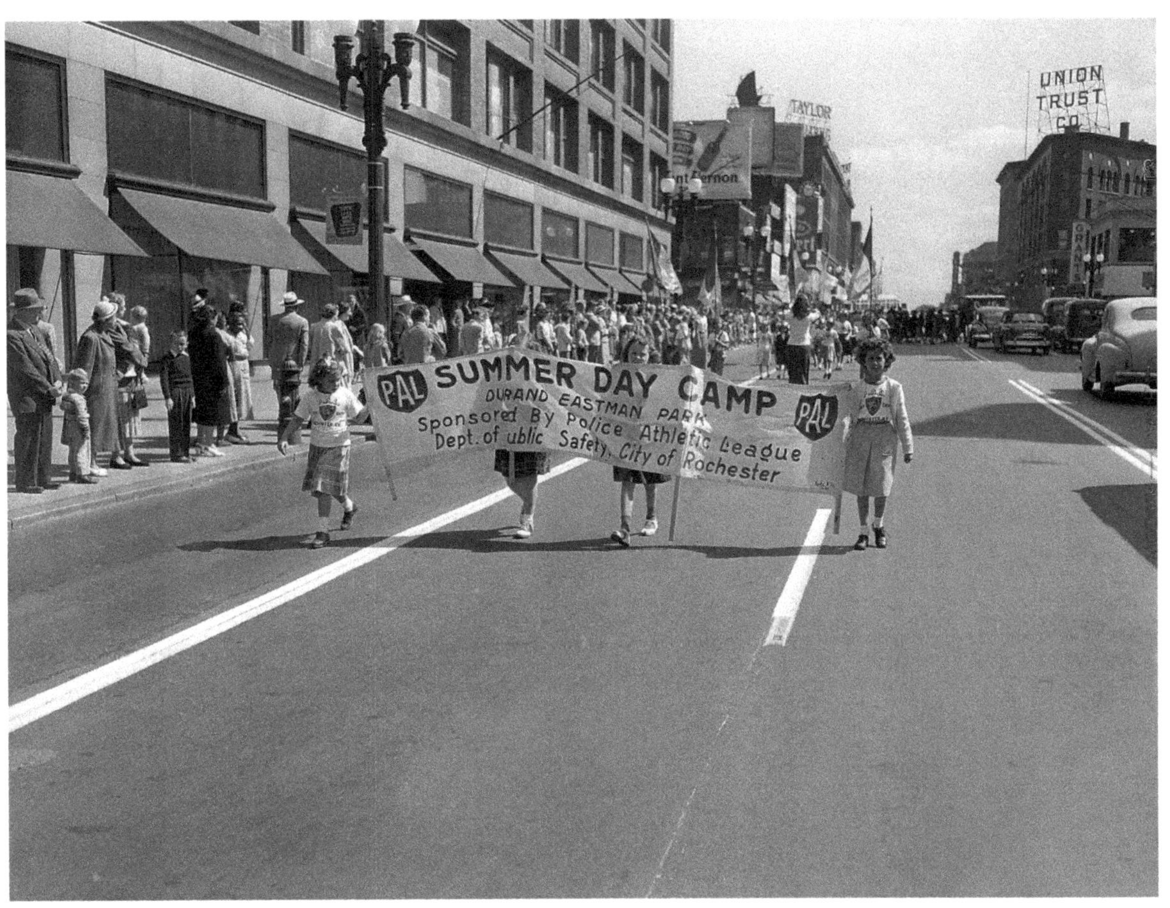

Youth members of the Police Athletic League carry a banner in a parade in downtown Rochester during Police Athletic Youth Week.

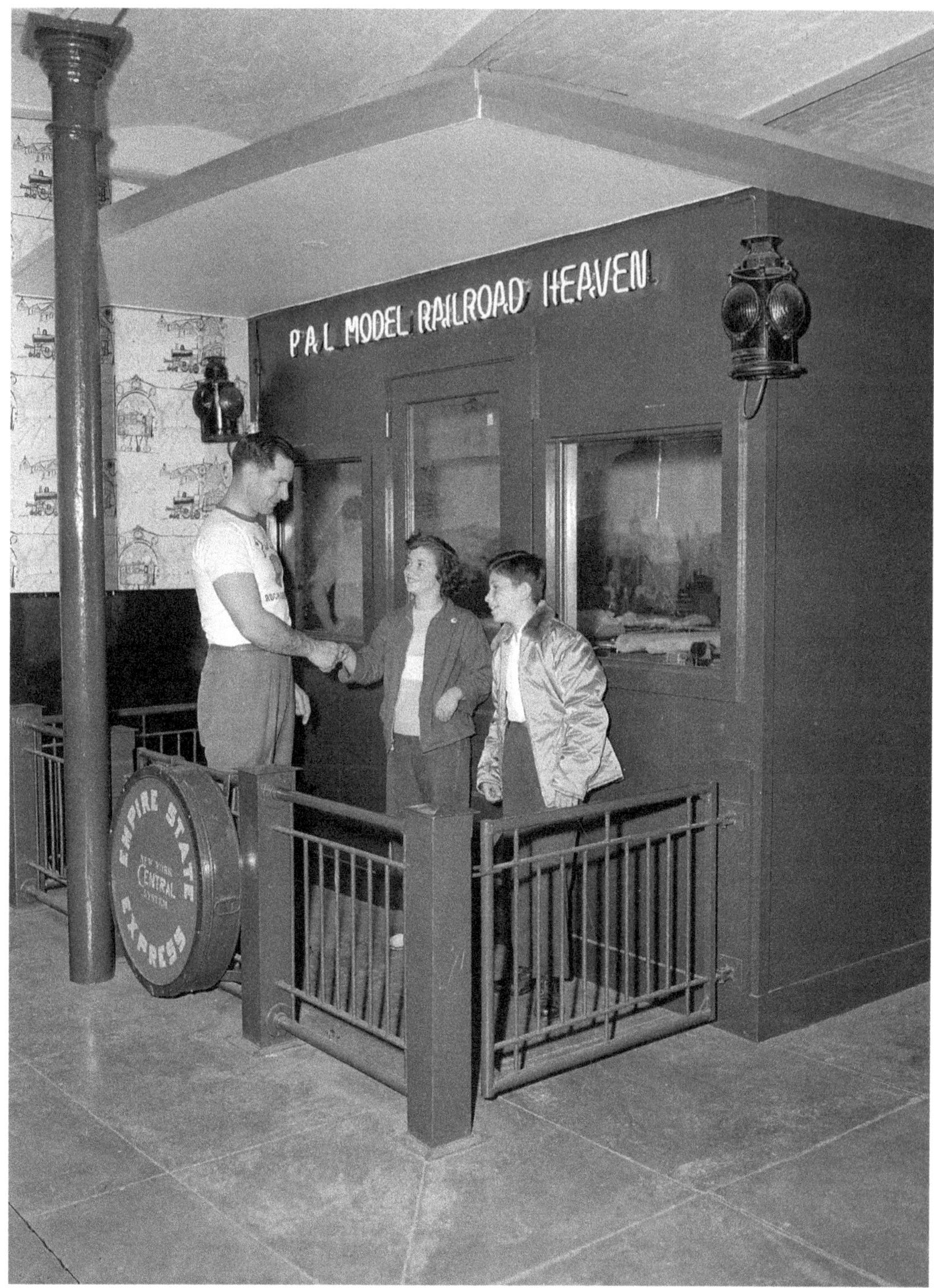

On October 27, 1950, Governor Thomas E. Dewey dedicated a set of four O-scale model railroad scenes that depicted the four seasons along the Genesee River. The Genesee and Kodak City Model Railroad Club laid out $5,000 worth of trains donated by Lionel Trains. The layouts were valued at $50,000 when completed. Named "Model Railroad Heaven," they were built for the youth participants of P.A.L., the Police Athletic League.

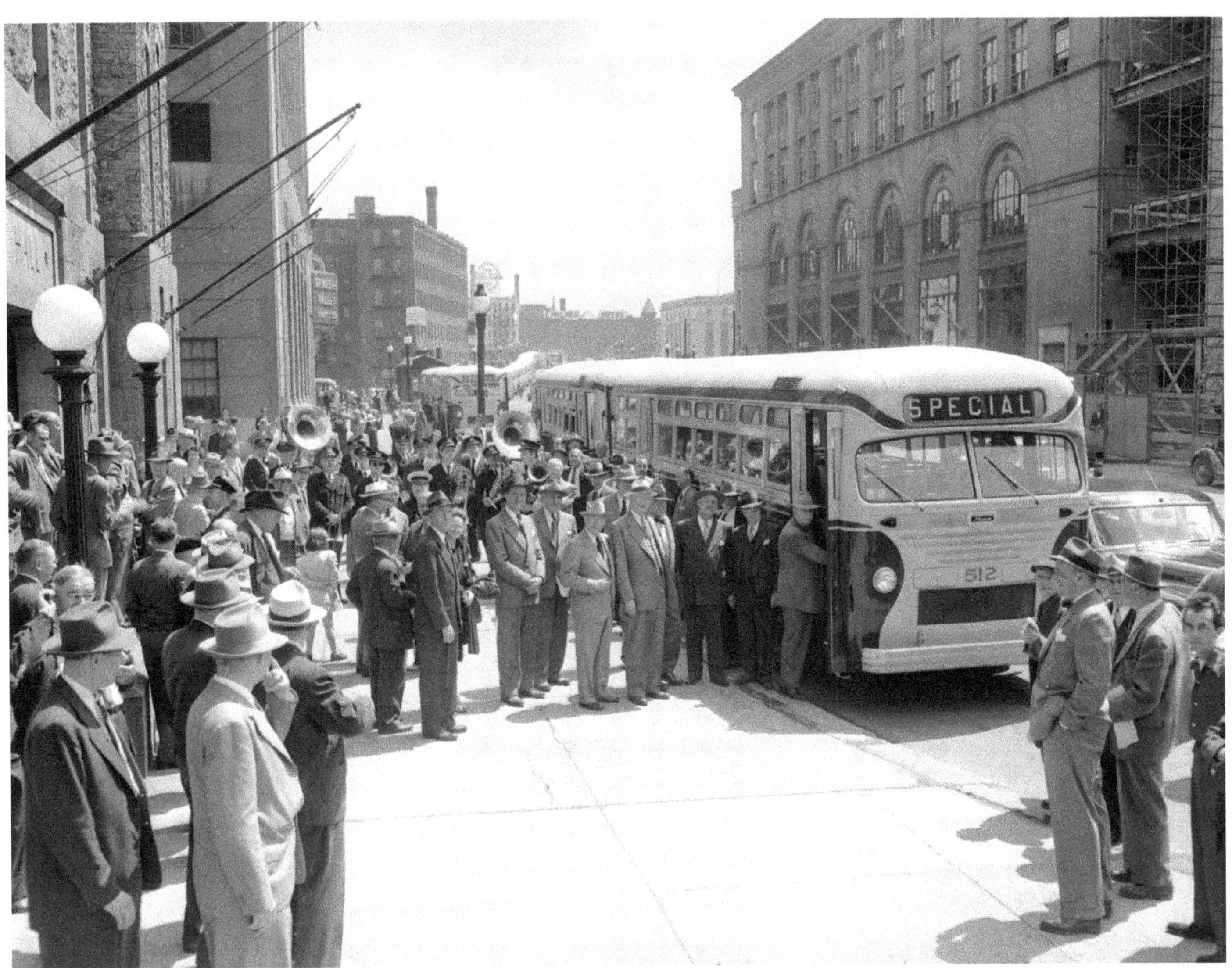

After rationing and tight postwar budgets, people gathered at Broad and Exchange streets on June 1, 1950, to unveil a new fleet of city buses. The 54th Regimental Band played as people celebrated. Boarding the new buses are Rochester Transit Corporation president John Uffert, RTC attorney Howard Woods, and Monroe County Republican leader Fred Parrish.

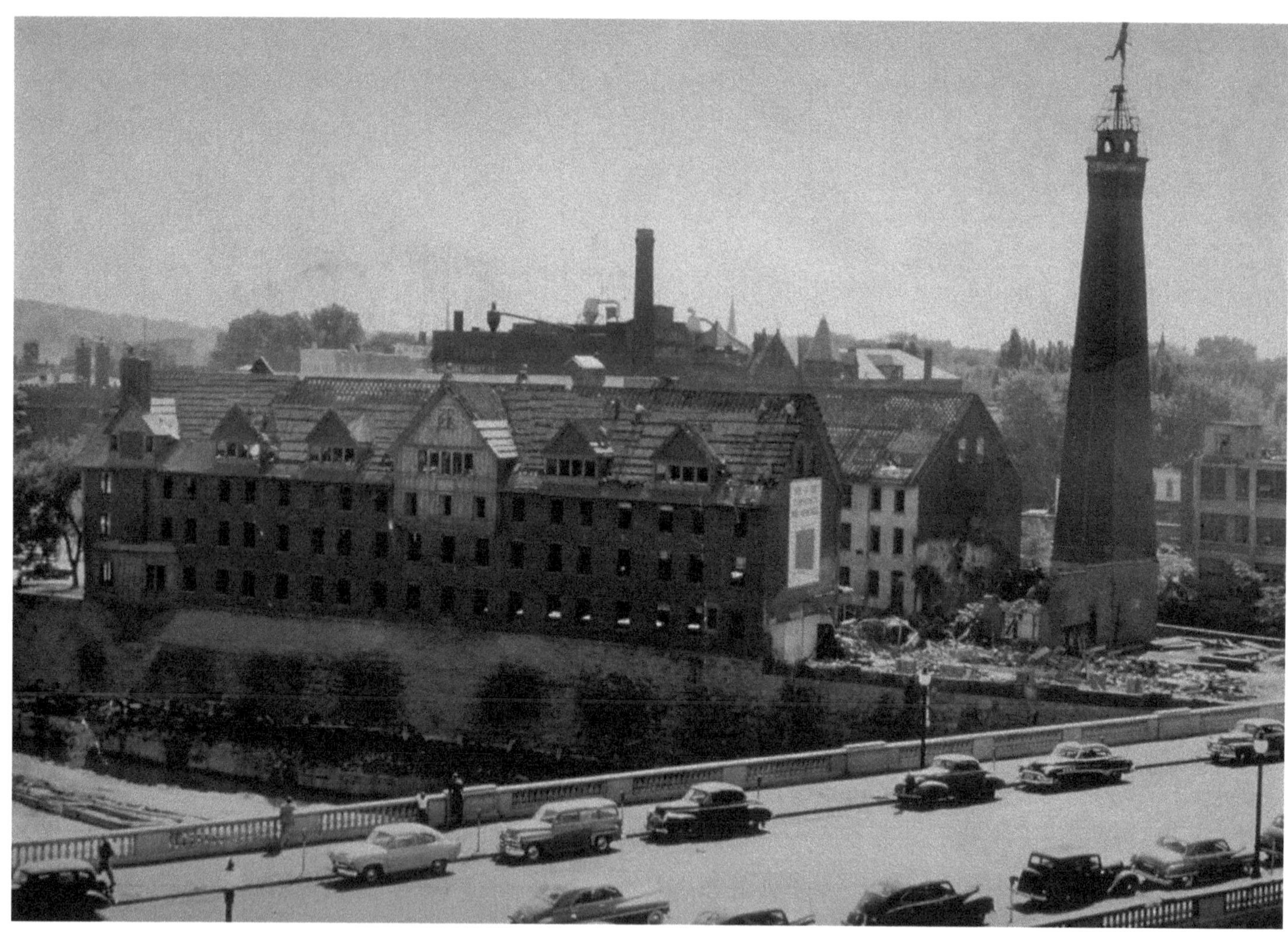

The Kimball Tobacco Company was built by William S. Kimball in 1880 near the Erie Canal aqueduct that is today the Broad Street Bridge. After Kimball's wife complained about the smoking stacks on Rochester's skyline, sculptor J. Guernsey Mitchell was commissioned to create a work of art. The result was a statue of Mercury, pictured here adorning the smokestack at top-right. In 1924 George Eastman acquired the building and leased it to the city for a City Hall annex and Central Library.

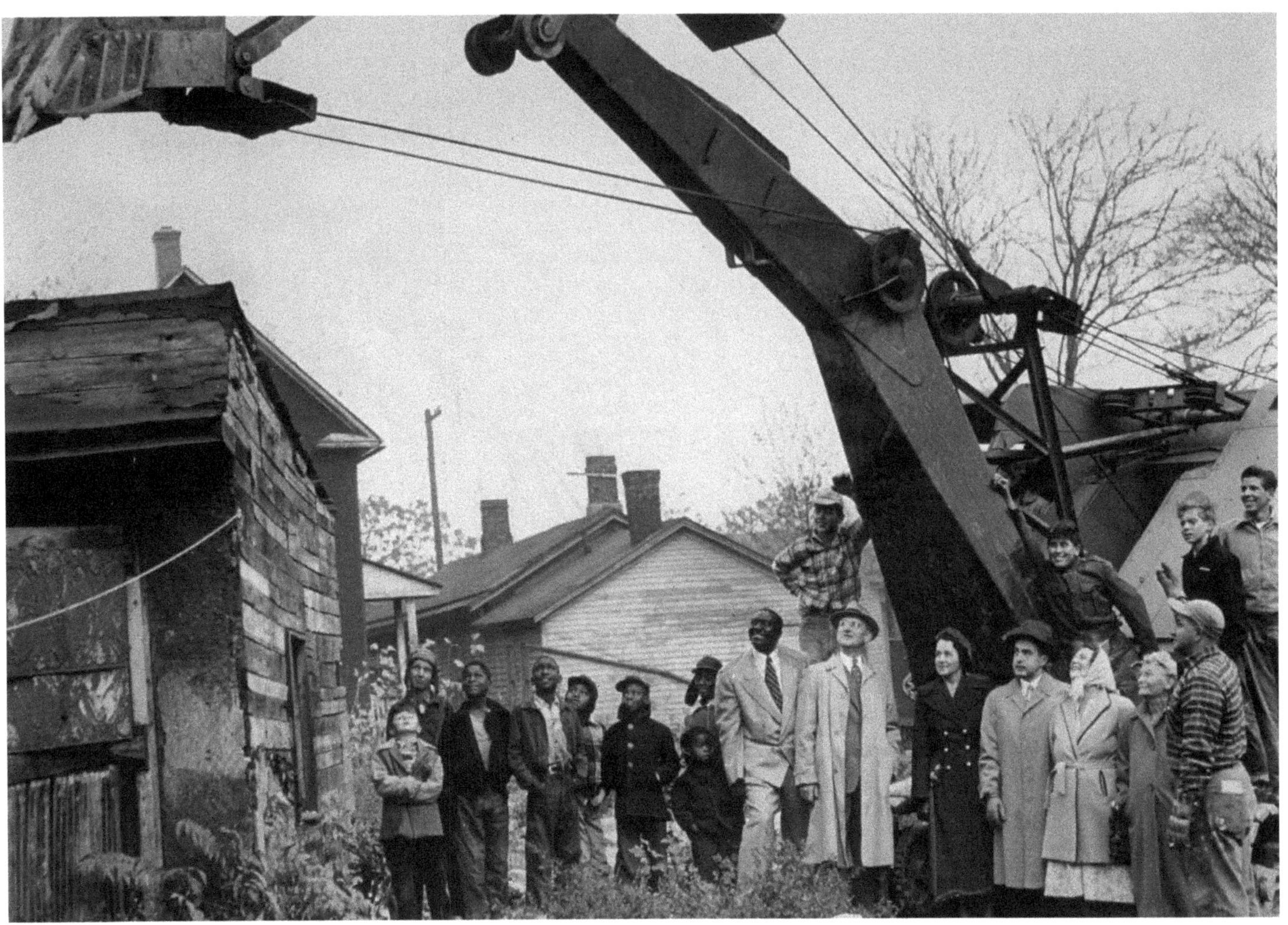

People watch as a backhoe stands ready to demolish a house in the Baden Street neighborhood. Dilapidated private homes were replaced by subsidized housing projects in the multi-million-dollar redevelopment project. These 1950 demolitions signaled the beginning of more than a decade of urban renewal in the city.

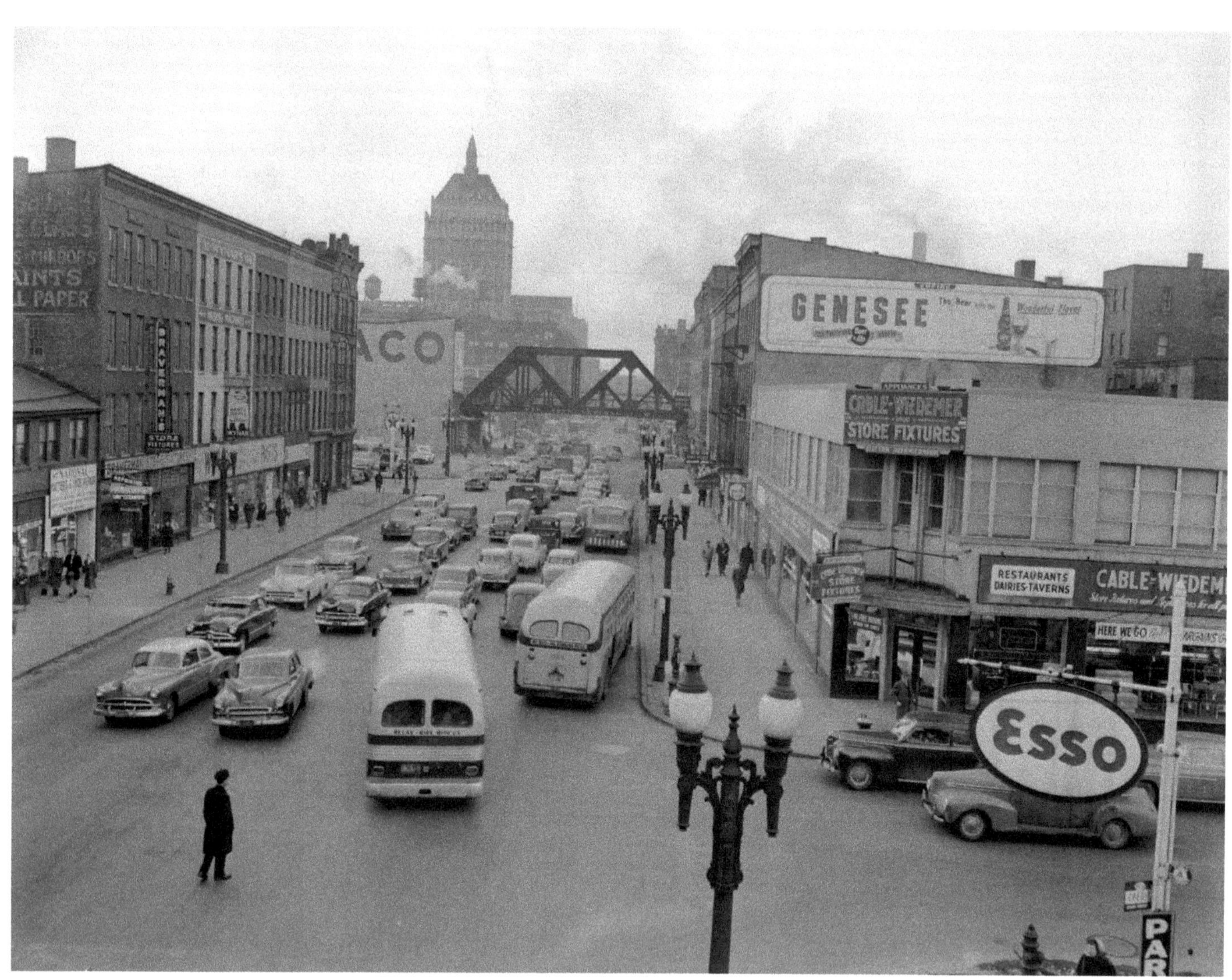

A traffic policeman stands at the intersection of State and Andrews streets. The Kodak offices are in the distance. The railroad bridge crosses above State Street and Braverman Store Fixtures and other stores are across State Street. The Cable-Wiedemer Hotel and Restaurant Supply occupies one corner. The Genesee Brewery advertises, "The Beer with the wonderful flavor."

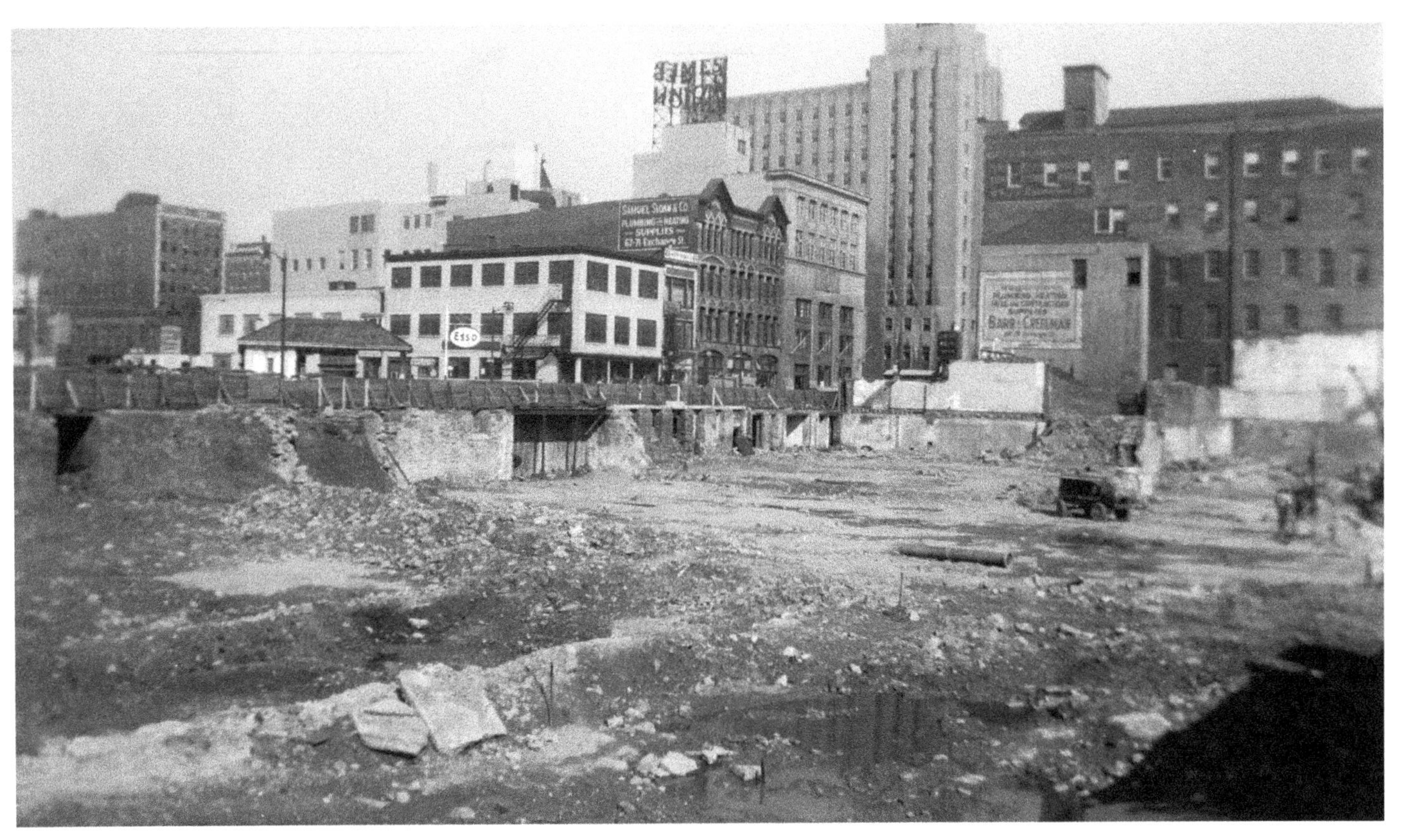

In this view looking northwest across the former site of the Kimball Tobacco Company, the site stands cleared for the construction of the Rochester War Memorial. (April 1952)

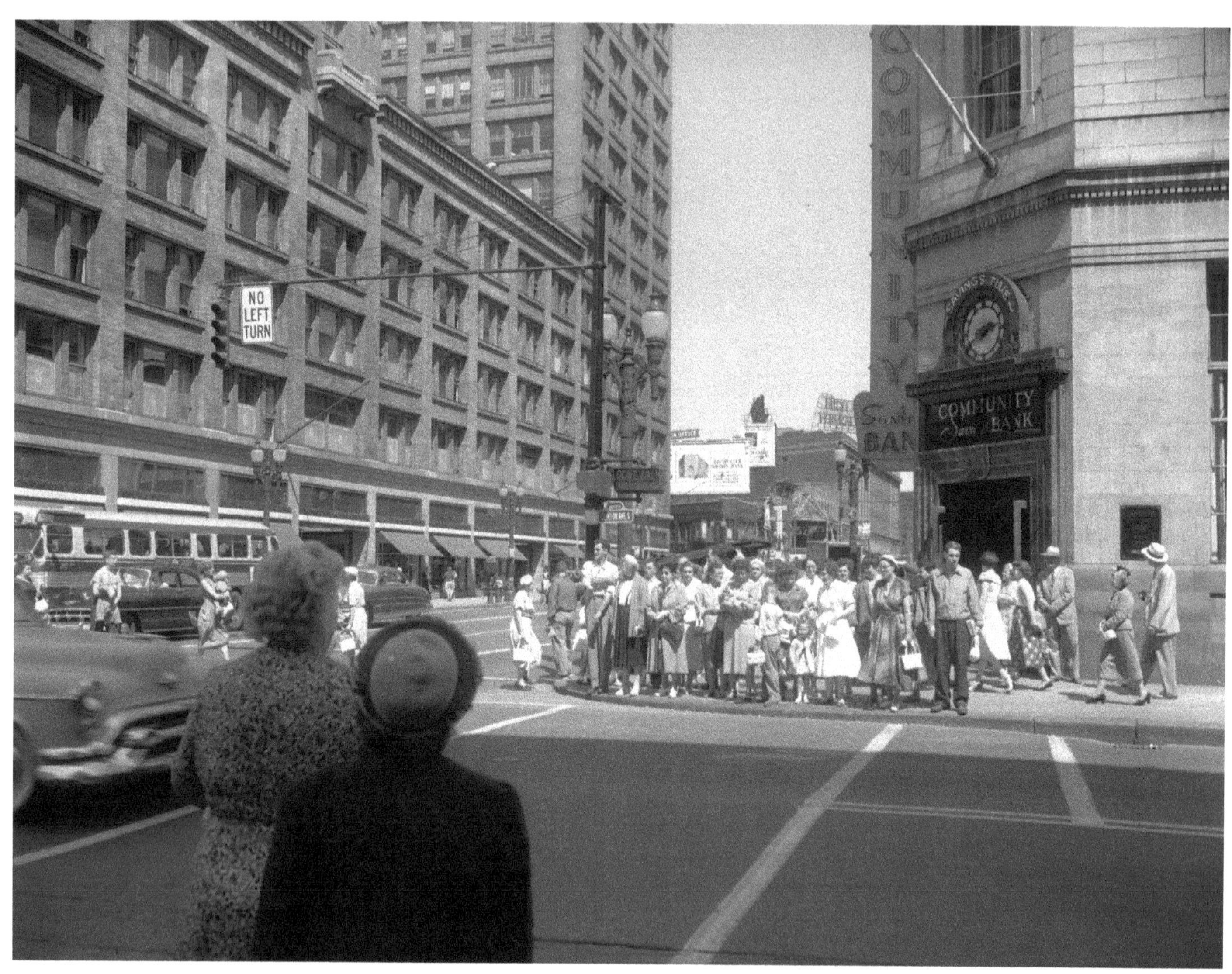

Sibley, Lindsay & Curr Department Store is on the left as people stand ready to cross Main Street near the Rochester Community Savings Bank on August 16, 1954.

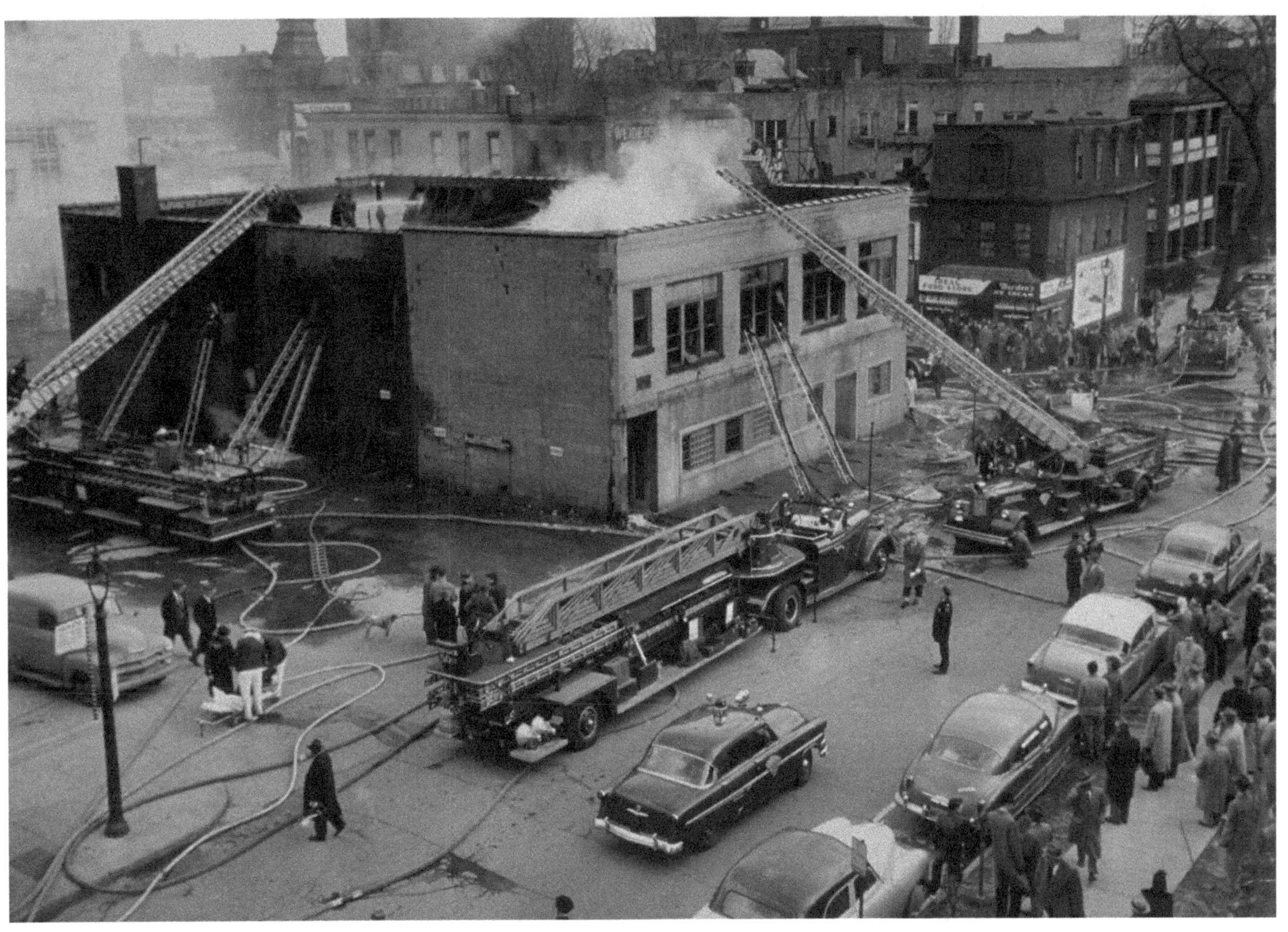

Fire destroyed the Fay Building at the corner of Fitzhugh and Broad streets in early 1955. The building was used as a City Hall annex. Though fire engines worked the sides of the building and firefighters climbed to the roof, the building could not be saved. Crowds look on from a safe distance across the street.

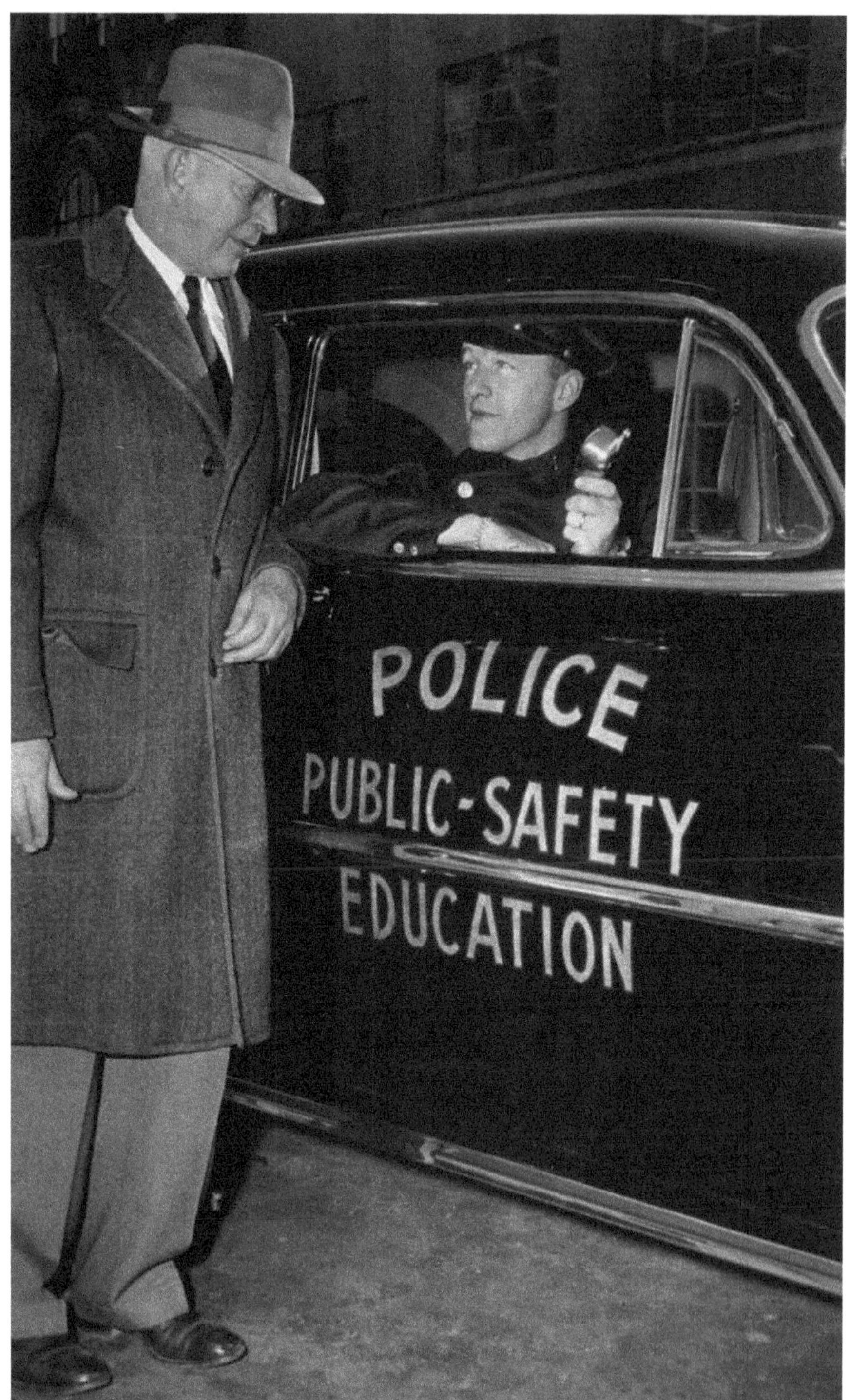

Public Safety Commissioner Kenneth C. Townson speaks to police officer Edward H. Jensen, who shows a microphone he plans to use to warn pedestrians of the dangers of jaywalking. Townson was the commissioner between 1950 and 1960.

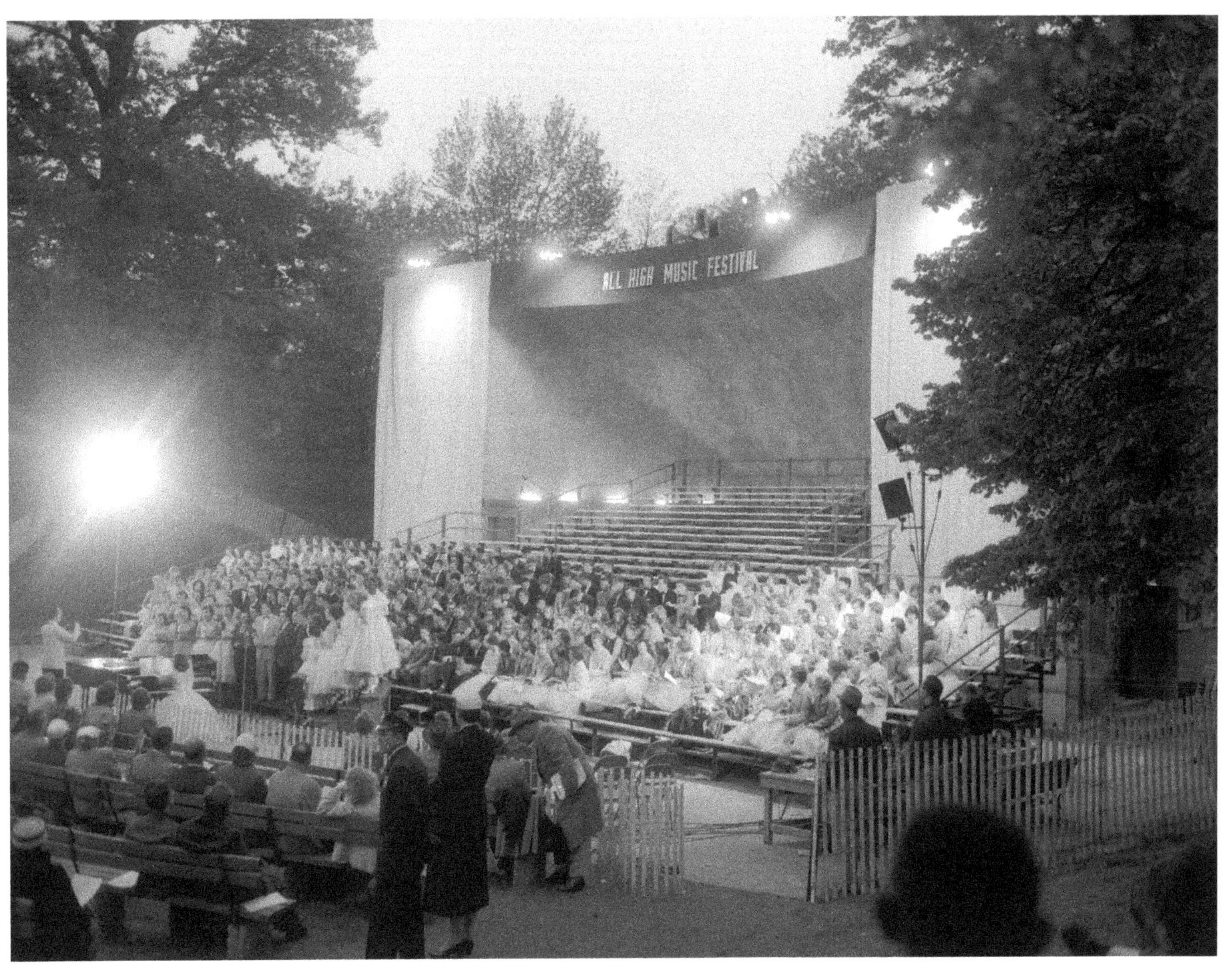

Five hundred students in the 9th annual All-High Music Festival perform the final event of Lilac Week in two nightly concerts at Highland Park. Six hundred instrumentalists from nine Rochester area public schools presented a special concert June 1, 1956. The choral concert included students from Brighton, Brockport, Irondequoit, East Rochester, Penfield, Spencerport, and Webster high schools.

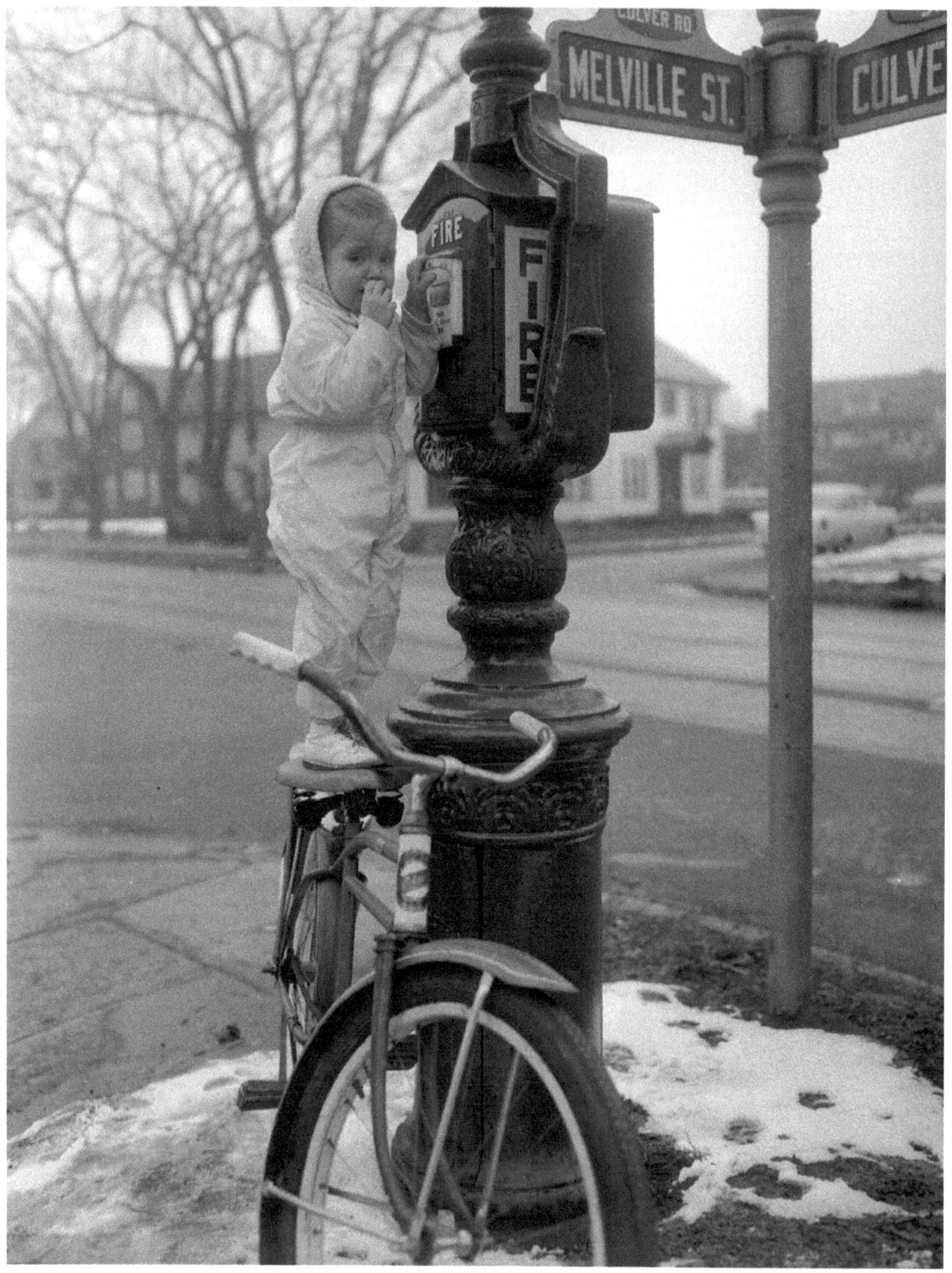

A little girl stands on a Raleigh bicycle to demonstrate the new fire alarm call boxes installed at Melville Street and Culver Road. Call boxes allowed the public to call in an alarm quickly to the fire department. (February 1958)

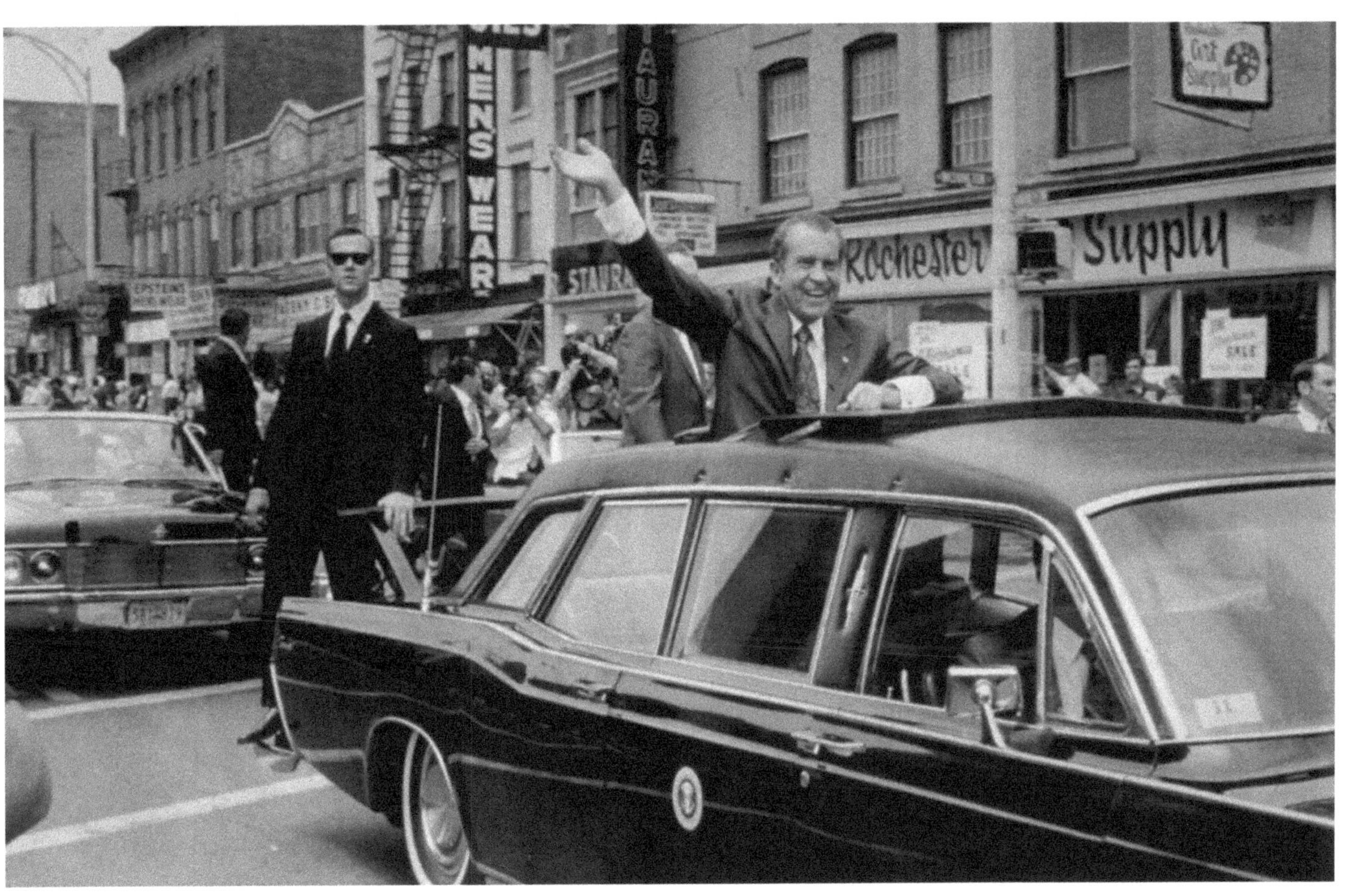

President Richard M. Nixon waves from an automobile as his motorcade passes along Main Street near Washington Street on June 18, 1971, as Secret Service officers stay nearby at the rear of the vehicle. In the background is Gil's Men's Clothing.

Notes on the Photographs

These notes, listed by page number, attempt to include all aspects known of the photographs. Each of the photographs is identified by the page number, photograph's title or description, photographer and collection, archive, and call or box number when applicable. Although every attempt was made to collect all data, in some cases complete data was unavailable due to the age and condition of some of the photographs and records.

II **Court Street Bridge**
Rochester Public Library
Local History Division
rpf00635

VI **Lower and Middle Falls**
Rochester Public Library
Local History Division
rpf00219

X **Snow on State Street**
Rochester Public Library
Local History Division
rpf00096

02 **Main Street Bridge**
Rochester Public Library
Local History Division
rpf00798

03 **New York Central Railroad Station**
Rochester Public Library
Local History Division
rpf01887

04 **David Upton Locomotive**
Rochester Public Library
Local History Division
rpf00684

05 **Andrews Street Bridge**
Rochester Public Library
Local History Division
rpf01740

06 **Floodwaters 1865**
Rochester Public Library
Local History Division
rpf01744

07 **Civil War Arch**
Rochester Public Library
Local History Division
rpf00500

08 **Flight of Hyperion**
Rochester Public Library
Local History Division
rpf00318

09 **Rochester Evening Express**
Rochester Public Library
Local History Division
rpf01556

10 **Indian Day at Maple Grove Park**
Rochester Public Library
Local History Division
rpf01629

11 **Ice Skaters on Erie Canal**
Rochester Public Library
Local History Division
rpf01103

12 **Old Elwood Block**
Rochester Public Library
Local History Division
rpf01558

13 **View from Powers Building**
Rochester Public Library
Local History Division
rpf01516

14 **Reynolds Arcade Interior 1877**
Rochester Public Library
Local History Division
rpf00403

16 **Four Corners 1880**
Rochester Public Library
Local History Division
rpf00578

17 **Main Street 1880**
Rochester Public Library
Local History Division
rpf00544

18 **Original Firehouse**
Rochester Public Library
Local History Division
rpf01798

19 **Milk Delivery Sleigh Rochester Public Library**
Local History Division
rpf00640

20 **Steam Sawmill of C. C. Meyer and Son**
Rochester Public Library
Local History Division
rpf01645

21 **Main Street from Four Corners**
Rochester Public Library
Local History Division
rpf01137

22 **Horse Race at Rochester Driving Park**
Rochester Public Library
Local History Division
rpf01111

23 **Coggswell Fountain**
Rochester Public Library
Local History Division
rpf00971

24 **Horse-drawn Street Car**
Rochester Public Library
Local History Division
rpf00449

25 **Main and Aqueduct Streets**
Rochester Public Library
Local History Division
rpf01086

26 **Upper Falls**
Rochester Public Library
Local History Division
rpf00288

27 **Policeman on Main and Fitzhugh**
Rochester Public Library
Local History Division
rpf00922

28 **Funeral of Frederick Kislingbury**
Rochester Public Library
Local History Division
rpf00548

29 **Glen House Boat Landing**
Rochester Public Library
Local History Division
rpf00891

30 **Storefront of Joseph Shatz Millinery**
Rochester Public Library
Local History Division
rpf01080

31 **Carriage at Bartholomay Cottage Hotel**
Rochester Public Library
Local History Division
rpf01545

32 **View from Court Street Bridge**
Rochester Public Library
Local History Division
rpf01555

33 **Sylvan Stream Sidewheeler**
Rochester Public Library
Local History Division
rpf01714

34 **West Avenue Lift Bridge Over Canal**
Rochester Public Library
Local History Division
rpf00992

35 **Monroe County Court House**
Rochester Public Library
Local History Division
rpf00044

36 **Main Street 1888**
Rochester Public Library
Local History Division
rpf00519

37 **Storm Destruction**
Rochester Public Library
Local History Division
rpf00866

38 **Plaza Near City Hall**
Rochester Public Library
Local History Division
rpf00503

39 **Monroe Commandery No. 12**
Rochester Public Library
Local History Division
rpf00874

40 **Main Street and East Avenue**
Rochester Public Library
Local History Division
rpf00520

41 **First Electric Streetcar in Rochester**
Rochester Public Library
Local History Division
rpf00463

42 **Home Stretch**
Rochester Public Library
Local History Division
rpf00166

43 **Horse-drawn Fire Engine**
Rochester Public Library
Local History Division
rpf01792

44 **German Theological Seminary**
Rochester Public Library
Local History Division
rpf02091

45 **Men Atop Dome**
Rochester Public Library
Local History Division
rpf00934

46 **Rochester School for the Deaf**
Rochester Public Library
Local History Division
rpf01900

47 **Elephants Parading Along Main Street**
Rochester Public Library
Local History Division
rpf00977

48 **Lyceum Theatre**
Rochester Public Library
Local History Division
rpf01211

49 **Smith and Holister**
Rochester Public Library
Local History Division
rpf01554

50 **Main Street from Water Street**
Rochester Public Library
Municipal Archives
e0000016

51 **Dedication of Soldiers and Sailors Monument**
Rochester Public Library
Local History Division
rpf00946

52 **Six-horse Team and Fire Truck**
Rochester Public Library
Local History Division
rpf01785

53 **Man Observing Genesee Floodwaters**
Rochester Public Library
Local History Division
rpf01116

54 **Steam Engine**
Rochester Public Library
Local History Division
rpf01634

55 **Two Boys in a Pony Cart**
Rochester Public Library
Local History Division
rpf00954

56 **Bicycles in a Fourth of July Parade**
Rochester Public Library
Local History Division
rpf00182

57 **Funeral for Frederick Douglass**
Rochester Public Library
Local History Division
rpf00197

58 **John A. Schueler Blacksmith Shop**
Rochester Public Library
Local History Division
rpf00851

59 **Main Street Looking East 1896**
Rochester Public Library
Local History Division
rpf00516

60 **Lower Falls Framed by Driving Park Avenue Bridge**
Rochester Public Library
Local History Division
rpf00932

61 **Rochester from Arsenal Building**
Rochester Public Library
Local History Division
rpf00914

62 **Main Street 1896**
Rochester Public Library
Local History Division
rpf01046

63 **Snow Removal at the Four Corners**
Rochester Public Library
Municipal Archives
e0000473

64 **Elwood Building at Four Corners**
Rochester Public Library
Municipal Archives
e0000287

65 **Fitzhugh Street Bridge**
Rochester Public Library
Local History Division
rpf01326

66 **Monroe Avenue**
Rochester Public Library
Municipal Archives
e0000292

67 **St. Paul's Church and Parish House**
Rochester Public Library
Local History Division
rpf01494

68 **Rochester Street Fair Arch 1899**
Rochester Public Library
Local History Division
rpf00270

69 **Erie Canal in Winter**
Rochester Public Library
Local History Division
rpf01800

70 **Soldiers Leaving for Spanish-American War in 1898**
Rochester Public Library
Local History Division
rpf00041

71 **Ontario Beach Park**
Rochester Public Library
Local History Division
rpf00852

72 **Erie Canal Near South Avenue**
Rochester Public Library
Local History Division
rpf00935

73 **Bradstreet School Hockey Team**
Rochester Public Library
Local History Division
rpf01067

74 **Charlotte Boardwalk**
Rochester Public Library
Municipal Archives
e0000013

76 **East Main Street 1900**
Rochester Public Library
Local History Division
rpf00524

77 **East Main Street**
Rochester Public Library
Local History Division
rpf00508

78 **Women Bicyclists**
Rochester Public Library
Local History Division
rpf00468

79 **West Main Street**
Rochester Public Library
Municipal Archives
e0000299

80 **East Main Street at Water Street**
Rochester Public Library
Municipal Archives
e0000340

81 **Central Avenue at the Train Station**
Rochester Public Library
Municipal Archives
e0000337

82 **West Avenue and Brown Street**
Rochester Public Library
Local History Division
rpf01859

83 **Civil War Veterans with Cannon**
Rochester Public Library
Local History Division
rpf02066

84 **Triumphal Arch Honoring General Otis**
Rochester Public Library
Local History Division
rpf00385

85 **Empire Theatre at Main and Clinton**
Rochester Public Library
Local History Division
rpf00782

86 **Sidewalk Accident**
Rochester Public Library
Municipal Archives
e0000306

87 **Smallpox Patients at Hope Hospital**
Rochester Public Library
Local History Division
rpf00652

88 **North Side of East Main Street**
Rochester Public Library
Local History Division
rpf00929

89 **May Day in Seneca Park**
Rochester Public Library
Local History Division
rpf01408

90 **Park Superintendents in Carriage at Highland Park**
Rochester Public Library
Local History Division
rpf01423

92 **Group Portrait**
Rochester Public Library
Local History Division
rpf01471

93 **Main Street at Parade's End**
Rochester Public Library
Local History Division
rpf00969

94 **Main Street 1906**
Rochester Public Library
Local History Division
rpf00507

95 **Rochester Trust Company**
Rochester Public Library
Local History Division
rpf00655

96 **G. J. Wagg's Meat Counter**
Rochester Public Library
Local History Division
rpf01878

97 **East Main Street 1907**
Rochester Public Library
Local History Division
rpf00512

98 **South Clinton Avenue**
Rochester Public Library
Local History Division
rpf01114

99 **Main Street 1910**
Rochester Public Library
City Hall Collection
v0000038

100 **Labor Day Parade 1910**
Rochester Public Library
Local History Division
rpf006003

101 **Swan Boat at Seneca Park**
Rochester Public Library
Local History Division
rpf01254

102 **Mr. and Mrs. Sharp in Front of Their Business**
Rochester Public Library
Local History Division
rpf01007

103 **Lee Private Hospital**
Rochester Public Library
Local History Division
rpf01255

104 **Genesee Valley Park Bandstand Dedication**
Rochester Public Library
Local History Division
rpf01431

105 **John Frisbie's Flight 1911**
Rochester Public Library
Local History Division
rpf00604

106 **President Taft**
Rochester Public Library
Local History Division
rpf00811

107 **Steamboat Pier on Lake Ontario Shore**
Rochester Public Library
Municipal Archives
e0000089

108 **Church of the Blessed Sacrament**
Rochester Public Library
Local History Division
rpf01527

109 **Centennial Parade Float at Exposition Park in 1912**
Rochester Public Library
Local History Division
rpf00610

110 **Dewey Avenue**
Rochester Public Library
Municipal Archives
e0000381

111 **Genesee River with High Water**
Rochester Public Library
Municipal Archives
e0000023

112 **Hotel Rochester and View of Main Street West**
Rochester Public Library
Local History Division
rpf01591

113 **South and Court**
Rochester Public Library
Municipal Archives
e0000469

114 **Erie Canal**
Rochester Public Library
Municipal Archives
e0000468

115 **Curtice Street Paving**
Rochester Public Library
Municipal Archives
e0000459

116 **Duffy-Powers Building**
Rochester Public Library
Local History Division
rpf00672

117 **Demonstrators for Prohibition**
Rochester Public Library
Local History Division
rpf00967

118 **Pedestrians on Exchange Street 1916**
Rochester Public Library
Local History Division
rpf01734

119 **Red Cross Canteen Workers**
Rochester Public Library
Local History Division
rpf01630

120 **Sibley's Department Store**
Rochester Public Library
Local History Division
rpf00664

121 Boys Swimming at Durand-Eastman Park
Rochester Public Library
Local History Division
rpf01457

122 East Side Savings Bank
Rochester Public Library
Local History Division
rpf01867

123 South Avenue 1917
Rochester Public Library
Local History Division
rpf00637

124 Crowds on Lilac Sunday, Highland Park
Rochester Public Library
Local History Division
rpf01442

125 Bausch & Lomb Glass Plant
Rochester Public Library
Local History Division
rpf00847

126 South Union Street
Rochester Public Library
Municipal Archives
e0000470

127 Children Check Books Out
Rochester Public Library
Local History Division
rpf01821

128 Inspection, United States School of Aerial Photography
Rochester Public Library
Local History Division
rpf01232

129 Mrs. Bertha Pendexter Eldridge, as a Minute Woman
Rochester Public Library
Local History Division
rpf01230

130 T. H. Symington Company
Rochester Public Library
Local History Division
rpf02033

131 Patriotic Fervor
Rochester Public Library
Local History Division
rpf01229

132 Parade of Gold Star Mothers 1918
Rochester Public Library
Local History Division
rpf00966

133 McFarlin Clothing Company on Main Street
Rochester Public Library
Local History Division
rpf00088

134 Horse Show at Rochester Exposition
Rochester Public Library
Municipal Archives
e0000405

135 Rochester Exposition
Rochester Public Library
Municipal Archives
e0000396

136 Barge Canal Construction
Rochester Public Library
Local History Division
rpf00884

138 Exchange Street Interurban Station
Rochester Public Library
Local History Division
rpf00363

139 Home of Thomas Hart Rochester 1920
Rochester Public Library
Local History Division
rpf01227

140 Prince Street Campus of University of Rochester
Rochester Public Library
Local History Division
rpf00759

141 City Hall and Fitzhugh Street
Rochester Public Library
Municipal Archives
m0001177

142 First Universalist Church
Rochester Public Library
Local History Division
rpf01539

143 Rochester Dental Dispensary
Rochester Public Library
Local History Division
rpf02090

144 Construction of Rochester Subway at Broad Street
Rochester Public Library
Local History Division
rpf01917

145 Lawless Paper Company Fire
Rochester Public Library
Municipal Archives
e0000221

146 Officials Unlock Gate at Exposition
Rochester Public Library
Local History Division
rpf01754

147 Brick Presbyterian Church
Rochester Public Library
Local History Division
rpf01510

148 Broad Street Bridge
Rochester Public Library
Local History Division
rpf01751

149 Neisner Brothers East Main Street Store
Rochester Public Library
Local History Division
rpf01783

150 Monroe Avenue 1920
Rochester Public Library
Local History Division
rpf00553

151 Eastman School of Music and Eastman Theatre
Rochester Public Library
Local History Division
rpf01024

152 Intersection of Main and North Street
Rochester Public Library
Local History Division
rpf00514

153 Air Mail Airplane
Rochester Public Library
Municipal Archives
m0000042

154 Aerial View
Rochester Public Library
Local History Division
rpf01033

155 Osburn House
Rochester Public Library
Local History Division
rpf00711

156 University of Rochester Library
Rochester Public Library
Local History Division
rpf00707

157 Kodak Park
Rochester Public Library
Local History Division
rpf00762

158 First Reynolds Arcade
Rochester Public Library
Local History Division
rpf00761

159 Storefronts on Clinton Avenue
Rochester Public Library
Local History Division
rpf01919

160 Education Building
Rochester Public Library
Local History Division
rpf01397

161 Shoveling Gangs in Main Street
Rochester Public Library
Local History Division
RPF00628

162 FDR Visits Rochester
Rochester Public Library
Municipal Archives
v0000125

163 Court Street Bridge and Rundel Memorial Building
Rochester Public Library
Local History Division
rpf00697

164 Audience at Rundel Memorial Building Dedication
Rochester Public Library
Local History Division
rpf00718

165 Coca Cola Billboard on Main Street
Rochester Public Library
City Hall Collection
m0001147

166 Sibley's
Rochester Public Library
Local History Division
rpf02229

168 Street Car Crosses Clinton at Main
Rochester Public Library
Local History Division
rpf00088

169 Women Boarding a Street Car
Rochester Public Library
Municipal Archives
m0000174

170 Victory Book Campaign
Rochester Public Library
Local History Division
rpf02043

171 Street Car on Main
Rochester Public Library
Municipal Archives
m0000178

172 P.O.W. Camp at Cobbs Hill
Rochester Public Library
Local History Division
rpf02045

173 P.O.W.'s
Rochester Public Library
Local History Division
rpf02047

174 Barge on the New York State Barge Canal
Rochester Public Library
Local History Division
rpf01927

175 Main Street at Four Corners
Rochester Public Library
Municipal Archives
m0001120

176 Stores on East Main Street
Rochester Public Library
Municipal Archives
m0001185

177 Snowstorm
Rochester Public Library
Local History Division
rpf01926

178 City Hall Subway Station
Rochester Public Library
Municipal Archives
m0000092

179 Main Street at St. Paul Street
Rochester Public Library
Municipal Archives
m0000007

180 Susan B. Anthony House
Rochester Public Library
Local History Division
rpf02255

181 South Avenue and Main Street
Rochester Public Library
Municipal Archives
m0000022

182 Children Wait to Board Bus During Nature Hike
Rochester Public Library
Municipal Archives
m0000429

183 Airplane at Rochester Airport
Rochester Public Library
Municipal Archives
m0000047

184 Fire Prevention Demonstration on the Court Street Bridge
Rochester Public Library
Municipal Archives
m0000323

186 North Wing of the Former General Wadsworth School No. 12
Rochester Public Library
Municipal Archives
m0000341

187 Summer Day Camp
Rochester Public Library
Municipal Archives
m0000550

188 Part of the Police Athletic League Model Train Layout
Rochester Public Library
Municipal Archives
m0000572

189 Celebrating New Bus Fleet
Rochester Public Library
Municipal Archives
m0000074

190 Kimball Tobacco Factory Building Demolition
Rochester Public Library
City Hall Collection
v0000074

191 Urban Renewal 1950
Rochester Public Library
City Hall Collection
v0000019

192 Traffic on State Street
Rochester Public Library
Municipal Archives
m0001132

193 War Memorial Site Excavation
Rochester Public Library
Local History Division
rpf00584

194 Pedestrians at Clinton Avenue and Main Street
Rochester Public Library
Municipal Archives
m0001138

195 Fay Building Fire 1955
Rochester Public Library
City Hall Collection
v0000137

196 Public Safety Commission 1950s
Rochester Public Library
City Hall Collection
v0000133

197 All-High Chorus Performs at the All-High Music Festival
Rochester Public Library
Municipal Archives
m0000347

198 Pulling the Fire Alarm
Rochester Public Library
Municipal Archives
m0000303

199 President Nixon on Main Street
Rochester Public Library
City Hall Collection
v0000043

HISTORIC PHOTOS OF ROCHESTER

By the late nineteenth century, the city of Rochester had risen to become a vibrant cultural center of the North. *Historic Photos of Rochester* captures this journey through still photography selected from the finest archives.

Join author Ruth Rosenberg Naparsteck on a tour of this great American city's illustrious past. See the first Reynolds Arcade as it appeared in 1877, the Erie Canal relocation project, Coggswell Fountain, circus elephants on Main Street in the 1890s, the Lyceum Theatre, penny farthings on parade, a John Frisbie test flight, and many other remarkable and unique scenes and events.

Published in vivid black-and-white, these images spotlight historic events and the everyday life of two centuries of people building a unique and prosperous city. *Historic Photos of Rochester* is sure to delight all visitors and every citizen interested in learning more about his hometown.

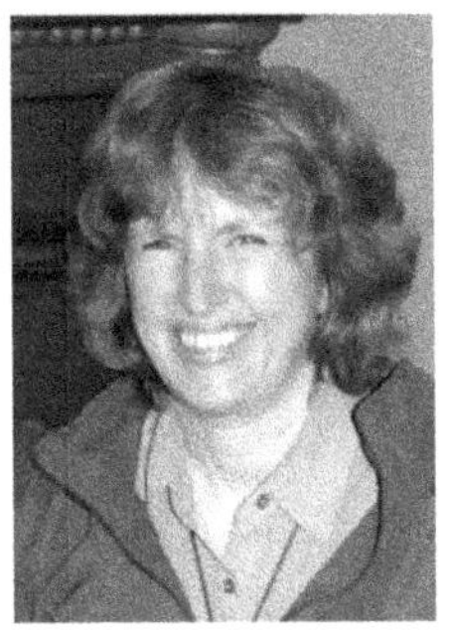

Ruth Rosenberg Naparsteck is City Historian and Records Manager in Rochester, New York. She holds a master's degree in American History from the State University of New York, a bachelor's degree in Sociology-Anthropology from Lycoming College in Williamsport, Pennsylvania, an associate's degree in Journalism and Mass Communications from Point Park College in Pittsburgh, Pennsylvania, and a certification in archaeology from Tel Aviv University in Tel Aviv, Israel. She has written several books on Williamsport and Rochester history and loves to garden, bicycle, hike, and explore the rivers and canals. She has two daughters, America and Molly-Maguire.

WWW.TURNERPUBLISHING.COM

www.ingramcontent.com/pod-product-compliance
Lightning Source LLC
LaVergne TN
LVHW060613110826
845154LV00003B/78
* 9 7 8 1 6 8 3 3 6 9 3 6 3 *